Feb. 2002

WORLD ENOUGH

for Goldie Williams —
May you enjoy my travels,
& join me in the delights of
places "way out and gone"!
yours very fondly,
Chuck Stickney

WORLD ENOUGH

▼

Travel Memoirs

Charles Stickney

Authors Choice Press
San Jose New York Lincoln Shanghai

World Enough
Travel Memoirs

Authors Choice Press
an imprint of iUniverse.com, Inc.

For information address:
iUniverse.com, Inc.
5220 S 16th, Ste. 200
Lincoln, NE 68512
www.iuniverse.com

ISBN: 0-595-18474-X

Printed in the United States of America

Contents

Chapter 1

Introduction:

Most of my travel writing was done right there, in the place I wrote of, with the grit, the shit, the smells and people there for me to copy raw, to let the place itself filter or plow into my words. This year I'm home, writing at my desk , here in Manhattan, world city itself, yes, but the smells, the language, the signs and lights and darks do differ from the rest of the world. (Though more and more the rest of the world begins or continues to mimic Manhattan.) The Nepali porter carrying cooking oil for sale to a remote village is wearing a bowling shirt from lanes in Fairlawn, New Jersey. The Indian in Pushkar in Rajahstan wants to buy my umbrella (made in China which I bought in Nepal) and asks me how many "bucks" I want for it. He means rupees, but wants to be "Western" and up-to-date for me. Pico Iyer wrote a travel book called "Video Nights in Kathmandu" in which he shows the clashes of contemporary Western culture and technology with the traditional or primitive or pre-technological societies that are now getting so easy to visit.

I remember going overland from England to Kathmandu in 1978 when you could still go by local buses through Iran and Afghanistan. The festival of Ramadan (they called it Ramzan) was on that August, and no good Muslim could eat during daylight hours, the heat was brutal, the land was brown and cooked. Then there was Pakistan and the military was stopping buses and trucks, and searching for guns because they feared a coup by the supporters of the jailed Ali Bhutto, and finally there was India, green and friendly.

(1978) "Everyone's skin here's a strip of dry ground. Brown with a smearing of grey. Irani, Afghani, all. Even me. Tan and dirt compounded a month with visions of dry dust browns me like a desert. Till Pakistan the brown went on, how brown, till Pakistan.

Then green! Wet smells of mud and leaves, and glistenings from monsooned flats to double the lights and sky and smells. A prism shifted and green pours in the bus's windows. Underwater I swim through green ponds, green roads, green cows, green flesh. Green hopes too. London to India—a month of travel, dreaming of water swimming-pool deep. Tired. No more dry dreams. Now just green and wet ones!"

Then Kashmir where in 1978 they hated the Indians, and the hatred is deeper now in 2000, and then Delhi and Agra and then all along the northern part of India, and then into Nepal where just over its border the tiny shops were lighted by kerosine, and by bus, ferry, jeep taxi, and at one point I jumped on a water buffalo's back and asked the startled buffalo's owner if this buffalo could take me to Ruxaul on the way to Kathmandu. And when I finally got to Kathmandu, almost three months after leaving familiar England, I had amoebic dystentery, had shed weight and comfort and time, and here I was in Ultima Thule, Nepal, and my ragged exhausted self noticed some few fresh and clean middle-aged middle-class middle-westerners saying, "Say, Doris, why don't you stand there in front of that temple, and I'll see if I can get that water buffalo in the picture with you."

You can get to the other end of the world fast and easy, or slow and with difficulty. I've done both. (From 1978 in Kathmandu) "BEE DANCE: I am here, now, describing that great arc we all travel. Istambul gives a taste, then Ezurum, Teheran, Mashad, Herat, Kandahar, Kabul, Peshawar, Lahore, then we're poured into India to disperse.

But still we trail from Delhi to Agra, Khajuraho, Varanasi, and finally Kathmandu. And so forth. All on the same trail of tourist sweets, like ants. But in Kathmandu we meet those who started from the East, and trade like hive bees secrets and secretions in a dance. What we've done, they want to do, and we their deeds too. "Deeds." Too adventurous a word for things too many have done. But why not see things guaranteed to be great before the risk taken, the chance of a wasted day? (Of course, like in all poems, there is the analogy with life. The stages: school, love, job, marriage. Learning at different rates, from different angles. The poets carrying things too weighty for them, pouring out their honey as they, pushed, pricked, dance their sticky steps."

We travelers, distinguishing ourselves from the despised tourists by our low-budget long-term-traveling ways, reveled in our adventurous linguistic distinction: travelers. But we usually followed each others' pathways or the ubiquitous Lonely Planet Guide despite our pretentions to independence. Layering in the magical exotic names, the way Walt Whitman did in his long catalogues of American Indian names or names of American rivers, spices the tale with foreignness, but it is a cheap generalized way to do so. Khajuraho may to the initiate evoke erotic sculpture of early India, but to the person who was there it may evoke fatigue from the immense heat, plodding around the old temples, the annoying post card sellers, the anxiety over one's bowels rather than one's vowels. Herat in Afghanistan now is a bombed-out wreak from the Russian war, but for me it was a small darkened street with friendly tea or "Chai" shops, the hippie meeting places where we, like bees, could exchange information about where best to go next.

Once an adventure happens or an exotic place is seen, and then described, the words remain and begin to take the place of the experience, as a photo begins to subsume the place of the place itself or the actual way the person looked, frozen into that mere second's slice of the moving colorful reality, declining from the vivid to the vapid, from color to black words on white paper. What I want is to convey is not merely the meanings, but also the converse, the thing-ness of the place and the experience itself, not what our minds can reconstitute it into, what Wallace Stevens wrote of in his poem, "The Man on the Dump"—"and you see/ As a man (not like an image of a man),/

You see the moon rise in the empty sky." Empty of all human mental additions. And Stevens finishes the poems with the shortest sentence about the specific I know: "The the." Not the "a" which could be any one or thing, but the "the," specific and sui generis, itself alone. All this when I can only remember a few of the actual things happening around me at the time of my trips and so I must rely on letters sent to parents and friends which were saved for me, or on poems or prose or notes written at that time, and so have to reconstitute with the fluids of current memory to try to get back what once was fresh. The notes may embody my misunderstanding of what I had seen; the letters to parents and ex-wife did not include stuff about sex and danger; the ones to friends may exaggerate. Not only names may be lost, but whole episodes forgotten or re-shaped by the story-telling since the trip or by the individual memory tailoring itself to fit the whole cloth of my life.

What unity do I find in the bricks of this book? What shape or architecture do I impose? From here to there, a geography? From early to later, an aging autobiography? Several themes—death, growth, sex, loneliness, odd cultures— and variations? One theme and a deepening? Or chapters on different countries, mixing poetry, remembrance, sniffs and touches of the places? Shards like pottery pieces, like chunks of broken chocolate, for the snacker on travel and on lives? A mosaic with one central design? Juxtaposition of seemingly unfitting episodes, and let the reader struggle to discover the puzzling country of this book, or smooth and straight-forward transitions between incidents? What motifs? What motives? What moves?

Zero to sixty in my lifetime. (In the year 2000 I did turn sixty.)

During the 1600s in Japan, Matsuo Basho wrote many haiku, very short evocative poems, self-contained lyrics which earlier in Japanese literature were part of linked verses. In Basho's famous travel book, "The Narrow Road of the Interior" he embedded these haiku in his travel narrative of a trip around Japan, an addition to the kind of poetic travel diary which had been common for 800 years. I have decided to do the same— to cannibalize my own words written on the spot and at the time and insert them into this travel narrative. These words are closer to being a part of the original experience than would be words written now, digested in the sack of memory.

Do I organize my book like a trip: following a particular desire—e.g. to see great art or monuments or archeological sights—or just flying or plodding from country to country till I get home? A book, unlike a journey, can use flashbacks. (Let me take that back: during a journey, your mind churns over what now you see, mixing it with what in your past was similar, or different, or connects. So often we live so often in the house of memory.)

Yet to take the journey is all in the now. (As Walt Whitman, the poet of the open road, said—"Do I contradict myself? Very well then, I contradict myself? I am large. I contain multitudes."

Hey, me too!) You plan and go from place to place, perhaps changing plans, but eventually you arrive home. To write right now of all my journeys is to be in the past, the layered past, then and more then, and the memory may go from place to place with each place in a different time, each place differently colored by my feelings while writing then or now about it. An Uncertainty Principle more complex than Heisenberg's. The world is stripped naked, but our minds as we age add the cobwebs of meaning; the spittle of chatter as we tell others what we saw and begin to embellish, our mouths open in speech, departing from the original experience, that drool of internal-mind open-mouthed contemplation, open-mouthed often in stunned silence.

Some of our most vivid and exciting images come now from the movies, and we are used to being calm observers while watching films of the most violent action which we may see from the protagonists' perspectives. In 1987, I started to write a novel in which the main character (me) was put in jail in Guatemala for a murder. I had just spent more than eight months traveling around Latin America, and so was full of all sorts of verisimilitudinous details of those countries. But I went back to another memory, of time I had spent riding around with police officers in the south Bronx, the infamous "Fort Apache." Let me insert a piece of this narrative, taking place after the main character has just been beaten up soon after he arrives in jail. "Forty-seven years old, always playing at slumming, hitch-hiking, sleeping in crummy hotels, traveling around the world on the cheap, dropping his middle-class-ness with ease because he could always easily pick it up again, Clayton still felt that this being in jail was not serious, was more like a good story to be told later on in New York to his friends, was like a movie which would end like all movies, with the theater doors being flung open, and a return to the late-afternoon street with just the smells of movie-house air and popcorn and the adjustment to the natural light and to real time. He remembered having felt like this when, as part of a project pairing professors and police, he leaped out of a patrol car in the Bronx and, while the two cops with him moved around behind parked cars toward the junk yard where three robbers had just been reported, one of whom had a shotgun, he ran right down the sidewalk straight toward the open junkyard gate because he somehow could not believe in the reality of those three robbers, and of that shotgun. It was just like a movie to him. But that was not a movie, nor was this." If an exciting movie can "distance" one from reality, how about poor pale words?

And how much can I remember of what actually happened? How much ought I remember? Think of the up-side of Alzheimer's Disease—the more you forget, the more surprise and wonder you can have each time you see something because it is always new. I remember my parents and I had a joke about every new place we went to : "Oh, it's just like Lake George." Joyce Carey noted that an infant can be endlessly fascinated by a wind-ruffled newspaper noting the continuously shifting shapes. Adults would just dismiss it with the thought, "Oh, just a newspaper blowing in the wind." The words dilute the experience. The words dilute the experience by themselves becoming the experience. Time too can dilute the experience when we've literally "been there, done that," when we've seen the place before. Even the Taj Mahal did not elicit the "Oh, wow" it did the first time I saw it. Traveling is through new and then older nations of feelings too. The splendour in the grass changes after the rusty lawn-mower and the aging gardener have been at it.

Barbara Tuchman, in her book "A Distant Mirror" on the 1300's in France and England, said, "As individuals as in nations, contentment is silent, which tends to unbalance the historical record."

So too with my writings—I write a poem or story most often when I'm not happy , and the words reflect that unhappiness. As Yeats said about his unrequited love for Maud Gonne, had she understood the purpose of his words, which were to make her love him, "who can say/ What would have shaken from the sieve?/ I might have thrown poor words away/ And been content to live." Sad to say, it really is lucky for regular folks that poets don't get laid as much as they'd like.

And while I'm quoting, the poet Wendell Berry said, "Don't own so much clutter that you will be relieved to see your house catch fire." What is clutter? The specific tangible clutter of details of the place, if left out, will leave the lesson of the place mere asbstract bleached cardboard. I thought I might start out this book-trip with the image of my shaved head. In Officer Candidate School in the Navy in 1961 our stripped scalps made us all look alike, which was the point. But it was also a metaphor of removing our civilian-ness. In Poona, India, in 1979, my shaved head was to conjure the monk-ishness of the spirit I was trying to elicit there. In Fire Island, in the mid-1970s, I often wrote of the sand-stripping and sun-burning off of my past in my poems. At times, here at home, I've shaved my head to embody (or en-head) a psychological symbol of my desire to make clear and clean and simple my life.

Zero to sixty in my lifetime. In the year 2000 I've lived for sixty years and travelled a lot.

SCOTLAND:

Scotland didn't sound so foreign in 1964, and it is less foreign now. Less foreign to all Americans not only because of speaking the same language, but because everywhere is less foreign in the year 2000. More people fly there, and everywhere else, on vacations. And American culture has seeped and stormed all over the globe, so really foreign and unfamiliar places are harder to find. Anthropology has had to turn to the study of our own culture or sub-cultures to find the shrinking pockets of the unfamiliar.

Less foreign to me too even in 1964 because I had majored in English as an undergraduate at Brooklyn College, and when I decided to do graduate work in English literature, I applied to universities in Britain. Oxford and Cambridge wanted me to get another B.A. at their universities, which would take an additional two years, but Edinburgh would let me start out as a graduate student. I finally chose Edinburgh over Berkeley, because Berkeley was so detailed in where I should show up and what I had to do in its acceptance letter, and therefore reminded me of the Navy I was just getting free of, and Edinburgh was so very casual and friendly in its acceptance letter I wasn't certain I was actually accepted. Why not study British literature in Britain?

So in October 1964 I landed in Scotland, moved into my "digs" at Mr. and Mrs. Grant's who had two other lodgers, and started my studies. For five guineas {5 pounds, 5 shillings) per week I got a small room with a small sink in it, breakfast and dinner, no heat, one hot bath a week, a nice view of Arthur's Seat, a wee pretty mountain, and an understanding of the Scottish stereotype about landladies from Aberdeen: they're stingy. Not thrifty, but bloody stingy. When I first arrived from America, I asked to take a bath; I was then told about the rules: once a week. The first hint of the unfamiliar. So I learned to immerse into my tiny sink whatever portions of myself I wanted to wash, whether those portions fit or not. Sinks are also, I learned, very useful on late and cold nights for peeing into. And that saves lots of water rather than flushing a toilet (a word to the environmentally friendly). I learned the same thing in China for the year, 1984, where hot baths were even more inconvenient than in Scotland. By the way, the Scots will call the toilet a toilet rather than our euphemism, "the bathroom." Scots also call it the "bog," no doubt from pre-plumbing days. Or they call it "the loo," from (the battle of) Waterloo, i.e. water closet. We Americans say "take a shit"; an English girl said she was "going to have a shit." Why I go on about this is not merely to show you the unfamiliar habits of speech, nor to disgust you nor to make you laugh, but also to pre-figure or fore-shadow a prominent motif among travelers in Asia, where the state of one's bowels is a constant topic of conversation and occupies an inordinately large portion of one's consciousness.

Speaking of multi-culturism, Mrs. Grant's favorite dish for us lodgers was a chicken curry, which we would eat in a dining room in which the electric fire was just turned on, and so we three lodgers started out our meals in winter with frosty vapor being emitted from our mouths into which we forked our mild curry. Usually later on of an evening I would wander over to the fish-and-chips shop and get six pence worth of chips ("salt 'n sauce?") or a mince pie and chips for one shilling, six pence. The reason I mention the prices unfamiliar to travellers now, because they're so cheap, and because the shillings, half-crowns, ha'pence, have been jettisoned for simplicity's sake. For thrift's sake, most places in Scotland then seemed to be heated only by electric fires, so all shilling pieces were sedulously saved and put into these electric appliances, and in my room I would hunch over this fire, my front crisping with the heat, my back chill as the room, the room temperature being basically the same as the outside, except with less wind (or perhaps not, depending on the intestinal effects of Mrs. Grant's curry).

After several months, Mrs. Grant asked me to leave her "digs" as I was receiving and making too many phone calls, and had had girls up in my room, so I moved to a residence hotel, the Salisbury Hotel, run by a Polish couple, where I paid 3 pounds, ten shillings a week for a room in the basement, a sink, hot baths whenever I chose, and a substantial Scottish breakfast joined by lots of doctors, often Indian, who were studying for the Fellow-of-the Royal-College-of- Physicians exams. Much more freedom and privacy and comfort than at the Grants, and I could more easily and with less guilt sneak in more women.

Most days in Edinburgh were grey and dour, chilly, with a characteristic smell that I smelled again in Prague in 1993, in a small courtyard that was being re-paved. The smell pulled me back three decades in an instant, faster than a Cray computer. But mostly in Edinburgh I lived more in the rest of my head, rather than merely in my nose, or even in the rest of my body. Studying literature of 1700 to the present kept that nose of mine pressed into books. That academic year of 1964 and 1965 was the most free and the best year of my life up till then. The Navy was behind me, though my reserve duty would last till 1967. In Edinburgh the travel was mostly in my mind.

But adventure did come, albeit in small things. On the birth date of Robert Burns, I had my first haggis—buying several at a fish-and-chip shop, and taking over the honours literature library in the David Hume Tower to recite, from a very early edition of Burns's poetry, Burns' "Address to the Haggis" to the other scholars. Several Brits never had eaten haggis before. I rarely ate it again, but felt proud to do the proper Scots thing on that proper Scots night. Another week it snowed about two inches and I my well have been the only one to ever have a snow-ball fight (one snow-ball) in the honours English library. A note from a letter says, "I beat a big brawny ox of a Scot in an arm-wrestle in the library," so life I see was not merely mental.

Speaking of libraries, I also worked a lot in the Scottish National Library, where one day I, a student of modern literature, decided to read

William Burrough's novel, "Naked Lunch." Easier said than done. In order to take out the book, I had to bring in a signed note to prove I was a real graduate student of literature, to indicate I already was deeply corrupted. There was only one man who had the key to the locked room in which the pornographic books were kept, and he was not there the day I asked. However, patience was rewarded, and eventually the book was in my moist depraved hands, the book not of course to be taken from the library's precincts.

To read this randy racy book in the staid Victorian Dickensian atmosphere of the Scottish National Library was so cognitively dissonant that I began to laugh, barely controlling myself. Around me were my fellow scholars, one with fingerless gloves, all battened down and serious. And here was Burroughs writing, "he stuck his_____ into her _____, after which the donkey stuck his_____." You get the idea. While I was chuckling, bent over with laughter, several friends also laughing at my laughing, an Indian, utterly furious, whispered to me, "How dare you laugh at me!" He was apoplectic, but I was not apologetic because I assured him I was laughing at what I was reading. I had to take him out of the reading room, and then he exploded. He accused me, and all Scots and all English, of staring at him, of ridiculing him for trying to dress like an Englishman (he looked perfectly well-dressed, certainly better dressed than I almost ever am), of, in short, being a foreigner, an Indian in a British land. Finally I convinced him that I and my fellows weren't making fun of him, and then he burst out with all of his foreigner's distress, wanting to take me out for coffee to pour out more of his sadness and troubles. I had too much work to do, so declined, and we parted friends. Fourteen years later, when I was in India for the first time in 1978, I realized how even the most mild-mannered Westerner can go beserk because of so many Indians staring at us. How infuriating it is to be seen as some freak of nature, some creature with no feelings, no privacy. Then I understood the sense of not belonging, of being the odd one, the one so foreign that gawking at him is not impolite.

For me in Scotland, I could and did blend in. My face, my race, my name, my language, soon much of my accent—I was not unlike most people in Edinburgh. One proud moment was when, in a shop on Princes Street, while listening to a very American woman with a very American accent having trouble with the currency, I exchanged surreptitious grins with the shop lady, implying, "what dorks these Americans be." I felt wonderful. I felt like a Scot. Were I that American woman in the shop, and had I noticed the grins, I would probably have felt like that Indian in the Scottish National Library.

Furious. And foreign.

And fore-shadowings of my future while in Scotland. One day in the zoo in Dundee, my friend Mike Gordon and a couple of others were staring at the chimpanzee, when suddenly the chimp spat at me. I spat back at him. My friends, the crowd and the chimp were alike stunned. Fair's fair, I thought. Later on—in Bali, India, Nepal, in Bandung and in Penang—I spent much time with monkeys in the wild and in zoos, and felt they are like us, like me. Not so foreign at all. Why be surprised that I returned the spit with this chimp?

I travelled around Scotland on my academic vacations, hitch-hiking and meeting people, getting to the islands of Skye and Arran, the highlands and the lochs. Once a group of us honours literature students had a working vacation at a small 18th century place called "The Burn," right alongside a lovely burn (stream). On the way there, at a Chinese restaurant in Perth, I was the only one wielding chopsticks. Foreshadowing my year in Kunming, China, teaching British literature to graduate students? No. Rather it shows my being raised in New York City where chopsticks are not an unusual dining implement. In the days at "The Burn" we hiked and played soccer, and nights we discussed the poetry of Wallace Stevens and Robert Lowell, two American poets (we believed in multi-culturism even then). One night, from 1:35 a.m. till 5 a.m., we took a walk to "a small country cemetery along a blue, moon-lit (full moon) road telling ghost stories, etc." My letters to my parents now remind me of this walk, but I have no real recollection of it. And think of what lurks underneath that casual "etc." What words exchanged, what ideas and observations during that romantic and probably chilly walk! What loads of life lost, buried or jettisoned from our feeble memories! What pitiful semi-resurrections from letters or photos. What distortions from the filter of our memories. What color anyway can pale words bring to absent life. What the hell really happened in our pasts? What are foreign places really like?

The few photos I took that year, like all photos, freeze the real moment, that one instant. That one real instant in the photo begins soon to absorb, because of its very tangible reality, the real moments surrounding that photographed instant. Begins to absorb the plethora of instants and impressions of that longer time we knew that photographed person until his or her other expressions, the other characteristic movements and gestures of the person in the photo, begin to fade and we forget. Reality's multiplicity becomes simplified, and the photo becomes our memory. The photo freezes an instant, but also freezes out all other moments not photographed. Our technology takes over our memories.

Can we trust our letters to our parents as telling of the real things that happen? I never told my parents about my sexual exploits, and they were some of my most thrilling times those years. I never told my parents of the time I broke up what looked to be a very big fight between rough "townies" and medical students in Dundee—about one of the "townies" who kicked me, while another was brandishing two broken bottles, and I faced them down and got them to quit and leave. Those details of what really happened would only make them afraid and uncomfortable. Lucky for me I was kicked in the thigh, not in the testicles as the fighter intended, and that I didn't know which of the three opposite me had kicked me, so I challenged them all, and began then to threaten them, and I don't know if my iron balls, my American accent, or my turning from peace-maker to someone who was beginning to get annoyed and threatening back finally made them leave. They left. I couldn't write down those details, but they are engraved on my thigh as well as my mind. An uncomfortable situation.

Foreign places are often quite uncomfortable, part of the discomfort coming from the odd food, the lack of clean toilets, the heat. But discomfort is not just physical. It's also the unknown language, the strange customs, the stares. Now with literature, I should be used to the strange, reading about so many different lives and other times and cultures. But reading is not being there. Watching a storm at sea in the movies is more vivid than reading about it on the printed page. Being in that storm at sea is not felt so much as vivid, but rather as terrifying. It is easy to misunderstand something read about in a book; something actual can also be confusing, but it will write its reality directly on your body and mind with most powerful pen.

In Edinburgh I saw lots of plays telling of other times and places. One piece of a letter from 1965: "Saw a good funny rendition of Aristophanes' 'Lysistrata,' met the editor of a literary magazine & he said he was going to include one of my poems in his next issue (a humorous 'gimmick-y' one dedicated to Walt Whitman—my more serious ones he either didn't like or didn't understand. Too bad.)" Not only might we misunderstand other places, times, and people, but also others' poems. Once this poem had been published (I just typed "punished"—appropriate!), I spoke to the editor who chose the poem, and mentioned what a newspaper reviewer of my poem had missed—that each line of the poem had a pun on a musical instrument. "What?" said the editor. "That's the point of the poem," said I. "Let's see," said he. Once he looked the poem over, "wow!" or several words to that effect said he.

I thought then, and often thought since, that even when someone likes your poem or work, and even publishes it, they do so for their reasons which may miss the deeper delights of what it was you did.

Then what deep reasons made me want to teach in deepest Africa? I think mostly for adventure, new and strange countries, and as I put it in a letter in April 1965, "since I'm eventually going to Africa anyway, I may as well do it now while they need and appreciate me, than in 10 years when they won't." I mentioned also the opportunity to climb Mt. Kilimanjaro, because of the stories of Earnest Hemingway.

Flash forward in time. I had applied for a job at Makerere College, in Kampala, Uganda, one of the best colleges in Africa at that time. The British Council told me that the college said "they would not need the assistance of the British Council at this time" which meant they probably filled the position with a native Ugandan. In a few years Uganda would be run by Idi Amin. I also met the Principal of a college in Sierra Leone, through the help of one of my instructors, Paul Edwards, who had taught for several years in Sierra Leone. When I asked Edwards what the place was like, he paused, looked at me with a grin and said, "the white man's grave." He gave me no other details. Edwards was white. So was I. At any rate, the Principal of this college told me that the English teaching there would consist chiefly of language and remedial reading practice. Not for me. Sierra Leone is presently in a vicious civil war. I've never been in sub-Saharan Africa, and may never get there now. So much for plans, and so much for adventure. I would not like my appointment in Sammara to have been my appointment in Stanleyville.

Now gypsys are also supposed to be dangerous. I spent two weeks in Ireland in April 1965, the first week motoring around Ireland with Michael Gordon, who was working in a medical "locum" in Derry (Londonderry to those Protestants who like London, Derry to the Catholics—the troubles in Northern Ireland were waiting to happen in 1965, with bombs already in Belfast—troubles that, like Africa's, were tribal and religious, would get much worse, and would still be burning in 2000). The second week I spent without Michael in Dublin, "dear dirty Doyoubelong" in James Joyce's coinage. The dangerous gypsys—so many housewives take their laundry off the washing lines when the gypsys come to town for fear of their clothes getting stolen. The gypsys who rented horses to Michael and me for an hour's ride, and traveled in their horse carts, and kept to the roads, vagabonds who keep separate and are alien and very mistrusted in most every land. By me too, I might add. But they are picturesque.

Another picturesque moment: the steep sheer Cliffs of Moher, Michael and I alone at the Cliffs except for a beautiful white horse grazing in a meadow right behind the Cliffs. So picturesque even I took a photo of it. Classic. Corny. Beautiful. So many people would see the same white horse and pale cliffs, and think, "Boy, is that beautiful! Must get a picture of that." So many of us think the same things. The white horse. The cliffs. The gypsys. I wrote down that the Cliffs of Moher were "like the vertical steeps of the Isle of Capri." Traveling gets you to comparing, and seeing one place, think of another, arranging all in the filing cabinets of our brains. Most towns in Ireland, I wrote in a letter, are depressing, but belied by their gorgeous names. The word ill-fitting the deed or the place.

Ah, to match the word with the place. Ah, for the gift of eloquence that the Irish say can be gotten from kissing the Blarney Stone at Blarney Castle, where other tourists and I slobbered over the stone embedded in the castle wall 83 feet above the ground, and you must lean over backwards, iron bars and a keeper's hand keeps you safe over this picturesque abyss. The stone actually has been worn away by the kisses of tourists. I French-kissed it a couple of times to make certain I caught the spirit of Demosthenes and caught a cold from the other kissers.

Maybe I didn't gain eloquence from the Blarney Stone, but Michael and I took a couple of women hitch-hikers for a day's drive down the southwest coast, and one of them was Judy Golding, the daughter of William Golding, famous then for his novel, "The Lord of the Flies," and one day to win the Nobel Prize in literature. In a letter, I wrote, "She's a nice girl whose father also has a beard. When I put my grizzly cheek against her soft flabby one, she said she was nostalgic for daddy. Just think, I reminded her of W. Golding. Wonder if my writing would too?"

Back to Edinburgh, to my thesis on the poetry of Stephen Crane, the several three-hour exams, and finally getting my Diploma in English Studies and finishing up this academic year. I gained a tolerance for almost constant grey skies and a liking for colorful plaids. Scotland—gently different from the U.S.A. Foreign and familiar and comfortable.

ENGLAND:

England felt too familiar to be foreign. The language, the faces—in 1961 the faces were English in the racial sense, not merely as citizens. London in 1961 seemed so friendly; people would walk you around the corner to see you were going the right way. In 1978 and 1979, there seemed to me less friendliness, less Englishness, and in my disappointment I wanted out of London, and headed out to my favorite place in England: Cambridge. I spent about three weeks there, writing poetry, reading, and researching old poetic manuscripts for their variants. I wanted to see the way the poets' minds worked, their first and second and third ideas and the changes they made in the lines of poetry. John Milton in "Lycidas" mostly got his lines right the first time. Thomas Hardy, who had a rolling circular handwriting, crossed out his errors by a backwards twirling roll of his pen, very nearly obliterating his original line—very difficult to see what he originally intended. Here my original intentions were this first Sabbatical year to travel to exotic locales, and here I was disappointed that London is not the familiar London I at one time loved, but rather is familiar the way New York City is familiar—too busy and bustling, more a multi-cultural world city than an English one.

But the familiarity of Cambridge hurt. Too much of it reminded me of being there with my wife Joyce in the early 1970s—our trek to Grantchester, our punting on the Cam River behind the colleges. The first nights there in 1978 were terribly lonely—not only missing Joyce, thinking of the passing of time and love, but also dreading the next 14 or so months in front of me of travelling alone. If I felt this lonely a couple of days after leaving home, and in a land where most everyone spoke my language, and in Cambridge where with my doctorate in literature I shouldn't feel too stupid or "out of it," how would I feel in some country where few spoke my language, and neither the food nor

the customs were palatable, and the natives unfriendly. No question
mark on that previous sentence, because it was not a question to me
then. I felt sick about leaving my friends and my home, and considered
my idea of travelling around the world to write poetry a very bad idea.

However, the next few days blew away most of this faint-hearted fog
and I settled in to a routine of reading, research, thinking, and writing
poems. I met a few people, saw lots of plays in the gardens of the colleges,
drank lots of beer and discovered sage derby cheese at the Cambridge Folk
Festival (spent some hours with Richie Havens there because I told him a
song of his was originally a poem by Yeats), and had a one-night affair
with a descendant of a famous Swedish religious philosopher, the best part
of which was the wonderfully silly and romantic two-hour walk back to
her place very late at night (which we could have done in 20 minutes if we
had been less silly and romantic). There is nothing like a lovely woman
with long and very blonde hair to dissipate my blues. But I really don't
remember her face nor her hair; for this, I rely on my journal of 1978. Her
face, I realize, is getting mixed up with the face of Margareta, another
Swedish woman I had a short affair with in 1964 in Alicante, Spain, when
I was the temporary Assistant Shore Patrol Officer when my ship stopped
there for a few days. And the reason I remember

Margareta's face, is that I have a photo of her. How feeble is our
unprompted memory, how quickly our past slides down the chute and
out of sight.

The price of travel is the fact of farewell. Farewell not only to the people you met and the place itself, but to the you you were while you were
there. Travel is in space and in time.

In Cambridge in July 1978, I wrote, "Vaulting over thirteen years,
Edinburgh street-smell tweaks me by the nose, asks me how I've grown,
reminds me what has passed. It caught up with me in Cambridge, though,
at one a.m., smelling of smoke and old homes. You've aged, it said, while
I'm the same.

Broken veins in British cheeks map all our roads. I've been here before. My first wife Joyce and I lay behind King's College and watched the sliding punts. In our punt, I didn't use the pole as rudder, and wove hapharardly down the Cam. I sweated and we both laughed. Eight years ago. My first wife. I've had no second.

Birds, excited by the coming dark, chirp like tinny typewriter keys around King's Chapel. I remember flocks of starlings netting Westminster or crows weaving around Uppsala's Cathedral spires behind sad Pia's room. Cathedral spires sink as time's total rises. I once wrote a poem about the crows in Uppsala and so saved something.

Poetry is wonderful. Just with words (with just words) you can make connections between things, like, oh, time the spider and wisdom the web he weaves, or poison the draught he pours for us all. Like Socrates. Always connecting. I'm soon facing forty. At the entrance of St. John's College by the Cam is an old Queen's head opposite a King's. Old ivy stretches up like arthritic fingers putting out her eyes, making her like, oh, Homer, or any old bard whose powers are failing. They say that then, blind, they speak the truth in places where ivy, parasitic web netting old truths, prospers round foreheads like prize wreaths, or, sagging, slips round sagging silenced throats."

Now in 2000 I've already faced sixty, and it's defaced me, and arthritis is no longer merely a metaphor. Travel is distance and travel is time and travel shows you some truths about yourself. Paul Theroux, in his book on train travel, "The Great Railway Bazaar," noted that "the further one traveled, the nakeder one got." And "all journeys were return journeys." He saw that "the scenes changing in the train window...are nothing compared to the change in himself; and travel writing, which cannot be but droll at the outset, moves from journalism to fiction, arriving as promptly as the Kodama Echo [a Japanese train] at autobiography. From there any further travel makes a beeline to confession, the embarrassed monologue in a deserted bazaar." Using the metaphors of travel—arriving, beeline—Theroux sees the travel writer as traveling in himself, and exploring his own sights and sites. Theroux sees also the trammels and tangles of truth-telling: "And I had learned what I always secretly believed, that the difference between travel writing and fiction is the difference between recording what the eye sees and discovering what the imagination knows. Fiction is pure joy—how sad that I could not invent the trip as fiction."

In Cambridge in 1978 I studied the first tries that John Milton, George Crabbe, Thomas Hardy made in their poems, the crossings-out in their manuscripts, and their new tries to get their poems just right. Some corrected more than the others. Because my divorce to Joyce had just come through in 1978, and we had spent time in Cambridge together, I thought of her and of the other women in my life, and my own tries to get the lines that my life run on just right. So I wrote a poem:

I
Breasts, like searchlights, blaze through the
fog of years I've wheeled through; seeing
false pairings, odd stops, repeated infatuation
end, I wonder at all the breasts spun
like wheels of fortune dry of all lactation,
like safe tumblers; hope sex is more than peeing,
hope love will magnify me through her.
II
We were off-rhymes, me and Marianne,
ragged rhythms. Hung up by her long blonde hair,
I was reminded for years by this string tied to her breast.
Why? Beauty not quite had, then left for the Navy,
was inflated by the void. Her absent body gave me no rest,
overlay even my wife's. Her breasts were some pair,
though we couldn't be. I tore up her photos and felt like a man.
III
First time I had Pia, she thought we made a baby.
For this I hitched from Spain—to be a Swede?
My life like her legs began to close. It should have taught

me. But what? To make love only for love?
Pia, melancholy dame, we ran together to make you abort,
and came together and laughed, before I left. We did the deed
and might have married. Another, a better, life? Maybe.
IV
Susan was already married. But not to me.
She was sensitive, intuitive, dainty; me—man.
I was a bit of a clod before she breathed in my ear,
a clod too on principle. She opened my senses
and my wallet for me. She curbed my leer.
She changed from Sue Ann to Susan to Suzanne.
I stayed Chuck. She closed her door. I lost the key.
V
Joyce was my wife. Now she's my ex-. A distinction
she insists on. O.K. For six and a half years,
"twin stars constellated," we whirled around each other,
sometimes flaming, shining, or smoldering. Then—out!
Children? She wanted to want to become a mother,
but neither wanted choking ties. Her therapy seems clear,
putting many in place of me. As I do, in commitment's extinction.
VI
At times my loss seemed to have no bottom,
the hole seemed too deep to dare. But the holes
were there, and bottoms without end. I grabbed my share
and more. Did I say my loss? Again and again,
like a miser I collected. Into holes like a snake to his lair
I slid. Getting girls was my need. I was a mole.
Then, tired of caves, wanting sun and air, I left Sodom.
VII
But I'm not ready for a son and heir.
Kathy is. But she really was not ready
for her marriage to go, then her aching back,

then nearly her job, then her favorite house burnt.
Then I left. She and I both learned from her lack
of luck this year. Making love made our bodies heady,
but our hurtings helped us more to strip ourselves bare.
VIII
Now what? Now is surely the moment of truth:
Is it Plato or Aristotle? The one or the many?
The central problem of thought, the truth about beauty?
I sampled all—matrons domestic, girls sybaritic.
One thing I know, it won't be out of duty
I'll do it. But it better be soon before there aren't any
as daily gets me shorter in the pecker and longer in the tooth.

These rhymes echo the sounds in previous and in future lines, as one
experience in love can also echo in the future. Marianne I knew in
London, Pia I knew on the island of Ibiza, and in Stockholm and Uppsala.
Most of the others have been in New York, my home. But Joyce I knew
not only at home, but in Spain and France, Morocco and Switzerland, and
as I said, in Cambridge.

Memories of now in 2000 echoed sadly those of then in 1978 which in
turn echoed those of earlier years.

Travel for me has often been to escape from my New York life and com-
mitments. But sometimes travel can snag you on the past.

CZECH REPUBLIC: ON THE CHARLES BRIDGE IN PRAGUE, 1993:
Because the priest John Nepomuk [Czech for "never tell"] wouldn't tell
the king what the queen had confessed to, the king dumped Father
Nepomuk over the railing of the Charles Bridge in Prague to his death in
the Vltava River. As the priest hit the water, stars were supposedly seen
glimmering around his head, and soon after he was canonized, lots of statues were put up to him with gold stars halo-ing his head. The one on the
Charles Bridge kept getting the stars stolen, so they stopped putting them

up, and now the statue stands, stone alone, greying under the layers of soil under the eyes of the tourists.

But look now at the sun-spattered Vltava River in Prague. Look at the glisten of gold on the river—why not like stars as the splash of the priest caught the sun? The world does reflect what is there as well as what we hope for. The stained glass windows of St. Vitus Cathedral reflect in the glass doors with no distortion, like Monet's garden in Giverny where the sky and trees so glaze the pond with themselves, that the pond like a mirror converts the water into whatever surrounds it, like the hollow-bamboo mind of a buddha.

Yet clouds on the 16th century cathedral doors are carved like the beard of the saint in a museum: curled, like the clouds carved in Chinese temples. Or flower petals can look like cogs in a gear, the natural and the manmade. The far-off sound of motorcycles heard in Cesky Krumlov gardens is perhaps the nearby sound of innumerable bees. In Krumlov in southern Bohemia in the old castle are some panes of glass in the high windows which are new, and so don't ripple and distort what they reflect the way the old panes in some of the windows do, the way memory will twist what did happen to suit our purposes, as poets will. The mind under the soil of all cultures and ages is the same, a mirror too of itself.

I reflect on my past—my past is me. St. John Nepomuk or the drowned sailor we now eat in our filet-of-fish sandwich, the soil burying us is that out of which springs all we know and are. In Vietnam and Laos, people used bomb craters for ponds to stock fish in, they drank water from spent shell casings, they got strong from lifting parts of cluster bombs as weights on an iron bar. Anything dead is useful as food for something else.

In Cesky Krumlov, the heraldric shield of the Swartzenbergs shows a severed Turk's head being pecked by a raven after a battle. The raven has its claws in the Turk's eye. We may assault our past so we can change ourselves. Or we can love it, rub ourselves against it till we scrape it bare by retelling it over and over, polishing it like the silverware we eat with till the pattern is level.

Silverware rather than stone as metaphor for the erasure of time and telling. Other travelers travel the same lines as I do; I often hate to share out the light from the stars over Annapurna, cram the mouth-damp mountains in my pockets to take home as we travel the same arcs, the same arks. As in Pompei, the past is preserved in a poem under layers of lines, lines of soil, layers of dirt. Excrement, dirt under the nails, our adventures and their distillations. Standing on the Charles Bridge in Prague, thinking.

Poor Father Nepomuk, whatever full humanity he had, is now just a circle of stars and a clasped mouth. So much for "immortality." A bridge is supposed to go somewhere. A white bird sitting on the head of a statue is incubating the past.

I remember a flight of cormorants or maybe pelicans from somewhere long ago—distorted in memory like the old hand-made glass in Krumlov Castle windows—who flew like an unstrung necklace, not linked together tightly as in a poem. Birds like the ones swooping near me now.[Today, as I copy this over in Jaisalmer in Rajahstan, India—26 July, 1993—other birds—ravens of black and brown, and sparrows and pigeons like the ones in New York City perch near me on the roof of my hotel as I write, and look at the old yellow fort in the sun.]

Helen was born of a bird, and who must, when old and all adventure past, muse on how now she can't launch even an admiring glance, how the gold of her beauty is all spent, how years have added anklets of her flesh to her slim ankles, how her hair has declined in value to silver, how squint lines around her eyes mimic the sun's rays, how her eyes don't dazzle any-one now. Lines are written on her only by age and on her forehead. But lines still circle her memory in poems. But the past piles up. No bird can fly faster nor escape. Circles.

Brueghel showed the crucifixion small and the picnic-ers big. In one painting of his, there are more than five crosses on that hill, and one guy is off in the bushes taking a shit. Real life. Coils of shit connect us to our bodies and to what we did earlier in the day. Can the pentecostal bird swoop down now on the Charles Bridge? Can I flirt with the muse now and not be sued for sexual harrassment? Can I bump into the power and the glory in the twisted surprising streets of Prague? Kafka, Borges, the written and the unwritten.

The smell of some Prague streets threw me off into the middle of my memory: Edinburgh, Scotland, some 28 years ago. Took some time to place it. Maybe it was the asphalt they use in paving, but I smell it often here in Prague, and stop, and sniff, and remember. Only glimpses of what was, and what I was, then.

And what could I expect? That memory or art could resurrect the moment long ago? In a museum here I saw both the Archangel Gabriel and the Virgin Mary painted by the same artist had exactly the same distinctive face with the same tight V of mouth. That mouth said to me that the painted saints and carved gods of myth and art look like the real models who sat for these artists.

Botticelli's Venus was probably his lover, Rembrandt's Old Testament women were all just Henrietta. Writers too, like Jonathan Swift's bees, were converting the world to their own brand of honey, or like his spiders, to venom. Or like Jesus, water to sparkling wine.

Under the Charles Bridge, the Karlov Most, float dead fish belly up looking like swans' feathers, below the weirs of the Vlatava. Or maybe they are swans' feathers. Christ on the cross, one of the statues on the bridge, is surrounded by Hebrew letters, like Nepomuk maybe with his stars. I think of the skeleton at the astronomical clock a few hundred yards away in the old square, turning on the hour his hourglass to remind us of the past and of the present passing. The universe swallows each of us with a yawn.

In Cesky Krumlov Castle, there is a ballroom where masked figures are painted on all the walls as though attendees at a ball. The painter himself painted himself, as well as one surprised character peering as though in a mirror, his face peering back at him and at us. There are also real mirrors for the real attendees (us) to see ourselves and our own masks. Borges and

Kafka and Prague and I wander the streets leading down narrow alleys opening up into the past right now.

Nepomuk. Jesus. In Guatemala a haciendado sucked the poison out of one of his worker's legs where a snake had bitten him, and died in agony because of open sores in his mouth. It took him two days to die, said his sister who told me this. I imagine in Auschwitz a man giving mouth-to-mouth resusitation to someone who had just bitten into a cyanide pill, and who would probably also die of the poison. How can one imagine Auschwitz? Only the smell of almonds in the cyanide, and none of the raisins of the cakes of his past Jewish life.

In Telc (pronounced "Telch"), an old medieval town where I spent a week in June, 1993, in the Czech Republic, the wind and rain rub lovingly against the gravestones in the churchyard in a timely embrace to erase the names till all the dead are spelled the same. In the cenotaphs of the dead rajahs in Jaisalmer in India it is the desert sand and wind that rub the memory out of the carved rock. Behind the self-conscious Rennaissance facade of the houses on the wide main square of Telc, the TV antennas call down the present moments. In the main square, tasteless cones of cheap ice cream fill the mouths of us all as we promenade in the evening slowly going grey against the still bright tops of the houses.

In Jaisalmer, India, on August 7, 1993, I finally wrote TELC:
"Embarrassed Adam cringes on Telc Castle wall,
sorrow in his face, his hand over his genitals.
I saw beneath the sculpted hand: no balls at all
What really does he cover up? What really is his motive?
Phallic or theological? Embarrassed at his Fall?

Above the garden wall, a head glides by.
A cyclist sure, but I can't see. A fly
buzzes like florescent bulb; against the sky
T.V. antennas behind Rennaissance facades of Telc.
My motive here is rhyme: Telc rhymes with belch.

What lies behind? The lies are all up front.
Krumlov's medieval parade with king and votives,
had runt for baron, for queen a gum-chewing slut,
for priest a lustful drunk. All true. *Ubi sunt?*
It's just a play. What lies behind the hand and eye?

Whatever race, Down's Syndromes look all like brothers.
Punch and Judy shows; ancestral portraits line the hall;
Death gets Punch, but new babies pour from mothers
and the artist fights time with puppets made of dust
(our dust), seeing the impotence of all the others."

In Cesky Krumlov, on the summer solstice eve (June 19, 1993), below
the castle, men dressed in medieval clothing brandishing and circling
torches over their heads, and young girls standing with sun-like halos over
their heads. There were fireworks, and candles were sent floating down the
Vlatava River, much narrower than when it flowed through Prague.
Lights, lights! Then came two rafts floating down the river, with Bacchus
presiding over one filled with blazing torches, mermaids, and other
Bacchic figures, pagan, one woman with a breast bared—cheers from the
crowd lining the banks, delight, the sun celebrated. Even at 10 p.m. the
sky above was still blue and light. Humans saying to the universe, "Me
too! Me too!"

I met someone on the train from Prague to Frankfurt, Germany, in July
1993, who knew me when I was the president and a leader of hiking and
biking trips in the Brooklyn College Open Road Club in 1960 and 1961.
Call him Marvin. He was wow-ed we should meet this way, and kept
shaking his head: "Wow, the great Chuck Stickney!" Naturally I was flattered. He had Tourette's Syndrome which, he said, was diagnosed only
recently. He had lost his job at a college teaching computer stuff, and was
just traveling around in Europe. Marvin had also been in Cesky Krumlov,

and, like me, had liked this old town. Krumlov had many gypsys and some had sung gypsy songs during a parade and festival of the old culture in the beautiful and ancient town square. The parade was of a medievally costumed king and queen, and their court, and had speeches and sword fights, as prelude to the summer solstice ride down the river. The gypsys were a distinctive part of the town. A local Czech told me that gypsys had been there for many generations, and that there was no problems with them in Cesky Krumlov. Marvin told me on the train that when in Krumlov he had asked a gypsy where he could get something to eat. The gypsy said to follow him. After walking for a while and traversing some desolate parkland, Marvin got suspicious, and said he'd like to return, but the gypsy said the restaurant was only a little further. After another gypsy joined them, Marvin was afraid, and when one of them hit him from behind and knocked him down, he pleaded with them only to take his money and not to hurt him. They took his money and took off. He walked back to the main part of town. I loved Cesky Krumlov because nothing like this had happened to me there. Marvin couldn't say the same about this place. My experiences with gypsys, especially in Spain, but also in the U.S. and elsewhere, make me very wary and untrusting of them.

Another example. I only ever spent a few days in Pakistan, but they were so filled with nasty experiences that I have always disliked their whole country. Is this fair? Is this the truth about a country or about a people? Of course not. Is it natural to feel such emotions and make such generalizations about peoples and nations based on such little evidence? Of course. Experience often trumps statistics. And when one's own experiences, however few, matches many others' experiences which you discover in conversations, and also matches statistics, it is hard not to make favorable or unfavorable stereotypes. In fact, I'd say it is foolish not to make such generalizations, yet one must be able to change these generalities about peoples if one of these particular people shows you it is not true about himself or herself. But travel shows, if anthropology didn't show you already, that people of one culture usually act differently from another culture. And some cultures have customs which displease those of another culture. A Mexican likes to have less physical distance between people than does an Englishman. Neither is wrong or immoral. But both may dislike the other's culture—the Mexican feels the English are cold, the Englishman feels the Mexican is physically overbearing. Human beings trying to get it right, understand, and protect themselves. Personally, I don't trust gypsys. Do you?

HUNGARY:

Dangled as bait in the river of time, outside a curio shop, a young Hungarian stands, old-fashioned dress designed for reeling tourists into time and till; resigned simper and blush show his real feeling for Szentendre's past; our American Williamsburg self-conscious but no simper; Rajahstan not even self-conscious. Szentendre's old cathedral perched above the Danube—the steamer from Budapest let us off here for a few hours of looking, before returning to Budapest, itself straddling the Danube.

Halfway up on the inside of Prague's St. Vitus Cathedral, there are stone busts of several heads, above them cut stone explanations, I trust, of who they are. Their faces echo faces I see in the streets. But immortality and renown, though stone doesn't rust, evades them as no one can read them. They're up too high. Though of Prague's upper crust, this crust is over the barest of air. To be remembered, our species' specious lust we take in at our mother's bust, yet our best hope is a bust. Yet I see the echo of their faces and their wants and mine in the streets today. We rhyme with each other.

St. George, killing pagan superstition in churches, forgot that dragons are dangerous. What once was called a poet's "elfin grot" is still a cave, a hole in the ground, like another hole in the ground.

George always looks too calm, here now in Szentandre, as in the Swedish church, Storkirchen, I saw in 1965. A lot too calm. Hungary's patron St. Stephen's right hand is in a gold and silver casket in a cathedral, and you are told that light will illumine it for only 20 forint, a sight that shows bold angels standing on demons on the casket. Sold on Stephens' plight, we watch his hand clutch tight a thousand years of cold. The demons are the base. We try to get time by our throat. The pattern breaks. Churches are meant to be familiar to the worshippers, meant to echo each other like rhyme, to call up the same emotions and rituals whereever they are. The McDonalds of the spirit.

In Budapest the McDonalds there opens early, and is popular for breakfast with the hungry Hungarians. The toilet too is classic American. After a savory breakfast, the toilet is my morning saviour and reliever of pain. In a Peter Breughel painting in a Budapest museum there are four guys crucified upon a hill. Four. Church fathers close in for the kill and pronounce the fourth false. To simplify the scene is to lie, but life just ambles on while significant stuff just whizzes by. Near Mary and other mourners, a man takes a shit upon a hill.

To rhyme is to help remember.

One evening in Budapest on the Danube's shore, a Japanese guy borrowed the violin from a gypsy street musician and proceeded to out-gypsy the gypsy with marvelous gypsy melodies. People stopped to listen. The gypsy was not happy about this. Later, the Japanese told me he had lived in Budapest for a year or so a few years back, and things then seemed much cheaper. It was now 1993. We talked about money, and about change.

ITALY:

I've been in Italy about six times. The second time, in 1963, I had taken leave from the Navy while my ship was at Naples, and ended up spending my days in Rome with two women, one blonde from New York named Joan, and one dark-haired white woman from South Africa named Jane. (Me Tarzan? No. This was platonic, except till the very end when I had a passionate clinch and kiss from Joan.) So the three of us went all over Rome together, seeing the sights.

Once when I told them to go ahead of me for a few minutes while I looked at something, I found them swarmed by young men, fairly slipping in their drool over two foreign seemingly unattached women—and one of them blonde! I disengaged these Lotharios by claiming one as my wife and one as my sister. Another time one soldier walked over to us and noted to us that there were two women and one guy, and couldn't he make our party more balanced. I used the "one's my wife, and one's my sister" bit on him, but he wanted to know which was my sister, so he could squire her. The Italian men were parodies of themselves, seeking to conform to the stereotype of the Italian "wolf," and succeeding. But it was all good-natured, almost as if it didn't really matter if they got the girl, as long as they played the game well.

Once, in 1971, in Rome at night with Joyce, my wife, we had a big argument over something. It might have been in, but not about, the Piazza Navona, one of the most romantic places in the world. At one point I stalked several yards away from Joyce, and then I noticed that another man started to go over to her. I stalked back, and asked him in English: "What the fuck do you want?" I would have been delighted to smash him, and recognizing this, he walked quickly away.I was not good-natured at this moment. How our mood, who we are with, the weather, our luck—how these color our times in places, color even the places themselves. Piazza Navona—dining there once, with the Bernini tritons and fountains, the church, the scattered couples, the stars, Joyce and I were flowing with good feeling. But not that night. In 1982, during the day, the Piazza Navona was crawling with homeless hippies, lethargically hanging around the fountains. Not romantic.

Also in 1971, on the island of Ischia, we both got covered up with the dark volcanic sand on the beach, sand supposedly therapeutic. The beach looked dirty, but it was just the color of the sand. We had a private terrace at a pensione on the beach, and went rowing and saw caves and, according to a postcard I sent my parents from there, there was a "full romantic moon." Without the postcard as prompt, I only barely remember the private terrace, and certainly not the full moon.

Yesterday, August 30, 2000, I stood on the Brooklyn Heights Promenade with Joyce, now my ex-wife, and mentioned Walt Whitman's poem "Crossing Brooklyn Ferry," and its lines, "I am with you, you men and women of a generation, or ever so many generations hence,\ Just as you feel when you look on the river and sky, so I felt...\Just as you stand and lean on the rail, yet hurry with the swift current, I stood, yet was hurried...." So many people have had the same experiences that I have had in Italy, and elsewhere, and will have them in the future, yet all countries are changing so quickly now, even Rome, the eternal city, dedicated to keeping its history fresh, is changing. The sound of Rome today with its squealing of tires as drivers speed around corners is not quite the same as the carts creaking at night in Juvenal's Rome. And so many churches were "chiuso," for restoration, and seemed never to be open or finished.

1978: "In Santa Maria del Popolo in Rome there are two Caravaggios. Helping to hoist Peter, the wrinkles in the forehead of one older man are admirable. Peter, being bourne upside down, looks uncomfortable. People look at this crucifixion, ignore the ordinary altar. This is what they came to see. A priest, impatient, counts the house. A brown curtain drapes half of a cherubim's face high on a wall. Stone ignores its flaps. Head hid beneath a booth, a medieval figure in the floor looks up skirts as they confess. In the dark niches where these paintings are, you must offer something for illumination. Ten lira in the machine, then push the button. Light."

On the island of Capri in 1971, Joyce and I tried to get into the Blue Grotto, to see its famous blue light. The first day we tried, the tide and the sea was too high to get in, so we bobbed about on a boat, looking at the hole in the cliff where the cave was, angry that the boatman, who must have known we couldn't get in, but took us, in two senses, anyway. Next day, Joyce and I set out again by boat for the Blue Grotto, and this time the weather and tide were okay. Having read Richard Halburton's Book of Marvels about his travels and adventures, I wanted to follow in R.H.'s footsteps (in this case, his watery wake) by swimming into the Grotto, not going in by boat. Our boatman said it wasn't allowed, but I told him I'd pay him as though he had taken me in anyway, and that I was going to swim in no matter what. He saw which way my own tide ran, and accepted. I dove off the boat, and swam through a narrow crevice in the cliff, and suddenly there was the famous blue light, coming in from beneath the water, and shimmering all over the cave. I dove deep and liquid fire came off my arms as I swam. Joyce jumped in once the boatman rowed her into the cave, and we swam together with blue churnings and shimmerings of light coming off our legs and arms. Here the water is pure, but lots of garbage littered the rocks and beaches of Capri that summer; one beach had swimmers contentedly paddling among bits of cartons and fruit peels. Someone told me that they clean up the beaches once the summer and the tourist season is over. Tiberius had his bodyguard throw off the cliffs near his imperial villa on Capri any of his boy lovers that displeased him. (Who cleaned that mess up?)

Venice in June of 1961 stank of old cheese, but it was the most romantic city in Italy. I couldn't get badly lost there, because signs are everywhere pointing either to the Rialto or to San Marco. But you can get lost just enough. Wandering in daylight or, even better, at night, with few people around at night (I hear that's changed with so many more tourists there in summers) is mysterious and redolent of antiquity and beauty (and old cheese).

Speaking of food, I discovered pesto sauce on spaghetti in 1973 somewhere near Genoa. Loved it so much I had another plate of it. What I didn't love was driving in Italy. Joyce and I had bought a car which we picked up in Paris, but once we got to Italy, driving became terrifying. Around the Italian lakes of Como and Garda, these two lane roads had Italian drivers coming around the blind curves on my side of the road, either because that was the straightest distance between two points, or because they were suicidal or homicidal. I have always tried to follow the "keep to the right" rule while driving (except in Scotland, Japan, and once upon a time, Sweden). It is a current obsession even while walking in the city on crowded streets. Did this current obsession date from the terror I felt while waiting for some nut-job Mille-Millia racing-car reject to come barreling around a curve on the left side of the road as though all traffic had been cleared off the roads to help him attain a speed record?

It would be easy to set a speed record eating in Italy because, compared with the USA, the portions are quite small. Ordering a meat dish, you can hold up the slice of meat to the sky, and see light through it. Or maybe it was the cheaper restaurants I ate at. In Stresa on Lago Maggiore in 1973 I don't remember where Joyce and I stayed, but we liked the place. In 1979 when I was divorced and had just finished more than a year on Sabbatical Leave, mostly in Asia, I stayed in Stresa at a pensione where I paid $16 per day for three very good meals, plus a room with two beds and a terrace, with a bath and toilet just outside my room. Even after Asia, I was impressed by the good value, especially when my cousin Lou Stephens, his wife and two children, were paying for two rooms, but no meals, about $120 per day. A much nicer hotel, naturally, but the competition is intense among travelers in Asia of who can see more while paying less, and I was so in that mode of cheap travel I included these prices in a letter to my parents. Stresa in 1979 was chilly and cloudy this late June and early July, with temperatures in the 50s, while I was used to temperatures in tropical Asia in the 90s, and in Egypt just before I returned to Europe, the temperature was about 119 or 120 F. The airplane shatters any sense of slow creeping by degrees (of temperature or of latitude) toward a destination. After a meal and an in-flight movie, we're in another country and climate. Abrupt. No transition. Disconcerting. Like after Strauss, rap. Perhaps one or more of these short chapters should be fragmented like this—like programatic music, with a turbulent style while writing of a storm, or as in shaped poetry, the shape of the page to look like a backpack or a valise or the shape of the country on a map. These words try to mirror or mimic the subject in a semantic sense, surely, both of the place and of the observer (me), and then try to slide into your mind as you read this, distorting the experience as little as possible.

From a letter of July 5, 1979: "In Stresa, working on Louie's book [on the painter Maxwell Gordon]….Arrived here on July 2—pouring rain, and that after 2 days & 2 nights on a bus! But I met and sat with and ETCETERA with a nice Canadian (French) girl, so the time passed through Greece and Yugoslavia and Italy quickly enough." What was left out of this letter? This girl and I had made love on the bus with all passengers asleep (we hoped), and had a good giggle over our exploit. (Several times over the next year or two she visited me in New York, and we had more leisure for our sexual grapplings.) Couldn't tell my parents about the sex on the bus. What is also missing from this letter? Anything about the three countries I traveled through on the bus. Granted, much of the time it was dark outside, but what facilitated the sex prevented the sight-seeing, not that I was as interested in what was going on outside the bus as I was on the inside. How much is left out of letters, poems, notes, journals. And even with the best notes in the world, and the best observing mind, and the best knowledge of the history and customs of those places, and the most time to revel in and reveal all that occurs, an even more than Proustian leisureliness, how much of what passes will not be known by the observer himself—by me on that bus, slicing through the darkness, past darkened fields and houses, and asleep or in conversation with someone, turning my head away from the landscape and all that is outside the bus and me. Even Borges's character Funes the Memorious, who remembered everything, would have missed so much.

In 1982 I spent several days in Florence, one of the most picturesque cities in Italy. What do I remember? The crowds in the Piazza della Signoria and the copy of Michaelangelo's statue of David, and then the real sculpture of David in the Galleria dell' Accademia, where I stood measuring with my eyes for about two hours this sculpture which was so perfectly balanced and yet with so natural a stance, I thought a student of sculpture should just study this David carefully and his education would be sound and complete. It's rare I feel moved to this extent in head and heart by any sculpture or painting. One statue out of all I saw in Florence.

Then there were the bronze doors of the Baptistry, the old palaces, the Ponte Vecchio and its fancy leather shops. I felt in Florence a glut of tourist bustle, a glut of churches (a common feeling among many travelers and tourists), a glut of art.

So off to Siena for a quieter day of sightseeing. A vertiginous over-view of the town from the tower of the Town Hall, and at its feet, the Piazza del Campo. A meal in a side street where the proprietor tried to cheat me, and the meal was lousy too. The house where St. Catherine got her stigmata, and a church where her authentic portrait is. Staring at it, I tried to feel myself into her life and her time, before she became a saint, before, when she was just a person trying to figure it all out. I wish I could see a photo of her, and all the other people who existed before photography, so I could see what they really looked like. Shakespeare at a party, and Shakespeare writing. Shakespeare thinking, not posing for the camera, as many of our celebrities do, aware of being observed, adjusting their faces to fit with how they think or we think they should be seen. The truth of them, even though it would only be the truth of one moment, of one mood, of one's outside. I liked my day in Siena, and felt then that next time I go to north-ern Italy I'd stay there instead of in Florence.

In 1963, while in the Navy on the U.S.S. Taconic (AGC 17), we sailed through the Straits of Messina a couple of times. The Straits separate Italy and Sicily, are narrow and turbulent, and so we set, as I remember it, the Special Sea Detail, readying our most competent watch to deal with any problems. I was on deck, looking at the myriad boats navigating the Straits, noting the high electrical wires above us bridging the water, and thinking of the strong currents of this sea. Many years later teaching Homer's Odyssey, reading of the many actual places commentators try to connect to Odysseus's ancient mythical journey, the Straits of Messina were often seen as the home of the monsters Sylla and Charybdis. We in the Navy sailed our ship (no sails at all, but the verb is used) more toward the center of the Strait, needing deep water as Odysseus did not. The Straits are never so narrow that Odysseus could not have easily sailed or rowed between these two monsters. Real life versus art? Like the portraits of St. Catherine, especially after she became a saint, what resemblance to reality? What resemblance these words, these ineffable thoughts?

GREECE:

In the summer of 1971, Joyce and I went to Greece for the first time. I was teaching ancient Greek literature at John Jay College, and so I thought to saturate myself in Greek culture, and to see for myself places like Mycene and Delphi and Athens. A anti-democratic junta was running Greece at the time and many people, to protest this, were not traveling there. If I waited till governments were to my liking I would never go anywhere, so we went. One good thing the junta did was set up tourist police to see that tourists were not cheated, and once we used them to get the correct price after the hotel owner switched it and raised it on us over our protests. The next day we complained to these policemen, and they called the hotel owner back to town from another town where he had gone, and got him to refund to us the difference. He was scared, but angry with us that we had had him running back to town in such a lather.

That same summer I ran five and a half times (1 3/8 miles) around the stadium in Delphi, where they held the ancient pan-Hellenic Pythian Games, "to thunderous applause of the birds. Delphi is magnificent— stark gorges seen from our window." Later on also ran in Olympia. In college, where I ran the mile and the two-mile run in track, and the five-mile cross country run (I was the Captain of the Cross-Country Team), I dreamed about becoming an Olympian and setting world records in the distance events. Here I was, actually running where the ancients ran! Me! A kid from Brooklyn! In Greece! Imagination raises the dust of this dusty flat bit of Grecian ground to the height of my old dream. Adventure is usually discomfort and danger filtered through one's imagination. Here in Greece there was little danger or discomfort.

Well, not quite. Joyce and I stopped first in Greece at the island of Corfu, and went to the beach at Paleocastritsa, the place a woman in the information bureau said was the most beautiful on the island. Small bays there, and we chose the one with a small hotel overlooking the beach, and with a small island a little more than a quarter of a mile out. One day I swam out to it by myself, and indulged in mooning about on it and exploring. Swimming back in, I saw Joyce coming out in a rowboat with a fisherman. She was frantic because she hadn't seen me and thought I might have drowned. Angry and relieved, she. Ashamed and reminded not to drift on my own thoughts, me.

Another night, Joyce and I joined some other tourists and some Greeks on the adjacent bay for a moon-lit, big-beach-fire-lit dance (I forget if there was a barbecue, but we did drink retzina). Sweating, arms around each other, we all danced till very late, and I remember staring up at the stars, listening to the waves slap, and thinking how simple the greatest pleasures are, how wonderful fellowship and the crackling of fire and the shush of waves (and even retzina) are, and how I could see why so many have loved the Greek islands.

In Greece often there were no menus in the restaurants we ate at. We would just be ushered into the kitchen, and peer into the pots on the stove. Not the words to describe the food, but the thing itself, sometimes hot, sometimes cold, but no surprises (till the bill comes).

Tours don't usually interest me, but we wanted to get around the Peloponnesus, and without a car, a tour is best. So we signed onto a sort of "hippie" tour for five days for low-budget travelers (a category where I always put myself). Stopping at gift shops often and leisurely, stopping at beaches often and lingeringly, and seeing the ancient Greek sites that Joyce and I really signed up for—quickly and perfunctorily. We complained that we wanted to see the ancient sites, but we were out-voted. Still, we saw the Lion Gates of Mycene, where Schliemann in a tomb found the golden mask over a ancient king's face, and saw that face crumble as the air hit it, and he said, "I alone of the living have seen the face of Agamemnon." (It wasn't really the face of Agamemnon, but what a great line!) We saw the stadium at Olympia, where I ran. We saw the sacred oaks of Zeus at

Dodona, where the wind's voice whispered truths too low to hear, even when I got away from the rest of the tour. Sacred Dodona. Sacred Delphi. Just the wind and light and silence. The gods knew what they were doing when they chose to live in these two places.

Often when you travel, you don't choose. In 1978 I was traveling alone across Europe and Asia to get to India by bus. The Magic Bus was heading to Athens from London, but in the middle of the night, semi-stuporous, we stopped on the road and those going to Turkey and points East were told to get out here. "There'll be a bus to Thessaloniki soon. They run all night," we were told. So out we got in the center of no-place, and off went the bus to Athens. There were six of us—me, a classic hippie from California, and four Brits (Tony, his girlfriend Cath, Keith—he pronounced it 'Keiff' as a good cockney would—and Brian). No buses came. No anything came, except the rain, so we slept under a highway bridge till morning, and hiked and hitched into Thessaloniki, staying till midnight when we all caught a train to the Greek/Turkish border, refused to pay the customs guy a lot of money for him to drive us to Edirne, so we walked there, then by bus to Istambul, where we stayed, all six of us in one room, in the Gungor Hotel in the Sultanhamet district behind the Aghia Sophia.

We did have the choice to separate, but we liked each other and I went across Turkey, Iran, and Afghanistan with them, three weeks together because we happened to be heading in the same direction and were put out of a bus together. One meets people casually, and ends up living with them for days or months. The day in Kabul, Afghanistan, we all split up, they were going north to Mazar-i-Sharif, and I wanted to continue on toward India. The manager of the hotel put me in a room with a Spanish woman, who he informed of this, waking her up, and putting me and my pack in the room. She looked at him, at me, grunted yes, and went back to sleep. Sharing rooms and even beds on the road was a casual thing in 1978. The next morning we ended up making love in a fast no-speaking way, and then got chatty and friendly. Casual, as I said.

Back now to Greece and to 1971 and being married. In Delphi, Joyce
kept watch while I climbed into where the Castalian spring flows, the
spring that is supposed to furnish inspiration for the poets and play-
wrights of the ancient Greeks. I gulped the water quickly, afraid I would
be chased away from this forbidden spot. Like from the Blarney Stone in
Ireland, inspiration flows from natural sources, and while I don't believe in
the gods, the muses, the magic that percolates down through history and
folklore, I tinge my disbelief with a touch of ritual and do it anyway.

If you love something, do it more than once. Joyce and I went to
Lindos on the island of Rhodes on the way to Israel in 1971, and returned
to Lindos on the way back. It was the archetypal Greek place. A small
whitewashed village, with Greeks and Swedish tourists and donkeys
ambling the twisting streets, cheap rooms to rent (ours had a view over the
beach), restaurants serving the omnipresent and never boring tomato
salad and moussaka, a small finger-nail-paring-shaped beach, and best of
all—at the literal top of the town, a Crusader fort surrounding an ancient
Greek temple with a well-worn statue of a goddess peering down hundreds of sheer feet to the sea. Major romantic and gorgeous! And on the
other side of this escarpment from the town, a tiny, round bay, with a
small white-washed chapel in its shore, known as St. Paul's Bay because
Paul was supposed to have landed there while spreading Christianity.
History, myth, pagan and Christian, and also upholding the myth of what
touristed Greek islands are. Perfect.

But we never went back after that 1971 trip. Later we divorced, and my
later trip alone to Greece in 1978 and then in 1979, showed me a Greece
far more European than it had been. In 1971 it seemed much more Greek
and foreign. The Archeological Museum in Athens still has those marvelous Mycenean bronze cups and small Cycladic figures which in 1971,
leaving the museum, I felt that all of art has gone downhill since then. I've
heard that Lindos now has a lot of hotels and condos, and I don't want to
go back to spoil my 1971 memories of it. Returning reminds you also of

the changes in you, and of time passing, and how you, like art, like the sea water, go downhill.

SWITZERLAND:

In the summer of 1961, between graduating from college and going into the Navy's Officer Candidate School, I spent five weeks in Europe and got to see the Matterhorn. Growing up, I was fascinated by mountain climbing. Not so much to do it, but to read of the danger and the endurance of it. I had climbed cliffs in Arizona before, and a few 12,000 foot peaks in Arizona and California, but thrilled to the real-er thing of climbing Annapurna and Everest and the Matterhorn. So now in 1961 I looked up and, standing above the town of Zermatt, piercing the sky, was the Matterhorn.

There were several routes to the base of the mountain. I took what I later found out was the difficult route, but it wasn't dangerous, just scrambling up a steep slope till it leveled off and then the Matterhorn was ahead of me. I took my simple camera, and a few photos, some taken by me of me grinning and one of my finger pointing toward the mountain, and one taken of me by a woman hiker. A misty rain wrapped the mountain round, and I had a sweater wrapped round me, but I was getting wet and so climbed up on the foothills of the mountain till I felt close enough, and turned round and went down. I still had my childhood dream of some day climbing the Matterhorn, but was not so enthusiastic of its reality, and was somewhat afraid of heights.

In Luzern, if I remember correctly, there is a bridge, crookedly built over some water, painted with scenes of the medieval dance of death, death pictured as a skeleton leading many citizens of all classes and ages and professions in the rhythmic parade toward becoming their own skeletons.

In 1973 I remember seeing a small sparrow trembling under a tree, not flying away even though several people were staring at it on the ground. I picked it up, and out from between my fingers scurried many lice, or what looked like lice. I put down the bird, not wanting the lice on me, and discussed with some of the onlookers about what to do with the poor bird. The bird seemed doomed, we felt, and whether to kill it or leave it was the question. Joyce and I left, but I still remember the poor shivering despairing bird in the street of Luzurn near the water over which was the bridge with the medieval paintings of the dance of death.

How neat was that image! Pairing the dying bird with the dance of death. But they were paired naturally by happening close together in time and space. Let me also connect these with the glacier in Grindelwald, the most beautiful place I saw in Switzerland in 1973. We got right to the foot of this blueish-white glacier, with its cracks, crevasses, and groaning. I won't anthropomorphize that glacier, but groaning was what it sounded like as it shifted and moved slowly forward. Sometimes the glacier, so I understand, seemed to move backwards, but this was because the weather might have been warmer that year or too little rain or snow had fallen. But it suits me that this glacier slowly, but inexorably, moved forward, a great symbol of cold unfeeling death to tie in with the dying bird and the painted bridge. The glacier ignored me completely.

In 1973 the Japanese were traveling. They were now rich, so differerent from when I was stationed in Japan in 1961 and 1962, and were willing to buy up everything and anything at almost any price. People told me gleefully that they would cheat the Japanese, and charge them outlandish prices which they would pay with a smile. (I remember when that was said of the Americans.) One Swiss man was lambasting in English this slight Japanese man about how dare they come here and buy up everything in sight. The Japanese was sucking his teeth, smiling, and bowing, although he must have known even without any knowledge of English that he was being royally insulted. We were all standing on a spur of a mountain looking down on the valley of Grindelwald with the north wall of the Eiger to our right. The view was magnificent.

Mostly it rained the time we were in Grindelwald. One night we were camping and the rain was so heavy it collapsed our tent, and we moved into our car, draping the wet tent and all our gear in the trunk and back seat. We decided that we had had it with the rain, and soon headed back to France, where no sooner had we crossed the Swiss-French border, than the sun shone full on again. Mountains are beautiful, but they usually come with rain.

Same with glaciers. The bridge in Luzurn, with its doglegs of shape, with the dance of death painted on its ceilings, prettily reminds us of our final destination. But Switzerland can make the journey sweet. In Zurich once in early September 1965, I wrote: "The weather cleared, but remained (and remains) cold . Went to the Art Museum. Walked a lot through the town, eating bratwurst, tagesuppe, etc., and chocolate at every opportunity. Soon no doubt my bowels will de-Spanish-ify and solidity will return….Am staying at the Youth Hostel….I try to struggle by on my incredibly elementary German." This may have been the youth hostel where guys all slept in one huge bed, and it was crowded. If the guy next to you turned over, you had to turn over too. All in the same bed or boat, the dance continued even at night.

Swiss chocolate was a staple of my diet there. But the best pastries Joyce and I had was from a little pastry shop on a lake in Zug. We sat in our car, looking out over the lake, eating pastries, and when they were finished, we went into the shop again and bought more. We stopped only when they had run out of pastries. One day in Jaisalmer in Rajahstan in India in 1993, twenty years after being in Zug, in a small rooftop restaurant, I met two young women who were from Zug, and I mentioned that little pastry shop. They couldn't get over it, that someone from America knew their town. They also were so sweet.

Behind Grindelwald stands the north wall of Mt. Eiger. During the 1930s especially, the Germans tried to climb the face of this mountain. Many climbers died trying. I walked up to its base one day. The clatter of rocks falling, and the wind, and the chill off it, and my knowledge of all the struggles and deaths on this north face combined to make the mountain seem terrifying and malevolent. I felt it was evil, that it wanted to hurt me. The rocks clattered down its face, and the wind swooshed, and the distance to the top took away my courage. Once before I had such a feeling of panic, and it was when I was sixteen and in the spring of 1956 I walked through some snow toward the foot of Yosemite Falls. I was alone, and could feel the spray and wind and roar of the falls. Suddenly I felt I was near something very evil. Turning around I could see nothing. But the roar and the spray made me retreat toward the safety of the Awahnee Hotel and my parents. The great god Pan was in those woods. He was also at the base of the grand and dangerous Eiger the day I was, another reminder of the beating of time in that dance we all learn.

SWEDEN:

From letter 16 Sept. 1965: "The next day got as far as Manheim [Germany], then remained for several hours in the rain, my forlorn sign saying "Copenhagen" sodden, my spirits the same. Hitchhikers in Germany are very friendly toward each other, a somewhat startling fact after the animosity (concealed, of course) between us in the U.S.A. The situation grew even grimmer, so a British lad and I took a train to Frankfurt where we stayed at a hostel. Frankfurt is crammed to the rafters with American servicemen and nasty Germans—glad to get out of it." A note about Frankfurt in 1993—every German in Frankfurt I spoke to was very helpful in showing me where places were I wanted to get to. Very nice—like Londoners in 1961. Except in Frankfurt where I stayed near the train station. Druggies and pimp-y types in and around the station, which is also right at the red-light strip-joint area.

To continue on Frankfurt in 1965: "Then met two Japanese fellows, one who hitched to Heidelburg to get some money for fixing his car, which was in Alsfelder. And which, when fixed and paid for, was headed for Stockholm [where I was headed too]. And they said they'd take me. So I hitched with Akira to Alsfelder where we waited for Tak. He arrived in two days." Now I remember Akira was treated very well by all sorts of Germans. They bought him beers. Hitching with him was amazing! When he say a car coming, he stepped out and waggled his thumb in an almost panicky movement, and nearly every car screeched to a stop for him (and therefore also me). Whether he communicated a frantic need, or the fact that he was Japanese, who had been allied with Germany in the last war, the German response to him was so much more friendly than toward me then in 1965. And it had been much less friendly to me in 1961.

"Leaving Frankfurt at 6:30 p.m., we set off for Stockholm. We slept in the car while waiting for the Travemende—Gedser ferry, then leaped across to Copenhagen where I seized one letter from my Swedish girl, Pia____, and left Denmark via Elsinore ferry. We slept off the road halfway through Sweden and arrived, haggard-eyed in Stockholm in the morning. I got in touch with Pia and there I've been for five days....I'll probably stay in Sweden till Monday and then head for Oslo to see a bit of Norway and find work on my ship."

But things changed. I made love with, and fell more in love with, Pia, and so followed her up to her university in Uppsala. I had met Pia on the ferry to the island of Ibiza in Spain's Balearic Islands, and was infatuated with her, but she held off anything sexual till, as she put it, if and when "I'll love you, I'll give you everything." In Uppsala we made love, and once had a magnificent orgasm at the exact same time, and burst out laughing, hugging one another. A problem though. Pia was fertile when we made love for the first time on the sofa of her parents' apartment, and she thought we had made a baby. When she told me that she may be pregnant, I thought over my options. I could marry her, live in Sweden, maybe teach English, and manage somehow. Suddenly I might be a Swede! Or we could get an abortion. Or maybe cause a spontaneous abortion, and so we ran a lot together, and jumped, and hopped, and hoped. Or another option, which appealed especially after we had an arguement, why not just get on a train to Oslo and go home. Run away from this complication. This all did not stop us from making wonderful sweet love a lot, but what to do about this possibility of a baby weighed on us, and pressed out of our minds much of Pia's studies of art history, and my concerns about

what to do with my life when and if I got back to the U.S., and pressed us
together, closer, connected from belly to brows.

About a church I wrote then: ST. GEORGE AND THE DRAGON:
Sometimes they said more than they knew, these craftsmen, whose work
one sees in museums now, or in churches; Storkykan in Stockholm, for
instance, has a wooden carving of St. George and his inevitable dragon at
the moment before triumph; the dragon lanced into agony dips his claws
in the horse who rears above him, both are gore-washed, wild-eyed, all
muscles cramped in mortality, all chocked with the other's pain, completely awash with the other, but George, whose arm carrying sword raised
automatic before the abstracted thwack, the curious pale blank of his face
reflects nothing of the birds who twirl and flash above these spring-sur-
rounded woods near the bat-packed towering castle, reflects not red-raped
grass beneath the dustless tussle, reflects no flesh-fed fumes from the nostrils of this dying myth, does not feel the sweating horse jogging pranceful
his thighs, nor the blue of sun-stroked sky quivering on his empty eyes,
because in all that colored senseful place and time, George was a saint, and
this the carver knew, and so formed him insoluble with the outside which
peered ineffectually into his skull through the linking holes of sense."

This was about something with a guaranteed outcome. The dragon
could not win. I, however, felt that I could very well get swallowed up by
my dilemma. The rest of the world went on while Pia and I pondered in
the fall of 1965.

Later in 1965 I wrote WINTER IN UPPSALA NEAR THE CATHE-
DRAL ON A SUNDAY:

"The rook-ridden towers were quiet today; no birds circled swooping,
none wavered high, nor swept the clean air round their sorrowful tips,
none now made a playground of these two thick spires. But this abandoned church was filled with Sunday people, heavy doors enclosed their
talk and the music, as on the walls thick shields of gold enclosed the heads
of the saints, painted halos like hoods, shelter from the wind which
whipped brown branches and thrust tattered twigs in amused imitation of

the churches' fine spines, twigs quivered with laughter in the immaculate sky, in the bird-botched, cloud-washed sky, where despite the snake-voiced wind swished hissing against them, the undeviating thorns atop the church swayed not, altered not, swayed not, altered not, but pressed instead the cloud-skimmed, skin-like sky, till the relenting year bled tearful snow, laughing, soothing, weary snow, on its torpid, brittle limbs."

The world went on, dipping toward winter, and one day Pia woke up bleeding, and hugged me tight, and announced her period had come. So I guess had mine, and so I made preparations for leaving Sweden. I would miss Pia, and I would also miss a wonderful berry jam called "lingonsilt." Lingonberry jam, spoons of it, are part of my remembrance of Sweden, one of the few Swedish words I could pronounce with the right accent. From a letter to my parents (25 Sept. '65): "The weather here is not bad for 60 degrees north latitude: real autumnal, smokey evenings, crows whirling about like charred bits of paper, air like a washed window. Pretty quiet life, this. Spend a lot of time walking to and from eating places (by the way, have eaten enough hot dogs to keep me from camping at Nathan's door when I get home. The novelty of the plebian sausage can, strange to say, wear off." "Warme polser" is either Danish or Swedish for the reddish frank served in carts throughout these lands. In this same letter: "Less interested in travel for travel's sake than I used to be in the days when my thumb was law and movement a physiological necessity," referring to my desire to hitchhike all over the USA when in college.

Another psychological necessity was American food. After my one year in China, I was desperate for pizza. Laid up with a high fever in Trincomalee in Sri Lanka, I had fever dreams of a soft salami sandwich on seeded rye bread with Gulden's Mustard, because this symbolized Brooklyn where my mother would take care of me. Once in Penang in Malaysia I stopped in at the new McDonald's and had a vanilla milk shake, and in Kuala Lumpur I had some cole slaw and an A&W root beer. Home on a bun or in a cup. Food is not just physical.

Pia painted an American flag and the word "Oslo" on a sign to help me hitch, "and they worked. Very easy hitching across Sweden which is supposed to be about the toughest place in Europe to hitch. I'll keep using the flag. Because tomorrow I'll head for Lond. I arrived in Norway to find the situation well nigh impossible to get a ship which will terminate in the US. Jobs to and fro—yes. Just 'to"—no! Even Norway has succumbed to rules and regulations—damn little adventure a man can have. If a boy goes to sea, he has to come back, otherwise no job. Oh, well, I guess it'll be a plane trip from Scotland now." So after hitching back to England, staying with a friend in London, and then to Dundee to stay with another friend, I flew back to the States. I had hoped to get some job as an ordinary seaman on a freighter to America, but ended that trip like any other tourist. Which I guess is what I really was.

DENMARK:

In 1961, my first trip to Europe, I was sitting in a small cafe in Copenhagen when I noticed a big headline—Hemingway tot! Earnest Hemingway had just blown his brains out with a shotgun.

Most people in that cafe were (according to my guide book "Europe on 5 Dollars a Day" which shows you something about inflation of prices) intellectuals and could speak English, and I remember discussing Hemingway and his work with them that afternoon.

On the train up to Copenhagen from Munich, I met a Swedish girl and we "huddled on the very windy and chilly deck of the ferry to Gedser watching the sun come up (and it took its own sweet time about it). In Copenhagen, I went to Tivoli [a huge amusement park] and saw free shows and concerts inside. Really an excellent park. Met two American girls and we went to Vingardens Bar, and danced, etc. after a tour of Ny Haven, tough waterfront honky-tonks. Vingardens—a crowded sweaty throbbing place that costs nothing to dance. Nightlife here is cheap too." From this snippet of my journal of the trip, you can see two obsessions of mine: money and women. Then and now.

These two make the world go round for very many of us men.

Speaking of a common tie, in Copenhagen suddenly there was a bunch of activity in the street and along came a parade. And who should be sitting up on the back seat of a slowly moving car but Walt Disney, waving to the scattered caught-off-guard pedestrians. I was so startled and delighted that I ran out to greet him and shake his hand, shouting "Walt Disney!" He shook my hand, asked me where I was from, and said "Well, it's nice to see another American."

One of the main things I hoped for in Denmark was to have a love, or at least a sex, affair with a Dane. They were supposed to be "easy" and rarely could I find that in American women at that time. Sex didn't happen for me in Denmark then. Sex and money. Makes the world go round. Anyway, the pursuit of it certainly does. Round and round. Lately (in 2000) I run around a lot less.

PORTUGAL:

Portuguese sounds like a troubled Yiddish speaker with a excess of saliva in his mouth. Lots of "oy-sh" sounds. It began to be annoying after a while, although my Spanish made me generally understood by them. One time when I was not, was when I, in Lisboa (or Lisbon), asked directions to get to the famous "Torre de Belem." This tower, on the riverfront, was a main tourist attraction in Lisbon. Several people converged around me, pronouncing, as I had, "Torre de Belem?" Scratching heads, genitals, what have you, they stared at each other for a few minutes in semi-mute incomprehension, till finally one man in a burst of eureka burst out with an "AHH! Torre de BelENG!" At least it sounded like that to me. Then they all knew where I was going and could direct me. It is as though a tourist in New York City asked for directions to the Statue of Luberty.

You'd think people would figure it out without excessive cogitation.

Another bit of incomprehension on my part was when the hotel desk clerk in Lisbon presented my bill for the several nights I spent at the Hotel Francefort. He charged me not only for the "nights" I was there, but then doubled the amount by charging me also for the "days" I stayed there too. I fought him on that once I realized he meant it seriously, not as a joke. I don't remember the outcome, only the disbelief I felt when the bill was given to me. Oh, for the Greek Tourist Police to have been there to adjudicate it all!

In 1965, after my graduate studies in Edinburgh, I spent about six months traveling around Europe and doing some writing. Mostly hitch-hiking, which is the best way to meet people and travel cheaply. I was picked up somewhere in northern Spain by a Portuguese ex-matador and taken to Madrid for a couple of days, and then we drove to Lisboa where he was originally from.

Spain's countryside was speckled with old rather shabby white houses, but as soon as we crossed the border into Portugal, the houses were all blue and white, everything much neater and prettier than in Spain. In Lisboa, many of the streets have mosaics in the sidewalks—small rounded stones spelling out the name of the company which they front, or with lovely patterns. Clearly a place meant to last, one that treasures its history. From a hill ascended by a funicular you can see much of the city.

In 1970 Joyce and I spent some time in Portugal—in Lisbon and in the Algarve region, with beaches separated by tall handsome rock pinnacles. Lovely towns down there as well. However, one older guy started up a conversation with me—he in Portuguese, I in Spanish—while Joyce and I waited for a bus by the side of the road. I wasn't concentrating much on what he said, but nodding and smiling and looking out for the bus. Suddenly he grabs Joyce and tries to kiss her on the mouth. She pushed him away, and I grabbed him by the collar, and somewhat disbelieving what I had just seen, I pushed him to the ground with my stiff right arm. He got up and ran, without me saying a word to him. I could barely believe what I had seen (I still can't grasp it, but I did grasp him). Perhaps he did ask my permission to kiss her, thinking I'd agree because I didn't understand what he was asking. I was thirty, he was perhaps in his fifties. Did he assume I would not hit an older man? Neither Joyce nor I had a clue.

In 1965 while in a very lovely fishing town north of Lisbon, Nazare, I wrote: "BLUE MONDAY FOLLOWS EASTER SUNDAY IN NAZARE: Off the back of the damp Atlantic the wind whips up a smell of sweat; the spirited sea in its bed rises and falls and rises again in an orgy of copulation—silvery fish spawn from every pore and water boils at the edges with their heat, all this for silver to fleck the wounded sides of the fish that feed the men of Nazare.

Now the golden meat of sunny tourists proves a tastier dish. I see gourmands prowl the windy streets looking for the edible scrap. Our town like all the rest is surrounded by an empty belly.

Overhead, a rumbling plane divides the sky with a counterfeit cloud, and a fishnet embraces a beach-bred red-sailed boat to slowly draw the mender into its web. Behind the town, the sea slips up the beach to re-lick its line of weeds and wet.

Only at full of fall of night can the tidy lovers deal in the coinage of inedible moon."

In 1970 we went to Sintra, a town near Lisbon with a marvelously grotesque castle, baroque to the max. Beautifully carved, but the carvings often are of monstrous shapes and faces.

I'm ambivalent about Portugal and the Portuguese.

SPAIN:

Heinrich Boll, in his short story "Action Will Be Taken," writes: "Wunsiedel's factory was swarming with people who were obsessed with telling you the story of their lives, as indeed vigorous personalities are fond of doing. The story of their lives is more important to them than their lives, you have only to press a button, and immediately it is covered with spewed-out exploits." With a computer, e-mail, desk-top publishing, instant messaging, these life stories are now even more rampant. Yeats's choice of the life or of the work is, at times for a writer, real.

Life in front of a flashing computer screen composing an autobiography or a travel book is a life of memory, of meditation, not to be confused

with the acts of living, of traveling itself. Writing is not even the life of an
observer looking on or over others' actions.

While I was a Lieutenant (junior grade) in the U.S. Navy in 1963, on a
cruise to the Mediterranean on my ship the U.S.S. Taconic (AGC-17), an
amphibious group command ship, we spent a few days in Valencia in
Spain, where I was designated Assistant Shore Patrol Officer under Major
Selby, a Marine from our ship. There were several other Navy ships there
at the time, and since I spoke some Spanish, I was meant to be a liaison
with the Spanish police to make sure our men didn't cause trouble. We
had American shore patrols out, but primarily my job was observing, of
walking around to bars where sailors hang out as a reminder to all that
sailorly wildness should be somewhat curbed. When not being driven
around during the hours of "liberty" I was at a Spanish police station waiting for trouble. One evening we got a call and I and a Spanish cop and my
driver sped over to where shore patrol from my ship were holding in cuffs
a sailor, Kazok, from the engineering division, nick-named the "snipes," of
my ship. Kazok was in tears, having started a fight with a marine and bitten him on his finger. Kazok, like most sailors on liberty in a new or even
old port, was drunk. I asked the shore patrol petty officer what the story
was, then asked Kazok. He tearfully told me that he was very sorry, would
never do it again, and asked if he could have his cuffs removed. The shore
patrol said if he promised not to cause any trouble, it was O.K. with them.
I told Kazok that he must go straight back to the ship with the patrol and
that I would talk to his division officer about the appropriate punishment
for him. He agreed, thanking me profusely and ashamedly. The Spanish
cop I was with just stood there observing. After all, no Spaniards were
involved, this was all just US Navy and marines business. We ere surrounded by a fairly large crowd, all of whom were quiet, non-threatening,
just observing intently. They wanted to see how we did things. The cuffs
were taken off the sobbing Kazok, the shore patrol and I waved each other
off casually, and I sped back to the police station or toward our rounds of
the sailors' bars. No problem. All calmly done. I remember thinking that

my efficiency and calmness must impress the many Spaniards watching. I was playing to an extent to the crowd. This was during the despotic years of Franco, but we were taking care of common business, and didn't concern ourselves with over-arching dictatorships or politics. But we did concern ourselves with how we appeared to the ones watching us.

Ordinary life continues no matter what government is in power, and so does sex. I was dancing with a Swedish woman, Margareta, who had just finished leading some holiday-makers to Benidorm further up the Spanish coast, and we decided to have sex. In the midst of this copulation in the hotel room which Major Selby and I shared, suddenly there was a knock on the door. "Is that you?" (I forget the Major's first name), I asked. "Yeah. Can I come in?" Pause. "Chuck, you got a woman in there?" "Yeah." "Look, I'll walk around for a bit and then come back." "Great. Thanks." So he did, and I kept doing. Later on, I was still doing, and a knock came again. Finally,

Selby said, "Look, Chuck. This won't be the first time this has happened. I just want to get some rest. So I'll come in, and just go to sleep. You can then carry on." "O.K." So I introduced him to Margareta, he got into his bed three feet from ours, and lay there as though he were asleep. Maybe he even was. But, despite doing some more copulation, etc. I never quite felt as free as I had when the room held just Margareta and me. Being observed or overheard or even the possibility distorted the sexual experience, and though we giggled about our having to do it quietly, neither of us could whole-heartedly forget the presence in that other bed. Like the Heisenberg Uncertainty Principle, the mere observation can change what is being measured. A measurement of six erect inches might, under the eyes of an observer, shrink to a mere two.

From drinking, sex, and military discipline which could fit into any country and be essentially the same, not especially Spanish, we go to military exercises between the USA and Spain. My ship was in Barcelona, and I had met and invited to see me on the ship several members of the Bentiber Ballet, some stunning ladies. I was taking them around the ship and awe-ing my drooling shipmates when I got a message from the Executive Officer of the ship who gave me less than an hour to be ready for two weeks temporary duty as the liason officer of the US fleet to the Spanish Amphibious Force. I was supposed to explain all aspects of the combined forces' landing at Almeria on the south coast of Spain to the high command of the Spanish naval forces. But who would explain it all to me? I was ship's company, not the staff who planned these exercises. However, the clincher was that I spoke some Spanish and so I was it. I was handed the OpOrder, a thick folder labeled SECRET, which would tell me everything. But if I didn't understand some of it, I would have to improvise. I didn't understand all of it.

Here we were in Spain, but as you must have noticed, there is very little of Spain in these pages so far. Sailors, both civilian and military, when ashore, tend to get drunk and try to get laid. Sailors know the sailor bars in places all over the world, but very little of the world around those bars and ports. A sailor's guidebook to the world would be short and repetitive, only as thick as a whiskey glass. But a combined-forces Naval exercise is serious and complex.

I flew to Cadiz on the east coast of Spain to a Spanish Naval Base to embark on the ship "El Almirante Lobo," their Amphibious Command, the "Admiral Wolf," a fine war-like sea-going name which had been re-fitted from a ship that in its civilian incarnation had hauled coal. Captain de Benito was the mild bespectacled man in charge of the Spanish forces. His Chief of Staff was a short young-ish polite gentleman. The other officers on the staff and on ship's company, all in grey uniforms the color of their ships' sides, were all gentle and friendly to me, and had little need of my assistance. There were three American enlisted men under me, one translator and two radiomen. The Almirante Lobo steamed around Gibraltar, with me observing the action on the bridge, and got near Almeria on the the south coast, and stood off the land waiting for the exercises to begin. The Spanish forces were mostly made up of small landing craft, while the Americans had much larger ships and more of them. How other countries must have been impressed by and envious of or even annoyed by our military capabilities!

One command decision I had to make was when the Chief of Staff asked me about two different coordinates in two separate parts of the Operation Order; it seemed that some Spanish ships were to be starting for their attack on the beach from two different places at the same time. What should they do? Which coordinates were correct? he asked. "Yesterday the exercise went smoothly? No one complained about where you started from?" "No," he said. "So have your ships start from the coordinates they used yesterday," I said. "Good, we'll do that," said the Chief of Staff. And we did as I said. And it was good. My first really big command decision, and me only a Lieutenant (jg).

While these joint naval exercises were going on, President Kennedy was assassinated. I was having dinner in the wardroom along with all the other Spanish officers when one of my men asked if he could interrupt my dinner. I said, "yes," and he told me he had heard on the cook's short wave radio the B.B.C. announce that President Kennedy had been shot in Texas. Was he alive? My man didn't know, but he would keep checking on the short wave for news. Almost no one of the officers spoke English, and when I told them what had happened, their shocked horror knocked them back in their seats. I excused myself and went up to tell the Chief of Staff and Captain de Benito who headed the Spanish forces. They also were dismayed and shocked, and asked me if I thought the joint amphibious exercise would be called off. I told them I doubted it, that the presidential succession was clear in our country, but I would try to find out from the American command. Captain de Benito wrote a message of sorrow about this to the Americans, I translated it and spoke it "in the clear" (meaning without encryption) over the radio. When I walked around in the ship later in the night, after I heard that the president was dead, I was aware of all eyes observing me, and so could not indulge my grief, which was real, without a certain histrionic tinge because I represented America and its feelings to these Spaniards. Like the Heisenburg Uncertainty Principle, the very act of observing changes the thing observed, and not just on the sub-atomic level, but also on the human level. The Chief of Staff told me that if their leader (Franco) had been assassinated, all their ships would break off whatever they were doing, and head back to their bases in Spain. I assumed probably for fear of a coup.

The next morning there was an all-hands ceremony on the Spanish flagship to mourn President Kennedy's death, and the Captains shook hands with me and saluted, after which we went over to the American ships for a conference with the leaders. The American amphibious group commander, Captain Boyer, told us they would go ahead with the exercise, and we should too. Later, one of my men on the American command ship, the Taconic, told me that when our Captain announced the assassination, his voice was shaking terribly. Shock all around, but the amphibious assault exercise would go on.

During the several days of amphibious exercise, I went with several of the Spanish top officers on to the beach, and got them an impromptu helicopter ride over the assault beaches in a U.S. chopper. On a lazy day after the assault I went over to the town of Almeria, and wandered around with some of the other Spanish officers. The fountain in the center of the town was dry, but in honor of me, the town turned on the fountain. Ah, the thrill of it all. Here was I, a junior officer, yet important because I was the link with the American forces. I found the Spanish Navy most considerate to me, yet here were these "fascistic" far-rightist anti-democratic state's people, dedicated to upholding the government of the state, i.e. Franco, behaving like gentlemen to me, and not solely because I was an American officer on joint exercises with their country. I found the same thing when I was in far-left Communist China, even dealing with most people in the government, that most people are decent, whatever their government. Especially if these countries need what you can give them, whether Naval power or literary knowledge.

Both Spain in 1963 and China in 1984 were rather poor countries. Spain was not quite European then, being behind the curve of economic and political developments in the rest of this continent. Bar food was often not those wonderful tapas, but was rather dry bread with hard cheese or salami, with nothing to mitigate their dryness. A good symbol of the country, like the stiff Spanish ruff around the throats of 16th century conquistadors. Think how a little bit of mayonnaise could make life softer! Once hitchhiking in Andalusia in 1963 in civilian clothes, I was picked up by a truck, and got in the back along with a whole party of Spanish workers. Asking discreetly but not too discreetly about how people felt about Franco, some of them volunteered answers. One man said Spain was about divided equally between lovers and haters of Franco. It seemed, he felt, your view of Franco depended on which part of the country you came from. Now this reminded me of a man in Iran in August 1978 who told me about half the country was for the Shah, half for the still-exiled Khomeni. In a few months, the lovers of the Shah were outlawed. So the tides of history. Obviously, one didn't discuss politics publicly in the Navy's wardrooms whether that Navy be Spanish or American.

Women was another taboo subject during the wardroom meals in the American Navy. Once in 1965, no longer in the Navy, I was hitching outside of Barcelona toward France, and got a ride with three gypsies, a Flamenco troupe, one of whom, the leader, was called "El Sali." The blonde Norwegian woman driving was his wife, and I'm sure the men would not have picked me up. I was chattering in English with the lovely lady and getting these jealous cut-your-throat looks from El Sali, and after I told her I wanted to get back to America by working on a Norwegian freighter, she gave me some names she knew in the shipping business in Oslo, and assured me it would be easy to get work on a ship back to America. Women and ships—not always smooth sailing for me.

In August 1965, I went out to the Balearic Island of Ibiza to relax and write, and I wrote a very short story about it: "Another Stroke of Luck": "Although they had been on the boat together, he had not managed to meet her until after they had docked in Ibiza. He saw her through the indiscriminate dispersal of the other voyagers, spilling , like multicolored

billiard balls, ahead of him through the town. He saw a slim brown line
curved away from the green square of suitcase as she advanced on a table
outside a small sun-quelled cafe at the head of the pier. Trying to simulate
indifference, his eyes nailed on a chair nearby, and he walked up to it,
unloosed his grip on his case and settled down luxuriously.

The chair was very hard and uncomfortable. "Ahhh," he breathed. No
answer. He glanced across at her. She watched him, her mouth a hemi-
sphere of white. "Hello," he said. "Hello." "You're English?" "No,
Swedish." "Perhaps you have the same problem as I do. I'm looking for a
place to stay." He then outlined what made him come to Ibiza, his plans
for writing, his desire for quiet and solitude, his need to force himself to
try to create, away from all other distractions.She also needed a place to
stay, so after coffee and rolls, they walked toward the early sun into the old
Barrio of the town.

The one- or two-story white houses had the grey of shade on their
fronts while the sun set a hedge of sharp yellow along their roofs. The
women, old with black dresses, mostly fat, were slowly beginning their
morning. A small girl, gold drops in her ear lobes, snot bridging her
mouth and one nostril, barefoot, short pale yellow dress, skipped in front
of the two of them as they climbed up the street, looking for rooms. A
short burst of hoarse sound, possibly a name from a black bent figure
behind them, and the little girl whirled and darted past them. "Like a
bird," he ventured. She nodded, a lip-closed smile. She was really quite
lovely, even more lovely than he had thought on the boat. Her hair was
short, blonde and light brown, both colors distinct. Softly brown, her
body was athletic, young. She laughed openly, delighted, round. Her
wrinkles were those of the sun.

He considered himself lucky to have met her, to be walking with her in
the new morning, to be considered by the old women as her husband, or
lover, or even companion. A vague tenderness wrapped his feeling for her,
almost brotherly. They stopped to inquire of a woman who was scrubbing
her front steps if she knew where they might find rooms for rent. The

woman straightened up, stood, wiped a forearm over her light brown forehead, and pointed to a door. Her sister, she said, sometimes took in guests, especially during August, the busiest time of year. But her sister did not have any room, nor did any of the places they tried in the first two hours.

Everyone was pessimistic. "This island is filled with tourists," one woman declared expansively. "Rooms are very difficult to find anywhere near the beaches." They continued walking. She had come for a quiet place with sun and swimming, and if Ibiza suited her, she might stay for a month. He, on the other hand, had come for work, had come to bury himself in tunnels of thought, beneath miles of paper, dimly lit by the blue light of poems. Now must be the time to submerge oneself in writing, , away from all others, away from the aimless tracks of life and into the orderly paths of art. Traveling tired him now, and he felt that he was ready.

This would be a test, not only of his competence, but of his determination and discipline as well. He must, he felt, above all, avoid immersion in life, in external events, in external beings. The time was past when he would merely experience. Now he would create and combine events in language, into a significant structure. And to do this he knew took solitude. It required an absence of books, of things which he could use to occupy his time. He wanted to write, but this desire had elements in it akin to the desire one has to take a cold shower because, unpleasant as it might be while happening, the effect is beneficial, And now here was the most pleasant distraction, a beautiful girl, to keep him from solitude.

Of course, he admitted, he would not expect himself to write all day and all night, but with such a girl, how pleasureable and easy to spend the days talking in cafes, walking through the narrrow street, swimming lazily, talking. Time would drift easily by, twisting slowly, without purpose, like a wooden slat on a turgid river. But to write, to think, one must be alone, must shun the life around him, for there is not time for both. And he wanted to be a writer.

"Oh, Lord, how hot it is," she moaned, scraping and slipping her sandalled feet against the cobblestones. "Well, why don't we go swimming?" he asked, "We can look later for a hotel."

They went swimming and later on found rooms not far from the beach. Two rooms at the same Pension. Quite lucky. And in the evening, they had supper at a Bodega which had wonderful wine. It was one of the nights of a big festival and there was dancing in the streets. They danced very close, and held hands while they walked home. She said she would like to meet him for a dance the next evening, but he also got her to consent to a picnic and swim at a beach seven kilometers north of the town. It would take up the whole next day. And he felt very happy when she agreed to his plan. "Really quite a stroke of luck meeting this girl, "he thought to himself, as he stared out his window just before going to bed at the empty, darkened streets still barely bluely lit by a thin sliver of moon."

As Yeats said, the choice is often of the life or of the work. Right now at this keyboard, the choice is still before me. This story is mostly true. The narrator is me, the girl is named Pia, the room I finally got was in a different Pension than hers; in mine, I shared a room with a Spanish workman, and it cost me 42 cents a day. (The cheapest hotel in Spain I ever had was a large single room in Jaen with a large double bed in1965, and that cost me about 35 cents a night.) An English artist friend who had just bought a small house for 1000 pounds in the town of Ibiza told me he could get me one for the same price. Tempting, but not tempting enough. I didn't want to be tied to any one place by my property. Still feel like that now at age sixty. More so. I don't remember the dance that night in 1965, but I do remember vividly every night after saying good-night to Pia at her Pension, having to walk back through the darkened sleeping town and hoping to get to my toilet before my bowels burst. A small cafe we often ate at was cheap, the food generally tasty, the dessert flan home-made, and diarrhea followed the meal as relentlessly as did the bill.

Diarrhea is my least pleasant travelling companion, but he seems to sign on to a lot of my trips, especially in Asia. Once Pia and I went off to the small island of Formentara, and spent the night sleeping in the woods. Another time we went off to Portinax (probably the place in the story seven kilometers to the north of the town of Ibiza) and also slept in the woods. I remember finding purple grapes in the fields near one of these spots, and the the two of us guzzling these dust-covered grapes and then having the most fiercesome shits. I also recall feeling so sorry for myself because Pia wouldn't make love with me that I decided to scare her by swimming way way out, actually toying with the idea of drowning so she would feel sorry for me and maybe then love me. Way way out, I changed my mind and swam back and didn't let on about my plan. I had it bad for Pia. Love and even infatuation can be dangerous.

Love and art took up much time in Ibiza for me in 1965. Most time is spent on more mundane things: From a letter of 14 August 1965: "A little playing on the harmonica, and an entire morning spent washing clothes in a basin." "That's right—I now can occasionally turn out drawings of people, boats, houses...which...at least are roughly recognizable, and I have fun doing them. Dad, I see why you like it [drawing] so much!" And "loving the mask and snorkel I bought. Fantastic! You'd never think all that went on under the water, except for undersea films a la Walt Disney. But why did I wait till now to learn this?" Of course, I was twenty five when I complained about waiting so long. Now, at sixty, what if I discover now some wonderful new thing or career? Ought I bemoan the "wasted" years or celebrate the new possibilities to become, say, a bowling instructor or a researcher into orang-utan behavior? (Actually, the little experience I've had with the higher primates, besides us, has made me consider that if like my new-age friends I believed in reincarnation and I had another chance to start my life over again, that might be an exciting and compatible new career. But bowling—forget it. If that were to be my next life's work, I would contentedly choose death.) I discovered by the time I reached Ibiza that I liked writing poetry more than I liked writing prose. But how to then make a living once I get back home to Brooklyn? Advertising? I'd see. Prose—short stories etc.—demands more attention to the physical details of a place, and so these details of the town crop up in the stories more than in most of my poems.

Talk about old and new lives. From a letter of 26 August 1965 about Ibiza: "Dug around in an old Carthaginean tomb up in the ancient necropolis. Found lots of pottery shards and one bit of very old glass. Lovely colors from chemical changes through the years. And lots of bits of bone. Four of us—1 artist, 1 potter, 1 seaman, 1 poet (me) went down into moldy chambers with candles and a rope. Great adventure." Now the poem (made into a prose paragraph): NECROPOLIS: "The Carthagineans, so I was told, planted corpses in their olive groves, and here In Ibiza the trees still stand, not knowing of Punic Wars and of salt sown in fertile furrows. But these trees are ineffective, for all the graves are open and sifted again and again for goldden amulets and pots, while they, impotent guardians, convoluted to tear themselves from the bone-brown disappointed ground. Yet olive roots slink down willingly and feel for flesh, ancient fingers suck warmth from callow rot, and these twisted eunuchs, agonized for ages, can breed (like all men's history) out of green decay, phoenix boughs at the top." The prose of the letter with more precise detail than in the prose-poem. The world as it is, or the world filtered through the imagination into a form of meaning. Both are necessary, and not incompatible.

The North-African Carthagineans in Ibiza. The North-African Moors in Spain in Granada. After traveling to Morocco in the summer of 1970, Joyce and I went up to Moorish Granada on what we called our "Moor Tour." We also called the diary of our trip our "diarria," a reference to the state of our bowels. Granada has the magnificent Alhambra which of course in deluged with tourists, among them us, in summer. The most exciting part for me in Spain is Andalucia, and the best part of Andalucia is what the Moors left behind when they and the Jews were kicked out of Spain in 1492 or thereabouts.

Seville is for me the loveliest place in Spain. First time I was in Seville was when I took a day or two from my Naval duties in 1963 and went there from the coast at Jerez de la Frontera where my ship was anchored. I went to see where Sherry was made, a typical Navy thing to do. But I also fell in love with Seville and its beautiful ladies (another typical Navy thing to do), its lovely old streets and wide plazas. I'd also been there as a civilian in 1965, met a German artist named Marianne, and strolled the Barrio de Santa Cruz with her in the soft romantic nights. Nothing sexual with her, not for my lack of trying. In 1970 I was there with my wife Joyce, and the place had the same romantic feel, with groups of old-fashioned black-costumed students guitar-ing and singing their "Sevillanas" through these winding narrow streets. The Barrio de Santa Cruz used to be the old Jewish quarter. Later it became the new tourist quarter. In the past thirty years I've not been back to Spain, and have heard it has changed very much, become more generic contemporary European than particular "puro" Espana. (On my computer I cannot make the mark of the "tilde" so the name sounds like it should be spelled "Espania." Even my computer makes words and names more generic.) Seville one day I may go back to, but with a fear of my remembrances clashing with what now is there and what is missing in Spain and now in me.

FRANCE:

Sept. 4, 1965: "Then slow hitching until about 9:30 p.m. when I was left off in the middle of no place just over the French border [from Spain] eleven kilometers south of Perpignan. A small ghost town. Wooden shutters flapping in the (very cold) breeze, a figure seen silhouetted against a lighted room and then shutting the shutters, etc. [I remember now in 2000 that I tried to sleep—no sleeping bag—just lying down near the road and trying to rest, but feeling rather spooked.] Cars went by there at speeds never exceeding that of sound, but approaching it. Got thoroughly disgusted [and a bit scared] and, to prove myself, decided to walk into Perpignan with one heavy suitcase and one overnight case. So off I trotted and in two hours or so I arrived. [I thought that since my legs could take walking fast more than my arms could lug this heavy suitcase, that I'd better speed-walk, and it worked.] Then the walk through town. By this time, both arms were lengthened by a good five inches. "But now," thought I, "I'm in shape for all the walking I'll be doing in Switzerland." The prize of valor.

"Rather perfunctorily, I hitched through town, stopping and airing my thumb whenever my arms were too tired.[Note: Americans simply stick our their stationary thumbs; Europeans move their whole arms with thumb extended in the direction they want to go.] A car stopped and I said that I was going to Narbonne, the next big town on my route. He said he was going to Zurich. I began laughing hysterically (cut to next day when I arrived in Zurich)." Whether I actually laughed or merely felt that wonderful upwelling of joy that a hitchhiker gets when a car stops and it's going very far along the route you want, I don't remember. A letter is a document like some newspaper reports and letters and first-person accounts, all of which may be exaggerated or self-glorifying or self-justifying or outright lies. This one probably wasn't.

Here I just went through France to get somewhere else. Sometimes you travel fast; other times, you stop and stroll and savor. One time I almost was killed because of my speed. My first time in France in 1961, a five-week trip between my final college exams and my showing up in Newport, Rhode Island, for Naval Officer Candidate School, I was in Paris and spent a little time with two college friends, Peggy and Barbara. From my journal: "As I was leaving Barbara and Peggy's hotel room at 4:30 a.m. or so, the hotel owner caught me at the door and told me he had almost shot me (he showed me the revolver!)" I remember he, just having been woken from a doze, shouted at me in the darkened lobby of the hotel, and that he, not recognizing me as a hotel guest, took me for a thief. Had I run faster or not stopped, he might very well have shot me. He was very upset. What a thrill! Real life in Paris! Ah, youth! Ah, romance! Ah, real bullets! Ah, luck!

Later on that pre-dawn night, on the Champs Elysee, walking across Paris to get to my hotel, a not-too-bad-looking woman asked me "Vous aimez?" When I waved her away, she said. "No, no, no, no. Pour l'argent!" I waved her away again, and having continued on a ways, stopped and thought over what she had said. To me at first it sounded as if I would pay her, the usual solicitation. Later I thought she might be offering to pay me which was so foreign to my experience and expectation that I didn't take it in. I looked back toward where she stood, about a block or so away in the pre-dawn light, and decided not to go back and ask her exactly what did she mean. I often regret that decision.

In 1963 during a Mediterranean cruise when I was a Naval officer, I took several days leave when we anchored off Cannes, and I went to Juan-les-Pins, staying in a Pension, trying to live as civilized and civilian life as possible. Wine with meals, calmly strolling the town, letting the tide of Naval affairs recede a bit. Who should I meet but some young lady, Susan, from Brooklyn

College who I noticed first for this terrible Brooklyn-accented French washing up from a cafe.

We ended up much later necking a bit in the hall outside her room, but she didn't invite me in because, as she told me later, she had to go to the toilet—bad. I remember feeling grateful that I wasn't invited in because I had enough gas in my gut to power the city of Chicago for a week, and naturally was too embarrassed to fart in front of a new girl friend. The body— it wants to copulate and wants to excrete, and some times you have to make a choice.

Sometimes the choice is between copulation and laughter. In 1965, I was traveling around Europe after my graduate year at the University of Edinburgh, and hitchhiking (*faire l'auto-stop*) through southern France, when I was picked up by a woman. That alone is rare. Single women for safety reasons ought not to do that, and usually don't. Anyway, we drove for a while, stopped for a drink in a cafe, and continued until she pulled over to the side of the road and said she had something in her eye. I tried to help her ("mettez votre lids des yeux comme ca" in my wobbly French) until she whimpered and leaned her head against my shoulder. I patted her reassuringly, and kissed her forehead, and she turned to me, and we grabbed at each other. Since we were right at the side of a well-travelled road, we needed to get off it for some privacy. She drove the car off on to some dirt road, then on to some even smaller dirt road, and we proceeded to take our clothes off rather frantically. Naked, she then lay back on the front seat of the car with me standing up outside (all of me standing up), the car door open to shield me from some cow herd or other wandering down this lonely track. At each pump of my hips, however, the car door opened and then swung back against my legs and butt.

This rhythm and this whole wild situation was begining to amuse me, and when I thought of some cow herd seeing us in this most indecorous position, I started to laugh. Now nothing removes lust faster than finding it funny, but this woman then started to cry because she thought I was laughing at her. I explained my laughter, and we decided to continue on past her village and get a place to stay that night in Angouleme and take our time over love-making (which we did). In bed that night, she told me that she was married to her first real sweet-heart and that I was only her second sexual partner. Her husband had recently left her and their small town where she was a school-teacher, and that she still lived a few houses away from her parents-in-law, and the scandal of taking a lover in that small town would have been too much for her. Here I thought this was an experienced woman, but my laughter had crushed her at that moment. The next morning we said sweet good-byes, she going back to her emprisoning village, and me heading on toward Spain.

The wildest time I had was in Paris on the 13th of July, 1965. The letter I wrote to my parents just before that, dated 12 July '65, described the usual delicious tourist Paris stuff: After Rouen,

"Then to Paris where I'm staying in a hotel near the church of St. Germain-de-Pres on the Left Bank, where all the artists, students, and other colourful types come (like me). I've been to the top of the Arc de Triomphe, strolled along the Champs Elyees often, seen the Louvre and Jeu de Paume museums, sat in the gardens of the Tuilleries and wrote a short story on a quiet Sunday, walked hand in hand with two American girls (one of them a Negro) along the Boulevard St.

Michel, saw the Eiffel Tower puncture the clouds, drank *vin ordinaire* with French workmen, sang folk songs with every nationality you could name on the Ille de la Cite and along the Seine, and so forth." "And so forth" is right. Every tourist ever in Paris probably did more or less the same things. And yet how excited we feel, as though we are the first to do this, or excited because we now have joined those sophisticates who have experienced Paris, the obligatory scene of the drama of romantic travel.

But the wildest time I had was on the night of the 13th of July, the night before Bastille Day. Letter of 21 July, '65: "On 13 July I stayed up all night. Events: (1) Met another friend from Brooklyn and we tried to pick up girls at this big dance near the Place St. Michel. We finally succeeded and danced the night away in the clutches of two French girls whom we left at 5 a.m. to go and eat onion soup at Les Halles (P.S. Have tasted better). (2) we both climbed to the top of a griffin (statue of one, not the real non-existent thing) and watched as people rioted for Bastille Day and splashed in the fountain. Someone took the French flag down from the top of the fountain and dropped it in the water. I asked for it, got it passed up to me, and standing atop my statue, waved it to the cheers of the crowd [many thousands of people], shouting "*Vive la France*' at the top of my galli-fied lungs. Next night, took my clothes off and jumped into the Seine (left my underpants on). After the third jump [from the embankment] and much splashing around, a gendarme told me to come out as he said I was indecent. I pointed to my sodden underpants, but he was not convinced, so out I climbed and retrieved my clothing from an English girl I had just met. Nice swim. Nice girl. Oh, la, la." [I remember now necking with her on a train, and then later necking in a park near where she was staying. The whole two days—wonderful, wonderful, wonderful.]

In 1967, while I was working as a copywriter for Needham & Grohmann, an advertising agency in Rockefeller Center, I took a short vacation to go over to Paris for my cousin Charley Stephens' wedding. The night before the wedding the guys—cousins Charley, Lou and James and one or two others and I went out for the evening, naturally hitting a strip club, where I was invited up to do a strip along with the stripper. According to the others, I looked as though I had found my metier. As on the night of Bastille Day in 1965, now in the spring of 1967, taking my clothes off in public seemed to be a natural (*au naturel?*) for me. Paris brings this out in me.

Not just Paris. In 1973 Joyce and I were driving around all over France, and decided to go out to the Ile de Levant, a nudist island off the Riviera. Beyond a certain point of the island, one had to be totally naked in order to proceed. Joyce and I stripped down and went out of the beach with the widest variety of naked people I have ever seen assembled, looking like a comfortable circle of Dante's Hell. Sprawled out, the men's genitalia pendant, the women's vulvic wounds open to sun and men's eyes, most bathers baked in the sun, some flaunting their sexual apparatus; some observed slyly, some openly. But the general sense was not of sexuality, but of somnolence and ease, like seals basking. The crew of the boat that took us over to the island appeared on top of the bluff looking over this beach, and the whole beach erupted in shouts of "stop looking at us and take off your clothes and join us!" When one of the crew took off all his clothing, we all erupted in cheers. This was before the Riviera was filled with topless women bathers, and breasts became ho-hum. Now on Bali the European women go topless on Kuta Beach, and only inland in small villages can you still see older Balinese women walking the paths topless. Civilization now bares breasts that once only the more exotic 'uncivilized' cultures in Africa bared. How times change.

Which is the most civilized pleasant way to travel? No doubt—the car. Hitching gets you to connect with the people. Same with public transportation. But in 1973, Joyce and I bought a car, a Renault, with the front seats able to recline so we could sleep in the car. And we did! A postcard from Quimper in Brittany, 19 Aug.'73: "Medieval cities! Brittany is wonderful. Cliffs, moors, the smashing seas, festivals. The car is a superb convenience—we sleep in it, travel in it, eat in it (would that we could also excrete in it). Tonight we stay in our first hotel in 6 weeks.[Sleeping usually in our car and in our tent in camp grounds, or as Joyce called them "cramp grounds.] We have never eaten so luxuriously, however, as on this trip. Just had a 5-course dinner. We are in le Faou just above Quimper. Tomorrow to the west coast of Brittany." Luxurious eating and pauperish sleeping—it worked out well. With a car you can get to small places and rural places, and get to the greatest tourist sites earlier than any one else because you are awake with the sun, and just need to start the ignition— no packing, no bills to pay—and you are off, smelly perhaps without a shower, but on the road quickly.

Bittany has the *Pardon,* a Catholic festival where Bretons come from all over, the women wearing the distinctive headdresses which show which towns they are from, much as the Guatemalan Indians do with their clothing, each small village with its own patterns and styles. Our car let us get to the smallest villages easily. I took communion in one *pardon*, unbeliever that I am, because I did want to deepen the experience.

We picked up the car in Paris. The man who gave it to me gave me only the most cursory instructions about its operation in barely graspable French, and then we were in it, just in time for the Paris rush-hour at the end of the work day. And it was a car with a shift.. So—madness on wheels, but finally we got out of Paris undented. We had heard that Paris traffic is terrifying, found it to be true, and so were worried the whole trip about how we would negotate the streets to get the car back to its drop-off point. We bought the car, guaranteed re-sale, and had to return it after two months. A large German guy we later ran into told us, "I haf been in Africa, shot lions, climbed mountains, and nothing I fear as much as driving my car in Paris!" So we were warned.

Generally, driving in the rest of France was not a problem. Small cities were easily negotiable. Small towns and many monuments and views were only accessible by car. And cars let us get to *le camping,* the campgrounds that the average French family spends their vacations in. In campgrounds and in small towns, the French are very polite and friendly, especially if you speak French to them. One person told me that he thought I was French, although he couldn't place the accent exactly, and so thought I was French, *"mais outre-mer."* I was very flattered, but realized that had he listened to me for a little longer, he would see my grammatical ineptitude and my vocabularistical emptiness. Speaking the native language helps tremendously to connect to people and gives the natives of any country the psychological advantage of seeming intelligent and knowledgeable, and the inept non-native speaker (me) the feeling that he is a dope.

Outside of Paris, the food is much better. We asked in each town where the locals would eat if they had their choice, and never got a bad recommendation. In Brittany, in the several-course lunches or dinners we had, the first course usually gave diners a choice of either a large plate of mussels mariniere or a small glass of tomato juice. We had mussels coming out of our ears, and happily so. We had in about six weeks only one really bad meal in France. It was somewhere in the Loire area. But it was spectacularly bad. Nothing turned out well. The place we stayed in required that we eat there, and so we did. Course after course came, each served by the cook/ hotelier's daughters, sweet and delicious (the daughters, not the food). The meat course brought us each a blueish-red slab of meat, passed within a block of the oven, essentially raw. We contemplated it in silence, then looked up at each other, and burst into laughter. It occurred to both of us simultaneously that this meat came from the shop we passed down the block: the *chevaline.* We were looking at a raw chunk of Trigger. I ate a bit around the edges, Joyce ate more of it, and we protested our lack of hunger to the sweet serving daughters for why we didn't clean the plate. Even the dessert was awful.

Another bad dish, but just a single dish, was the *omlette au Mont St. Michel* that Joyce was served. Mont St. Michel is a spectacular medieval town out in a watery plain that the tide over-runs twice daily. The sheep who graze on these salty march grasses are delicious to eat, and we had this dish another time. But we ordered the omlette because it was a signature dish of the place, and we had seen the whipping around of the eggs in a copper pan till they were airy and frothy, and so seemed appetizing. Joyce's omlette came first, and we contemplated its blackened exterior in silence. But—hey! If that black outside was the way the omlettes came, then we were surprised, but ready. After eating much of the omlette, mine was brought out. Yellow exterior. I told the waiter to either get Joyce another omlette like mine, or else not charge us for the blackened omlette my wife had partially eaten. O.K., no charge. When the bill came, he had charged us for the omlette, and I told him to re-calculate the bill and leave off the charge for the eggs. He returned, with the omlette off the bill, but a few other spurious charges added so the bill came to the same as with the omlette. At this point I was furious, and as frothy as the omlette. I told him I wanted to see the manager, and had a huge argument with her. She: But your wife ate the omlette. Me: I thought the style of the correct Mont. St. Michel omlette was black, and if so, were willing to eat it. I demanded the police. Et cetera. I didn't pay for the omlette.

This was a very rare instance of French impoliteness. Almost always, in the small towns and cities, the shopkeepers and people are positively courtly, which of course brings out your own courtliness, which adds to their courtliness. You all practically bow to each other in these exquisitely polite exchanges. Paris, which to so many tourists is all of France they know, is a different story. Gorgeous places like Annecy and the Loire region and the people who inhabit them, if seen, would change many tourists' ideas about the "brusque" French.

Joyce and I went to the Loire with its chateaux and beautiful little towns in 1971 (hitch-hiking) and in 1973 (with our car). With car is better. You are on your own schedule, and if you can't find a hotel, you can always sleep in your vehicle. Chambord, Chenonceau, Azay-le-Rideau— these perfectly jewel-like places are small enough not to overpower you except with their beauty. A must-see in France.

As is of course the Louvre. "Taking off from the top of stairs, (the crowd watches) Winged Victory, headless, et cetera, toes the heights of perfection, while her laundry flaps between her legs, scooped like a clam shell out behind, braces holding wings apart, up her buttress, keeping her headless up. Nearby, her hand in a case showing a few nail-bitten fingers. Nearby, the Venus of Milos with no arms at all. Perfection based on the broken and parted."

For an American, so much of France seemed in 1973 so bound by the past, by its tradition—glorious, gorgeous, and solid. In 1973, I wrote BASILICA AT VEZELAY: "In the medieval basilica of Vezelay, the arches, groined, still braced against the weight of above like bow-legged horsemen off to war. Across the ceiling the arches grasp like talons, jealous of escape, or webs a spider spun, the sealing of the out-of-date. French fetes utilize the sky for fireworks, *feu d'artifice,*

less durable tales than stone, but beautiful as trails of sparks then smoke crisscross the sky lacy as lingerie a spider weaves to hide and to attract. Smoke tails lazily hang above us in the night, a Portuguese man-of-war, a spider web designed to stop the bleeding."

In France the past sometimes traps and submerges the present, but we as tourists often go to a country now to see it as it once (or twice or thrice) was.

NAVAL OFFICER IN EUROPE & U.S.A.:

After a one-week school in Combat Information Center tactics in Norfolk, Virginia, where my new ship, the U.S.S. Taconic (AGC-17), was home-ported, I flew down to Guantanamo Bay, Cuba, to join the ship. Spent a morning and afternoon frying in a small boat with a friend from OCS, Tom Swerski, exploring up a river from our military base toward a hostile Cuba. As we went up the river, our marines were driving pilings into the water, and we were told to get back in an hour or so, because these pilings were designed to block the river from infiltrators from Cuba, and we too would be blocked from the getting back down the river to the base in a couple of hours. (1 June '63): "everyone uses it [the river] to fish on and we passed 3 boats within 2 hours. Then around the bay and some more frying. I'm still peeling from that day; my back looks as though ants have lunched on it!" Just a couple of years back, I had spent almost a week in Cuba as a civilian. Now Cuba was definitely Communist, despite what everyone in Cuba had told me in 1960.In October 1962 there had been the Cuban missile crisis, and before that, the failed Bay of Pigs invasion. Cuba was a "hot zone" and not just from the tropical sun.

Not just Cuba. (1 June '63): "Well, we're back from Haiti! Spent 2 days getting out to the ship [from Norfolk]—plane to Cuba, ship and helicopter to the Taconic, and 4 hours after I arrived, we turned around and headed back to Norfolk. Three days of steaming and back where I started from!….The Taconic is full of spit and polish and the uniforms are always being changed. We had a Vice Admiral aboard." He was the Admiral in charge of what was planned to be an invasion of Haiti, so I was told, to stop "Papa Doc" Duvalier from killing so many of his people. We had lots of marines, a helicopter carrier, and many amphibious vessels. Here I was—brand-new on the ship, not knowing where anything was, and I was supposed to relieve the Assistant First Lieutenant and the Gunnery Officer of his duties, and a war was about to start! Glad that it didn't. Many years later I did get to Haiti as a civilian, but this time in the Navy I saw Haiti and Cuba from afar

(but in both cases, too damn close).

Seeing foreign places while in the Navy is different from seeing them as a civilian except when one is on leave. In August 1963, while the Taconic was anchored in Cannes, France, I took leave for five days and stayed at a pension in Juan-les-Pins. It was the Pension "Capucines,"and cost about $6 per day for a room and three good meals. The town catered to the young and rich, and I sunned on the beach, and at night danced "the twist" and listened to "le jazz hot." (1 Sept."63) "I went on an afternoon to Monaco and the ride there was worth more than the gilt palace of Rainier and Grace. Beautiful scenery. I also went to Nice twice and found it to be a lovely city with a beach of smooth rocks which are "lie-able" on if you arrange the rocks beforehand to fit your anatomy." I remember lying on this beach and noticed that a lovely woman lying in front of me was slim enough to have her hip bones stick up above her flat abdomen so I could see down the bottom part of her bikini. I maneuvered into a better position. At some point she realized that her bikini was almost two inches above her abdomen, and so she put a small rock on her bikini bottom, this eclipsing the view so desired by a woman-deprived me. No way to get these rocks off! That's the Navy!

I had met three English girls from a ballet company at the Club Rio in Barcelona, invited them to see my ship, and almost as soon as they came on board, I was detailed to fly off to Rota, Spain, for liaison duty with the Spanish Navy for a joint amphibious exercise. From a letter of 23 Nov.'63: "I kissed them all good-bye—twice! The next day in Rota I was free and went to Seville where I had a wonderful time and met a German artist named Marianne Lautensach who gave me a wood-block print and a very stimulating evening of looking at her etchings (Damn it—real etchings!) and talk. She really is a talented and interesting girl. I've even written a couple of poems to her to go with her drawings." Barcelona. Seville. Fascinating cities.But what do I remember? The women. Too little time to spend with them there. "The needs of the Navy are primary."

On 6 August 1963, I wrote to my parents, "Just a short note (it's after midnight—I won't set foot on land for about 17 more days) to say how much I liked Spain and those Spaniards. I spent some time in Jerez de la Frontera and Puerto de Santa Maria, where Columbus set sail from, near Cadiz in Andalucia in southern Spain....Got to a corrida de toros, a couple of coach and horse rides, two hours of horse-back riding, a thousand miles of re-tracing my steps in Jerez, a trip to a distillery (Bodega Gonzales—for Sherry [named for Jerez]), political discussions about Franco and the Guardia Civil (Falange): consensus of opinion—they stink!" At another time, I hitchhiked and got picked up by a truckload of people, and in the back of the truck, in the dark, I asked also about Franco, and one man told me he himself hated Franco, but the country was about evenly divided among Franco-likers and haters. I disliked Franco. Yet I in the Navy was working with and for Franco's Navy, to help them integrate and coordinate with the American Navy, to teach them our tactics. The politics of anti-communism. "He's a bastard, but he's our bastard."

While on that liaison duty with the Spanish forces on our joint U.S.— Spain amphibious exercises, President Kennedy was assassinated [I wrote of this in my chapter on Spain]. This was exciting duty for me with the Spanish. (23 Nov.'63) "From getting helicopter rides for the Spanish officers [and for myself, from our marines on the assault beaches], to sitting in on the conferences that decide how the landings will take place (and helping to make a couple of pretty big decisions also!), to driving a Spanish boat alongside the Almirante Lobo [Spanish flagship] (didn't tear up anything—congratulations were given me for this noble exercise in boat handling). It's really been some fun. Translating is very tough especially if you consider that I can't really speak Spanish! But everyone says I'm doing fine (even behind my back), and Capitan de Benito [the Commander of the Spanish forces] wanted me to stay for the whole operation and Commodore Boyer [U.S. forces commander] said OK."

I remember my last night on the Almirante Lobo—we all had a party to celebrate the success of the joint amphibious landings, lots of wine was drunk, and I got tipsy. Many of the Spanish officers as my escort got into the boat which was to bring me back to the Taconic, and the whole raucous, somewhat drunken bunch of us headed off through a rather rough sea, so rough in fact that we could not use the Taconic's gangway, and they had to put a cargo net over, the kind that marines clamber down on amphibious assaults. Our small boat rose and fell alarmingly near the Taconic, but I refused to put on a life jacket the American sailors demanded I put on, and I kept shouting in Spanish, a bit more than tipsy, that I was assigned to the Spanish and I didn't need no stinkin' American life jacket. Now the trick was to wait till the boat rose high on a wave, then jump and grab the cargo net and immediately climb quickly up it. If you grabbed it too low, or didn't climb up fast enough, the boat might slam into the side of the ship with you between the boat and the ship, and you would be crushed and die. I was not so drunk as to not be aware of this at this time. Timed it—jumped—grabbed—climbed fast. Made it safely, and turned to wave my Spanish compatriots off with much Spanish compliments on both sides. Great way to end an exciting experience.

Another exciting and unusual place we anchored was Malta, a small island between Sicily and Tunisia. (21 Sept.'63) "We've been in Malta for 3 days now....Went on a tour to the more historical points on this island. From Neolithic stone age man building his "dream chambers" where dreams are analysed, to the Roman artifacts of the governor's palace when the power of Rome extended to Malta, to the associations of the Knights Templars who guarded the way of the Crusaders on their way to the Holy Land—a very deep sliver of history has this Malta! 6,000 years worth in a small area. I bought you some Maltese hand-woven handkerchiefs (wonderful lace)....

We'll be at sea for a long time after leaving Malta day after tomorrow. Next we go on an amphibious exercise to Turkey (no getting on the beach though), then maybe a fast trip to Spain to drop off some people and pick up others (probably no liberty ashore), then Malta again, I believe, for 3 days....Enclosed is a picture of me and the Rock of Gibraltar where I saw Africa's coast. I'm in the foreground, Rock in the background." Much of the time in the Navy we never get a chance to get ashore. Gibraltar, the Azores where I could smell the land—how sweet. And how unreachable. Can I count these places as places I've been? No.

Some places I did reach shore, but just barely. Sardinia is one example. "Right now we are steaming around slowly in a setting sun not far from Golfo di Aranci, in the northeast corner of Sardinia. We'll play [Navy] games for 2 days or so, then start off for Malta." A later letter (16 August '63) states, "Well, here I am sitting off the southernmost point of Sardinia swaying at 90 fathoms of anchor chain out through the port hawse. The weather is hot and the water is a clear blue. Got ashore a couple of times for short periods. We had about 94 men go over for a beach and beer party which ended up, as these things do, with sailors fighting with one another, throwing everyone into the water (me included, but I didn't mind), getting drunk on beer and wine that they bought from some peddlers, propositioning all the women they could find on the beach, etc. Typical Navy party....We'll be on this amphibious exercise another 4 days." Grandfather of Tailhook! With alcohol not permitted on U.S. Navy ships, what most sailors and officers do when on liberty is go out and drink alcohol. Wine was served on the Spanish ships for the officers, and so they did not seem to have the need to equate liberty with booze.

Mediterranean cruises were full of amphibious exercises for our ship. Off the northeastern coast of Sardinia again in mid-October 1963, we achored out and did some more practice amphibious landings on the way back from the eastern Mediterranean. On 27 Sept.'63, I wrote, "We are now off the coast of Turkey (Saros Korfezi Bay in Thrace near the Bosphorus). We will get underway for Rota, Spain, on Saturday and arrive there about 4 Oct. There for a day and then to another exercise. We just had lots of Turkish brass as well as the Commander of our Sixth Fleet aboard here yesterday. War games for the last couple of days (and today!)." Lots of travel, and what did we see? We saw the sea. That's often the Navy.

We also saw Norfolk, Virginia, home port of our ship and much of the Atlantic Fleet and much too many sailors. What to do there? (24 June '63): "I've been running a bit since I've been entered in a track meet to take place in a week. Something to do, anyway. The past week and a half I've spent in classes in Officer of the Deck refresher training. Navy schools almost invariably put me to sleep. ...Been reading a bit... thinking about taking several of my philosophy books back to the ship with me for those long sea-wracked nights ahead. Norfolk has made me nostalgic about Japan." Tepid describes my feelings about the place. Other Navy courses I took over the nest year and a half were on cargo-handling and the Combat Information Center. The cargo-handling school had us part of the time on an old de-commissioned ship and we actually worked the winches and gave the signals ourselves instead of just giving the orders to our petty officers and they giving the orders to the men under them.

The lack of "available" women here was depressing, but there were bright moments:

[29 Jan.'64] "Last Monday went to a song-fest—we sing to the accompaniment of a piano and other officers and NURSES!!! where I actually talked to an intelligent sensitive pretty girl! Yes, here in Norfolk! Must have been a dream. Things here are not the best." Another way to escape was to go to Williamsburg, which I did with my old LST buddy, Carl Bowler, who was now in the Navy on the East Coast. To go to Virginia Beach to swim and run, where once I had a Portuguese Man of War wrap itself around my forearm (hurt like hell). To dance in "The Jolly Roger," a disco as savage as its name implied. Often fights there, more than one inspired by a woman who tried to get me embroiled in a fight once. She asked me while I was dancing with her if I were Italian, and when I said "no" she, a few minutes later, brought three tough Italian guys to our table and pointed me out to them as the guy "who said he doesn't like Italians." I pulled the leader of this pack off to the side, told him one friend at my table was Italian (the dentist from our ship), told him we were three and they were three, so if they wanted to fight us, it was fair, and also warned him about this woman who then I could see was a liar, bad news, and just wanted to see guys fight. He and his fellows walked off, and we were saved for another day. A couple of weeks later I saw another fight break out at "The Jolly Roger," and this woman was standing looking on near the table where it started. Too few women in Norfolk, but in this woman's case, one of her was too many.

Speaking of women, but only metaphorically here, (23 Feb.'64) "At midnight tonight (and for 12 days after), we are undergoing a test to see if we can be physically penetrated, a test of our security procedures. People from other Navy ships who are conducting this exercise try to slip aboard under false orders, in a working party, etc. The loss of our security "virginity" is a commonplace thing. Most ships fail. Just another annoyance for me, though. This past week I've been the First Lieutenant, in charge of the Deck Department (93 men) while Mr. Coyle is on leave. Very busy week. A crash program getting Staff spaces ready for a deadline this Wednesday…..Now to get ready for "8 o'clock reports" and the 20—24 watch [as Officer of the Deck on the Quarterdeck]. Got a good program of poetry for watch this evening." I had been reading and discussing poetry with my Bosun mate and watch crew on slow night watches on the Quarterdeck in port, while we huddled under our coats in the February dark and wind. The men seemed to enjoy it, I wrote. It passed the time, kept my mind alive, and may have been my first experience of teaching literature.

So much for *mens sana*. *Corpore sano* is kept so by [30 Dec.'63] "Lately I've been playing a lot of Squash with Dr. Art Bankhurst [Taconic's physician], and combining this with sit-ups, push-ups, and running….we're both improving our game and getting into shape. This is about the most enjoyable thing to do in this city empty of all except sailors. Doing a bit of reading in Existentialist philosophy. Today, besides 8 hours of work, 8 hours of watch. No reading today."

Corpore sano is usually the department of the marines, the leathernecks, jarheads, grunts. [15 March '64] "Yesterday (Sat.), 4 marines, another Naval officer and I went out hiking in a state park near here. We got clawed by briars, fell into swamps, got foot-sore, wet from the rain, got a little lost—in short, had a great time! For instance, I was following one of the marines through a swamp, getting from log to patch of sodden grass, from hummock to slanted tree trunk by leaping, swinging, or stepping, when I came to a patch of fairly open water about 3 ½ feet across. On the next little patch there stood a tree of a diameter of under a foot. Biting my lip, I jumped, right leg stretched out, and grasped the tree. Pulling myself to it with both hands, I thought with relief of another time having just missed falling in. Just for a second, however, as the tree, with me still clutching it, my feet against its stump at the edge of the dry patch around its roots, toppled backwards and dropped me to my knees into the dark brown water. The tree just missed clubbing the marine following me as it collapsed into the water with a squashy "smack." Highlight of the day! I'll have to do it more often."

Or best yet, to head off to Washington, D.C. to spend the weekend with my cousin Charles Stephens, who was there writing speeches for Senator Smathers of Florida. Lots of blow-out times with him! I could practice being a civilian there, and wanted to keep practicing.

My main job on the Taconic when I first arrived was as First Division officer, having in my Deck Division about 37 men as well as a junior Ensign, my assistant. Soon, in May 1963, I was promoted to Lieutenant (junior grade) and began to feel like a bit of an old salt. One and a half gold stripes now on my sleeves and shoulders. No more "boot Ensign." On December 10, 1963, after "a long rough trip of eleven or so days from Spain to Norfolk ...all the Deck people are swathed in whatever wool they can procure and chattering away [with freezing cold as well as with talking] as they discuss our landing....It looks as if many of our officers will switch positions due to new ones coming aboard, leaving, etc. and I'll be taking over the after part of the ship (Second Division). Same type of work and about the same number of people."

Two things, among many others, that made duty on the Taconic less pleasant than duty on board the San Joaquin County. On the Taconic, because of our propinquity to the top brass, we often had to wear our summer whites, a uniform which attracted dirt like a vacuum, rather than the more casual khakis usual on the LST. Another was (from letter of 11 June '63) "The food is pretty poor compared with what we got on the LST. The crew here eats better than we do—much better. On the LST we ate the same stuff as did the crew. Poor officers!" And we had to pay for our food as well.

In June 1964, I was appointed Mess Caterer (probably because I had been on watch during the deliberations) in addition to my other duties. "I relieved a Lt. and began immediately to initiate changes in our menu. I am now also responsible for four decks of officers' country, and am feeding 100 people just now. I only have 18 regularly assigned men plus extra men the embarked Admiral's Staff provide. Now I have two divisions: S-3 (Stewards) and Second (Deck). I work to administer the officer's Mess, staterooms, berthing, etc. (Including our embarked staff). There will be better food served than ever before! I work directly with the Executive Officer who is President of the Mess." Changes I instituted? Asked the officers what foods they actually wanted to eat! And I had noticed that while not one officer ate the brussel sprouts, the first-class petty-officer steward in charge of making up the week's menu for the officers kept ordering brussel sprouts. When I stopped him from doing this, he complained that that was always what he had done. Not if we were paying for it, said I. When the word got out that I would really give the officers what they wanted, lots of officers confided their cravings to me, and I set out to re-make the wardroom's menu. Real steak, Italian night, fried chicken, green peas—no more brussel sprouts. They all seemed happier, but after a couple of months, just before my getting out of the Navy, the job was taken over by the Supply Officer, and brussel sprouts made a come-back. Still, I tried.

Other jobs and titles I got sounded like more excitement than Mess Caterer. "I am now [15 Oct.'63] the Taconic's Landing Party Commander which means in the event of trouble in some out-of-the-way town, or police action against mobs, or showing the flag in a parade, I and my 45 men all armed to the teeth storm ashore and quell the disturbance. Actually, it is rarely used. But the training might be fun. Play at being Marines, take hikes, fire weapons, etc."

I discovered, when I assumed the duty as Landing Party Commander (the title certainly has a ring to it!), that for years it seemed the landing party had had no training in weapons or tactics at all. So I decided we all would have at least some weapons training, and so broke out the weapons we would use and organized a firing training day on the fantail [after end—back end] of the Taconic. Steaming along in the open sea, we fired sub-machine guns—this weapon had no kick, but did ride up, so I had to aim low— and M-1 rifles—and light carbine rifles— and my own side-arm, the 45 caliber pistol, which I was familiar with from carrying it on my courier runs in Japan.

We tossed over the stern small targets attached to lines, and fired at them. I took the carbine from one of my men, and aimed at one of the targets, a small rag bouncing along erratically at the end of a line a couple of stories down off the fantail. Several men and petty officers watched. I fired and hit this bouncing rag spot on. Knowing I could never duplicate this great shot, I handed back the carbine to the admiring sailor, and walked off casually to what I of course hoped was the rightly-so awe-struck silence. Who knows what my men did actually say. "Lucky shot" probably. But that shot made my day.

Speaking of shooting, I was also the officer in charge of the main battery during General Quarters, to be called when we were attacking or repelling an attack on our ship. Our main weapons were a 5 inch 38 gun forward, and 40mm anti-aircraft guns along our ship's sides.

With the 5 inch 38, we practiced firing at a long sleeve towed behind a plane, and one of my jobs was to assure we did not fire at the plane itself. I and one phone talker were in the Gun Director's Mount, both wearing headphones to keep in touch with the bridge and the Captain, the anti-aircraft batteries, and with Combat Information Center which would feed us new targets, or tell us which were the "friendlies" so wouldn't fire on our own aircraft. The 5 inch 38, when fired, has a terrible "crack," and is a little like firing a 44 cal. Magnum pistol—almost frightening to fire. At the end of this one particular firing practice, my phone talker had bleeding out of his ears. Almost all the Gunner's Mates had great hearing loss, and we used to make fun of them putting their hands behind their ears to hear better. I'm sure I lost some of my hearing from this Naval gunfire.

At this one particular exercise, we fired at this sleeve towed by a plane, and hit it dead on. I and all my gun crew cheered and slapped each other on the back, but then I thought that in a battle we would have just splattered a pilot all over the ocean, killed someone, and I lost some of my joy. But this helped me understand something of the noise and exultation, but not the terror, of combat, and of how when you are doing your job during battle, firing at the enemy, you think of your firing from the ship as a technical problem, rather than as a moral one with deaths caused by you. You with these big guns are immersed in the details of lead angles and fuse settings rather than in the picture of a dead aviator.

Smaller guns were what I carried as Assistant Shore Patrol Officer for three days in Valencia, Spain in May 1964. "Spent most of my time in Valencia touring all the joints and keeping the sailors [from several U.S. Navy ships as well as the Taconic's] out of trouble. It was fairly quiet and I got to see some of the floor shows as a duty. Valencia's most interesting attribute is its people. It is an old city, but without the scenic attractiveness of Seville. The people are friendly, the streets are very clean, and the weather is golden and warm. I saw Litri (2nd best in Spain) fight a couple of bulls on Sunday in the Plaza de Toros. One of the best I've seen." I had toured around the city with two Swedish girls I met one evening, one of whom I slept with that night. Nice perks of this little bit of shore duty.

"Both coming in and leaving [Valencia], the Captain asked me to translate the wishes of the Spanish pilot who helped us in and out of our berth [at the dock]. The pilot, an elderly Spaniard, dumpy and somewhat slow, would make violent motions with his hands and mutter "De tug" and from this ambiguous exchange, I was supposed to tell the Captain either to cast off, slack off, change the sides the tug would push, and so forth." It would be funny if so much did not depend on getting these commands right. (It was funny to me anyway even at the time.)

I was appointed as one of the five judges of a Special Court Martial on the Taconic underway to the Med in April 1964, to try a man accused of stealing a car in Norfolk. He admitted stealing this car, but at one point in the trial I tried to get his Defense Counsel to explain to him in front of us the difference between stealing, "grand larceny"—the intent to defraud the owner of this car of its use permanently—and "wrongful appropriation" which essentially eliminated the "permanently" from the previous definition. There was no evidence of this seaman's intent to keep this car permanently, nor did I believe he actually did intend to keep it. The difference was explained to him in court in front of us, but he did not take the lesser offense of "wrongful appropriation" I offered to him. Here I was, as a judge, acting as his Defense Counsel. No one in this court was a lawyer. We were just Naval officers, both line or supply corps. (By the way, I was a line officer, which means eligible for command at sea, and we disdained all who were not line officers.)

One of my jobs as Second Division Officer was also to be the Brig Officer, and so if we had a prisoner it was my job to provide a secure space to hold him in, and to provide guards and to see he was fed properly, etc. We of this Special Court Martial found the sailor guilty, and sentenced him to 6 months forfeiture of pay, reduction to lowest enlisted rank (he didn't have far down to go), and 6 months in Portsmouth Naval Prison once he was taken off the ship when we arrived on land. Checking one day to see if he was all right, and if his guard was awake, I went into his cell and asked him why he did not take the lesser offense I had essentially offered him during the trial. He told me that he had been screwing up most of his life, and even in the Navy, and so he felt to turn his life around and get straight, he needed some really stiff punishment. Then perhaps he could break the habit of being a "fuck-up." I said I understood.

At least one Chief Petty Officer had told me that one of the best things that happened to them to straighten them out when they were young in the Navy was that one of their senior petty officers, noticing that they were messing up, took them down to the Bosun Locker or one of the holds and beat the tar out of them. It stopped them from going bad, they told me. It is strictly against Navy regulations to do this, but it is done often, and senior people including myself often turn a blind eye to it. Once I came to 0800 quarters to check on my Division, and I saw one of my men with terrible bruises on his face, and a bad black eye. "What happened to you?" I asked, and he mumbled about having fallen down a ladder. After dismissing the men from quarters, I asked my leading petty officer, Hillman, what the hell actually did happen. Hillman told me that Short, one of my brighter, but very aggressive, men, had some of his gear missing, and conducted a locker inspection and, finding his gear in someone else's locker, proceeded to beat the shit out of the owner of that locker. The whole division and its petty officers knew of it, and now so did I. Hillman felt the beating was justified, and I went along with him on that. Here I saw a clear infraction of Navy regulations, and a serious one to boot, and yet I let it go by. The Navy has a code beneath, and sometimes contrary to, the regulations that it also adheres to. A thief on board ship is a terrible thing, because in such cramped quarters, you have to be able to trust each other more than civilians can ever appreciate.

Talking about fighting, sometimes it can even be encouraged on board ship. In a letter of 11 May,'64: "Here we are, one day out of Naples...after about two weeks at sea....Our trip across [the Atlantic] was fairly uneventful. We just stood watches, worked, read, slept, saw movies, etc. Last night we had a "Smoker" which denotes boxing matches plus assorted entertainment. I was Master of Ceremonies [introducing the fighters and singers, making witty and insulting comments during the bouts, keeping things moving]. It went off very well (many told me it was the best Smoker they had ever seen). A couple of people asked if I did this professionally. The Admiral, Chief of Staff, our Captain (plus everyone not on watch) were there."

In the same letter, I wrote, "After a week in Naples, we go to Santa Manza, Corsica (southern coast) for about 4 days of amphibious landings. If the alternate plan is used (foul weather plan), I will be a "Wave Guide Commander" i.e. control one wave of LVT's (amphibious vehicles) on their way to the beach. Although I've never done it before and have had no training except what I could dig up myself out of publications, I think and hope I can bring it off. It is supposed to be done by a specially trained and experienced officer cognizant of LVT's and their peculiarities. Hope we use the main plan so I don't have to do it, but it should be interesting at the very least." Line officers are supposed to be able to do any and every job, and I'm an officer of the line.

On 29 July 1964, I was the Senior Observer on the Casa Grande (Landing Ship Dock—459 feet long) for their replenishment at sea and their man-overboard exercises. It reminds me of one high point of my time on the San Joaquin County, my LST in Japan, which was a man-overboard exercise where I was the officer who had the Conn, and I gave all the right orders—if the man goes over the starboard side, you stop all engines and order a right full rudder to throw the stern away from him, then order the boat away to pick him up, making sure all the lookouts keep the man in sight. I was relieved of the Conn because I was also the boat officer, who had to supervise the lowering of the duty boat, get the men and gear in it, and motor off to pick up the man. My Deck Division were also the ones responsible for the boat and davits for lowering it. We did everything smoothly, and set the ship's record for the fastest man-overboard drill ever. Was I proud! So when I was the Observer on the Casa Grande, I felt I really knew what I was doing.

On board the Taconic, we had a Navy helicopter detachment (just one helicopter, tied up aft on the small flight deck). As Second Division Officer, I was also Flight Deck Officer as this space was my responsibility. Before a Med cruise, on 10 April '64, "we had a surprise "flight quarters" as a helicopter came to us to deposit some mail. I was the flight deck officer and, in the absence of any aviation personnel aboard, I gave the helo the proper arm and flag signals to land him myself. As they left, the pilots both gave me a friendly wave and several people on the flight deck gave me a well- done." It's nice to feel that you are not in over your head when something out of the ordinary come up for you to do.

Helicopters were exciting to fly in. (6 June '64) "While underway we had our helicopter hold local operations, circling the ship and making touch and go landings.One afternoon, he hovered over the flight deck and lifted a few of us from the deck and into the helo by means of a cable and sling affair. I rode up and down several times as well as circling the ship in the helo between lifts." I still have a photo someone took of me being hauled aloft by the helo, as well as some photos I took while circling the ship, my feet hanging out of the open helo door as we clmibed quickly to about 500 feet above the ship and circled it. Scary to be hanging just by one small belt as the helo circles and you look almost straight down! But those moments were the best.

In May 1964, I wrote, "The weather is quite good here in the Mediterranean. Coming across the Atlantic we had rain and dreary days although we didn't roll or pitch much at all. Just grey skies and grey water. By the way, because of my work with the helocopter on board ship, and my bringing it in for landings, etc., the helo detachment conferred on me the title of "Honorary Airdale" meaning I'm welcome in their flight deck shack and are considered capable of being a flight deck officer cum laude." I was anxious at that time about my up-coming 5-day leave to Rome. "Soon—on to Rome! If someone asks me the question, "Quo vadis?" I now can give them a properly Biblical answer!" No matter how exciting life on the ship could sometimes be, I always preferred to be in some place foreign, and on leave.

"Honorary Airdale" was a pleasure to receive, because all ship's company, line officers included, respected the Navy pilots, feeling that that was most challenging and dangerous duty in our service. But my greatest honor was more official. On 11 April '64, "I received a letter sent to the Commander Sixth Fleet, Vice Admiral Gentner (3 stars!), sent by the Conde de Pentaflores, a big wheel in the Spanish Navy, who said that Charles Stickney is to be specially commended etc. for his enthusiastic, competent etc etc performance during his duties with the Spanish forces. Admiral Gentner received this "with great pride" etc etc. and sent it to Capt. Buell, Taconic's Commanding Officer, saying that it was to be put in my service record and fitness report. Our skipper endorsed it with "congratulations etc etc.. Wow! I'm a bleeding commendable hero! Enough of such self-laudatory praise." I was very proud of this commendation.

Another moment I'm very proud of was when I saved our ship. Let me explain. In the Atlantic on the way to Cannes, France, I wrote on 16 August 1963, "Three days more and then Cannes—and leave. The days here are fairly monotonous after the days underway when we picked up the formation [six other ships that were deployed in a circular formation with us with senior officer present in the center of the circle]. Underway, we had evasive steering with all the ships darkened completely [no lights at all showing, so we couldn't be seen by an enemy] all around us going at 13 knots, zig-zagging, odd course changes, and so on. At night, just before I relieved the junior officer of the deck, the officer of the deck, who had been on watch for four hours, gave a wrong rudder command, which I countermanded [without telling the O.O.D.. He said "come **left** to new course —" and gave the order for **left** full rudder. The Bosun on the helm repeated his order with a slightly questioning note to it, and the Lieutenant as the O.O.D. said again, "Yes, **left** full rudder. Come **left** to new course ———." I had not yet relieved the JOOD, but I realized that the new course we were to come to in our next leg of the rather complicated zig-zag was to the **right** of the course we were now on. I could literally feel the tension on the bridge. Others must have realized something was wrong, but all of us froze. I thawed first. "I changed it [the wrong rudder order], made it right [put on hard right rudder to compensate for the left turn we were even then beginning to make], compensated for the previous error, and brought our ship to exactly where we were supposed to be in the formation." I had put my hands on the shoulders of the helmsman when I changed the order, and worked the rudder to get us where and when we were to be. I could feel his tension relax while I was issuing the new orders, and told the phone talkers to tell Combat Info Center what I was doing, and to have another of the watch check our radars to see if we were still maintaining 1,000 yards between ships. It came out perfectly. Had we continued with the OOD's wrong order we might very well have smashed into one or more of the ships on our port side who were turning right while we were originally turning left right into them. "The O.O.D. thanked me [when I told him of his error—he said "Didn't I say Right Full Rudder?"] and he meant it too! It's pretty easy to make a mistake that could sink a ship or two when all the pressure is on [especially at the end of four hours of night watch]. Only essentials count then. Made me feel just one shade a hero. Fairly routine error in formation, but dangerous as hell. That is what is appealing about the Navy. Adventure —not the continual petty hogwash that is usually one's lot aboard here." Another proud moment. These very busy watches at sea where you understand everything and are on top of everything that happens—those go the most quickly and are the best.

While in Cannes, I had the in-port O.O.D. watch: "just before leaving Cannes, we had a fire on board, three of our boats were not yet back, and the Special Sea Detail was to be set at the same time and we had 45 minutes before we were to leave. Now there was a busy watch! Now you know why I have grey hair. All was taken care of expeditiously and in time, however. Navy always muddles through somehow."

But the watches underway are more dangerous and exciting. Once I had the 0400 to 0800 CIC watch heading to the Straits of Gibraltar, but once in the Straits we were to set the Special Sea Detail of the most experienced officers and men to get us safely through this extremely busy place. It was before eight o'clock, we were now in the Straits, and Bayley, a Radarman 2nd Class, and I and a couple of other seamen decided we were handling all the ship contacts so well and were into the work of plotting their paths to see if any would get too close to us that we wouldn't bother to get anyone to relieve us as yet. Cocky is what we were. Suddenly we get a report from the bridge that a nearby ship was Russian, and that the Captain wants to launch the helicopter to take some pictures of it. I had to get on the phone to the Captain on the bridge to get his instructions to relay them to the helo pilot who I had to talk to on another line a few yards away from the captain's phone. We didn't have enough people to do all the tasks here, and couldn't spare anyone to get more help. Meanwhile, the chopper pilot was annoyed at me while he was airborne because he needed both hands to keep his helo hovering over the Russian ship, and didn't want to interrupt this to talk to me, while the Captain was yelling at me to tell the damn pilot to get some other shot, while I ran between phone lines to speak to them both. Plus we were also trying to notice the many other ships in the area so we would not collide with them. Usually the ship traffic in the Straits of Gibraltar runs either east-west in and out of the Mediterranean, or else north-south between Europe and Africa, so there are general shipping lanes keeping it from being too chaotic there. Too much to do with too few people. One time crossing the Atlantic there were only two qualified Combat Information Center watch officers, and I was one of them, and so had to stand "port and starboard watches," which means one watch on, the next off, the next on, and so forth for a couple of weeks. Not one night did I have more than four hours sleep at a time. That can wear you down so that you don't recognize day from night. Busy, busy!

Once, on the way to Rota in Spain and then to Gibraltar, I wrote, "It is about 8:20 p.m. now and I've just been on watch on the bridge. I had the Conn (in charge of controlling the ship's movements) although I was Junior Officer of the Deck. We received a message of a merchant ship in distress about 55 miles away and we came to another course (close to the one we were already steaming on), and rang the engines all ahead full. The Captain and Executive Officer were on the bridge. And I had the Conn as we steamed to rescue a disabled ship! Wow. At any rate, there are probably other ships that will reach her before we do."

"We've been at sea for about ten days and I've been standing at least eight hours of watch a day either in CIC (with all the radars) or else on the bridge, plus working hours….boy, am I pooped!...

This ship is a real run-around as often as not. Many extremely petty things are worried over, and people get frantic about the smallest stuff at times. All the other officers say that this is the way it has been for a long time. I'm going to get some sleep now because I have to get up about 3:15 a.m. to take on another watch, and if this ship in distress is located and we have to help—well, there goes another night's sleep down the drain." The trivial and the tremendous, all in a day.

We rendezvous with other ships for more pleasant reasons. [11 Oct,'63] "We just spent a day replenishing off the southern coast of Sardinia. Ships have been coming alongside each other all day, sending over provisions, oil, etc. by lines and by helicopter." Another time [21 April '64] "I was sent over to a Destroyer by a high line while we were conducting exercises with it (a line is rigged between two ships traveling fast so as to make steering easier; they were alongside each other about 180 feet apart and going at 12 knots). A chair was rigged and they shuttled it back and forth. For a little adventure, I asked to be put in this chair and was hauled over to the Destroyer." When I arrived, one officer asked me to come on down to the wardroom for a cup of coffee. I was going to accept when my boss on the Taconic screamed at me to "get back in that chair!" I did, said good-bye to the Destroyer folks and was pulled back aboard the Taconic. Wish I could have stayed longer—or stayed for a few weeks.

In July 1964 the Taconic steamed into New York harbor for a little rest and recreation—it was the year of the World's Fair in New York, and we sailed under the Verranzano Bridge still so new that they were paint chips and debris falling on my clean decks as we sailed, all sailors at attention on the weather decks, all spit and polish, to our berth on Manhattan's West Side, "arriving 21 July at 3:45 p.m. at the northside pier 90 forward, and will leave N.Y. on 27 July." My orders were to be detached from the Navy about 14 August, so I could prepare for my graduate studies at the University of Edinburgh in Scotland.

Once while I was the Officer of the Deck on the Taconic tied up to a pier in Barcelona, my parents' cruise ship, the "Christoforo Columbo," was due in Barcelona that night. I had the 0400 to 0800 watch, and had my crew keep tabs on the cruise ship to find out where it was going to berth. It came in just around the pier from us very early in the morning and tied up. Not too long after this, I heard a small voice down at the foot of the gangway, asking, "Request permission to come aboard, sir!" I looked over the ship's side, grinned, and said, "Permission granted, DAD!"

My mother and father came up the gangway, looking very happy, about as happy as I was, and I embraced them both on the quarterdeck, then took them around the ship when my watch ended. Here in New York in

July 1964 they welcomed me back into our Brooklyn house, and when I left the Taconic and the Navy for good in August 1964, I was once again welcomed into civilian life.   Lots of traveling in the Navy, sometimes to other countries and seas, sometimes just steaming around in the ocean. A good taste of salt water in my mouth, enough to let me know that I prefer water much more fresh and free.

NAVAL OFFICER IN JAPAN:

After graduating from United States Naval Officer Candidate School [Class Fifty Six, November 17, 1961], I was sent for duty to LST-1122, U.S.S. San Joaquin County, home-ported in Iwakuni, Japan. The four months of OCS was very difficult, and I was ready to get to a ship to use what I had been studying. From a letter to my parents just before I graduated [all quotations in this section are from my letters to my parents which I now have]: "I hope my orders take me to Japan, Australia, and Hawaii. I won't want to waste my time not traveling. Want to study overseas (England or Scotland). This place [Newport, Rhode Island, & OCS] is a pain in the ass, and I hope I get good orders." A slight obscenity and an obsessional repetition of "good orders" shows you my psychological state at the time.

On the way to Japan by plane we stopped at Hawaii "for a couple of hours; it was dark and I saw nothing" and at Wake Island ("hot as hell, flat as Texas, and small"), and then on to Yokosuka near Tokyo. I had visions of future travel: "May get to go to Hong Kong, Bangkok (?? In Burma?)...." Seems like I didn't know my geography of the Far East, but I had enthusiasm.

Also I planned on buying a motorcycle "soon to save taxi fare. Most everyone has one. The country around here [Iwakuni south of Hiroshima on the island of Honshu] is supposed to be quite pretty & when the weather gets warmer I'll take trips all around, to Tokyo, etc." And so I did.

The most touristic trip I took was a week with my uncle Lou Stephens, aunt Laney, and cousin Lou Stephens Jr., who was also a Naval officer on a destroyer. From a letter of 31 March, 1962:

"I flew up to Tokyo on a Sunday and went up the Tokyo Tower (taller than the Eiffel Tower) before meeting the Stephenses as they returned to their hotel. Lou Jr. came in about 4 a.m. The next day we went to see the Kamakura Buddha, after which we went off in a private car with a guide and driver to Hakone National Park where we donned kimonos and shuffled around a rocky garden [a beautiful rock garden, not as I boorishly put it, a "rocky" one], then took a "hotsi bath," then had tempura (raw fish—urgh!) [unsophisticated 21-year-old me, confusing tempura with sashimi, and disliking raw fish which now I like. Ah, hopeless youth! How things change!] and sukiyaki cooked by geishas. They danced, played the koto [from the photos they also played a samisen], and then we played games. I won the horse-back ride [sounds sexual, but I don't remember what it was], and Louie lost in the game of "baseball" (ritualistic strip poker). He refused to take off his drawers, so the game ended. The whole evening was very special. [I remember lots of sake drinking, lots of giggling at the sexual innuendos, and giggling at the whole delightful playful evening with these geishas.]

"Next day we went to Ago Bay and Ise. Women pearl divers and beautiful inlets are the highlights of these pearl islands. We went to Kyoto and Nara, which have great shrines, temples, and parks. Louie and I had a lot of fun exchanging "l's" to "r's" ("schline" for "shrine" for example). Kept us in stitches." [How politically incorrect I once was—and often still am. I also remember going to Kyoto's Ryoanji Temple with its famed rock garden. Louie and I spent maybe 20 minutes at most in it. We met two Japanese young women outside who said they planned on spending the whole afternoon in this temple contemplating these rocks. Superficial materialistic American tourists—that's us! "Just check that shrine off our list, Martha! Only three more to go and then we can eat!"]

"Met the Duke and Duchess of Beford on our trip also. The Duchess is French and smokes small cigars. She told me that the last time they got their names in the news it was for doing "the Twist" in the Peppermint Lounge in N.Y.! A very nice trip and so great to see the Stephenses!"

Another time, in February 1962, cousin Lou was in Yokosuka Naval Base with his destroyer, the Mullany, but had left the ship by the time I arrived. I went with some other officers to a hot bath and massage—the young, cute girls "definitely not over-dressed. And yet strictly on the up-and-up, a family type of thing with no funny business....Then, about 1 p.m., sitting in Club 88 out away from the center of Tokyo, who should walk in but Louie." The Navy world is a small one, even in the biggest of cities, and it often revolves around bars. I should not have been so surprised to see my Navy officer cousin.

On January 9, 1962, my 22nd birthday, I wrote my parents of my plans to get down to Tokyo "one of these weekends. However, it is a big city devoted to entertainment mostly (according to my fellow officers) and supposedly quite expensive." This at a time when Japan was a poor country and one dollar equaled 360 Yen. In August, "I just got back from a day in Tokyo. I flew down to Atsugi Naval Air Station as a Navy courier (handle all sorts of important documents) and then, after delivery, I en-trained into Tokyo. This student asked me to accept him as a guide (for a fee—he was Korean) which I did. We went to the Imperial Palace (only can get into it two days a year—these weren't those days). Then to Ueno Park which has all sorts of museums, a zoo, etc. A Buddhist shrine and a Shinto temple and then to a kimono shop where I bought four of them....the belts are inside the sleeves, but there is an extra red fancy belt thrown in. Also a square of cotton used by Japanese for carrying things. A present from the lady. They are best for bathrobes although the Nipponese use them in public all the time." I wonder if many Japanese wear kimonos in the street now. So many places in Asia are filled with American-style jeans and tee shirts. Whole types of national dress are now often used only on special holidays or occasions.

Speaking of generalizations, I made one in that August 1962 letter: "The Japanese are a very friendly people. However, Iwakuni-ans are the worst types—where a city, or a large part of one, is dependent on a military base and its needs, they turn out the biggest collection of whores, cheats etc. to satisfy these needs. At any rate, Japan is a nice place—outside of the bars!" I have found this to be true in an even wider sense. The people who speak English and are the most "Western" in many Asian countries, are in my experience much less nice and decent than the less educated and more ordinary typical countrymen. Whether this is because the English-speaking and "Westernized" folk feed on the tourists as their prey, or whether they gain some hardness from us and our culture—I don't know.

On 15 November 1962, I wrote, "Flew up to Atsugi for a day [as a courier] and on the way back we flew over Mt. Fuji. I went up to the cockpit and the view was absolutely fantastic! No camera, however. Darn! The leaves are changing color down here [in Iwakuni] now, but nothing comparable to the New England autumn." The majesty of the unchanging countryside compared to changeable people. The seeing of a iconic landmark through a wider window. The absence of a photo to seize the moment as momento. The seeing of another country through the familiar filter of one's own culture and country. The nature of travel.

All other countries, naturally, are compared with our home country. On 26 Dec.'62, I wrote, "I went down to Atami which is a hot springs resort on what is known as the "Japanese Riviera" (Izu Peninsula just south of Tokyo). Scenery is sort of modified Monterey Peninsula with similar, although somewhat slighter, rugged wave-cut cliffs. After Atami, I went back to Atsugi Naval Air Station where I spent Christmas Eve in the sack sleeping off the hikes and sulphur hot baths." France and California and Japan—reminders of each other.

Iwakuni, my home base in southern Honshu, is a couple of hours or less by motorcycle from Hiroshima. Close enough to go to when weary of the Iwakuni bars and U.S. marines. In May 1962, "We (Walt Gardner, my dept.

head and me) went into Hiroshima on our motorcycles. We wandered around town, went to the Peace Museum (relics of the atomic bomb blast of 1945), and met some (4) girls from Hiroshima University. They, like many other Japanese students, want to talk to Americans; they like to practice their English. We took them out for ice cream and left with the possibility left up in the air with regard to our coming to their university to speak about America! Possible." [Never did get to speak at their university.] In August, I wrote, "It is pretty hot and sticky here in Japan too. Went into Hiroshima last week with Walt (Operations Officer) and met a couple of cute girls at a movie ("Jazz on a Summer's Day" filmed in Newport, R.I.). Went out that night and next day went to the island of Miajima. Going out this week too. Rare to meet a girl who doesn't work in a bar. My girl's father is very much against her going out with me ("a foreigner"). Also, her mother died in the atomic bombing of Hiroshima." Kind of a Montague—Capulet situation here, only more so.

Never had sex with any woman in Japan except for women who worked in bars, who were very often, but not always, prostitutes. There were military bars, and all American men and some very few (terribly too few) American women in Iwakuni were military. We were forbidden to go into Japanese civilian bars, but I did discover a coffee bar which played European classical music, so I headed for that. Once I ran into our Hospital Corpsman, an enlisted man, in this bar, and we agreed not to report each other. Here I was, feeling guilty at being in a tea-drinking classical-music-playing place, while I was encouraged by the military rules to frequent boozing whore-full bars. Certainly the question of security about military secrets being exposed in foreign haunts may have been part of this rule. But if ever we wanted to know about where or when our aircraft carriers were going to visit Iwakuni, a secret matter, we had only to ask one of the bar girls. They would all know because their American boy friends would write to them when they were coming, and the bars and whores would prepare a big and expensive welcome. The bars were divided yet again into officer's and enlisted men's establishments, an informal classification. The enlisted men's bars were rougher, and usually played "Country and Western" music, or as we called it, "shit-kicking music." The officers' bars played jazz or any other music that would get us melancholy enough to drink a few more beers, and look longingly at the girls behind the bars. Two of the ten officers on my ship eventually married Japanese bar girls.

In a letter of 15 Oct.'62: "There is a very tiny bar (no one who has not been to Japan can imagine how tiny a tiny bar can be!) in Hiroshima called "The Pad" where Jazz is served up piping loud and the cool cats and chicks really dig it. Met some interesting people there last Saturday. One invited me to a Sports Club dance (the sport is Karate, the art of crunching an opponent's head with your hands)." In Iwakuni one bar I went to was a small one called "The Town Pump," to which I gave a sexual connotation rather than than the place townspeople would gather around for water and gossip. The Pad with its Japanese beatniks reminds me of the musical show in Tokyo I once saw where one young weedy Japanese guitarist sang "Home, Home, on the Range" which he of course pronounced (no kidding!) "lllange" and a very tiny Japanese girl belted out in a very Ethel Merman way the songs Ethel sang. American culture was percolating into Japan. On 5 July'62: "This past weekend I went to Kure, a shipbuilding port about 20 miles on the other side [north] of Hiroshima. The trip by motorcycle was exciting (sore ass!) Although Kure itself was nothing too special. The inn where Kirk and Dave (2 officers on the LST) and I stayed was very Japanese. We took a "hotsi bath" in a rock garden type of bath, and our room overlooked another rock garden with a pool of fish in its center. We slept on tatami mats in a futon—a quilt type, very warm and heavy. Flies kept us awake all night, though. For breakfast, we dined on cold egg, seaweed, bamboo slivers, rice, green tea, and some other stuff I won't even hazard a guess about what it was. I stuck to egg and rice!"

"The Japanese are very polite, friendly, and kind people (generally) once you get out of Iwakuni and its military-base-hustler attitude. The school children all in their uniforms love to take your picture, shake your hand, speak a little English, giggle, and be cute. They are really something—so anxious to talk to you and ask questions. Well, now to duty!"

I did get to more than one of the Japanese islands. In a letter of 25 Feb.'63: "Friday, Saturday, and Sunday, I spent at Beppu on the island of Kyushu at a very excellent Japanese "Ryokan" (Inn). The second night a couple of guys from the ship shared it with me, but the first night it was just me, the tatami mats, scrolls, and sliding wood-and-rice-paper doors. The people there could not speak any English and my "Nihon-go" (Japanese language) is poor, but we had a good time anyway. Like shuffling birds, the girls go about making everything exactly the way you like it, and giggle at your attempts to speak Japanese, and at their own to speak "Eigo" (English). The maids enter bowing and smiling, and shuffle around getting your "atsui furo" (hot bath) ready, folding your clothes, lighting the gas heater, pouring out cups of "o-cha" (tea), green and hot, and putting the fragrant charred wood in the "hibatchi." Always so polite. No other people quite like this one (that I ever came across, at any rate). Outside Iwakuni and all military-base towns, Japan is an interesting and worth-while country to visit."

"On Friday night, I sat and read, watched some T.V. (Private T.V., bath, etc. for 2000 Yen—$5.60 on an individual basis. No tipping.). And wrote poetry (or verse). I felt it was incumbent on me after giving me the quiet atmosphere of the Japanese inn. The poetry was mediocre and uninspired.... On Saturday night, Hank, Rich (my assistant), and myself were treating ourselves to a sukiyaki dinner in our room. The maids were charming, the sukiyaki was delicious, the beer slightly inebriating, and the evening really fine! We shared the beer with the girls who cooked and served the food and they got ever so faintly tipsy. In Japan it is the custom for all barriers to be let down and everyone sing, pinch fannies, dance, and get plastered. We did what we could to uphold tradition without tearing down the place. Dignity is supposed to "go by the boards" during these parties."

"The next day we went to a mountain on which is located a miniature replica of Nikko, a shrine city near Tokyo. Also, there was zoo where I had great fun (and a large crowd) as I played "Cowboy" and raced around a track on a tiny horse whooping and carrying on (per Hollywood style). Also, I rode on an elephant and attracted a bunch of young girls in school costume (sort of like a sailor suit in blue). The man who owned the elephant had me get on him with two girls, and he (the elephant) did all sorts of tricks like waving the Japanese flag, etc. Me—a carnival shill! One is called upon to fill many different roles as an American abroad and attracting customers could be one. I also played "throw the ball at the bottles" type of game, and made all sorts of baseball noises, winding up, etc. which drew a crowd. Did pretty well at that after missing the first ball after much elaborate spitting on the hands, looking at second base, winding up….Went over really big! Send you some pictures when I get them developed." Did my performance that far-off day in 1963 inspire some young Japanese students to shuck off their school uniforms to become the professional baseball ("beso bor-u") players of Japan who can match our American professionals today? Very doubtful. I was better at the wind-up than the pitch.

In June 1962, I was flown down to Itazuke Air Force Base in a small Beechcraft plane near Fukuoka on Kyushu by three Navy pilots all senior to me, because I had mentioned to the Naval Commander of the base that it might be fun to see it. He detailed those three to fly me down so that they could get their flying in for that month in so as to be eligible to get their flight pay. Ah, the Navy! So, from a letter of 15 June '62: "In Fukuoka, I met a Japanese businessman who took me around, showed me the sights; we ate sukiyaki together, and went to this cabaret which was decked out in [Second World War] war-like decorations, the waiters wore [W.W. 2] Japanese soldiers' uniforms, played military music. He (the Japanese) did not like militarism. I'm glad of that! Most Japanese are very dedicated to peace." I remember that a couple of the waiters had only one arm, which I was told they had lost in the Second World War. There was not one iota of animosity that I could feel against me, even though here I was in the once-enemy stronghold. Old Japanese rising-sun battle flags.

Medals on the waiters' unifroms. And here was me, a U.S. Navy officer and known to be so. Yet I was treated royally with authentic friendliness. A most amazing place! (And people!)

The other large island in the south is Shikoku, smallest of the four main islands of Japan. On 23 May'62, I wrote: "Last weekend John Bole Kirkpatrick and I went to Shikoku, and to Takahama by a 4-hour ferry boat weaving through the other islands in the Inland Sea, and then spent the night in Dobo, an ancient hot springs resort where we had two "atsui furo" (hotsi baths), and after wrinkling up like prunes, we walked through the streets of Dobo. Stared at by all, we seemed to be the only white people in town. We are taller than most of the Japanese (Kirk is 6 ft. 4 in.) and stood out in the crowds. It was packed with high school students who were there to play athletics (big games) and take "hotsi baths" (a national institution like Hara Kiri and raw fish). In the morning, we went to Matsuyama, a pretty large town, where we listened to Bach in a coffee shop (surprised us also!) and bought a few things in stores. Then the boat ride back."

Traveling around Iwakuni itself was easy once I got my Honda 55cc motorcycle. In a letter of 30 January 1962: "My motorcycle is a lot of fun to drive! This past Saturday I and 3 other officers took our cycles up and into some rugged hills. Skidding along in low gear through snow, gravel, and mud, we climbed way up to the top of this mountain. We passed through small villages, men trudging along the road with timber on their backs, women working in the fields with primitive tools. The road up the mountain slithered around with sharp curves and steep drops while we gunned our cycles along it. Lots of fun. And even better when it gets warmer.

"On Sunday, I went with another officer (Ltjg Hank Heredia) on a "Military" sponsored tour to the Shuhodo Caves, Tokuyama, and Prince Mori's Castle. The caves are like Luray Caverns, except smaller. Prince Mori's castle is quite a lovely delicate spot with gardens in back where I took some shots with 3 Japanese girls in kimonos. They all giggled, I laughed, and we had a good time. Except for the fact that we took off our shoes in Mori's house, and therefore developed frostbite of the toes (there is nothing so cold as a Japanese house in winter)."

The archetypical Japanese island of Miajima was less than an hour by motorcycle from Iwakuni, and I went there often, climbing Mt Misen, and contemplating the famous big red Torii gate in front of its Shinto shrine on the Inland Sea. In February 1962 I spent a typical Sunday when I did not have "the duty" aboard ship with "riding my motorcycle up in the hills [behind Iwakuni], down stream-bubbling ravines, through small farm-villages, etc. This coming weekend—perhaps the same sort of thing." My motorcycle gave me mobility to get to tiny and very old-fashioned villages where people dressed and lived as they used to a century ago. This old Japan, which I do not doubt, is now in the year 2000 completely gone except in self-conscious ceremonies and festivals.

If anyone wants to see local old-fashioned customs anywhere in this contemporary world, you better get to these places very fast. It's so easy to travel to the ends of the earth now, and everyone is doing it, thereby making every place more like every other place, and every place looks more like here and now.

In April 1962 Japan was still often a very foreign country. "It is getting very balmy out and the sun heats up the land and the breezes are fresh. This past weekend, I went out to Kintai Bridge on the outskirts of Iwakuni. It is a very famous span curving over the Imazu River in about four arches. Everyone was wildly staggeringly drunk [it was the Cherry Blossom Festival], the Japanese were falling all over themselves and us, boozily spewing out what English they knew (usually "herro, boy-san" and then they'd giggle and lurch around some more). It seems they seize on any straw for an excuse to have a binge, and cherry blossom time is it. The trees still have quite a few blossoms on them near Kintai. I took out a little rowboat and rowed upstream against the current, and then roared off downstream, and then up again. Meanwhile, everyone was staggering around the cherry trees, and pic-niking on the banks of the river." [I remember that one U.S. Marine got drunk, took out a boat, swamped it, and drowned that day.]

"The next day some of us went up to Miajima Island, not too far from Hiroshima. Here again, all the Japanese were celebrating. Walt Gardner (Operations Officer) and I walked up to the top of Mt. Misen and saw just below the top at an old Shinto shrine a very weird and ancient religious ceremony. Chanting priests shaking bell-like rattles threw sticks with prayers (?) written on them into a fire, after which all the people walked barefoot through the cold ashes. The costumes, shouting, fire, etc, made it an exciting spectacle. The view from Mt. Misen is really terrific. We could see our ship and Hiroshima plus many miles in all directions. The day was clear and warm. We went on our motorcycles of course." Seeing this overall view did not help us understand the symbols and purposes of this Shinto ceremony. Seeing is not always really seeing. But my motorcycle got me to the old Japan hidden from most foreigners.

My motorcycle almost got me killed too. Many drivers in Japan seemed to want to emulate the wild Kamakaze, to run you off the road whatever the risk to themselves. But we Navy and Marines were not slouches in the "taking risks" department. Once, I was riding over a bridge into Iwakuni, and decided to go straight, but suddenly shuffling in front of me crossing the road was an old "Mama-san" and so I turned to the left to keep from running her down. My foot brake had bent up from a spill on a mountain road, and so was hard to get at. One of my hand-brakes had broken off (from another mountain spill) and so there I was, trying to avoid Granny, fumbling with both feet and hands for a brake, and trying to turn left at a fairly high speed. I found the brakes, but a bit too late, so mounted the curb and smashed into a storefront, made of thin wood and then starting halfway up, of glass. BLAMMM! My motorcycle was part-way into the store. It had knocked out the wood panel and smashed out some of the glass, which then slid down the groove in the wood like a guillotine. Had I gone into the store a little further rather than just with part of my front wheel, my arms on the handlebars would likely have been sliced off. I was shaken, and turned to the old Granny I missed. She shuffled by, looking at me, but continued on her way. I walked into the store, using the door this time, and who should be the only in it, but a Down-syndrome boy watching it for his Dad. He was smiling and going "duh—duh" which was pretty much the way I felt. Then a crowd formed, his Dad came out hearing the crash, and we all bowed at each other, me saying "Gomen nasai" (please excuse me) a lot, and bowing some more, and offering to pay for the broken store, and handing him what money I had, which apparently was enough, and so we parted, me Gomen nasai-ing and bowing, and he bowing and smiling, and me picking up the motorcycle and finding it still worked, and drove off very carefully in a flurry of bows and shakes and shame.

In 1994 at the top of a volcano in Bali, I met two American emergency-room physicians on vacation, and they told me the emergency-room slang term for motorcyclists: donors. Yes. Several pairs of trousers and a couple of layers of skin I left on Japanese dirt roads, and I'm lucky. When I left Iwakuni, I sold my motorcycle to a Maine officer, and a week or so later I heard he had totalled it. He lived. Once I needed a driver's license for a jeep to run courier documents, and so I had to get a Japanese driver's license. (Never needed to take a driver's test, neither military nor Japanese, for my motorcycle license.) I show up, and am told to get into a very large Marine truck and drive it around this parking lot. I told the Japanese examiner I never drove a truck before, much less at the very time of a driver's exam, and I said I just wanted a license for a jeep. He told me "drive" and so after he told me how the gears shifted, I drove it around for a while, not very well or smoothly. He told me that I passed, but pleaded with me to "practice. Please practice." He probably figured another American maniac at the wheel would not make much difference in Japan where fast wild driving was a national sport.

The Japanese language is difficult to learn, but we in the Navy used certain Japanese terms as part of our daily conversations even with each other.

In a letter home I said, "Tell Grandpa I'm glad he is feeling O.K. and hope everyone else is "dai jobu" (all right) and "ichi-ban" (the best) and "genki des" (is fine)." From another letter: "Dear Mom (Oka-san) and Dad (Oto-san)...Mele Kalikimaka (that is Merry Christmas in Hawaiian). [One of my fellow officers was an indiginous Hawaiian, Ltjg Pete Patacsil, who we would sometimes call "Pineapple."] "Since working on my Seamanship course, I have radically increased my nautical vocabulary to where it includes the following phrases of inestimable value to a Naval officer: "Kampai" ("Bottoms up" in Japanese),

"Yum sing" ("Bottoms up" in Chinese), "Okole maluna" ("Bottoms up" in Hawaiian). My education is now complete. The money spent on my college education was not wasted."

My linguistic education certainly was not complete. On my Christmas leave, staying in the Gohra Hotel in Hakone National Park, I wrote on 26 Dec.'62: "I went up to Hakone National Park and spent a couple of days hiking and snapping pictures of Mt. Fuji. Met the Executive Officer [second in command of a ship] of the "Tillamook" (ATA—auxiliary tug) with whom I had shared a BOQ [Bachelor Officers Quarters] room my first night in Japan." Notice here how many abbreviations and phrases that are not understandable to a civilian. I then go on: "He and the corpman for the tug and I spent some time wandering around a mountain lake, struggling to buy some edible chow in a Japanese restaurant where no one spoke English. Example: "Well, rice is "gohan." That's a start....."

Certain things can partially transcend language. From another letter: "On Saturday night, about 6 of us went to a Japanese restaurant, got a private room, and had sukiyaki prepared by some geishas who afterwards played instruments, played games, and sang Japanese songs, and we sang American ones. Pretty wild evening. Well, I'm going to "rack out" as we say in the Navy (go to sleep, a "rack" being a bed. Tomorrow I have the duty as C.W.O. Good night!" C.W.O. means Communications Watch Officer. Who says knowing English is enough to speak Navy?

In a sense I lived here in two countries: Japan and the U.S. Navy. The Navy always and obviously took precedence. "The needs of the Navy are primary," as the saying goes. (17 July '62)

"I've been extremely busy what with I & E [Information and Education officer], Electronics, Operations Division Officer, and Communications Officer (the last two for about 2 weeks). Now we are alongside the U.S.S. Ajax (AR-6), a tender which repairs stuff on board that we don't have the facilities to repair ourselves. In the past week we've been underway for two days…fantastic! We "rubber docked" i.e. threw a red barrel over the side and then turned about and bought it alongside dead in the water abeam to starboard (listen to that nautical lingo!). At any rate, I did quite well both days. The Exec said I did it better than he did, and the Captain gave me an approving nod and a wink, and told me, when I wanted to get even closer, said, "It's perfect just where it is" (or words to that effect). Then too, I took the helm (steering wheel) and responded to orders instead of giving them. That also is fun. Great days—made me feel like a ship-handler and an officer rather than a harried, ink-stained, clerk-psychiatrist-policeman etc.

"Last weekend I had the duty— a hot, lazy weekend with sun-bathing on the 02 level (2 decks above main deck) and reading and meeting boats etc. Last Wednesday and Thursday I made a trip down to Atsugi Naval Air Station on Navy business. Didn't go into Tokyo…." A mixture of routine and excitement, relaxing and hectic, anchored and underway—life on my LST-1122 (Landing Ship, Tank), the San Joaquin County.

Underway once, just about sunrise, Ltjg Carl Bowler and I were the only officers awake and we had "the Deck" (controlling the ship's routine) and "the Conn" (controlling the ship's movements through the water). Carl and I would switch being the Navigator and giving the steering and engine orders, and at this time I had the Conn. We were steaming along and saw in front of us to our port side (our left) a small Japanese fishing boat that was going to cross our path. The range was decreasing (we were getting closer) and the angle of the boat on our bow remained the same. That meant we would collide with the fishing vessel unless one of us modified our course. Now accord-

ing to the Inland Rules of the Road (rules governing ships' behavior when
not on the high seas, and we were on the Inland Sea) we were the "privileged
vessel" (the vessel coming along on the starboard side of the other ship) and
so were obligated to continue our course and speed, and it was incumbent on
the other vessel, the fishing boat in this case, to change its course or speed so
as to avoid crashing into us.

But they didn't change their course or speed. "Range decreasing, angle
remains the same," said Carl. "Shit," said I. Finally I told Carl I didn't think
they were going to change course, that what the hell could we expect from a
damn Japanese fishing boat anyway, that they'd go by the rules? So I suggested (Carl was senior in rank to me) that we turn to starboard (the right),
speed up, and sound one short blast on our horn to warn them we were turning to starboard. Carl agreed, and I gave the orders. Carl had trained his
binoculars on the fishing boat's wheelhouse and saw no one till the horn gave
one short and loud blast. Suddenly he saw a man lurch up and rub his eyes,
look around, gape in horror as he saw us, and start swing the wheel frantically
to port. The fisherman had been asleep. Had we obeyed the Rules of the
Road and held our course and speed we would have sunk the fishing boat
and have caused an international incident. Whew!

Another situation with us and fishing boats was when I had the Conn
and the Captain was up with me in the wheelhouse. There were lots of
boats around us and we were concerned. We had one boat on our starboard side who would come close to colliding with us if we continued our
present course and speed, and as he was the privileged vessel, it was up to
us to change course to avoid him. I suggested speeding up and passing in
front of him, not quite kosher but effective as he could see us well, but the
Captain told me to give the orders to come (turn) right to cross his path
behind him, the more proper Navy way, but as we turned to starboard and
gave one short blast on the horn to inform him we were turning right, the
fisherman panicked seeing this big Navy ship turning toward him, and so
he turned left toward us which made it very likely we would collide with
him. There was less space between the two ships now and it was lessening

very quickly. The Captain grabbed my shoulders, pushed me out of the way, and shouted out orders to stop all engines, then to reverse them. We missed the panicked fishing boat, but here was another example of when or if we did the right nautical thing, we would have sunk another ship. What works in the book or among Navy vessels does not always work in the Japanese Inland Sea.

Life on board the LST is generally routine and unexciting. Work hours are from 0800 to 1600 (8 a.m. till 4 p.m.) And after that we often have "the duty." From a letter: "Last night I had the duty and "stood by for" (i.e. assumed the duties of) the Command Duty Officer and the Communications Watch Officer. Woken up in the middle of the night to get traffic over the teletype in Radio II, to give the keys to the 2nd Division watch-standers, to answer questions, take reports, etc. Last Thursday, I navigated the ship into its anchorage. I navigated for about 45 minutes. Not too badly, either. And I am learning!" Another time (letter of 2 June'62), "Dropped the anchor right in the hole (perfectly)!" Not all was ship-handling and work, though. On the Marine Air Station I played some tennis, swam in the pool (the Inland Sea's water was pretty filthy), went sailing, ran, played handball, badminton, and even one game of golf. Once I ran in a track meet and "came in third out of nine men in the 1320-yard run."(Got a medal for that.) Sports, reading, riding my motor-cycle, going to movies, or going into town to bars to listen to music, escape the ship, drink ("lemonade occasionally"), sometimes pick up a semi-demi-prostitute at the officers' bar-cum-semi-brothel, take her home, and have sex and talk and tea. That's life there in Iwakuni.

But mostly life is on the ship. (3 May 1962): "Tonight I have the duty and am sitting down in the cryptocenter in the semi-solid bowels of the ship...listening to a radio dimly heard through the steel bulkhead...the ventilation system humming and blowing...a hatch slammed shut...some-one walking on the deck overhead...two men laughing about an incident on the beach [ashore]...the "word" over the 1MC [public address system for the whole ship] for "Sweepers, sweepers, man your brooms, sweep down all decks and passageways, empty all trash containers on the fantail [at the stern]"...common sounds aboard ship...It is just about time for taps and the 2200 [10 p.m.] boat to be called away, and I have to see that it is done....It is about 2237 now and the LCVP [Landing Craft Vehicular Personnel—boat] has returned, the troops have mostly turned in except for the men on watch, I hope, Sweepers have been held, the communications gear is OK and the anchor chain moored to the buoy is slack [means no strong currents or waves]. Things are pretty peaceful."

Things are sometimes too quiet. (15 June '62) "Rain and overcast skies are the order of the day. Last night I had the duty and we were "souped in" by fog. We had to ring the ship's bell to guide our boat back. We had the radar on to locate our boat and the boat of a fleet tug anchored not too far from us. We tried getting them on the harbor net (radio), but "no dice." The the fog broke up and we could see again. For a while there was a little excitement, but soon it became the same old routine again." Another ship pulling in to Iwakuni can make for excitement—the Ajax for ship's repairs, or a fleet tug in from Hawaii that I was the senior observer on (junior Ensign though I was) for their drills and tests on man-overboard, ship-handing, and navigation.

In April 1963 "here we are in the wide Pacific Ocean steaming at 7.5 knots on course 128 degrees true and 136 degrees per steering compass toward the island of Guam, in the Marianas Islands. As soon as I get there, I'll try to get a flight out to Hawaii [to join my next duty billet on the U.S.S. Taconic (AGC-17) [Amphibious group Command ship]. I've been standing O.O.D. [Officer of the Deck underway] watches.... Okinawa, where we stopped for a couple of days, was rather a grubby spot; however, the U.S. Air Force clubs there are terrific. The Air Force really gets the money and use it to make things awfully comfortable for their people." After being used to the spartan life of the Marines' clubs, the Air Force seemed to us to entertain in palaces.

All the way to Okinawa, the swells (the waves, not Air Force officers) came at us rolling from the port side, and the LST, being flat-bottomed, rolled constantly. Almost all the crew were seasick, and naturally, to prove their being old salts and therefore seasick-proof, the Captain and some of the Chief Petty Officers lit up cigars. This made the rest of us even more green, and only partially with envy. The first night out of the Japanese Inland Sea and into the Pacific (mis-named those nights), Kirk and I had the watch. It usually takes a few days to get back your sea-legs and your sea-stomach, and I was getting badly sea-sick. I had Kirk relieve me of the Deck and the Conn, a serious ritual, and I went below, threw up, felt much better, and returned to relieve Kirk. Saying "I relieve you" means all is now officially your responsibility, and so the words are taken very very seriously.

At the break of day one morning when I had the O.O.D. watch on the way to Guam, all the sea around me, it seemed the whole Pacific, was totally empty of other ships and of everything but green water and sky. In the wheelhouse with me I had two nearly dozing sailors, one my phone talker connected with the engine room and the radar spaces, and the other my helmsman. No one had said anything for some minutes, each of us immersed in our own thoughts. I could see the curvature of the earth, like in the Texas Panhandle. It was so peaceful, just the shussh of the ship through the water and the hum of the engines. As the sun rose, I noticed that it rose exactly at 090 degrees on our true compass, due East. "So East on our compass is really East where the sun rises!" Somehow this rather obvious insight seemed special to me that daybreak, connecting the Navy with the natural world. We headed east toward Guam, east away from my time in the Far East, east toward my next Navy ship, home-ported on the east coast of the U.S.A.

MEXICO:

I was thirteen when I first got to Mexico in the summer of 1953 to visit my relatives, the Stephens' family. They had a wonderful estate—several houses, a huge garden—in the quiet suburb of Coyoacan. In 1990 I drove past the house on Calzada Taxquena and the place seemed right in downtown—crowded, businesses around it, anything but the quiet un-trafficed street I remember. So many more people, the machismo of the Mexican male for producing children and the poverty of possibilities in the outlying countryside, have changed the city into a megalopolis, stuffed full of desperate and polluted competition.

A danger is romanticizing the past. The white-clad peasants of Mexico in 1953 didn't have it so good then. I remember, in a native market where I had gone with my Uncle Lou, an old dignified unshaven blind Mexican man standing by himself playing his guitar and singing. He had no boy to help him. After his song, he stopped for a short while, waiting for someone to give him some money. I waited till he started singing again, and till his next song was over. He stopped, and waited again. Meanwhile, the bustle of the market continued. No one paid any attention at all to him, walking by him as though he didn't exist, busy with their own lives. At this point, I walked over to him and pressed a small coin into his rough hands. "Gracias." "De nada, senor." I had to go to keep up with my parents and uncle. To this day I regret I gave him such a small coin. To this day I pity his alone-ness even more than his poverty. But his blindness was worse than all.

In India I learned it was best to give to blind people, not just because I pity that disability more than any other. If a beggar is blind, they cannot see who is giving something to them, and so the next time they encounter you they won't demand or petition you for more. I've had beggars, and not just in India, pester me with their petitions because once I was very generous. But in Mexico at age thirteen I was not generous, and this cheap gift of a small coin weighs heavy on my mcmory.

At thirteen my Uncle Lou Stephens let me work in Dorset, his textile factory, as a quill boy, putting quills in a machine that wrapped thread around them. It was a simple job and I learned it quickly, despite my lack of Spanish. You could hardly hear anything anyway, what with the constant roar of the machines. When I'd leave the factory, I couldn't hear for a few minutes, and I'm certain if I had worked at this for a long time, I would have been somewhat deafened. For a week I worked there, making

10 pesos a day, which should have been more like 6 pesos, but hey! I was the boss's nephew. This was my first paycheck and my only factory job, and I could see how boring it would be for a life's work.

Then I helped Elijio in Uncle Lou's garden. Here I lasted four hours, clipping around the edges of a flower bed. My back ached terribly. The sun was hot. I gave up and went back to being a kid who didn't have to work for this summer in Mexico.

Acapulco was a high point of that 1953 visit. There were few hotels there then, and we stayed in small houses at the Club Deportivo, a sports club my uncle belonged to. I had never felt tropical sun before, and we were all—my Mom and Dad, Uncle Lou and Aunt Laney, cousins Charley, Louie, Lizzie, Lolly, and Jimmy—admonished to wear tee shirts and broad-brimmed hats even into the water. I learned to water-ski—old films show me falling down again and again before finally staying up all around the bay, wobbly but up. Once, cousin Charley and I paddled over on a small "tabla," like a big surfboard, to the island of Roqueta where a Tarzan film had been made. On the way over to this romantic jungle island, we saw a dead fish with a foot-size hemispherical bite taken out of it, a reminder of sharks. Scary, but who thinks they'll die at thirteen?

In 1965 at age twenty five I was again in Acapulco, and this time decided to swim over to Roqueta, maybe 2/3 or a mile off the beach at Caleta. I asked a lifeguard what about sharks, and he told me there were some, but not too many. He didn't try to dissuade me from the swim. The current was strong, but I calculated the angles and ended up on the beach I aimed for. In the middle I lazed a bit, just floating, but watching out for those tell-tale fins, and by changing types of strokes, got to the island easily enough, where I rested for 15 minutes, and then swam back. Very proud of myself, so proud I told the housekeeper of the placed I stayed at, and she then regaled me with stories of the families in boats attacked by sharks who capsized the boats and ate all the families. Glad I didn't hear about these stories till I got back safe.

In 1986, aged 46, I was also in Acapulco, and took a boat over to Roqueta and swam back, the current pulling hard to the side sweeping me out of the bay, but I fought it and got back to the beach at Caleta. I'm 60 now. Enough of swims to Roqueta. Let time and better sense and more awareness of fragility and death let me find other tests for myself.

In the summer of 1969, Joyce and I drove our VW Squareback down to and around Mexico for two months vacation. I was working on my Ph.D. in literature and she was finishing up her B.A. in psychology, and we had the chance of a break from studying. Except for a carburator that caused the VW to stall in traffic or going up a hill with a drop-off into a ravine and no safety fence beside the road, it was great to have the mobility of a car. In Acapulco, besides para-sailing around the bay and marvelous swimming and food, there were also dangers. Once I looked up as a wave built up before breaking, and I saw a very long fish, maybe eight or nine feet long, travel just below the wave's crest. I grabbed Joyce without a word and pulled her in to shore, and then yelled to my cousin Charley to get out of the water, then ran up the beach yelling to everyone to get out of the water. A life guard at the hotel near where we were swimming told me that there were no sharks there, but whatever I saw was big and sleek enough to eat anyone he wanted to.

Swimming at another beach, Joyce and I both got stung by a Portuguese man-of-war, I getting a slash across the neck. It hurt, but nothing special except for the red mark. After we went off to Pie de la Cuesta, a beach with huge waves, I remember having the feeling that I was about to die. It wasn't painful nor nauseating, just a strong physical sense of death. I told Joyce and Charlie without making much of it, and they didn't realize how strong my premonition was. After an hour of so, the premonition vanished, but as you can read, the premonition stayed in my memory. Charley and I went swimming in La Quebrada which the high divers swan-dive into during the nightly tourist show. The waves funneling into this cleft in the cliffs pull you toward the rocks, but by swimming hard you can grab the rocks and climb up the cliffs a bit and then leap into the water from twelve feet up, not the

120 feet up that the professionals dive from. "Careful of your knees," one diver told me—lots of sea urchins clamp to these rocks. Seventeen years later, here in 1986, three times I watched the divers dive from 120 feet up. I stood on the other side of the fence put up to keep the tourists safe, and while I was there on the cliff, looking down about sixty feet, I felt many rats running past my legs, clearly agitated by my presence on this cliff. I stayed there watching, but I too was agitated. Reminders of danger even if only observing.

But we were tourists too: From a letter of June 3, 1969 about Mexico City: "We toured the pyramids and went to Lagunilla Market; picked up various pre-Columbian and post-L.B. Johnsonian heads (small), and are still looking for that serape, church door, and Mayan temple just suited for our living room....Writing letters when living so nicely has always been hard. But think that between letters, we're having more fun than pen in hand permits." As Yeats said, there's the choice beween the life and the work. As Tuchman said, contentment often doesn't get in the history books. And history books often don't speak of bowels: "I've had a bit of Montezuma's Revenge this morning, but it's being beaten back by the formidable artillery of Kaopectate and toast." Military metaphors and historical Mexican references to describe the common "shits."

Mexico was the first country on my Sabbatical Fellowship Leave of 1986 to 1987. Highlights?

In Mexico City, the World Cup of Soccer being held there, and the fever it sparked—when Mexico won a match, long lines of cars parading down streets using their horns to beep out "Mex-i-co" in rhythm. Being in Tepotzlan with Charley, Xenia, Gabi and Bret. Seeing and talking about Louie's paintings, with long late-night talks about life and philosophy with Louie and Karen. Wonderful taco places. Getting pickpocketed on a bus.

One week in Queretero, watching it rain outside and watching the World Cup on T.V. inside.

Ambling along the lovely Colonial streets, some—the *peatonal*—just for strollers. Written Aug.14,1986: "Dona Josepha, the heroine of Mexican independence from Queretero, has gotten better looking since she died. Her bust, milked by patriots for a hundred and a half a hundred years, makes the myth grow quiet and strong. The years buff off the rough warts of the face her mirror offered her, and offer us the handy face our simple need dictates. What of our faces after we're dead? A few incidents trapped in stories which change as the hands swing and the teller changes. And that is us in memory, or as the records number our lives on pages no one reads. But Dona Josepha, her words and likely likenesses are remembered, yet remembered as she barely was, simplified so that her veins run others' words and her blood is brighter when merely dyes on a poster, this heroines's angry spit at what she hated now baptismal water."

Speaking of mirrors and Mexico, Josepha and me and this book and all autobiographies, this was written on the same day: "The mirror on the breast of one of the saints fills her with my face as I face her, her own ceramic center given over to my incense-shrouded face. Before that, the church's undertaker had removed her blood and filled her with the pious wool of sheepish ideas. Her brittle self makes her real self immaterial which once was material, homespun as a faded shirt. This mirror shows the worshipper in this Mexican church and makes his prayer return into his own mouth. Pre-Columbian Mexican mirrors were pieces of obsidian, glass from the volcano, the bloody lava congealing to the color of night, so, say, the Aztecs could see their darker selves more clearly than in the moving rivers, and more clearly than in the splintered obsidian they used as sharpened blades on their bloody war hatchets." Language also can be seen through a mirror darkly and distorted. Menu mis-spellings rely often on mis-hearing: *Chateaubrian; Filetminong;* or an inability to distinquish between the sounds of v and b: *cebiche; se bende elotes.*

An updating: "Above the windshield is another mirror of the owner of this Mexican truck: it's named "Charles Bronson." Another truck is named "Fall Guy." Engines stuck out like chests, louding honking feats and fears."

Nine days in San Miguel de Allende, that beautiful but totally touristic town filled with Americans, all painting water-colors, collecting jewelry, drinking booze, living cheap. With me sitting in the main "jardin" reading novels, and all of us ogling each other.

Guanajuato for a few days, watching the folk dances near the Alhondiga, peering into the churches, and one magical time "parading through the streets at night behind costumed young men playing and singing old Guanajuato songs and reciting poetry." This old-fashioned evening reminded me of the young men singers in the Barrio de Santa Cruz in Sevilla, Spain, also marching through the dimly lit streets with the same sort of old buildings, followed by lots of people lucky enough to hitch on to this informal parade.

There's a different sort of parade, like the Dance of Death, also in Guanajuato. From July 11, 1986: "It's reverent, quiet, as we measure our paces, three or four, before we stop again to stare into these glass cases at these mummies once men at the Pantheon Cemetery in Guanajuato. Then on to the next case. The glass shows us, a thin skin on the light, turn invisible as we shift even slightly in our places. These mummies have proven that they last.

A homicide detective student of mine once told me that people are just meat. If he died, he said, his wife and kids would remember him for a while and then they would forget him. Dead men who exploded from their own rot gas. To see the mummy of the "eminent French doctor" and the miner and the beloved wife of the beloved husband, all names gone, all words, all flesh, yet immortal for another few years as the tourists file by, glass separating them from us, clear, colorless, undistorting, a glass to see the past, these dead from 1903 and 1878, and to see our future. Look in the glass.

So is the pace we measure in Patzcuaro, this chilly rainy Indian town, sliding along the Basilica's walls toward the venerated bones of Don Vasco de Quiroga. Mostly Indian women, brown enough to forget the white bones all colors are, two sliding in ahead of me and giggling, a family doing it too, *con permiso* the father asks and I glare but let him through, as the line augmented by the ones in before their time, shuffles toward the saintly bones. The 450th Anniversary of this Basilica de la Virgen de la Salud culminates in this *Peregrination* with the Patzcuaro local band in attendance, dominated by trumpets, playing all day, their mouths incised by their mouthpieces, they, their instruments' instruments.

Rockets are set off, trailing sparks, till bursting with bang, they vanish, leaving the stone church dark and enduring. The bones of Don Vasco are, of course, just bones, and I do not kiss the crystal case they're in, though others do. They are well preserved, but not gleaming despite all hopes, but pitted brown and dingy. The fireworks continue. The speeches and the Mass are in Tarascan, the native language of Patzcuaro. The Mass means the same in all languages. So do the bones. The fireworks continue.

If the line didn't move, if people didn't check out of their rooms, if cows didn't die so that hamburgers could be born, the wafer and the wine, the wayfarer couldn't wander. And the fireworks continue."

In Mexico's south, in San Cristobal de las Casas, there's a church, San Cristobal, at the top of winding steps, where they also had fireworks and a fiesta, with a band playing, hotcakes being sold along with a drink made of pineapple juice, sweet bread bits, and a shot of mescal or brandy, special for this fiesta day among the Indians there. Franz Blum's widow gave a lecture in her Museum Na Balum about the Lacandon Indians, now dying out, as indeed is Blum's widow. There's a great market in San Cristobal, and a fine Sunday market nearby in San Juan Chamula where the Chamula Indians administer their own laws.

"July 27, 1986: Went from San Christobal Las Casas to San Juan Chamula, a small Chamulan Indian town in southern Chiapas. The Sunday fair. Church filled with Indians (no benches; all sit or kneel on long pine needles; smell of pine, incense, candles). Put lots of candles stuck on the flor, then pray in their Indian language—monotonous quick chant, continual as long as breath lasts, then start again. Slightly higher pitched, but similar to Tibetan monks chanting. The sun is Jesus, the moon is the Virgin Mary. They look at the sun just after leaving the church (because the sun is their real and pagan god). Pour libations of mescal and Pepsi to the gods by sprinkling the liquids over the candle flames, and then they drink from the bottles. Quite friendly Indians here. Their "policemen" wear black or white tunics as do all the rest, but will carry black sticks of wood, 2 ½ or 3 feet long, with a thong attached, which they wear over their shoulder like a rifle.

On Sunday mornings, the village elders sit on a semi-circular stone bench , about 35 or 40 of them, dressed in the round-brimmed, be-ribboned (several colors of ribbon), pointed-top straw hats, white shirts, black tunics, and they judge cases and resolve problems of the village. The petitioner or suppliants or culprits greet several elder judges (one judge in particular this day) by graasping the black tassel of what seems to be their staff or cane of authority. They then discuss the case in front of the elder judge who decides it. They usually speak in Indian, but some words or sentences were in Spanish. They are all respectful, but sometimes the whole crowd laughs together." How long will these people continue to have the right to have their own customs and laws in Mexico? Same problem among many indigenous peoples throughout the world, including in the United States. One law for all? Or one controlling central power like the sun?

God's slow and quiet fireworks of stars are bright on the beach in Puerto Escondido, with French tourists sauntering on the main street, heading for the bright bars. In Tehuantepec, a *pistolero* struts, and the drunks stumble. Besides a great shrimp cocktail I had there, I tried something called *vida a la vuelta*, made of all kinds of fish from the sea. Delicious. All things are to fat us, and we parade on to fatten worms. Talk about recycling.

July 11, 1986, written in Taxco: "It's 3:40 p.m., I'm sitting on an iron bench in the Zocalo [central square of town] in front of the beautiful and intricately rococco baroque-o Santa Prisca Church in Taxco, its so-called rose stone facades turning toward beige, the white grey of the cement, the corroded stone, the pigeon shit streaks—all wither the rose toward white. So the words wither from their early freshness, like the rose, its freshness bled to a symbol even before the Middle Ages when it evanesced from flesh, the moist meat of sexual applause of wet bellies clapping…. (And as I write this, a blare from a restaurant's tapedeck plays Madonna's song, "We are living in a material world, and I am a material girl." Ah, the poem this world writes! Just listen to its fertile juxtapositions!)

I just had to switch benches because the man selling the balloons near me is setting up a machine to make cotton candy. How the noise and movement of life being lived, fragile and silly as this cotton candy, a deep rose color, even scarlet, certainly richer and deeper than the yellowed immemorial Museo de las Momias, than the word "rose" which doesn't fade like the stones of the church, but is so cheap that everyone uses this word like a rag to wipe their wet dreams off with…." Yet here a Swedish lady I met who had lost everything she owned in an earthquake in Mexico City, moved to Taxco and opened a pizza parlor. Samuel Beckett said, "I can't go on. I must go on. I can't go on. I must go on. I can't go on. I'll go on." Join the parade.

Writing then about writing, "my tension, hunting the fit word, the word bicep-tual, my tension, holding the breath so nothing, no air can get in, afraid of the outside, not wanting things, flying off to other countries partly to keep unattached, to observe, to lose the phone connections, the friends, to be a lonely Buddhist." Alone-ness is not always lonely, but alone-ness usually is freedom for me. There goes the parade.

In 1990 or 1991, when the Gulf War started, I was on a three-week winter break and spent it in Mexico—one week in Mexico City with cousins, one week in Tepotzlan, also with cousins and alone, and one week in Oaxaca alone. Tepotzlan was still a small Indian village even in 1990, but soon thereafter got dangerously "revolutionary" for gringo landowners. Oaxaca was pretty, and its surrounding Indian villages were still dispensing their own forms of justice in their public courts. The Gulf War kept tourists clustered around their T.V. sets. Justice, war, crime, the usual news.

I enjoy watching the parade.

GUATEMALA:

In July and August 1986, I went to Guatemala because I heard it was not as dangerous as it usually was with its guerrillas. It's a very mountainous country, with many of its most beautiful mountains volcanos, so danger comes not just from its politics and people.

But mostly it's politics, ethnicity, and social class. In Huehuetenango, fairly close to the Mexican border, there were lots of soldiers in combat gear patrolling the city, but many people told me it was *muy tranquilo* in the countryside nowadays. On July 30, I wrote, "Tonight, the crowd to get into the American movie about the U.S. Army in Vietnam was pushing too hard, so I left to go to the main garden where the Army band (in combat camouflage uniforms) was playing somewhat out of tune, but gaily, the old favorites of most Western countries. Few people stood around, and most who did talked during the tunes. No one applauded the band, who were relaxed, and who ignored the lack of reaction to their playing. I talked to two officers who were also listening to the band. They were on guard, as were the patrols with automatic weapons at the ready. The two officers were very curious about me and my travels, and we discussed politics and various languages, including (with examples) some words of Quiche, a native language here. Very few guerrillas now, they told me. We did all agree that for most people *es difícil para vivir.* It is difficult to live." Both of these officers, neither one Indian-looking, seemed well educated, sensitive, and decent. I thought of the soft sweet politeness of most of the Indians in Guatemala and Mexico, and also thought of the extensive killings by these same Indians, whether ancient Aztec or contemporary soldiers. Another distressing paradox of humans in history.

While I was wandering around in an open-air market, a older man, the retired head of education in the area of Huehuetenango, asked me if he could help me. Don Juan Luarca Ciani was known by everyone in the market and in the town, slapping backs, and greeting all boisterously. He had me to lunch at his place, he and his wife regaling me with stories of the town and of his life. He was once a dedicated Communist, but changed his mind and turned anti-Communist, so much so that a Communist tried to assassinate him; had he not stuck out his hand, getting shot in the arm, he would have been hit in the chest. He showed me the scar. When I, being the moderate balancer and "let's look at the other side's view" kind of person that I usually am, which drives most of my friends nuts, brought up the United Fruit Company and their exploitation of their workers, he told me his wife worked for them for a long time. "What exploitation? She was paid more than the average wage here, and yes, she had to work hard, but they had a swimming pool for the workers, a cheap but good cafeteria to eat in, and benefits more than other businesses here. So who is being exploited? Who?" Interesting man. I gave him my "John Jay College" tee shirt as a souvenir.

In chilly Chichicastenango (sounds like a song by Cole Porter), there are very colorful markets and very colorful clothing on the Indians here. Written August 14, 1986: "The well-watered gardens in Antigua's Plaza de Armas have more mosquitoes than Chichi's higher drier plaza. Chichicastenango is filled with drunks who chat you up for money and who sleep like dead men sprawled on the street. I sprawl, beholden to no one, all over the map, and drink from many steep rivers." I saw an Indian on the church steps praying out loud, looking up at the sun, and swinging an burning-incense-filled object, and was told he was a Catholic who prayed to Jesus and to the pre-Christian gods at the same time.

"White corn, red apples, booze sprinkled on it all," I wrote, "the rose petals, the long rolls of incense wrapped in tree bark, the candles stuck to square wooden trays on the ground (instead of right on the church floor as in San Juan Chamula in Mexico) to keep the floor of Santo Tomas Church clean of candle stubble. The Maya-Quiche language here full of sudden glottal stops. An inch-worm, red, not unlike the color of the rose petals, rose testing the air above the corn, the candlelight flickering on him, the mescal or tequila and light pushing him off the corn onto the cool and colorful petals."

A man took me out to the woods near the town and showed me a pre-Christian idol which had fresh flowers draped around its neck. On the way to this idol, we came upon a hut with a few anti-rebel militiamen in it, supposedly guarding the town, but all quite drunk. They asked for money, but we made jokes and said "no" and while they weren't happy with us, they didn't shoot us. Jokes, or better yet, self-deprecating jokes, are great for defusing dangerous situations. Drunken guards with guns constitute a dangerous situation anywhere, but especially in Guatemala.

Life is hard in Chichicastenango. One man was carrying a cross for the physical support of the frame for his market stall. Symbolic! So I wrote, "The cross the men carry here is the hardest and heaviest of wood and forms the base of all the market stalls in Chichicastenango. Bent over like Jesus, the barefoot Indian, red and white stripes on his short trousers, his shirt a patchwork of bright colors, every Thursday and Saturday, market days in Chichicastenango, sets up his stall and sells. The base of his baseness, the anchor that keeps his poles stiff and unsliding, the lines firm, is his work which feeds, robs, and robes him. Jesus would enjoy Chichi. Lots of drunks who beg, men without shame who, ragged, won't work. They lurch around by day, and sleep draped on the street at night, or vice versa. By our centavos we keep them alive, drunk, and unconverted. Work could firm them, dry them, bend them like the man under the weighty wood shaped and cut as all real carpenters do." Life is difficult here.

One of the most beautiful places in Guatemala is Lake Atitlan at 5,000 feet altitude, and its main town Panajachel. During the eight days here, I swam in the cold pure lake every day and, this being a tourist town, saw videos every night. The natural and the artificial, Nature and art. Just the right combination. Also walked around the lake to various Indian towns, Santa Caterina and San Antonio Palopo—magnificent views of the lake and of the volcano at the lake's far end. In Palopo, some Indian women tried to get me to buy a hand-woven shirt, and I offered to trade one of my tee shirts plus some money for their shirt. They assured me that they could only wear a shirt of their town's distinctive design and colors, and so couldn't trade for one of mine.In the 1970s and early 1980s in the Far East or Nepal they loved to get any old American shirt no matter how worn. Anything American had power and prestige built into the cloth, even if it also had dirt and sweat ground in too. Not here, though in some other villages around the lake, I saw some Indian men wearing tee shirts, but not the women who seemed to keep up the traditional fabrics and patterns. I saw this also in a Karen village in northern Thailand in 1978.

In San Antonio Palopo, I finally brought one of their shirts, a large red collarless shirt meant to be worn outside the trousers. Very handsome. Hand-made. Only 12 Quetzals ($4.25). The real thing. After wearing it for a few years, I felt tired of looking like some maven of ethnicity, and gave it to one of my women friends. What looks great on the road may look odd in my city.

Antigua has all of the best of Guatemala. Volcanoes flank it. Ancient Colonial buildings stud it.

The elevation cools it. (And there was a great Japanese restaurant right behind the main plaza. Sukiyaki in Guatemala! Talk about diversity.) What makes Antigua even more charming is that a huge earthquake knocked down many of the Colonial buildings and churches into romantic ruins. Written August 15, 1986: "The earthquake's voice is our two-hundred-year-old teacher's mutterings who let slip a thin layer from off the top facade of Antigua's cathedral. Under what could be stone, carved hard and deep, smooth, enduring, lies lies: brick and mortar, fitting ordinary houses, lives, with a skinny surface of brown plaster. Ah, lessons, lessons." Not all is as good as it seems.

These ruins speak most eloquently and beautifully of the natural dangers here. "Like a breaking wave, the purple and the orange flowers pour over the decrepit stone wall." In the mornings I'd write in the Church of Hermano Pedro. In the afternoons I'd read in the main plaza, annoyed by the peddlers and beggers as in all of the main plazas in Latin America, but reveling in the space surrounded by Colonial buildings. Many here may hate their Spanish conquerers, but they sure do appreciate their architecture. As indeed do the folks from the south of Spain for whom the Moorish architecture is their biggest tourist draw.

Lots of North Americans come to Antigua for lessons in Spanish, and one guy I met called himself "Climbing Star." He was a 54-year-old Norwegian who had been wounded in the Korean War, and was writing a book on his initiation to be a Sundance Ute Indian chief. He knew the Ute Indian language, and he told me that Tonto (which means "stupid" in Spanish) called the Lone Ranger "Kemo Sabe" and that means in two different Indian languages, "White Shit." That's great if it's true, but I feel like I'm Herodotus, telling as truth whatever it is I've heard.

And what do we really know of the people who built the temples and monuments of Tikal? Still smothered by the jungle, many of these ancient pre-Columbian stone buildings are in much better shape than the ruins of Colonial Antigua. I stayed the night near Tikal, in Flores, a semi-flooded city, a lake lapping at the houses. For dinner, I asked what's on the menu, and they told me, *"Hay tepesquinkli."* "What's that?" *"Es un animal pequeno que esta en la selva."* A little animal that lives in the jungle. Sounds fine. So I had it. Very tasty. The next night, having been through the ruins of Tikal, I asked for a dinner of *tepesquinkli* again. Again delicious. Many years later I learned that a *tepesquinkli* was a small dog that the ancient Mayans used to breed for food. Nice to know that the past is still present in Guatemala. The wind whirring the leaves in Tikal sounded a little like a rattlesnake, and rattlesnake is reputed to taste like chicken, but Guatemala—dangerous and beautiful—has its own special flavor.

COSTA RICA:

In the summer of 1980, I saw the city of San Jose, the volcanos, and the sea shore at Cahuita on the Carribean coast. The blacks there, speaking English but so thick with an unfamiliar accent I would rather speak Spanish with them, felt shunted aside by the powerful Hispanic mestizos in the capital. "Even when we vote in a black man, he becomes rich and then forgets about us," they said one day, sitting and gossiping around a small store in Cahuita. Earlier, I saw several men slaughtering a big sea turtle; its head was off, but its flippers still flapped hard. The next day I heard a tourist was robbed at gunpoint on this beach. I wanted to get home after my time here and in Panama.

From August 17, 1980: "A long low level flight of cormorants crosses the mottled hill like a water wave in air. A cormorant, like a plane diving steeply slants through water from out of the sun. What can we infer? That all connects, that even the wild corybants dancing down the hill are some pattern's slave, or like an unstrung necklace, if you prefer, like thirty cormorants flying, woven in a dance."

PANAMA:

In the summer of 1980, I flew down to Panama to meet my aunt Helen (Laney) Stephens on her yacht, a 53-foot motor sailer named "Queequeg." Late at night I showed up at a marina of the Carribean side of Panama, and her yacht was not there. No one knew where it was. A bartender told me to check with some friends of hers on another yacht, and so I did. Jack and Alma, Laney's friends, invited me to rendezvous with her if I would help them take their boat through the Panama Canal. You bet! On the way through the canal, in the Culebra Cut, I did the steering and was thrilled. At Toboga Island in the Gulf of Panama, we saw Laney's boat come in to anchor, and I dressed up as Jack with his hat and shirt, and kept my face away from the crew on Laney's boat till I boarded it. Along with Laney, who was asleep below, the crew consisted of Hank, Laney's boy friend and a retired professor of Biology, and two others, one a young man who knew sailing and boats, and another, a retired Army sergeant, who had spent a couple of tours in Vietnam and who helped with protection.

Hank recognized me, shook my hand, and we headed below to surprise Laney. Hank said Jack and Alma were here, Alma said hello, and I took Laney's hand. She turned over in bed, looked at me, and burst out laughing. "You're the only one who could have gotten out here and found me!"

"Here I am!" said I. So I transferred to Laney's boat for about three weeks of sailing.

Mostly though we motored, not always hoisting the sails. The weather for those weeks was generally calm, though once we motored through the night, and there was a storm ahead of us. We had set a dead reckoning track, and should have had no trouble with land or rocks in our way. But ahead the storm kept lighting up what could have been cloud banks, but could also have been land.

There were no lighthouses nor towns to give us any sense of where land actually was, and I called Laney up from below to suggest we come to starboard and take no chances. She agreed, we turned, and it turned out to be land after all we were originally heading toward. Without radar, our eyes alone in a storm and at night are deceiving.

Another time we had dropped the anchor off a small island and were sitting round the deck relaxing when suddenly there was a big bang on the underside of the boat. We stared at each other for some seconds. Then another big bang. I thought some large fish or turtle must be underneath

and hadn't a clue about what to do, when the young man on the crew said, "The tide's going out. We must raise the anchor quickly and get away from these rocks!" The banging on the bottom was the outgoing tide dropping us on the rocks under the water. The anchor was holding us down and as the water diminished, the rocks got closer to the boat's bottom. Lucky we had this young guy on board to figure it out. There's danger even when anchored in calm seas.

There were other dangers in calm seas. Very venomous sea snakes, and lots of them in the Gulf of Panama. Sailing by clumps of seaweed you can see them resting or foraging there. I was waiting to dive into the water once in a bay and from under the boat came a sea snake swimming right where I was planning to dive. Spearing lobsters one day, diving deep from our small rowboat—when you take the lobsters out of the water you can hear them, speared and in pain, creaking like a door opening—I was warned that sharks hear the lobsters in pain and come swimming, so we better just make one more dive. Laney, when snorkeling that day, saw a shark at the bottom of the bay asleep and still. There's danger in the water.

There's danger on land too. All the yachtees are afraid of pirates stealing their boat and dumping them over the side into the water. Lots of scary stories. One night there was yells from astern of us where we were anchored off a small deserted island. An open canoe, maybe 12 feet long, with an shut-off outboard engine at the back, manned by three blacks, two men and a woman, came alongside us. We rushed to get the 45 caliber pistol, the M-1 rifle, and a wooden club (my weapon) to aim at them while our youngest crew member clambered into their boat to help them start the engine. They made no moves, aware that we had them covered with our guns. When their engine was fixed, they motored off. If they had snuck up on us without yelling, we may have shot at them in surprise and fear. Lots of fear all around.

One day we came to another small island in the Gulf not far from where Panama ends and Columbia begins, and took the small rowboat ashore. A woman on the land saw us and ran. Soon after, an older man came down the beach carrying an old shotgun and a machete. The presence of Laney reassured him, and he told us they were afraid because just a few days ago on a nearby island, a neighbor of his was killed with his whole family—five people in all—most likely by Columbians, said he. He had the same prejudices as we did about the Columbians and the drug trade. On another island I went ashore with the two crew and found it apparently without human traces, but as we explored it we found a airplane landing strip with a small hut beside it. Pretty clear this was for trans-shipment of drugs, and if we were seen here we'd all be killed. So back to the boat and weigh the anchor and get the hell to a different island ASAP!

Very near Columbia, off the Darien jungle where there are no roads, and even the Pan-American Highway doesn't cut through (to keep the jungle ecologically pristine and to keep the drug smugglers out of the north), we found a river, got a guide, and in a small motorboat travelled up this river till we got to a small Indian village. Looked like palm leaves made up their huts in this tiny cluster of people, the women all bare-breasted, the men too shirtless, in loincloths as I remember, all quite friendly, we not understanding their Indian language, and our Spanish not helping much either. I asked by gestures if I could see one of their bows and arrows, which several of them were carrying. One Indian with a grin gave me his, and I asked if I could shoot it. Gleefully, they took me over to a place just outside the cluster of huts. The bow was very long, surprising since all the men were very short. I fired one arrow which made an almost 90 degree drop to the ground, and we all laughed at my ineptitude. Best way to get people friendly to you is if you show that you can't do what they can do well, and then you laugh at yourself. Their contempt for your lack of prowess makes them like you. My next shot was better, but still not so good, and we shared another laugh. It was a short visit to this village, and then back down the river, getting into our small boat, smacking through the surf till we got aboard the yacht.

I spent several weeks aboard my aunt Laney's boat, learning about the often serene skies and seas and fish and animal life of the area from her and by observation, and about the even more frightening human life of the area from what I had seen and heard in Panama.

ECUADOR:

In late September 1986 I flew into Quito, the capital of Ecuador, from Guatemala because I had seen Costa Rica and Panama once before, and once was enough, and Honduras and Nicaragua didn't interest me, and going into Columbia scared me. It cost as much to fly from Guatemala to Quito as it did from New York to Mexico City, a much greater distance. When I asked why such high prices, the woman who sold me my ticket said that their airline was the only game in town. No competition. Quito is an Andean mountain city, at a high altitude. Lack of air rather than great beauty took a bit of my breath away, although Quito does have some lovely old Spanish Colonial buildings, especially the churches. I am anti-religious, anti-colonial, anti-monarchist, but without religion, very rich people, and kings, man's world and history and architecture would look pretty dingy and petty. Wandering the chilly dark streets in the evening didn't make me want to linger here, nor did the advice given me by the front desk hotel clerk: distribute your money among a few pockets, and put some down your sock under your instep especially when riding the public buses. Mexico had made me distrust the public buses because of pickpockets.

Another city that has lovely old Spanish Colonial churches is Cuenca, in southern Ecuador, a pleasant place. Between Quito and Cuenca is the small town of Banos, named for its thermal hot springs, a reminder that volcanic activity and earthquakes underlie and imperil the Andes. Banos is certainly worth a visit, nestled as it is among hike-able hills. ("Nestled" is such a tourist-brochure word, but it describes the town's placement.) In November 1986, I wrote, "The coffins are not selling like hot cakes, so the funeral parlor in Banos, Ecuador, sells soft drinks too. Opposite the gilded coffins—the pale green of Inca Cola, the dark mahogany of Pepsi, the gilt of limon, the bubble, hiss and sigh of colorless carbonated water."

I got a haircut here from someone who wouldn't tell me how much it cost, despite my asking him several times. He was giving a haircut to a local policeman and they both wouldn't tell me the price. Having fun at the expense (in two senses) of the gringo. At the end the price seemed outrageously high, so I walked into another haircutting place, asked them, and they told me the regular and much lower price. I returned to the thieving haircutter, told him what should have been the correct price, and demanded he give me back the difference. He was reluctant. I moved very close to him, told him he was a thief, and demanded my money. Slowly he produced the correct change. Note: Always know the price beforehand. Same thing happened in Manaus, Brasil. There the barber told me "five" in Portuguese, but when time came to pay he said, "fifty" in Portuguese. It was about six dollars, but I felt cheated— everyone in the barbershop (it was filled) was amused at the foreigner who was duped, and I decided not to contest the crook. So much for the thieving barbers. However, pretty and pretty steep hills with nice Indians and mean dogs, hot baths and good food in town, and enough foreigners to give you a respite from Spanish made Banos a good place for several days, and it's also a good place from which to head down to the tropical Amazon basin, the east of Ecuador.

The low-altitude jungle was one of the high points of Ecuador for me. Taking a bus from Banos, we passed several "control" stops where police check to see that the Indians etc. remain in the part of the country they reside in, to keep them all from flooding into the cities. Finally arriving in the tiny town of Misahualli on the river of the same name, I hooked up with four Germans and two French who were about to leave for a trek into the jungle with a guide. They let me join them. From a letter of Oct. 19, 1986: "...a four-day trek into the Amazonian jungle along the Rio Napo (and others) with a guide and six others. Nary a nibble from a pirhana 'though I swam in a couple of rivers, nor a battle with a boa ('though I carried a tame 3-foot one for a while at a short stop at a tiny and deserted estate in the jungle). All animals have been either eaten by the Quechua Indians or have been sold to zoos, so except for the butterflies, a couple of turtles and lots of trees and big spiders, it was just us in the jungle. Very wet—we wore rubber boots and sometimes sunk into mud up to our knees. Learned something about what to do and see in the jungle." In another letter I note: "...sitting motionless and quiet at night in the jungle by a small pond waiting for small crocodiles (none appeared). I dozed off for a bit." And from my memory: we saw some Indians panning for gold on the Rio Napo, so stopped and talked. They let us pan for a while and I got some flakes of gold which I gave to them. Exciting! Signs on the river near small villages say, "Gold accepted."

Tired of crapping off in the jungle, I crapped in a river, and very relieved to do so despite worrying about the candiru, a small fish who swims up into any bodily crevice you have left open. I did not urinate in the rivers for this reason. One night we ate dinner and slept in an Indian's hut in the jungle. The Indian told me he didn't ever need anything in town except for a shirt or two, and he could always do little odd jobs like carrying stuff if he needed any money for these shirts. He was slowly carving out a canoe and had help from other Indians nearby which he paid back with his help building their canoes. A very simple life, with little point for saving money or having many possessions. Uncomfortable in the hut, but only because we are used to soft beds. Some butterflies in the jungle are drab on the outside, but once they unfold their wings to fly, there is this glint of iridescent blue that is exquisite, which glint abruptly comes to an end when they arrive on a branch or flower and shut their wings. We painted our faces in designs with a red stain from one of the pods of a plant, and with another plant I accidently scratched myself and numbed my flesh. This was a plant, according to our guide, that the Indians used as a pain killer. So much of tropical medicine there must have been discovered just as inadvertantly as I found it out.

When we got back to the little town of Misahualli, we danced at a bar till late, and I realized that I was very grateful to be out of the jungle. Some jungle there is thick bush, other parts are forested with little or no under-brush—lots of variation. But in my past fancies I've been frightened of the Amazon because I visualized it crawling with poisonous snakes and insects. Only the guide saw any snake this trip, and while there were lots of sand fleas, mosquitos, and spiders, they weren't so terrifying. Facing this fear and going to the jungle anyway made me proud and relieved to be out of it. The next day I planned on a ride up a different river in a public motorboat to some fairly remote Indian villages, but it was raining so hard and steadily that I realized I would see nothing and would just be chilled and soaked. So bus back to Banos for a day or so.

Another city I was glad to see disappear over the horizon was Guayaquil on the west coast. I was there to try to get a ship out to the Galapagos Islands, but was told that foreign tourists now had to go by plane (to give the government airlines money) and only Galapagos natives can go by Ecuadorian cargo ship. So I bargained with a travel company and got a good price to join a small tour and fly over to the islands. The tour company told me to please not tell any one how much I had paid, but at one point we all confided in each other and the price variations were wide, except that all the Ecuadorians paid about half what the foreigners—Swedish, German, English, and me— paid.

In Guayaquil, while wating for my flight, I stayed in the Hotel Boston, a "love hotel" where they ask you how many hours you want to stay rather than how many days. Lying in my room, solitary and often horny, and listening to the moans—"Ay, mi amor!"—from the other rooms is not fun. All the park benches along the waterfront are taken up by young smooching Indian couples, one couple per bench. In the central plaza, the benches are often taken by Christian preachers using bull horns to preach the gospel, and by aggressive shoeshine boys. As I put it on Nov.1,'86: "Far from the days of the duenna, Guayaquil on Ecuador's coast bounces on its tidal bedsprings, the afternoon lovers lunch on each other, the Malecon by the riverfront with upright two-backed couples so many so that me alone seemed half-complete. My hotel, the Boston, a whorehouse, banned nothing. In the Parque Centenario, bands of Christians coupled with microphones converted the quiet every night. Outside the Church of San Francisco the lottery hawkers hope you bank on a more worldly hope. Where do I go? Where is my place?" However, I did find a good Chinese restaurant and so was reasonably content.

The Galapagos Islands were perhaps the highlight of my entire Latin American trip. From October 8th to the 15th, eight days, we steamed around the islands on a 43-foot-long boat, the "Darwin." Late the first afternoon, we got on this small island where several sea lions were, and one tiny sea lion pup waddled over to me, and sniffed at my foot, then looked up at me with friendly interest. I was in love already! We could not touch the wild animals, but could let them explore us. Then two sea lions went swimming just off the beach, and I alone of the tour group joined them in a swim. They took little notice of me, though they swam close. I felt like I was accepted by these wild animals, was like one of them, a magnificent feeling. From then on every chance I got I went among the sea lions, swimming or just sitting, I sometimes calling out to them with their own *rouw rouw rouw* hoarse cries.A letter of mine reminded me that I "was assured by others that I must be part sea-lion." I took, and still take, that as a compliment. The sea lions and I "were diving and cavorting and ogling each other under water at a distance of a few feet." Once, however, I approached a "macho," a male sea lion with his larger bulk and more bulbous high-foreheaded head. He had with him two females, and so came toward me to keep me away from them. O.K. I backed off. But soon I was in the waist-deep water and these two females swam over to me to give me the once-over. The macho, now in the water, suddenly and very rapidly swam right at me and I figured this was going to be bad. But very close to me, he veered away, and I, taking the hint, got out of the water. Our guide said he probably just wanted to remind me of his power, and for me to leave. Clearly sea lions are my favorite animals in the Galapagos.

But sea lions were only one sort of animals there. Marine iguanas doing their push-ups, and then sneezing salt out of their nostrils, dark and completely poker-faced, rarely looking at you though you are staring at them from very close. A mocking bird pecking between an iguana's toes while he rose on them. Blue-footed boobies and red-footed boobies watching you as you amble near their nests. Red-puffed-out throats of the shrill frigate birds competing for mates. The lumbering up-foot down-foot dance of the huge albatrosses. The skittery walk of the many Sally Light Foot crabs. The glide of the spotted and golden manta rays and the white-tipped reef sharks we saw below our boat while anchored in the evening off a beach,and then seeing the Southern Cross bright in the sky. The amazing shapes the molten lava took on Sullivan Bay on Santiago Island. Getting soaked by the water squeezed out of the blowhole on Espanola. And to continue as though this were a sexual metaphor, the sighs of a giant tortoise copulating. Once, swimming in from the boat to an island (though the rest took the small boat in), I saw a massive thing in the water slowly approaching. Naturally I thought of a shark, and so increased my speed toward the beach. This thing turned out to be two sea turtles copulating and slowly swimming. Another time we went to a small inlet where there were more turtles copulating, and we could get close to them in our boat.

They weren't happy about our presence, but didn't stop their copulation. There were small sharks also swimming near them, but each ignored the other. Shades of the "love hotels" in Guayaquil. Men and animals. Not so different. And in the Galapagos so friendly with each other.

Another Eden for me.

PERU:

"Here comes another church, here comes another ruin!" It's the way I began to feel after traveling for a while in so many countries. In Guatemala in September 1986, I wrote in a letter, "Back to Antigua once again. About three weeks this segment in Mexico—Yucatan mostly, seeing Merida and Villa Hermosa, and the wonderful Mayan ruins of Palenque, Uxmal, Chichen Itza, Tulum. Then to Cozumel for a bit of swimming, and on to Belize—a Carribean Black place, something like Africa and Mississippi, for a day or so on the way back to Guatemala to see Tikal, the best of the Mayan ruins!" Names, names. Without photos or postcards or precise descriptions

how can we call each up in its singularity, in its own peculiar self-ness?

Trujillo, Peru, in the fall of 1986 has its own ancient ruin, Chan Chan. Almost no tourists nor anyone else out there at Chan Chan, and that was fine. Old yellow-brown adobe slowly settling back into the undifferentiated mud it started as—dust to town to dust, like memory, like flesh. Trujillo is a pleasant town, where I was robbed in a market at night, and just prior to a celebration in the town square, some rebel terrorists set off a bomb in a small truck parked there. No one was hurt; a policeman told me that the rebels probably didn't intend to hurt anyone, but just wanted to remind everyone of their presence. Whether these terrorists were part of the *Sendero Luminoso* that made large areas of Peru off limits to foreign tourists in 1986, no one knew.

In Lima, the capital, the weather was chilly and raw, with very foggy nights, and during the five nights I was there I woke up each night with terrible asthma, and could barely breathe. I'm assuming it was all due to the weather, but no "next time in Lima" for me. The Museum with the wonderful gold figures from Peru's early cultures was exciting to see, but I was glad to leave Lima.

November I, 1986 I arrived in Caraz, in the Callejon de Huaylas, along a beautiful road, but feeling a little weary of this all. From my journal: "It's 5:20 a.m. in Caraz, a small town near Huascaran Peak. Lonely and cold, its white top is left in peace unlike my white-ish top because so far the only things that function well are people's mouths at night when I'm trying to sleep. Let's see: on the way to Caraz from Chimbote the bus broke an axle and we sat in the desert for seven hours. At the hotel, first there was no running water and then my shower could not be turned off. Then the horde of teenagers on an excusion talked till midnight and then—like the adults in Trujillo—started again at 4:15 a.m. My shower, unstoppable, gurgled beneath their giggles. Then no buses were going to Laguna Paron [a lovely lake far above the town] except if you pay too much. And I missed the day bus back through the Canyon del Pato, which I missed seeing because it was dark after the seven-hour delay, and there wasn't another bus. Oh, even the thieves *no functionan bien* because when they grabbed me in a Trujillo street, wrestled me to the ground, thrust their hands in to my pockets, all they got out of it was my handkerchief. Which they dropped. Which was returned to me. And I didn't function well because I did grab one of their team, the one who jostled and blocked me with his back before the other two grabbed me. I jerked him around and yelled and hissed in fury a bit at him and then let him go. One week in Peru by then. Lonely and cold and perturbed, when I open my ground-floor window to admire the great mountain, Huascaran, a kid on the street stops and gawks in. I am in the Callejon de Huaylas, where in 1970 an earthquake dropped tons of rock off Huascaran which killed 80,000 people and buried several towns near here. I understand the mountain. I myself get disgusted at times."

Finally, we did get up by truck to Lake Paron, and got out of the truck and climbed up beyond it. The altitude must have been 15,000 feet or so, and while we were used to 12,000 feet by this time, the extra few thousand when we scrambled up a slope was exhausting, and left us all panting like dogs. The "we" I mentioned refers to a couple I traveled with for a couple of weeks—a German woman [who I started a slight affair with] and her Bolivian husband [who found about about our reckless but slight affair, and beat me over the head with his fists, I not resisting because I figured I deserved it] and their three-year-old daughter. (They are another story, but I'll not tell it here.)

And what is the real story behind the Nasca lines? Lines tracing the outlines of a spider, a hummingbird, hands, a fish, a standing man, a monkey. From a contemporary metal tower you can make out the designs, but from the ground, the lines just look like someone scraped rocks off the land. These lines are very shallow, not dug into the earth at all, but the wind cleans the lines every night of whatever sand blows onto them. A European woman, the world's leading authority on the Nazca lines, lectured to us about them one evening. A very dedicated famous old lady.

Talk about old! On the Paracas peninsula there is a tiny museum in the middle of a very desert-y nowhere with, as I remember, mummies and pots. But there's a great trip I took by boat out to some small islands— lots of sea lions and penguins, lots of seabirds and acres of guano on one island. The trip was somewhat seasick-ish rough, and at one point with the boat we went between two rocks through a narrow cleft. I waited to be smacked up against one of the sides by a wave, but it didn't happen. A very worthwhile boat trip.

Arequipa in southern Peru is also a worthwhile city to visit. The Church of the Company of Jesus is so golden and gorgeous, with baroque altars bedecked with paintings, and statues and—gold! There's the Convent of Santa Catalina, much less golden but also grand, and the usual plethora of churches less memorable because so many are around. Some white trousers that I took into the jungle in the Ecuadorian Amazon, scrubbed clean but still with jungle and mud stains on them, I gave away to a beggar here whose trousers made mine look immaculate (to use an appropriate religious term).

But Cusco (or Cuzco) was more exciting than any other city in Peru. The city itself is fascinating, with streets and buildings built on old Inca stonework, still unmoved after earthquakes, and still perfectly aligned, each stone shaped to fit another stone's shape. And the hikes out of the valley of Cusco to other Inca sites are well worth puffing over. From my letter of Nov. 23,'86: "Am now in Cuzco, Peru, marveling at all the Inca stuff here in the city, and the ruins outside it. Four ruins yesterday (Saqsaywaman, Tompumachay, etc.), and the day before in Pisac clambering around the ruins strewn all over a whole mountain. Both days solo." Most of these ruins near Cusco are just off the road that leads up the mountain. Can't get lost. All ruins come complete with Inca stonework. The Pisac ruins are way up a trail above the (surprise!) town of Pisac, where they had a small market the day I was there. On the way up this trail there are the ancient irrigated fields still in use and built up on paddies like the Chinese or Balinese made. Flattened fields with stone walls around each, steps up the mountains.

At the top of one of those mountains is the Inca stronghold of Machu Picchu in one of the most beautiful settings in the world. On November 25, 1986 (I have the ticket that allows entry to the site) I got up before dawn and walked alone along the Urubamba River along the railway tracks in the semi-darkness toward Machu Picchu. Going through a tunnel was the most frightening, because should a train come through that tunnel, there was little room for me to get to the side of the tunnel and avoid it. (And it was bigger than I was.) From the foot of the mountain I climbed up the steep switchbacks of a small trail, while all around me the light was getting brighter and the mountains surrounding Machu Picchu were getting more distinct. No one else was in sight during this whole trip from my hotel way down the tracks to the gates of Machu Picchu, and when I arrived at these gates, there was one other person waiting till the gates were open. He had stayed at the very expensive tourist hotel just outside the site, and a few minutes later as the light came up and the mountains around us were silhouetted, a few more tourists from the hotel wandered over, and the gatekeeper opened the site. I scampered up to a place overlooking the valley to the right of where I had climbed up, and I saw the "Buddha light" for the second time in my life.

My shadow was thrown by the sun behind me onto the low-lying mist or clouds in the valley below me. I moved my arms like a slow "jumping jack" motion, or like someone trying to fly, and the shadow below me, surrounded by a nimbus, an aura, a halo of bright light, moved its arms too. My silhouette spread out hundreds of yards across the cloud still cupped in the valley's hands. I yelled to a Japanese woman tourist near me—"Hey, it's the Buddha light!" and got her to do the same and spread her shadow like mine across the valley. We were like little kids, playing with the light until the clouds evaporated, but my delighted spirits did not. On Emei Shan, one of China's most sacred mountains, in October 1984, after I had climbed to the top, I also saw the famed "Buddha light" and exulted. Another continent and another religion, but here it was again. A mere optical trick of the light, but a most powerfully symbolic one.

I came up the next day to Machu Picchu too, but missed the Buddha light. I hiked the next day along the Inca Trail to the Winay Wyna ruins, and then also up to the steep peak above Machu Picchu named Winnu Picchu, the best view around the whole area. But the Buddha light shown over this ruin, this ruin the bright light highlight of my trip to Peru.

BOLIVIA:

Lake Titicaca, rather unfortunately named though it is, is at the border of Peru and Bolivia, and at an altitude of about 12,000 feet. The hills around it were brown and dry in the late fall of 1986, but the water scintillated blindingly and blue-ly as I went out on a short boat ride on the lake to one of the small islands. Some young men and boys were kicking a soccer ball around in a casual game, and they gave me a chance to kick the ball around too. There were a few huts on the islands, and some women, as I remember, were weaving. I am rarely interested in buying stuff, so there is less reason to hang around people who rely for their livelihood on purchasers. The air was chill and bright, and conjuring up the scene, I smell dust. After less than half an hour, my boat returned to the town of Puno in Peru. I did my duty as a proper tourist, had been on Lake Titicaca, seen the natives, and felt that that small quick tour was enough. Some things during traveling one does more out of duty than of love, or even interest, and at such times, one wonders why the hell even go to these countries? The high altitude can be exhausting, and so can the pillaging attitude of many people in Peru and even more so in Puno toward the tourist. At that point, I wanted to get to another country, and so did my Titicaca duty almost to get it over with so I could escape fascinating and dangerous Peru.

Once in Bolivia and still by the lake, we had a couple of hours in Copacabana, a small town with a lovely church on a hill. A procession of Indians, a few of them playing brass instruments loudly and not very well, were coming up the hill. Many Indians had been drinking heavily, and several were quite friendly. One told me they were parading on a pilgrimage to a cemetery way up the road, and he invited me along. A great opportunity to see the indigenous folk doing their indigenous things! But I felt a little nervous about going off into the countryside with drunken Indians, especially after Peru and its crime, and I was tired and a bus was leaving for La Paz, Bolivia's capital, I didn't know where I could sleep in Copacabana that night, and so declined his invitation. Afterwards in La Paz, I regetted this slightly, but the momentum of travel can itself drag you on to the next planned destination even when there is no time pressure on you and something perhaps delightful arises. "Perhaps." Joining the precession could be a highlight of the trip or it could end up getting you stabbed in a drunken brawl. Choosing the "perhaps" is the adventure. I didn't choose it this time.

La Paz is the highest capital in the world at 3300 meters, but by then I had spent many weeks in the high Andes, so my energy was not dampened too much. La Paz seemed small and easy-going, and Sucre much more so. Beautiful Colonial churches and buildings in both cities, but Sucre felt like a good place to live for a while, something like Antigua in Guatemala. Spanish Colonial churches begin to be hard to differentiate one from the other after some months in Latin America. I was never a "must-have-a-photo-of-this-moment" kind of guy, and felt less and less of this need as my trip got longer. I was rather "churched out" by this time.

Not too far from Sucre is the city of Potosi, famous for its silver and tin mines, and about 13,000 feet above sea level, chilly, overcast, and bleak. In the market, many Indian women, often nursing their babies, or having the infants asleep tied to the women's backs by a colorful shawl, sell coca leaves—about 25 cents for a half a kilo of them. Lunch for many men seemed to consist of coca leaves carried in a plastic baggie. I bought some, reputed to be good for altitude sickness, and chewed them. Not a bad taste, certainly not mood-elevating as cocaine is supposed to be, but they do numb your mouth slightly. People in Potosi use them as casually as we do chewing gum.

Many tin mines were closed down because the international price of tin was so low. But I got a tour through an official mine, and one through a mine that was closed, but many men, lacking work, were eager to burrow into any seam that could make them any money at all. With a few other foreigners, we put on mining overalls and boots, hard hats with acetylene lamps lit, and went way down to where men were digging, and explored some of the passageways for more than an hour. The smell of rotten eggs, of sulphur, was very strong, and most of us were coughing during this tour. What it must be like to work hard all day down here, taking great gulps of the stinking air (remember, we're at a very high altitude too), and then go back to the surface with its cold bleak weather. Much worse than what George Orwell wrote about coal mining in England in the 1930s in his book, "The Road to Wigan Pier." Several people during the few days I spent in Potosi made jokes about how awful the weather was there, but that's nothing compared to the weather below ground in the mines.

The rate of money exchange in Peru for my dollars was not good, so I waited till I got to Bolivia. But in Bolivia during that time my Visa card was not able to get any cash advances from banks or Currency Exchanges. I tried everywhere—banks managers, top hotels. Nothing. So I had to leave Bolivia before I was ready to. Sucre tempted me to linger, but decreasing funds pushed me out to Argentina. At the Argentinean border, I realized that my stash of perfectly legal and eminently respectable coca leaves accompanying me through Bolivia had to be jettisoned, and so I gave them to a friendly customs inspector on the Bolivian side. Many Bolivians told me that they also were heading into Argentina because there was no work in Bolivia at that time.

Argentina seemed so European after Indian Bolivia—the people, the service in the restaurants, the ambiance. And this was in Salta, northwest Argentina, where many Indian Bolivians had migrated to for jobs. Less interesting to me because more familiar, but comforting to have ice water at a restaurant and feel I probably wouldn't develop typhoid from it.

Then on by bus across the deserted Gran Chaco grasslands to Asuncion in Paraguay. Lots of stores selling electronic appliances in that city. The place seemed prosperous and unthreatening. One person told me quietly so no one else could hear when I asked him how things were in Paraguay, a nice general question requiring only a bromide as an answer: *Hay mucho miedo aqui.*

"There is a lot of fear here." General Stroessner had been dictator here for a long time, and dealt with his political opponents harshly. Lots of bill-boards around that said "Vote for the Colorado Party." The party of progress, long live democracy, blah blah, that sort of stuff. The Colorado Party was Stroessner's, and I guess he wanted to make it look like there was a loyal opposition party in a fair contest. I did not get a sense of spys and police and thugs walking around keeping the populace cowed, but shows you how a few days in a place does not qualify one to be an expert. Pity. But these few days in rather tame and modern unexotic Asuncion were sufficient for me, and I headed to its opposite, Brasil, via Iguacu Falls.

BRASIL:

In a postcard of Dec. 2, 1986, I wrote: "After Peru (5 ½ weeks), spent 2 weeks in Bolivia, 1 in

Argentina, 3 days in Paraguay, and am now in Brasil. Planning on staying here till March 4 or so (end of Carnival) and then heading home...." Coming by bus from Asuncion in Paraguay, a pleasant enough city that seemed dedicated to the selling of electronic goods, I first arrived in Brasil where Paraguay, Argentina, and Brasil meet: Foz do Iguacu. I was weary of Latin America with its crime, and each country's similarities of culture and architecture, and also because just one and a half years before I started on this year-long Sabbatical of Latin America, I had spent a little more than one year living in Kunming, China, as the graduate professor of British and American Literature. I was tried of traveling. I wanted to be home and in my own city and country. I was beginning almost to be homesick.

Carnival in Brasil I was certain would be an exciting experience. But I never even stayed till Carnival. Intimations of Carnival (and Brasil too) was starting to resemble to me the waterfalls of Iguacu—powerful, tremendous noise, danger, and coming at me from all sides. There is one V-shaped chunk of Iguacu Falls which is called "The Devil's Throat," and you can stroll out on some walkways below the falls to be splattered with their roar and wet. However, after wandering the walkways and taking in the views, it felt like enough for me. Also, I could only find a room for one night, and so went on by bus to Curitiba and Sao Paulo and then to Rio.

Rio's setting is stunning, and I did the usual tourist stuff such as going to the top of Sugar Loaf, and ambling along the beaches of Copacabana and Ipanema. After the Andean countries, I finally felt now that I could fit in with the people. Rio's inhabitants in the Botofogo section where I stayed wore shorts and tee shirts, and sometimes barely that, and so did I. Speaking Spanish got me around in this Portuguese-speaking country, and a few people thought I was Argentinian. Very friendly folk here. One day it poured, and the streets all flooded. Buses were stalled in the rivers of the streets, and in Ipanema I had to ford a street waist-deep in water. People took it rather casually.

But a tourist I must still be, and dutifully went off to the old and popular town of Ouro Preto, a mining town now mining tourists' silver. More foreigners here than I had been used to seeing, all wandering the streets of this baroque colonial town, well worth a visit, but for me, inundated as I was by months of old colonial buildings, and broken by so much baroque, a few hours were enough. Then off to Belo Horizonte (pronounced "Bell Horizonch"), where I tried to get a bus ticket to Salvador de Bahia. Forget about it. Long lines at the bus station, and all tickets already sold, because it was vacation time and the whole nation was travelling. One man in despair said there was no possibility to get where he and his family were going, and walked out of the station. I canvassed a few bus companies, but all tickets were taken, so I bought a ticket to Salvador for a couple of weeks later, and then tried to figure out what to do with the extra couple of weeks in Belo Horizonte.

Clearly, it was not to spend my time in Belo Horizonte, a name that I felt like translating as "Pretty Flat." So I checked my guide book and it mentioned a nice little diamond-mining town about six hours from B.H. up in the hills named Diamantina. So I bought a bus ticket and went.

Very glad I did. Calm, tidy, with pretty cobblestone streets, with many white buildings having blue trim on their facades, which reminded me of Portugal, Diamantina was a great place to rest up and mull over one's trip and one's life. On January 4, 1987, just before my 47th birthday, I wrote:

RULES FREE

I

The twin feet of time and heat press the coal to diamonds, **leaves**
bright after black. From my travels, what can I **wring**
from this night, from that view, beyond a fading square of **red**
and green, of face and pretty church. Last night a whiff of **carnival**
at the dance with the girls from Belo Horizonte when the sambas **rock**
us till wet and wasted. I hear the rooster deny it's night; time's **butt,**

I watch January up-end again for the 47th time as I **stand**
drooping in Diamantina, a town dead when diamonds **stopped**
in its veins, and left its bright painted churches and charm. I'll **mount**
up again soon enough and ride on. What is left—the story's point? The
photo's **interest**?
Divorced, no girl friend, no kids, I'm under no one's heel. I'm **free**.

II

But sometimes free winds blow a little too hard. I want them **stopped.**
Slim trees can buckle or whip in the stripping wind. I want to keep
the **leaves.**
There is treeless land beyond this copse, this little and last **stand.**
Tighter and straighter the banks, slower the flow now that once could
shove around a **rock.**
So rules are what I like more now, life enclosed within a **ring.**
February here in Brasil will shatter with its **Carnival.**
It now makes me nervous. Rather than do I'd rather have **read.**
Rather than sexy Nivea it's poems on walls I'd **mount.**
She chased and caught me at the dance with round mouth and **butt.**
But now not what's beyond the banks, but the banks now have the
most **interest.**
Older I get, the more mistress, the more wife, once cleaved, split, now
cleaved to, are **rules.**

A little depressed, but playful with the puns in this *semi-demi-sestina*,
I enjoyed Diamantina, where I was assured that their Carnival was a lot
nicer than Rio's. Nivea was a sexy psychologist, but had a couple of
large boyfriends, and so I didn't. Tininha was cute and a sweet kisser,
but didn't want to go further, so I didn't. So many Brasilian men told
me not to trust any Brasilian woman, that they would all be unfaithful.
Several Brasilian women told me the same thing about the men. Sex is
like the air here. Ubiquitous.

On to Salvador do Bahia, known for its African-ness, its colorful flair. There, on January 17, I wrote, "The fruit of man's sin is delicious. In Salvador, there's *umbu, abacaxi, caju,* fruits of that fecund juicy sin. "Look you conceive…." Ripeness is all, and rottenness follows hard on.(!) Black seeds and slime are out, milk is in…the fruit juice they call *vitaminas.*Teats are in the hands of babes. *Nossa Senhora do la leite.* They mistake the possessive for the plural: *Gem's* says a stone store, *Souvenir's* another. Burger joints multiply to feed the people of Brasil. Fruit juices sing with sugar, crackle with ice. How sinfully sweet the natural, the innate savor. For this we hazard the harp and all those airy nothings to which a name given is only breath, air, a sound. Pronounce the word "Hope": an explosion of air, inspired by fear of our own expiration. The parks here in Salvador have *capoeira* dancer-fighters, moving to the twanging of the *berimbau,* one string on a bow attached to a coconut's skull. Dreadlocks coil and flop on the fighters' heads. Water is not too safe to drink here. The churches are filled with the flashes of cameras. Heaven's sundae will never melt, we hope, but that one day all the stores are really closed."

Some of these *capoeira* fighter-dancers are very aggressive about soliciting money from anyone in the vacinity of their twirling, sweeping, slow-kicking demonstrations. I gave some coins, and the guy showed me his scrapped-raw knuckles from twisting on the ground, and asked for more. I didn't give more, since I was just hanging around this small park, and didn't like this extortion.

One afternoon I saw this *Candomble* religious ceremony in front of a church, with revered big fat black women, dressed all in white, several of them smoking pipes and escorted by young girls, watched by a large crowd of all ages. Then a bus came into the church square and lots of young men and women climbed up and were dancing on it, with samba music on some P.A. system or other, and the crowd was getting sweaty and excited. There was (I think the same day, but am not sure) a bunch of tables set out, and food and beer were flowing, and a small group of young men and women offered me a beer, and then I offered them beers, and one woman sat on my lap, and everyone was boozy and very friendly, and it was getting wild, and then one guy from another table near ours got into a running fight with someone and kept cracking this guy's head with a small wooden stool, deliberately trying to break his head. It was getting too much for me, certainly the fighting and even the drunken friendliness, because I saw how close that was from violence. I begged off from my group, and they swung away, reveling and drinking. Salvador was exotic and sexy and exciting, but dangerous excitement I had had enough of in Latin America by that time. While there, I wrote, "Nothing an ant likes more to eat than semen. A trail of them scuttles across the hotel sink this morning after last night's beat-off with my brain. Seven weeks ago I saw [in Peru] a buzzard emerge from the shell of a horse on a road high in the Andes, born again from its chest. The spaghetti squirms on my plate, my fried eggs wide-eyed in terror." I needed to get out of here.

Recife was my next city in Brasil, and I remember this place mostly for the attempted robberies. Olinda is its artsy beach-front pretty suburb, but an afternoon here at this point was sufficient. Brasil is a huge country, and these long bus trips up north on its Atlantic coast were wearing me down, whole nights on buses, stopping with other exhausted Brasilians to grab a snack, take a leak, and wait forlornly while the bus was getting gassed up and its driver rested.

Finally I arrived in Belem, and got a ticket for the boat trip way up the Amazon to Manaus. I traveled with a German girl I had met on the ticket line who was going to go up the Amazon and its tributaries into Peru, and who was feeling rather ill and worried it was because of pregnancy with a short-term boyfriend. An English guy named Jan who had met her a few days before was our third. We got tickets, but in order to keep the prices down (and perhaps some share for the Captain) about twice as many tickets were sold as there was room for on the big river boat. So the three of us pitched our hammocks (which we bought out in town) in the passageway. Mine was in an athwartships passage so every night for the five nights we were on the boat I was kept awake by people bumping into my hammock while passing down

the passageway to the toilets or the showers. Since this was Brasil, the toilets
were in constant use, and taking a shower was an interesting experience with
flaming homosexuals flaring loudly through the bathrooms. Not much sleep
on this boat filled to much more than capacity.

The good thing about going up the vast Amazon is that, to avoid the
current, the boat stuck fairly close to the banks of the river, so we could see
some small villages and the green jungle all the way to Manaus. The government of Brasil was building a road along the Amazon, but it had a long
way to go before it could take the place of the river to get people into the
country's heart. When going down the Amazon, the river boats take
advantage of the current which flows fastest in the middle, and so one
would see only the tiniest green fringe of jungle way off in the distance.
Most of the European tourists (I found no Americans on this boat) during
the days hung around the open-air snack bar topside aft, and I met a lot of
interesting travellers. A young Brasilian guy took me up to meet the
Captain, and I found him relaxed and easy-going. He told me that for the
meals, included in the boat ticket price, he provided lots of meat. He did.
Almost every meal was meat and manioc, but the meat was suspicious-
looking and not very tasty. Hence the snack bar topside where you could
supplement these rations. Most Brasilian passengers had supplementary
food in their bundles.

Finally we arrived in Manaus and got a hotel. Except for the old Opera
House, Manaus is undistinguished, so after a few days I headed up to
Venezuela with Jan. We had to hurry because the rainy season was arriving
from the south, and we needed to get out of the Amazon jungle before it
arrived and the roads became muddy and impassable. Jan got stopped at
the Venezuela border and told to go back to Manaus and get a visa. On the
way to the border, a few soldiers stopped our bus, and ordered everyone
out to get a Yellow Fever innoculation. We all complied. One man at this
stop was delirious, but it was from malaria. Several times we had to stop at
rivers on this road north till a ferry could take our bus and the few cars

across. Passing miles upon miles of jungle, you could not believe that the
Amazon was being deforested as quickly as it supposedly is.

After spending the night in the town of Boa Vista, I got a new bus
which took me past the flat-topped buttes of southern Venezuela up to
Ciudad Bolivar, a city on the banks of the Orinoco River. I got a hotel
room with a German named Bodo, who I had met on the river boat and
who was traveling around South America on his motorcycle till he had to
start his medical studies back in Germany. A great adventure! One evening
toward sunset we saw this huge fish leaping in the Orinoco; someone said
it was a kind of a dolphin. Romantic! That night I went up to Caracas on
a bus, hanging on to a seat, fairly unattached to its seatframe, hardly sleeping. Unromantic!

Once in Caracas, I decided just to go home, so bought a plane ticket out
for that evening, and by the next morning disembarked in a frigid February
in New York, about four days from being in Manaus on the tropical equator.
I had no warm clothes at all, so I put on all the shirts I had with me before I
went out and caught the bus, then the subway to my warm home, glad to get
back after eight and a half months in Latin America.

CRIME IN LATIN AMERICA:

Getting pickpocketed on a bus in Mexico City is the gentlest of crimes.
You feel stupid, but you don't bleed. I got on this bus in June 1987 right
by the Museum of Anthropology, prime site for tourist-nailing. Every
tourist who goes to Mexico City goes to this museum, so there's little dilu-
tion of potential victims by more cautious locals. This is the waterhole
that the jackels wait at for the arrival of their prey. And there I was, a foreigner, one who peeled off his bus fare from a wad of Mexican and U.S.
currency, then put the barely diminished wad back in his left front pocket,
but kept his left hand hanging by a thumb from that pocket.

Now I thought I was being street-smart. First, the money in a front
pocket; second, the left hand looped over that pocket. So, blithely using

my right hand to hold the vertical bar in the crowded bus, I felt my money was secure.

Then this guy on my right with a couple of people between us reaches over and asks me in Spanish to please pass this ticket to someone down the bus on my left. Of course I say yes, and, not having three hands, get the ticket from him in my left hand while still holding the bar with my right, and turn and flourish this ticket and ask, "Whose ticket is this?" in Spanish, and for about a minute no one answers. Count my hands: one on the bar, one with the ticket. None on the pocket.

Finally a short guy near me says, "That's mine" and takes the ticket. But he had seen me waving it before and just looked at me, but I'm still not particularly suspicious. So he's got the ticket and my left hand is back at its post, hung from my left front pocket. This contented state of mine lasts for only another minute or so. Suddenly the short guy I handed the ticket to starts poking me hard on my left arm near the shoulder—poke, poke, poke, poke. Really hard pokes. I turn to him and he says, "You've been robbed," and points to my pocket. I find my money missing, and my stomach vanishes too. He points to the rear exit of the bus and says, "He went out there, the guy who robbed you. He's out of the bus." Then he points outside behind the bus. The bus having just stopped, I pushed toward the exit and got off, ready to catch and bash the pickpocket. As the bus pulled away, I saw no one behind. (I was the behind. The horse's behind.)

The pickpockets, staying aboard, had robbed me and then gotten rid of me. Another foreign sucker cleaned out. My cousin Louis told me that it happens with everyone, including the cautious locals, on Mexico City buses.

Public buses are the playing fields of pickpockets. In Quito, Ecuador, the hotel desk clerk warned me to carry my money stuffed down in my sock. For a year in 1984 and 1985 I lived in Kunming, China, and I was often cautioned about the pickpockets on the buses. Pickpockets in Communist China? Ridiculous! Besides, I'm from New York City where street smarts come with mother's milk.

So wearing shorts with snaps on their outside front pockets, I took out money to pay for the bus fares of the two Danish girls and me, and then stuffed it back into one of those outside pockets.

Of course everyone on the Kunming bus was staring at us, we being *wei guo ren*, foreigners, to say nothing about these two gorgeous blonde Danes who would turn heads anywhere in the world, and had certainly turned mine. A turned head doesn't see straight, said the old feudalist Confusious, and that must have given this fairly short man, close-cropped head, dressed in dark blue, a fairly safe target. Suddenly I feel this guy against me, sort of leaning on me, although there were no crowds on this bus. I looked down at him, barely registering him: most southern Chinese look and dress like him. Also, men are very physically affectionate with other men; women with women. So I thought he just might be friendly, or like the young men in Burma, just like to veer into you so that they can touch you, see if you're real. In China this touching is not a particularly sexual thing, nor is it unusual. Only a bit later, when I reached down to pat my money did I realize what had happened. I didn't know the words in Mandarin for much of anything, leastways how to explain the robbery, but I told the Danes, and looked around at the other passengers cursorily, knowing that the casual view I had had of the thief wouldn't let me identify him. Feeling very foolish I got off the bus, not expecting to see the robber, unlike in Mexico City.

Now the Chinese pickpocket's "slow press" technique was quite unlike the Latin's lightning one. Several months into my Mexico stint in 1986, I was waiting around at a bus station in southern Chiapas, cautious about my fellow waitees, I alternating roving feet and eyes, on the lookout for my bus. One pulled in, stopped with a fetid roar, and its door opened. Wanting to check on its destination, I got on to ask the driver. Its destination wasn't mine, and so I turned and climbed down the few steps where on the way up was the guy with the clipboard. He too had been hanging around the station as long as I had, but seemed less like a traveler than the families huddled around their bricks and bags of luggage. So when I saw him, the soft alarm began in my mind. In a second, our trajectories crossed, the one bus step too full for the two of us. He, with his clipboard held up to his chest, both hands near it, squeezed past, and I felt two of his fingers enter my shirt's left breast pocket. Feeling that the pocket closest to my eyes was the safest, lately (too late) I had been keeping my money there. My left hand came up under his right hand's two fingers and simply pulled them up and out of my pocket, not even looking at him. Later on I had a very strong desire to have kept moving his fingers up, bending them back, and breaking them, but I was glad I didn't do that. Score one for me.

But the vigilance appropriate to combat fades between battles, and so in Sao Paulo, Brasil, in the midst of a crowded downtown street I wasn't prepared for why this young guy seemed to be keeping pace with me on my right side. Maybe two feet away, maybe for ten seconds, he moved when and how I moved, keeping the distance. I stopped, annoyed but not worried. He stopped, so I started again and suddenly there was a hand in and out of my right shorts pocket. The khaki shorts I was wearing would not be out of place in Rio where everyone wears shorts or even bathing suits in the section near the beach where I stayed, but in business-y Sao Paulo shorts were rare. Also, thse shorts had pockets which hung open like a billiard ball hole, like a yawn, offering their contents easy access to the outside air. And to hands who saw the square bulge in that pocket, that wallet shape, as a magnet. In and out went the hand, and I whirled to find the rest of the thief. I saw no one who looked suspicious, no one who did not keep walking toward me, no one who I could grab. Turning back, I couldn't see the guy who had been shadowing me either. The wallet shape in my pocket had been my handkerchief, fairly well used I am delighted to say, but cleaner than at that moment I wanted it to be. Score another for the thieves, but just by a nose.

Crowded places are the waters that pickpockets swim best in, and the most crowded are buses and native markets. I learned to keep my money in my socks or even under my insteps; spreading cash over several pockets and places reduces the chance of all of it being taken at once. Blending into the crowd, looking like a native, helped too. In Peru I shaved my beard, kept my moustache downcurved in Zapata style, wore long pants, and bought in Caraz an American trucker's red peaked cap saying "Hawaii" on its front, so I looked like all the other Peruvians and didn't get stared at much. But still in many markets I was warned by older women selling stuff to watch out for thieves, and I walked warily, turning every so often, slipping sideways through the lines of food sellers, standing with my back to walls, watching who was watching me.

But some losses are from pack, not pockets. Guatemala made my pack lighter by "disappearing" my sunglasses, travel alarm clock, and flashlight. Whether from a bus trip to Huehuetenango, or in the hotel there, I don't know. A friend bought me the sunglasses, cheap ones, aviator type, from a blanket on Broadway; the travel alarm I bought in Hong Kong; the small orange flashlight I got in India. Gone not only the things, but also the bits of life and memory that clung to them. Still—travel light, travel light. Let the past fall off like hair from a balding scalp.

So it's not just things that are taken, it's also your freedom to do certain things. In Rio, for example, people didn't wear wrist watches. One common thief's trick there is to ask the time of someone, and when they bring their watch up to check, the thief grabs the watch and pulls it off the wrist, breaking the band, and runs. Expansion bands are the easiest, but most bands break easily enough. My important stuff—passport, credit card, traveler's cheques, large amounts of cash—were kept in a money belt beneath my trousers with a leather belt keeping my pants from being pulled open or off, and my money belt snatched.

Once in India, wearing loose cheap drawstring pants and trying to stop a fight between some English and some Goanese fishermen, I had my pants pulled right off me, the ripped pants hanging by my ankles. Since I was barefoot, shirtless, and wearing no underwear in this open-air restaurant on the beach in Goa, I suddenly found myself quite naked, standing and arguing with the group of fishermen who turned their fury on me rather than on their original targets. No one paid any attention to my being naked in the restaurant. So often I wear strong belts now for reasons beyond the safety of my moneybelt. Experience timidifies.

The security of one's luggage, of one's wrist, of one's clothes—they vanish slowly or quickly on the road. A hotel room, a place to hole up in away from the burly and hurly burly of foreign-ness, a place one can domesticate and Americanize with one's own possessions and solo presence. But once in Puno, Peru, a very dangerous town on the banks of Lake Titicaca—there's a joke told by both Bolivians and Peruvians who say "They have the titi, we got the caca"—while I was in the hotel's public shower, a filthy hole with the hot water not quite the body temperature of a corpse, and being at about 12,000 feet altitude you need hot water, someone was in my room swiping $20 from my moneybelt, hoping by only taking some of my U.S. cash and leaving everything else I wouldn't notice it. But my moneybelt was tied up a bit differently from the way I did it, and my inner money holder was put back upside-down, and I knew exactly how much U.S. cash I had had, so I stormed downstairs to complain to the manager.

He was upset when I told him and when I accused the bellhop of the theft because he knew I was out of my room for a shower. (The only other person who must have known was a man who had a room down the hall who heard the bellhop and me speak as we left my room as he entered his, but I didn't think of him as a suspect then. Later on, after Puno, I realized he must have been the crook. He was the police officer who lived in the hotel, so the manager told me, as a watchman for it. He watched very well.)

Striding down the dark Puno streets at night looking for a police station was scary, but I was so angry that nobody would probably bother with me, although I had been warned of a lot of throat-cuttings down by the lake late at night. The police sergeant was amiable, but tended to dismiss the sum of $20 as being a trifling loss (it was) in the light of my being Norteamericano and therefore rich, and in light of this being Saturday night and of him being lazy and not wanting to fill out the papers on the theft.. "Come back tomorrow." O.K.

Tomorrow I came back. "Get the suspect." I went back and got the bell-hop. How about finger-printing me and the bellhop and seeing if my money pouch had his fingerprints on it? "We don't have fingerprinting equipment. Try the P.I.P." The P.I.P. is the Peruvian FBI and its members are recognizable by they're being very well dressed in civilian clothes and often carrying automatic weapons slung over their shoulders. [Remember, this was during the heyday of the vicious Marxist revolutionary group, the Shining Path, who relished cutting throats such as mine, and their presence kept me from traveling to several areas of Peru.] The P.I.P. have a lot of discretionary income, as a person had told me a month earlier, and love the latest electronic gadgets. But the P.I.P. told me they don't investigate any crime that netted below $100 and my crime was a mere $20, but I had had it with the Peruvian thieves and wanted revenge on at least one of them. So it was back to the police station for paperwork, and one policeman to come with me to the hotel and question the manager and the bellhop, and have me go through my pack to see if the money was misplaced in one of its crannies. The cop seemed to think I had made up this theft—possible shakedown of the manager, who knows? From then on I usually would leave all my valuables with the hotel manager in his safe, and get a receipt. [However, once in Agra, India, in 1993 I did just this, and one of the managers used my credit card and bilked me for $240 dollars or so, and I didn't find out about it till almost a year later when I got home to get my mail. If you can be cheated, you eventually will be.] A sense of even less safety burgeoned.

Banks are alleged to be among the safest places to be in, but the one in Sao Paulo harbored a staff of official thieves. A bank manager told me I would get the "official rate" when I received money from my Visa card; that sounded fine with me—no commisions, no bank charges. Of course, I thought the official rate was the one posted up in all the *casas de cambio*, the money-changing stores.

The bank needed time to telex to check on my credit limit, so I wandered around for a couple of hours till the hour set. The manager himself paid me out the money—but I had already figured out the number of cruzados I'd get from the rates posted at the money-changers, since you can only pick up your money in Brasilian cruzados and not in dollars. But the number of cruzados hand me was about the equivalent of $300 and I had spent $500 on my Visa card for this amount. So I was robbed of $200—without violence, without hands other than my own reaching into my pockets, without threats. Official rate: less than it's worth, but no recourse when credit cards can only be used in banks to get cash. Robbery with courtesy.

Still, violence does up the ante in any robbery. $200 lost, slipping between the official rate and the real rate at this bank, was my biggest money loss, but at other times the loss was potentially much greater because I could have lost more than money or goods. One night in the beautiful old Colonial city of Trujillo on the coast in northern Peru, I was wandering around a marketplace along some streets narrowed by carts and tables around which were women selling fruit and clothing and pans, moving in that peculiar light, a mixture of shrill acetylene and propane lamps, dim overhead city lights, and golden wavering kerosine lanterns. Suddenly, a young man stepped right in front of me and, as I was saunter-ing forward at the time, I had to brake hard and instinctively put my hands up to ward off this guy's back. As I did this, I felt arms around each of my shoulders, and two hands jam down in both my front trouser pock-ets. Smashing down quickly on the hand in my left pocket where I carried my money, I had to use my right arm and hand to break my fall because both thieves pulled me backwards toward the ground. We were in a nar-row street crowded with people, trucks and cars, and with all the confu-sion, I knew I didn't want to get run over.

In less than three seconds it was over. I got up off the ground and grabbed the guy who had stepped in front of me. The other two behind me went and went fast. I never saw them. But I did see the fellow in front of me and got him by the shirt collar and shook him with my right hand free so I could punch him if he or I need it, and screamed and cursed him in English and explained about him in Spanish so this quickly gathering crowd would know why I was manhandling this young adult thug. He was protesting that he had done nothing, and then some other young guy said that he had seen him do nothing and that I should let him go. He had done nothing: he didn't touch me, just blocked my forward motion just at the moment that his colleagues jumped me. No doubt he was one of the gang and, when I did let him go, both he and the fellow who had spoken in his favor ran off in the same direction. But I had only lost my handkerchief I had in my right front pocket, which, doubtless in the interests of hygiene—his own—the thief had dropped, and a young girl returned to me. I lost nothing. Just confidence and affection for Peru.

My right arm and shoulder hurt for about five or six months after that, and I had a hard time getting to sleep lying on my right side. I became much more careful about having my money spread around: under my instep, in my socks, in a breast pocket, as well as some in the same trousers' left front pocket. That time in Sao Paulo, the pickpocket also going for the square wallet-shaped handkerchief, a magnet for thieves.

Attracting those made to steal, filing toward me from all over the city, like iron filings, reached my most magnetic day, a January Sunday in Recife, on the northern coast of Brasil. A trinity of crooks went for me that day in the hot equitorial streets, sun-streaked, when everyone including the police were at the beaches, and the Sunday left the streets abandoned by the sensible.

My first confrontation came with two street kids, late teens, one with bathing suit and sneakers and nothing else, a suspicious-looking guy who I felt was following me in a street market, and so stopped and waited by a vendor, pretending to look at the goods, but really waiting to see if he'd go by me. He did, not seeming to pay any attention to me, so I forgot about him. Soon after, I wandered over to an open plaza I liked, close to the waterfront, and began to read. Who should sit down on my three-person bench beside me (beside me) but this kid with bathing shorts and sneakers. And speaking of sneakers, another kid sat down just then on a bench next to mine, same age as this guy, about 17 or 18, and they began talking to each other. Then the kid with the shorts asks me for the time.

Now any one in South America in 1986 knew that if someone asks you for the time, you never turn up your wrist and offer that he look at your watch because the common trick is to grab the watch and pull it off your wrist. In Rio, renowned for robberies, I rarely saw any people with wrist-watches. So I told this kid in Spanish mixed with a bit of Portuguese that I didn't trust him and told him to get the time from someone else, and told him to stop following me, after which speech I got up and walked over to another bench. The two of them left, probably feeling that no sur-prise snatch was possible with me then.

Who then should come over to me soon after, detaching herself from her prostitute colleague, but an exceeding jiggly, pudgy sloven of a lady, 30s going on 60, bits of her black skin peering or pouring out from the rips of her stained dress, about as seductive to me as a sow, and she proceeds to jiggle and suggest and attempt to fondle, and I'm not buying any of it in any sense, and tell her I just want to read and I'm not interested and please to leave me alone. Finally I move again to another bench after she began sitting on the arm of my bench and slurping her sounds and smells over me. She follows me to this other bench and continues with her pitch. Finally I grab her arm and tell her, more firmly, that she should leave me alone. Reaching into her purse, she comes out with a razor blade and tells me she'll "gillette" me if I make any trouble. Interesting verb she used.

Apparently my hand on her arm sparked this defense. So I tell her again, this time not touching her, that all I'm interested in now is peace, not a piece, and to please leave me alone. She leaves.

At this point I was feeling nervous about Recife on a Sunday. For one thing, I was wearing my watch and had my moneybelt under my trousers with all my money, passport, et al in it, and so was feeling very vulnerable. ("When you've got nothing, you've got nothing to lose" was and is a strong dark undertow in my life.) The manager of my sleazy hotel by the slummy waterfront was often not around, and since he was the only one who could get into the hotel safe where I had been keeping my valuables, and that night I was taking the bus to Belem on the Amazon River, a 36-hour trip, I didn't want to take the chance of not being able to retrieve my valuables from his safe. Therefore, I was feeling very unsafe carrying all this stuff around among the prowling predators, so I decided to walk back to the hotel, and get out of the sun and away from this shady bunch.

So I'm walking back, hot and sun-blurred, through the intricate empty back streets when I come to a long wide street with the waterfront way down at the end. Then I hear guys walking behind me. No one else is in the street. I hear their voices getting louder, so I turn my head and see two young men. I keep walking. Now one guy seems to be walking faster, trying to catch up with me, it seems. When his footfalls get very close, I turn to my left and step back against a wall. A second later he is alongside me and turns toward me and puts out a hand, but not for a handshake, aggressive and questioning, his chin stuck out. I go to push his hand away, and he grabs two fingers and twists. I pull my hand back, and suddenly am filled not with fear, but with the desire to hurt him. "You son of a bitch," I hiss—I've always had a hard time yelling or even speaking my aggression to anyone, and tend to hiss my words when I'm furious—and kick his still-outstretched hand, and start toward him, my fists clenched at my sides. He runs back down the block where his friend is, but then stops and looks around for a throwable rock in the littered street. I now yell at him in English—fury drives other languages out of my mind—"come on, come on," and I motion for him to come back. I did want to kill him or hurt him badly, all the past of that day, and these other days of fear, or being robbed and jumped, pouring into my body their pent adrenaline. He threw a couple of rocks, but they went wide; I barely remember the number of rocks he threw, so filled was I with my own anger, and the explosive pleasure of turning on him.

Turning on a robber can be satisfying, but fatal. When my ex-wife and I were robbed in 1971 in New York City, my fear turned me not furious but numb. Two Hispanic males with knives caught us in the foyer of our apartment building, between the outer and inner doors, and pulling knives on us, demanded that we go inside the locked inner door. I said, "We'll give you what you want out here, but we're not going inside." I wasn't angry, just numb. Thinking of them getting us to go inside out own apartment and then having the time to contemplate all the nasty things they could do now we'd be out of everyone's sight made me say "no." They got our wallets and they jammed their hands into our pockets—like in Trujillo, Mexico City, and Sao Paulo—to see if we'd given them all, and then said, "Watches and rings."

Our rings were our wedding rings, especially made for us, gold, and I thought—but without anger which meant I was very numb, which must have seemed to them coolness under fire, but I had had that spurt of fear in my stomach and bowels earlier—"These pigs can't have anything like these rings which are the symbol of our marriage and love," so I told the thugs, "The watches O.K., but not the rings." That seemed O.K. with them, probably because I was calm and they didn't want to push me into doing something angry which might force them to cut or kill us, they being professional thieves who don't escalate violence beyond what is necessary to get the stuff.

We gave them our watches, and just then a young black woman came into the foyer, looked around, must have figured it out, but continued hesitantly toward the locked door, and I said, "We'll go in with you." I didn't know her, but it was pretty easy to figure out who were the robbers and who were the robbed. We followed her in, and I closed the door quickly and bolted up the stairs to call the cops.

Besides money and two watches, what else did we lose? Joyce lost her desire to live in our building, even in the city. She lost her trust about our invulnerability. I lost any desire to wear anything that might be stolen from me that I would perhaps fight for or refuse to give up, such as my father's wristwatch which I got after he died in 1980, and only wore a few times till I realized I didn't want to lose it in a robbery or fight to keep it and likely lose my life. Or what if those two robbers had been less calm themselves, or really desperate for money or power over us, and they had said, "No, man, give us your rings too," and that had triggered my madness, in two senses, and I then told them "no" and wouldn't budge from that?

They can and did rob me in Latin America of trust, of money and things, of my watch in New York, making me more watchful and fuller of hate and therefore more hateful, watching them

waste my time filling out police forms in Puno, Peru, watching time waste me, stealing my hair, my desires, my years, watching robberies slowly diminish me. But metaphoric robberies are not legally indictable offenses. We watch the birthdays come pouring down on us and we begin to smother, to drown from their sheer numbing number. Instead of spending my entire Sabbatical year down south, mostly because of crime, I fled back to my home after only eight and a half months, back to February in New York and its cold. Whether sneaky or sudden and shocking, these robberies in 1986 and 1987 in Latin America swiped some of my enthusiasm for travel, swiped some more of my ease in the rest of the world.

HAITI:

The first time I saw Haiti, it was 1962, I was coming from duty in Japan, and had caught a Navy ship from Guantanamo Bay in Cuba, then flown by helicopter in order to relieve the First Division and Gunnery Officer on the amphibious group command ship which was ready to coordinate landing the U.S. Marines on Haiti (so I first heard when I arrived on the ship) to kick out the dictator of Haiti, Papa Doc Duvalier. Nobody had told me anything about what my ship was engaged in till I arrived on it. We were just steaming back on forth off the coast with various other ships, waiting for the word to invade. We didn't get that word, and a short while after I arrived, a deal must have been struck between President Kennedy and Papa Doc, because we all turned back toward Norfolk, Virginia, and steamed home. Never got to see Haiti then.

In 1967 when I was a copywriter for Needham & Grohmann advertising agency in Manhattan, we pitched the Haiti tourism account, and I worked a lot on it. Hearing about many of the corrupt and dangerous things about Haiti, the copy chief and I played with some headlines like "Go to Haiti—you'll never go back home!" and "Go to Haiti—you'll never be able to tear yourself away!"

The Haitian who worked with us from the Ministry of Tourism defected to another country before they decided which agency would get the account. We ceased pitching it. I had hoped to see Haiti if I worked on this account. But never got to see Haiti then either.

In 1976, I squeezed three weeks out of my winter vacation while teaching literature at John Jay College and finally made it to the land of Haiti. From a letter of Jan.17, 1976: "Very strange place, this Haiti! People are very friendly—one smile of mine elicits grins an acre wide. I met this Austrian girl at my hotel as soon as I arrived, so we've been wandering around together since. My hotel is the Holiday guest house—$5 per night [sharing a room with Brigette]. It's right in the center of Port au Prince— and what a center! Hurly mixed with beaucoup burly, and sired chaos! Like darkest Africa. It's right out of National Geographic. Everyone of course wants to be our guide or sell something, and Brigette wants to speak to all of them.

We've seen a voodoo ceremony—pretty authentic and rather exciting. Lots of fire eating and glass eating and chicken-head (live at first) eating. [One of the dancers in the ceremony gave the eye to another female dancer, and she then jerked off into a spirit possession. Not really believable to me, but this was put on for tourists. Another time I tried to find another more real voodoo ceremony, and ended up again at the same place, same dancers, same tourist thing. But it was worth going to anyway.] This is really Africa. It's very easy to get in solid with the Haitians. Just wager a couple of cents at one of the gambling booths on the sidewalk, and you find the whole crowd rooting for you. Seems to be no anti-white feeling here at all. Refreshing.

Tonight we're going to see the big dance for the tourists and upper-class Creoles at Cabana Choucounne. Hot stuff. Last night, high above the hills above Petionville [a ritzy suburb of Port au Prince] on the road below the night club of the Ibo Lele Hotel, we danced to the music of the club and didn't have to buy a drink or stop dancing except when the cars went by!"

Often the best dancing was in the streets. I'd be in my room, and would hear a small band passing by on the flatbed of a truck. Running out, I'd find myself in the midst of a crowd of people also running out of their houses, and we'd all start dancing, following the slow-moving truck down the center of the street, and soon there'd be a happy mob dancing and taking over the street. They called it "exercises for Carnaval." Usually I was the only white person in the mob, and all were delighted to see me. A few told me to beware of pickpockets. Once, behind this mob of dancers was a policeman with a whip, which he used to keep the stragglers at the back from straggling too much. I moved back to the back to keep others from being hit because I felt he would not whip me, clearly as though being a white tourist would protect me, as though skin color was a magic talisman. And this talisman worked this time. Several people addressed me as "blanc" or "barbe," "White" or "Beard." Once this mob of dancers passed in front of the Presidential Palace —Papa Doc's son, Baby Doc, was in charge of Haiti then—and as we approached the Palace, the musicians played softer and softer and the dancers danced slower and slower, and passing the Palace, which had bunkers in front with armed troops manning these bunkers, we all just shuffled along silently, just the sound of our feet moving, and after we got past the Palace, the music began again and so did the happy dancing. But by the Palace, only silence and nervous fear.

At the cemetery where Popa Doc is buried, there are several TonTon Macoutes standing guard over his remains. They are in civilian clothes, but carry guns and a very mean reputation. They watched me carefully as I inspected the grave. I smiled at them, and got no smile in return. Very un-Haitian response.

Haiti, like almost everywhere else, has typical hotels and very modern Western hotels. One of the most interesting is the Oloffson, where the most colorful and international people hang out at the bar in the evening.

Monsieur Joliecoeur who headed the tourist business for the government
was always in attendance, and one time at another hotel at a dance he was
buying drinks for Brigette, my Austrian girl, and me, dancing with her,
trying to get her away from me. It didn't work, but he sure turned on the
charm and cash. Another up-scale hotel up in Petionville that Brigette and
I visited to swim in their pool, had a big rat run along the pool's edge that
sent the swimmers scurrying. The pool attendants chased it until it
jumped into the pool, swam a bit, went under, came up, went under, and
stayed there. An attendant caught its drowned body in a pool strainer and
flipped it off the terrace onto an adjacent vacant lot, and we all went back
into the pool.

Brigette and I shared a hotel room, $5 per night [whether for each of us
or total I don't remember], but the partition between the small hot rooms
only went up about seven feet or less. (Same in a hotel I stayed in in Belize.
Cheap only gets you so much wall!) We could hear everything that went
on in the next room, where a Dominican couple were on their bed too. To
protect the mattress from being sweated on or semen-ed on, it was covered
with a plastic cover. Since only one sheet was provided, we had the choice
of covering up our naked sweating bodies modestly with the sheet, but
then sweating more being in contact with the plastic matrress cover, or
lying on the sheet exposing our bodies to the air. And to others' eyes. I
heard the couple next door say something, and then heard the bed squeak
in a different way than usual. Lying on the bed, I looked up at the half-
wall behind our heads, which half-wall divided our two rooms and saw a
forehead and a pair of eyes peering over the wall at naked us. I slammed
my fist against the wall and the forehead and eyes vanished. "Careful!" I
said in Spanish. We heard nothing from the other side again. Brigette and
I covered ourselves (and the plastic mattress cover) with our single sheet.
Modesty won out.

Modesty was not in the make-up of Roi Henri Christophe, who ruled
Haiti long before Papa Doc, and who built the Palace of San Souci
[Without Worry] and the Citadelle of La Ferriere in the early 1800s on

Haiti's north coast. I climbed to the Citadelle twice, once on foot and once by horse. Standing around and talking with some of the horse guides, a man pushed out of the crowd around me and handed me a button which he gave me as a gift. It was from one of the French or Haitian soldiers of the time of Henri Christophe, who excelled at massacring each other when the black slaves freed Haiti from the French. [I still have that button, as well as the slug from the execution ground in La Cabana Prison in Havana, Cuba. Grim souveniers.]

In 1976 "TRADES IN HAITI: The trades sweep the sweat from the mahogany boy who hope I will create my guide from his sad past. Who knows Haiti? Cap Haitien is unrolling very slowly, a city whose pattern we know when we saw it first far ago. So much of what it is is still what it was. Bone-white whitewash layers inches thick on one injured wall shows a historical partiality. I ignore the boy, slide into the past, away from his demanding present. The palace of the royal Empress Pauline Bonaparte, in ruins, is under my hand. No whitewash here. Coral fans forever open cool the white bones of the Empress. The palace? Of its bones are made of coral. I see pearls of piss on the grass that stipples the tumbled wall. That is new. I see a change of suffering to suffering, from slaves to beggars in a hundred and fifty years. King Christophe kicked the horrid French out, and built another palace, called Sans Souci. He was called "The Civilizer." Twenty thousand died of the two hundred thousand building his Citadelle. Another mahogany boy tells me fully fifty thousand died. He read it in an old book. He could be right, right among those dead if this day was then. *Plus ca change....*The sun is slipping, snuffing the flowers to the boy's color. I'm at the walls of the palace of the Empress Pauline. The coral fans do not wave. The trades sweep the island still."

Near Cap Haitien is a nice beach, Cormier Plage, that I went to a couple of times. It's a long walk along a deserted dirt road to get there, and once two young farm workers came out of the fields and walked close behind me. They both carried machetes, there the usual farm tool They must have thought I didn't speak French or that I couldn't hear them because they said something about *attaque le blanc*. As I had been called *Blanc* since I arrived in Haiti, and there was no other white person (or any person at all) around on this lonely road, I figured they meant to attack me.

So I watched their shadows behind me, waiting for one shadow to raise up its machete and kill me. After a few seconds, I spun around and asked them in French something perhaps about the beach or the weather or something. Then, smiling confidently, I looked them both in the eyes and turned around and continued walking at my previous pace (although I felt I wanted to run) toward the beach. They seemed surprised that I spoke French, but answered my questions politely. Soon, they turned off the road and I relaxed a little. A very friendly people, the Haitians, very polite, but violence has been central in their history.

From 1976: "REPETITION AND ROTE IN HAITI: The palace of Sans Souci an empty abstraction now, its floors which were ceilings gone, its Counts of Lemonade and Marmelade now null and sour while slaves freed into slavery who built it are also all now sans souci and the palace of King Henri Christophe where chambers go from cellar to stars without stopping had once a silver bullet administered in them to beat the paralysis of body and command of Christophe as his revolted slaves revolted and he chose to follow where he had led so many and now in the square in Cap Haitien on the steps of the Bibliotheque Roi Henri Christophe across from the statue to Dessalines and the slaves martyred by the French this time sit just about fifty little girls in three rows like uninterrupted waves uniform in their blue and white dresses like transient clouds and stable sky over this island always and they one by one or two by two recite in French in front of their teacher and the others lines of coversation and peek at me who is the strange *blanc* called *barbe* who listens and who ties their lines together in even such slack a sein as this where Christophe ruined stretched down from the Citadelle to his shadow on the square where these seven and eight year old girls whose white and blue uniforms were a short interruption between the black of legs and black of faces, black like the funeral which luckily passes at this very moment tightening like a line around these childrens' books, this poem, the necks of slaves here hanged in the square where time circles and all lines lead beyond choice and delay as a pair of these girls recite in French how it is hot today, but no today it is cold, as the funeral led by a small boy with cross and surplice is followed by lines of older school children in brown uniforms and then the hearse then family then friends who draw all eyes as they pass on into the cathedral as the children are learning their lessons by repetition and rote which will never finish."

I was part of the U.S. Navy in 1963 ready to set them "free" of Papa Doc. Ha!

CUBA:

Christmas vacation 1959, my age 19, one year after Castro took over Cuba from Batista (from my journal of hitch-hiking down to Florida and Cuba): "Slept across the road from a trailer camp on wet white clay ground [on Marathon Key, Florida]. Saw cars on causeway, and when woke up, saw heron as sun came up. Key West dirty, and flew to Havana.

Walking down Prado, with Cubans after me with words of sinful joy to be had for a few pesos. Stayed in Hotel Regina for four days [for $4 per night], and for last day and night, checked out as money was low. Large room, double bed with the saggiest mattress yet. No hot water, leaks, etc. Walked around, went to Morro Castle, then to La Cabana (in back of truck with soldiers for a ways), then needed a government pass, but soldier took me through without a pass. Took away my camera. We passed barracks and guards, and I asked him if I'd be shot if I wasn't with him and he grinned, and answered, "Si." He found a bullet slug at the firing range down in a moat where most of the political prisoner were shot by the revolutionary government under Castro.

I met an Arab named Khalil who said when he was 15 or 16 he was in the Arabian army fighting against the Israelis. He showed me a bullet wound in his leg, and described how he had machine-gunned Arabians for collaborating with the Jews. Good thing he didn't know I was Jewish! He told me he wanted to kill a rich tourist in order to get money to go to N.Y. I assured him that I was poor. He asked to borrow a dollar to buy a knife (for skin-diving, he said), and I had the idea that he would kill me with the knife my money helped buy. At night, I finally loaned him the money, but was not sure whether I would ever see him again. He wanted to "make his heart strong" which meant to develop enough guts to murder someone.

We tried to get into the Presidential Palace and were stopped by a guard with a sub-machine gun who let us into the anteroom where there were about 10 men armed to the teeth just lounging around or behind a desk. They would not let us in, but could if we came back on Sunday. I saw the Palace, Morro Castle, La Cabana military prison, El Capitolio, Columbus Cathedral, statues of Maximo Gomez, University of Habana, the Zoological Gardens, the Habana Hilton, police stations, El Templete; the governor's palace shown to me by a policeman from California who enlisted in Castro's army in the Sierra Maestra whose wife and child were killed by Batista's men. I went to a distillery with a newly wedded couple.

The night before New Year's Eve I met at a fiesta in the streets for "toys for the poor children"fund, a Negro who insisted on singing the songs of Johnny Mathis to me, and buying me drinks (bacardi and coca cola); a weird skinny balding curly-haired fellow who played the guitar and harmonized with the other fellow who was called Orlando. We all sang—I listened—when the band played the Cuban nation anthem. Two guys who were drinking invited me to go to the Victoria whore house, all expenses to be paid by them, but I refused, thanking them anyway.

I met Fidel Castro's nephew, a shy smiling nice-looking guy who seemed in a perpetual state of wondering happiness, and whose friend wrapped his arm around my shoulder and we conversed in Spanish and poor English about my views on Castro and how the Cubans loved him. A Negro who was talking English to me with a jazz bop flavor ("skin me, man" for let's shake hands) dragged me over to meet all his friends and girls, and told me he was going to start a N.A.A.C.P. organization to help the colored peoples in Cuba, and he had just spoken to Raul Castro about it this morning.

All these people had me dance with this girl who was dancing with this other guy who was persuaded to relinquish his very cute partner to me, and I danced for a while, and then a soldier and a girl began dancing, and it got wilder and wilder and everybody was watching them and it was getting sweatingly frantic and grinning and wild.

The next day I spoke to a young Negro soldier and his three friends and we walked all over the city, and I had dystentery and needed a bathroom. We went to a party where, after I got to a bathroom (too late), I went upstairs where I and my friends and a man and his wife told me of the bestiality of Batista and his Hitler methods and of the plaques and bullet holes in the streets where students were shot down, and he opened a bottle of champagne which I didn't take because any food or drink was too much for my intestines due to my eating food at the booths in the streets, where one day an old thin prostitute who had been grawing on some chicken came over to me when I ordered an orange drink, and she mumbled something intended as a"come on" but after I repulsed her offer twice with a "no, gracias," she went back to eating her chicken. She was thin, with lips made up to look as if the lips were shaped that way, but weren't. Poor horrible woman.

Probably hungry because hustling in Habana is best for a plump girl with a big rear, not as a skinny old woman of about 35 or less. Like crawling into bed with death.

It seems that Havana is chiefly known for sex. While there, a Negro pimp came over to me on the Prado, while I was reading the "Bhagavad Gita," and told me he had seen me in Times Square. They all have some line like that. I told him I wasn't buying, but he told me there was no charge to look. So we walked to a door down a dark, narrow, dirty street; he knocked, gave his name, and we went in. In one of the rooms a man and a woman were changing the sheets. The prostitutes sat in a sort of "waiting room." The pimp told me to sit down, pick a woman, and talk in

English so the women wouldn't understand. I sat down and looked them over. Most were too plump foir my taste. Some attempted a seductive smile, but others didn't seem to give a damn. The prettiest girl was half facing away from me with a blase bored look. I singled her out, the pimp told her to prepare, but I said I didn't have enough money (I actually had enough) with me, but if I got enough I would be back later. The pimp told me if I didn't want girls I could have boys, and he ran his hand down from my chest to my stomach. I told him if I wanted anything, it was girls. I didn't later go to meet him.

My four friends and I on New Year's Eve, celebrating the first anniversary of the revolutionary government of Castro, went to a party at the Cuban exposition near the Habana Hilton where I met the head of the Cuban secret service, a round pleasant fellow who took me in to the kitchen to speak to the chef about the new Cuba, and a waiter showed me many bullet wounds in his body after being shot by Batista's men. I saw a bearded famous commander with people hanging all over him. Happiness! A drunk friend of the secret service head was giving me "abrazos" to symbolize Cuban-American solidarity. They dislike the US government, US newspapers, and Eisenhower, but do like the American people, students, and Stevenson. I got on the plane to Key West early in the morning after my friends said good-bye, and met a man who climbed many mountains in the US, an amateur botanist...."

So went my journal. Whenever in Cuba I would mention that we were hearing that Castro was a Communist, everyone assured me that this was just US propaganda and simply untrue. I only met one acknowledged communist while I was there, and he said in English, "We are getting stronger, my dear." When I told them Americans were upset by these show trials held in a Havana stadium for the public that condemned many people to die, they assured me that all who were executed were murderers and well deserved to die. The execution ground against a wall in the moat at La Cabana Prison had in that last year something like 450 executions done in it. The wall was eaten out by all the bullets fired against it that didn't lodge in the bodies. Cubans thought that was great. I don't know whether Khalil was telling me his true story, not do I know who told me the truth.

But Cuba one year after Castro took over was very happy to have him as their leader, and I was very happy to have spent there five and a half days of my Christmas vacation.

MOROCCO:

In 1965 I went to Morocco for the first time, and felt it was a land out of a "National Geographic Magazine," a land from another time, much more primitive and exotic, a cliche of the colorful. From a letter of July 29,'65: while traveling through Europe after my graduate year at the University of Edinburgh, I returned to southern Spain from "Lisbon to Sevilla by bus, a full day of jolting with stops every half hour for the driver to talk to bystanders, pick up a melon here, a beer there; in the evening we arrived. Sevilla hasn't changed since I was there last. Still wonderful, and still flooded with Yankees. After a day in Sevilla, I caught a bus to Algeciras and then the boat to Ceuta]Morocco], then a bus to Tetuan. Another continent beneath the weathered heel of CJS [me]—Africa, Asia, Europe, North America—all down the drain of past experience.

"French Morocco is a fascinating place. [The northernmost part of Morocco speaks Spanish rather than French as its second language; Arabic is its first.] I wandered through native bazaars (where they sell natives—actually, I'm sure if you wanted one, you could buy him or her). Watched people weaving rugs, making shoes, making everything, watched people watching me, crept through narrow streets, and was lucky enough to be there [in Tetuan] when a festival was on.

Saw Berber tribesmen dance, and fire their old flintlock rifles. Took two photos even though a gun-bedecked Berber told me "no." Later on in the evening, I was surrounded by lots of them (with their rifles) and one fellow asked me, with a big smile, if I got any photos. I said "yes." We shook hands all around and I wished them well and they wished me well. All really very friendly. We spoke Spanish and French.

Saw lots of sights and bought three Moroccan hand-made wool caps. Keeps the cold out (even in August nights are cold out there in the desert, with lots of wind). Went to a fair later on in the evening, saw a Turkish-type show with belly dancers and the lot....the tea there, if weak, is extremely aromatic and tasty; if strong, is undrinkable. I've had both....

Then the boat back to Spain and hitched to Malaga; at Malaga I waited till the wee hours of the morning for a ride to Granada. I read poetry and cursed in the interim. About 3 or 4 a.m. I got a ride to Cordoba. Saw the Mosque ("La Mesquita") and the old winding streets. Lovely city. Then hitched to Granada....Traveling and writing are not too compatible."

Time. How to write while in motion, clutching luggage or while your thumb is waggling for a hitch? Time—the contemporary world of the machine lives right by the old Moroccan made-by-hand. The waiting on a line to check in at an airport in 1996. The hitchhiking, waiting for a ride from a car in 1965. The slow amble of a donkey in the streets of Fes is the same whether in 1996, 1965, or 1665. The djelaba looks the same. The face is the same.

The trip in 1965 was solo, but in August 1970, I traveled there with my wife, Joyce, and wrote from Fes: "So different from anything you've ever seen. Makes the colorful Mexican markets look like Boston Common on a Sunday. Wild, exotic, strange, and almost always friendly. We have for three days been staying just on the other side of this gate [Bab Boujeloud]. Fantastic colors, scents, cries, people, tastes, especially in Fes!" This plethora of adjectives and nouns fits the jostling together of so many different things in the medina [ancient native quarter] of Fes, even 26 years later in 1996, when I was there again with my friend James Greenberg.

In 1970, Joyce and I got a hotel room in a fleabag in the medina, and when we were first shown to our room, there were two young Arab men sleeping in the big bed. We woke them up, and asked the hotel manager to please change the sheets when this room was ready for us. An hour or so later, after a mint tea in a cafe nearby where we watched the passing show, we went back to the hotel, and found the sheets somewhat smudged, but at least our bed, if not so clean, was empty. What could we expect from a fleabag but a cheap price, but this room had a window overlooking Bab Boujeloud, a priceless view. In 1996, traveling with my friend James, we stayed in a fancy air-conditioned hotel with a swimming pool, way out of the old medina. Getting old and wanting a little more comfort this latest time in Fes, although in Meknes we stayed in a much cheaper place with fans, and in Rabat, James got an air-conditioned place, and I a walk-up hovel overlooking (and over-hearing the Muslim prayer calls several times in the nights) a mosque in the medina.

Men wanting to be your guides are in Morocco worse than mosquitoes. Persistent, in your face, never taking no as your answer, constantly pointing at things to see even after you insist on being left alone. That was also an unchanging part of Morocco, and it deters travelers from returning there. It was worse when I was with Joyce, because there was the sexual element too. Several men in the evening surrounded us in the medina of Rabat and began touching Joyce's blouse because it had "interesting material." The blouse was cotton. The only interesting material in the blouse was pure Joyce. I was picking off their hands like lint, warning them about touching, and we left the medina. Once, in Tangier, I asked directions of a fellow to some good restaurant. He said he'd guide us. I asked him please just to point out the way. He insisted, took us to a fancy restaurant, and proceeded to sit down at the table with us, ready to scarf up an expensive repast. I got the manager to get him to leave. Gall beyond belief! Tangiers in 1970 was the worst place. Beggars and touts throng the streets, and the place feels evil. By the time we had gotten to Tangiers I had eaten very little in the week since we had arrived in Morocco from Spain—the heat and food put me off, and we subsisted mostly on bread and bottled orange juice, and I must have gotten a flu because after paddling a pedalo boat in the Atlantic, I felt faint and spent the rest of the evening in my hotel room, Joyce nervously going out by herself to get something to eat. Often, traveling in Muslim countries with women, they have been sexually harrassed, and I have had to defend them. I'd rather now not travel with women in any Muslim country, as I spend too much of my time as their bodyguard.

In 1996, the guides were as persistent as ever, but James simply walked away from them, and I insisted I didn't want them, and eventually it did work. Once, one guy kept speaking to me as I walked through Fes's old medina, and I deliberately stepped on his feet as I continued walking down the street. With an "ouch" and a curse, he finally abandoned me. Before James arrived in Morocco, I was heading toward the old Fes medina when four young Chinese people, two men, two women, pleaded with me to help them get rid of these two Moroccan guys demanding they make them their guides. The Chinese said that nothing worked to get these two guys to leave them alone. I talked to the Moroccans and told them I knew how to get to the medina, and that the Chinese did not want their services. They kept following us, trying to explain the sights around them, but I deliberately took the Chinese in the opposite way the "guides" suggested. Finally they let us alone, after calling us all racists for not accepting Moroccans, and I yelled back at them that if they two were representative of all their people I could see it made sense to become a racist. Many people in the streets called out to the Chinese in pidgin Japanese, and I kept saying that they were Chinese, not Japanese, but the Moroccans were not used to the "poor" Chinese as tourists, and so assumed they were rich Japanese. Or maybe it made no difference to the Moroccans—Chinese, Japanese, same thing, rich Oriental tourists. (Talk to the Japanese or Chinese, see how they feel about each other, and then let's all discuss racism.) Why so many guides, and why so persistent? Simple. Morocco is a poor country, and unemployment is quite high. If I were poor, but could speak English or other languages, I too might hang around waiting for tourists, and badger them to employ me. I hate it, but I understand and sympathize.

Fes is fascinating. In 1970, guides were not the only problem. There were often packs of young boys who would eye our expensive camera and Joyce's bag, sidling toward us at times. But there was a heartening pattern to watch several times what came next. An older woman would see these boys and us, would know what was up, and proceed to yell at the boys. She and a bunch of other older people would surround the boys with us as part of the circle. Then a young man in the circle would kick one of the boys, and that boy would burst into tears. More yelling from the woman and other bystanders at the boys, and then all would disperse, with me thanking them for their protection. Happened several times. Now I never take a camera, and use postcards of the sights instead. Less to steal, less for me to worry about.

That August evening in 1970, just after Joyce and I had left the frightening Rabat medina, several boys were following us, and one touched Joyce's back with the palm of his hand, and took off running. This was probably just a boyish poke, meant to insult, almost like a dare. I turned and ran up the steep hill after him, the others boys scattering, and I honing in on the poking, but not pokey, boy, and I caught him. I grabbed his arm, and started shaking him and yelling, and I was quickly surrounded by a crowd. Here I was, a bearded foreigner, a lot taller than this kid of maybe 10 or 12 years of age. I must have looked like a bully, and aware of this, I yelled to the crowd in my rusty French that this boy insulted my wife, he touched her, what kind of place was this, how could they let this happen. Then the pattern once again emerged. An old woman berating the kid, a young man kicking him once, the boy bursting into tears, the crowd dispersing. I went off with Joyce feeling somewhat safer, that we could be protected by the people here. But we still stayed away from the medinas at night.

Inside this same medina of Rabat in 1996 there seemed to be no danger whatsoever. It was then daylight, noon-ish, so few people were out in the glaring sun. It had become an artists' colony, self-conscious of its old-fashioned low white-washed houses. Anything but sinister. At night it might very well still be different.

One difference in Fes in 1970 was how the police dealt with alcohol versus kif or marijuana. There was an abandoned shed in the medina, where several kif smokers were lighting up. No one seemed troubled by this. However, one drunken Moroccan who came over to talk to us as we sat on the sidewalk drinking orange juice from a bottle was quickly taken away by two policemen, perhaps because he was bothering us, but another person said how this was a bad man, and how it was bad to drink alcohol. To each culture its own narcotic. In Bolivia everyone munches on coca leaves, in the United States everybody hoists a beer or a triple cappuchino. Reality must have a mediator to dilute it. Our bodies sweat and can smell bad, and so we use deodorant to dilute or banish our natural stink. On a local bus once in Meknes in 1970 I remember that everyone, however ragged and dusty they were (and mostly they were—many people then wore ragged jalabas, and it was like the jeans of a hippie, lots of patches and pride in them) they smelled good, like sweet spices. Often you smell like what you eat—Joyce and I in Greece smelt like Greeks. Moroccans smelled like spices.

Even more exotic than Fes was Marrakesh. Both times I was there, alone, in 1996, I stayed in a cheap hotel on the Djemaa el-Fna, but had a room with its own private bathroom, so I could not only take a shower, but could wash clothes, which I did every two days so I could travel with very very little luggage. The Djemaa el-Fna is a large open plaza ringed by numbered orange juice stands, so if you've been buying from stand #47, you can find him easily. Each stand owner clamors for business, but I set up a relationship with one stand where when you buy, say, three fresh-squeezed juices you get a half a glass or so free. The juice is delicious and cheap (making it more delicious), and in the torrid climate of summer, it is necessary.

In the evening the Djemaa el-Fna turns wild. There are snake-charmers, sticking cobras in your face so you take a photo and the snake-charmer takes your donation. There are troupes of musicians who play, and dancers who dance. One musician had a American banjo, but most music, even his, is fairly traditional Moroccan. One popular dance troupe had a very effeminate man, front teeth all gold, dance like a woman and make sexual invitations to men in the crowd, and especially to me, which made the Moroccans laugh. I took up one invitation to dance in this circle of musicians and got applause and good-natured laughter. One of the best ways to get a bunch of natives from anywhere on your side is to do something so they will laugh at you, and then if you yourself laugh at your own antics and at the crowd's reaction to you, you have won them over. I've done it in China, Costa Rica, and now Morocco. Lots of food and drink booths also set up in the evenings in the Djamaa el-Fna. Great soup and hot aromatic drinks besides orange juice. There are theology lecturers, healers with powdered deer antlers and potions to cure everything, boxing contests for young boys, a whole carnival of noisy glittering circles of viewers around each act and stand and stall.

I spent two weeks in Morocco before meeting James Greenberg in Fes, and about a week of that was spent alone in Marrakesh. While sitting around in the largely ruined Palais el-Badi, I took notes on my impressions there—June 27, '96: "Storks make noise while flying like "huh, huh, huh, huh," at each wing beat a low chuckle. Storks lined up on ruined walls make big twig nests. When arrive at nests, storks clatter their bills like dulled castinets, reminder of Moorish places in Spain. Storks in flight have separated feathers at the end of each wing, like a wind-shredded ensign. Storks—bring babies. Small birds scoop water or insects from the one pool still filled with water, not just filled with blank memories. A small insect drowns, barely noticeable to me, beating the water in time to its panic. Thunder off to the south, a promise rarely kept, but that day it rains. The green globes hang from its orange trees; this world is not yet ripe."

A month later, alone in Essouirra after two weeks in Morocco with James, I shaped these notes into a poem: AT PALAIS EL-BADI IN MARRAKESH:
"Storks creak out a low chuckle when they fly,
a "huh" at each wing beat, and then the sharp clack of bills
on their twig nests, monotonous maracas (what Andalusian dance?).
The birds that bring babies, yet here the broken fountains
are dry except for one scum-green pool where flitter still the

tiny wings of an insect drowning. Mountains of marble and wood
were stripped from here for another palace of another ruler; new men
should be served. Green globes on orange trees, deceit of dying
worlds not yet ripe for us to grasp, not sweet enough till never.
Storks' wingtips, the separated end-feathers like a wind-shredded ensign
(for their nest building? A ruined palace? A laugh? A question?
Another chance?)"

The next day in Marrakesh—June 28, 1996—I sat alone in Ben
Yussouf medersa, and also took notes on birds: "the small birds, swifts,
wings like a sickle moon, a nervous nail paring, are easy to see as free spirits. Storks are clumsy, creaky, ugly—no fit symbol for the light-footed
soul. I was thinking such thoughts when a young Belgian couple joined
me sitting on the floor of the medersa. My eyes lighted up at cute Kathy,
and we three discussed the J.F.K. assassination. A bird shat on my left forearm. (Sorry I forgot you, oh souls!). The ruined Palais el-Badi and the
empty medersa teaches—the wooden Koranic teachings high on the walls
are barely legible after centuries of rain."

A week and a half later in Fes, I turned these notes into a poem, building and trimming the line endings to get rhymes and off-rhymes to once
again write of time and the destruction that follows

in its wake. A MEDERSA IS A COLLEGE OF THEOLOGY:
"Wheeling and sliding, the swifts pare the sky above the courtyard
of Ben Yussouf medersa, yet the blue square is not marred.
Bird squeak vanishes quickly to be replaced with more bird squeak;
wings like a crescent moon, these swifts, wings that meet
and part, meet and part, all this flitter just for back and forth,
while the sun twirls the shadows, and the moon awaits the moth,
and these scimitar wings, these nail parings, these sickles
designed to cut down our hope; to scythe; to cut, not a riddle.
Yeats' changeless birds have had to be restored. Teachings of the Koran
inscribed in wood below the roof teaches even the illiterate moron

what is the fate of all things. Six centuries of rain make the words illegible and so what it teaches us is never out of date. Birds shit still on this courtyard."

Birds—the soul free to fly? A more mundane and usual creature to ride in Morocco is the camel, and in Zagora, in June 1996 in the valley of the Dra, I got to travel on one. To get there from Marrakesh, you take a bus over the Atlas Mountains, and down the Oued Dra, passing golden (or yellow, if you're more of a cynical realist) square houses in small villages along the river. Zagora is a small town on the edge of the Sahara Desert. Naturally some locals met me at the bus station to try to sell me a camel safari, and I bought a three-day trip. The next morning I walked over to the Touareg guide's house with him, and had tea outside with his family in their courtyard while I waited. He also introduced me to a very old blind man living in a tiny hut made of woven-wood-branches slathered with mud, living on the guide's family's charity. What must it be like to live, old and feeble and blind, in a hut open to flies, snakes, and scorpions, brutally hot in the day, very chilly at night. Very sad, but at least you are taken care of, not by a relative, but by another charitable Touareg. I've seen lots worse in this world. The couple who were to go with us didn't show up so the guide sent me off with his younger brother and a camel. The several other times I've gone on camel safaris, I've had the reins and the control over my camel, but this time the Touareg held the reins as he walked in front of me over a hill and into the desert. O.K. It let me pay more attention to the scenery around me than I could if I were guiding my mount.

The desert at the beginning was the *hamada* type, all yellow dirt and stones. I had been given a black veil to shield my face, the traditional veil of the Touareg, and I had worn it for a while till the backs of my hands began to burn in the vicious sun. So I wrapped this veil around my hands instead. I knew enough to take a long-sleeved shirt and a wide-brimmed hat, but next time I'll also take gloves! Later, we stopped for tea and lunch and shade at a single small tree, and lying down to rest I noticed a maybe 3 ½ inch black scorpion a couple of feet away from me. I mentioned it to my guide who left off making the tuna (from a can), tomato, and cucumber salad, to see if we could kill it. There was also a big white scorpion, and they both went down their hole below the tree. We probed the hole, and finally killed both scorpions. They have a right to live, but I do not, nor did my guide, want to share a small shaded space with these.

We watered the camels at a well, and we drank from it too. I had bought along many bottles of water, but the well water was tasty and safe. As the sun was going down, we camped and ate. I was feeling very weak, and had no appetite, and realizing it was from salt deprivation, I licked up some pure salt and felt better. Mint tea was the liquid staple, and the Touareg made it as usual too sweet for me, cutting off chunks of solid brown sugar with his knife, and dropping them into the boiling water. The sun set, we spread out our bedrolls, chatted a bit in French, our common language, and lay back to watch the stars. The desert is the place to see the stars, far away from any light that diminishes them, until the moon rose over the mountains to my right, and the stars had to play second fiddle. Some flies annoyed me, and the night was cold, especially after the fierce heat of the day, and the bedroll was not so thick as to be able to ignore the hard ground, but I slept well.

Next morning, we went over to catch our grazing hobbled camel who had strayed a few hundred yards during the night, and I fed him dates and nuts and grass, while he sat patiently folded up on his belly back at our camp. Then on to his back, he standing up in that characteristic four-step unfolding unhinging (in two senses) motion that seems to want to pitch you off the back and off the front of the camel. Later that day we stopped at a few trees in the center of sand dunes which looked like the classic desert of the Sahara. My guide went off to see a Touareg family he knew nearby, and asked me to come, but by then I had enough of Touareg tea, and just wanted to sit under these few scraggly trees by myself. And so I did. That night we camped on the sand dunes, and watched the stars till I fell asleep. Next day, in the afternoon, we arrived back in Zagora, and I took a shower at my hotel, saw with shock my lobster-red face below my eyes where I I had neither beard nor veil to block the sun, and wandered into town to sit with a cold Coca-Cola and admire the passing Berbers, Touaregs, and Arabs. Touaregs come in all colors from one black fellow I met from Mali, and the lighter shade of my Moroccan guide. The Berbers are usually very light-skinned, many European in shade and features. Moors are not all swarthy!

In Fes, Meknes, and Rabat with James, we wandered the medinas, saw the old palaces and museums, tried to evade the guides, and I discovered the delights of pigeon pie flavored with sugar and cinnamon, and James the fresh vegetables and fruits of the markets. Morocco is, even in 1996 where most people now wear Western clothing unlike the ubiquitous djelaba worn in 1965, still so foreign and exotic.

James left after his two weeks with me in Morocco, and I went down to Essouira on the Atlantic coast for my last two weeks here. Essouira is an old Portuguese town with a fort overlooking the ocean, and thick Portuguese walls built which could be defended against attack, but now just serve as a lovely memory of not-so-lovely Colonialism, as indeed the wonderful Moorish fortresses and mosques in Spain do when the North African Moors conquered and occupied Spain for many centuries. (Turnabout is fair play?) Surrounding this formerly Portuguese, and currently European tourist, enclave, is the Moroccan part of Essouira, not frequented much by many of the tourists. Here it is the usual bustle, donkeys, people marketing cactus fruit and aromatic drinks in the streets, and the usual shops selling everything, and the shoppers almost all Moroccan.

Every day for the two weeks I would take long walks along the beach, watching the many wind-surfers on the beaches at the town, and then further on where there might be a couple of camels grazing near the sand, a donkey-cart trundling along to pick up seaweed or sand for cement, a fishing boat tacking against the wind. Lots of wave-rinsed silence and emptiness which I love. And then in the afternoon, for lunch perhaps sit at a fisherman's outdoor cafe at the port where you can buy small shrimp in its shells, or sea urchin and squid to eat. In the early evening walk up to the fort and watch the sun set over the water, making sure to wear your long-sleeved shirt because Essouira with its relentless wind coming off the Atlantic gets very chilly at night. Then off for a sandwich in the main Portuguese plaza to eat and watch the people relax, or off to the small Carnival at the outskirts of the Moroccan area, or wander these streets, or head back in the chill of evening to my room overlooking the Portuguese walls and the big clock, take a hot bath, and read poetry or write poetry, or just think over my trip and my life. Time passing.

One poem I wrote while in Essouira in 1996, but containing some notes I brought with me from my southeast Asia trip of 1993-4, fits this motif of my writing over the last decade or more, the motif of time passing and of death. The observations and meditations mix in this poem as they have in my mind and in this book, of different times and different countries and different feelings.

On July 29, 1996, I wrote:

"The dust we are and will be\ whirls and gets in our eyes.
Hamlet's ghost, desperate, cries\ "Remember me." Vanity. Blindness.

In a graveyard in Malacca [Malaysia],\ a stone "Sacred to the memory of Henry Kraal." Whoever.\ Gnats swarm around my eyes.\ Alarm clock buzzes:"Awake."

We'd love it if Shakespeare\ would only keep talking. We are
paying attention. Wind flickers\ like fire, moving the saffron cloth
over the old Thai *chedi* in Chiang Mai [Thailand].\ All the elements
speak except old bricks.
All the elements speak, especially old bricks.

Pythagoras tried to purify his soul\ where it could fly free of chains
of birth.
Hindus feel Nirvana is free of chains of birth.\ To what end? Escape or
remain connected?

Wind flickers like fire. Dust whirls.\ We want to move. We want rest. We slog through the sandstorm of ourselves."

A good Moroccan metaphor to end on.

EGYPT:

The dung beetle, the sacred scarab, of ancient Egypt was associated with resurrection and immortality. These beetles break down the dead organic waste into products useful for the soil and so for us. They turn shit into vitamins and energy. They make the dead stuff live. It is the trappings and decor of death that keep the ancient Egyptians alive for us, this paradox forefronted in our museums and high school history classes. So does writing about the past, like this book, like a beetle burrowing through memory and old letters, journals and poems.

In June 1979, after about ten months in Asia, I got to Egypt to spend one week there. I still had a bad case of amoebic dystentery, and probably weighed maybe 110 pounds, up from about 100 pounds when I was in Sri Lanka. I looked like one of the living dead from Auschwitz, all ribs and

knobs, but I felt fine. From a letter of June 28, 1979: I was around the Valley of the Kings near Luxor—"I spent from 8 a.m. till 4 p.m. riding a bicycle [from Luxor, then crossing the Nile River on a small local ferry], hiking across the desert over a small mountain [really just a rocky hill behind the Temple of Queen Hatshepsut, as I see from a postcard], waddling through tombs of the pharohs and temples too—during which time I had one tiny wine-glass of juice [because I was too cheap to buy more at the expensive tourist cafe in the Valley of the Kings. And there, of course, there were no free glasses of water.]. And the temperature was 115 degrees in the shade, and believe me, there was only sun where I was trudging. I felt a bit knackered, but no problem. So I'm in the pink (sunburnt a bit—a pun)."

I remember now leaving my bike locked up by the Temple of Hatshepsut, which was not open at the time. No one else was around. On the other side of the hill from the temple was the Valley of the Kings, but there weren't any trails to get down to it, and so I had to find my way through the dry wadis and gulches. Ther was absolutely no sound in that hot and dry desert. Absolute absence of life it seemed. The Valley of the Kings had some tourists around, but I wandered around and into some of the tombs-caves alone. Heading back to my bike, I walked back along a paved black road, sizzling in the heat. After the hike and bike ride back to Luxor, passing again the two Colossi of Memnon, solitary seated statues just off the side of the dirt road in a field, faces scraped by time and rain and blowing sand, crossing again the sluggish Nile on the ferry, I got back to my hotel where I proceeded to down a gallon of water. The manager of the hotel told me that this was a particularly hot spell in Egypt with temperatures that day at 46 degrees celsius.

Heat and dryness can kill you, and almost killed me that day, but heat and dryness can also preserve mummies and the colors on the walls. I was stunned by how fresh the ancient colors seem on these temples in the desert. The huge incised pillars of the temple of Karnack, the temples of Luxor, the Cairo Museum—magnificent! The pyramids of Giza ("over-rated heaps—no beauty") and Sakkara are interesting, but did not make an extraordinary impression on me. "I hitched from Giza to Sakkara, and an Egyptian fighter pilot picked me up. His wife is now working in Israel, and he is happy about that peace! Egyptians, while hoggish about getting your dollars, are basically really friendly and nice. I was pleased about Egypt and I thought I'd hate it. One never knows.

The Egyptians all ask me where I'm from, and when I say USA they all say "welcome." They love [President] Carter and are very happy to be at peace with Israel" In the summer of 1970, I stayed the night on an Israeli Air Force base with my friend Michael Gordon, who was serving as a doctor on that base, and he told me of having been told by one of his pilots that he had shot down an Egyptian MIG fighter plane with a Russian pilot in it. But most MIGs later on were flown by Egyptian pilots, and the guy who picked me up was pleased that peace with Israel meant he would not have to face an Israeli pilot in a dogfight. Now I was in Egypt after the Camp David Accords and so Americans were indeed welcome. While walking down a street in Cairo, I passed several young adult men who, smiling, watched me walk by. I was wearing orange pajama drawstring pants, and an orange Indian shirt, so I looked like an American hippie. One of them said, "Salaam" [greetings], and I, unthinking, returned the greeting, "Shalom" [Hebrew for Greetings]. Inside I cringed. All I needed was to be taken for an Israeli here in Egypt. Walking away I heard nothing from the group behind me instead of the furious curses I half expected. Were they too shocked by my Hebrew returned for their Arabic? Did it matter to them? I don't know, but I still cringe when I think how bad a spy I would make.

It was annoying to return from countries where there is no custom to tip waiters to arrive in Cairo where during my first elevator ride in my hotel, the elevator-boy asked me for a tip. I said no, that I had just come from Asia, not America, and that his was not a service we tip for. My hotel was of the middling sort, neither posh nor a fleabag. Traveling from Cairo to Luxor and back by train, I experienced both extremes of travel. Going to Luxor, I got the first train I could and ended up spending all night standing in the packed corridor of a coach. And what was worse I still had amoebic dystentery, and often needed a toilet. Problem was, the coach was so crowded that there were a few men sleeping in the toilet, so it was unusable. The only toilet available was in the next coach which was a first-class coach with a guard at the door. I had to plead several times during the night to get into that other coach's toilet to relieve myself. And with amoebic dystentery there is no way to control your excretory need. Your guts give you the "two-minute warning" and after that time, you shit in a toilet or you shit in your pants. No other alternatives. I had to tell the guard about my problems, that I had just been in India, and so was desperate. Not a fun night!

Returning to Cairo, I had time to make reservations for a first-class coach, traveling during the day so I could see the Egypt that previously had slipped by me in the night. Air-conditioning too.

I lorded it like a pasha in my roomy padded seat, watching the struggles at the second-class coaches, but remembering. No problems about the toilet now. No Egyptian dung beetle, no sacred scarab, needed to follow me around now. I digested the days in Luxor on that train trip, and am still doing that digestion now at this writing.

On November 5, 1979, after being home in New York for a few months, out came another chunk of digested Egypt:

"In Luxor I watched time plumb down from the still still blue attitudes of the ancient temple paintings through the white scarred 1725 on a pillar. I can hear the silence creating more sand. I can feel 1725 as old. This temple feels too old to touch.

Memories arise, bubbles from fermenting cider. I chew on them again, nourished anew, as I climb down toward the water in the well, roped to past lovers with fraying excremental lines…. How can I haul myself into or out of my body?

The hawk's shadow slides, a black boomerang, across the Egyptian hill, slicing the sand but scarless. If I could fly up, not fall, no rope needed, cut free like a bubble shimmering up, or be cool under the knife-like wing, take comfort in the shadow of the hawk's wing, passing over the old me laved by a woven blanket of sand."

Egypt is as old as it gets, and I was a mere 39 years old, but was feeling time deepen. Ancient places, full of sun and sand, remind you that you don't matter much, and that no one will long remember you. Authors—take note!

ISRAEL:

Now—October 17, 2000—the Palestineans are fighting the Israelis again. When Joyce and I were in Israel in late July and August 1971, there were only the scattered terrorist incidents and the so-called War of

Attrition which was an air and artillery war with Egypt along the Suez Canal. Nothing so big or fierce that Joyce and I were much worried. After all, the war of 1967 had been decisively won by Israel (but the Yom Kippur War of 1973 was yet to come). People were being warned about bombs being planted on buses, but life went on without too much fuss and fear.

We visited our friends Michael and Yael Gordon who lived in Jerusalem, a fascinating place, a condensed holy city sacred to too damn many religions; holiness is still being fought over from the medieval Crusades to the contemporary Muslim jihads. "It's my God!" "No, it's my God!" Hopeless. The quicksand of history pulling us down into hate and war. In Jerusalem, however, the history mixes with myth, and in the Old City, the Arab and the Chassid walking the lanes can't help sometimes walking side by side, not by choice but because the streets are often as narrow as Fundamentalist thinking. Strolling one day through the ultra-orthodox Jewish neighborhood of Mea Sharim, Joyce was shouted at and a rock or two was flung at her because she was wearing a sleeveless blouse. Joyce and I went to the Wailing Wall several times, but she had to go to the woman's section. Separation even here. Jerusalem was having a building boom, and we stayed in one of the new suburbs with the Gordons and their two young children. New housing, but segregated between Jew and Muslim.

Michael Gordon was doing some Air Force reserve duty as a flight doctor, and so one day we visited him at his Air Force base. Impressive and serious readiness for battle. Training which was being used as the War of Attrition continued. Beleaguered but confident seemed to be the mood in the country. They even seemed confident in their driving abilities, although I thought they were nearly as dangerous to others behind the wheel of their cars than behind the throttles of their tanks.

Bravely, I rented a Ford to see some of the rural areas, and drove up north to the Galilee region.

Wonderful waterfalls and oases like Ein Gedi, the hot trek up to and around Masada, the salt-stinging float in the Dead Sea where you bob like an apple in the thick brine, the usual and exciting tourist sights we did.

One road we drove down was unmarked except by one sign which was only in Arabic and Hebrew. But what the hell, we kept driving. Earlier we had seen burned-out tanks and sand-bagged bunkers, but when Joyce suggested we look into one of them, I noticed a 50-caliber machine gun snout sticking out of the bunker, and so vetoed the idea. The road was getting narrower and not having seen a sign or even a sign of life, I began getting a little nervous. Suddenly the road ended at a small rounded bare area, and there was a U.N. military officer who stopped us. I started to ask him questions, but he interrupted me with "You know, you're in no-man's land. There are lots of Israeli tanks over there" and then gesturing the other way, "and lots of Syrian tanks over there. You better get out of here." I still wanted to ask him questions about how the duty was to be camped between two enemies, but he cut me short, and told me where I was was dangerous and I'd better get the hell out of there. I did so, and on that drive back I was watching for snipers and drove quickly. We had an Israeli license plate on the car, and so this made us targets for many people.

Joyce and I also drove up to the Golan Heights with its burnt bunkers and spectacular views over the valley. Of course, these spectacular views were perfect to pour down artillery fire onto the Israelis living in the valley below, and I felt how dangerous for Israel it would be to cede them back to Syria. Many Israelis died four years before in 1967 when they took those Heights.

We also later on took a bus for three days into the Negev Desert and in Sinai. The Sinai baked and crisped, with lots of small rounded hills of reddish stone shards with not a green plant to be seen. This was the summer, and I can tolerate heat and deserts quite well, but I felt that to climb one of those hills—and they are not very high—would just about do me in. In the Gulf of Acaba we went swimming and snorkeling. Brightly colored fish scattered like light under the water, but once, standing on some rocks looking for a good place to jump in, I saw two moray eels, open-mouthed, swaying in the current, unblinkingly watching me. I moved further over. Then I heard a big slap and a big fish leaped up and hit the water. I didn't see what kind of fish, but a big splash meant a big fish which meant a big mouth. Still I jumped in, but didn't swim long.

At a beach filled with Israelis, I felt better about snorkeling. While I was watching the pretty fish, and Joyce was down the beach sun-bathing, I looked up and saw a fellow with a snorkeling mask gesturing to me to come to him. Must see something interesting, I thought, and continued snorkeling for a second, and then looked over to him again. This time he gestured frantically to me to come to him, and my first thought he must be caught by the foot by a giant clam (shades of my movie-going experience). I realized he was too far above the bottom to be so caught, and I thought maybe a fish has got him, but when I reached him I saw he had water filling his mask. He was drowning in his own mask, and was so panicked he didn't think to take it off! I ripped his mask off, and he, his eyes big with fright, grabbed me, his saviour, around the neck with both arms and we both went under. Into my head popped the words, "So this is how I'll die!" We bobbed to the surface and I pushed him away from me, trying to say comforting things and at the same time get his arm from around my neck. Finally, I held him off my neck enough to start swimming in to shore, still saying comforting things to this stunned bug-eyed man. I saw a woman coming out near us from the shore, and asked her to help me in with him, but not to get too close. She swam nearby and I pulled him finally to shore where he sat, slumped and voiceless and staring down at the sand. A relative came over to us and I explained the situation to him. Had I not gone over to him, and had he, panicked, gone unconscious before he thought to take off his mask, he would have been floating, drowned, but nobody would have gone out to save him, because he looked just like any other entranced snorkeler in the Gulf of Acaba. His relative thanked and told me that the almost-drowned guy did not speak English, and when I went to say "good-bye" to the guy I saved, he barely acknowledged my going, so stunned was he by the experience. Walking

over to Joyce I realized had I been drowned in my attempt to save him
(which when he pulled me under, I thought a real strong possibility), she
would have gone on sun-bathing little knowing her husband was dead.
How close and easy death can come on such a serene cloudless day!

In Eilat, a resort town on the sea, we spent a miserable night camping
out near the beach, alternately covering ourselves totally with our sleeping
bags to avoid the dive-bombing mosquitoes or uncovering our faces so we
could breathe in the still sweltering air. Any hotel would have been better
than this night in the open, but I was being frugal, and didn't dream that
in such a desert, even by the sea, mosquitoes could flourish. From this
miserable situation on this beach keeping me up most of the night and so
observing the moon-struck land, and the miserable historical situation of
this land, constantly being fought over even as I write these words, came
this poem I called THE BOOK:

"Sinai's strata are folded open, plain to see near Eilat. Read heat, read
bright here, read bare from these torn books, our oldest mounts. Hate
here roughed out these breasts of hills as brown as certain clay. Our early
old pages are burned and fused. Too today two many things face down
each other—Israel's Eilat and Jordanean Acaba. Sun and moon are jug-
gler's balls up and over the mountains. Now the sun is caught in evening
Eilat. Moon too, pale soldier leaping from behind the mountains, clay
pigeon shooting, jealous pale coin to set near Eilat at four in the morning.

"From the swamp at the frontier mosquitoes buzz the beaches at night.
The Red Sea is blanched by sun, but at night is warm and sticky. A salty
poltice to bring to heal. Moon, tossed on a wager, always comes up heads.
Sinai at night is charcoal, but burns again every day. Desalinated water
tastes not like fresh. Hate removed is still not love."

Israel is exciting, but until the Palestineans acknowledge that I was in
Israel and not in Palestine, it will be a land waiting for war to happen
again. When Joyce and I first arrived from Greece by ferry, there was a
mix-up, and a delay because some group of officials or other was striking.

We were very tired and annoyed, but when we finally got to our Israeli Customs Inspector, he did his "friendly Jewish waiter" routine and we were charmed, and while bantering back and forth, invited us to come and live in Israel. After all, it's such a wonderful place, he enthused over our meager backpacks. Yes, Israel is wonderful, think I, but too many people would like to clear the land not only of stones and weeds, but of other peoples' history and lives. As Yeats said about Ireland (a pun even in its name), "Much hatred, little room."

TURKEY:

Just after Joyce and I arrived in Turkey in the summer of 1971, an earthquake hit. We had come by ferry from the Greek island of Rhodes to Marmaris on Turkey's southwest coast, passing lovely calm rocky coves on a serene sea. Shortly after disembarking at Marmaris, we were looking at souvenirs in one of the shops at the port when suddenly there was a roar, and the shop started shaking, and the glassware in the shop began tinkling. I first thought it was because a ship was backing down—the roar and the shaking resembled that. Then I realized that we were somewhat inland from the piers. Not a ship's engines, but an earthquake! Others had started running from the store more quickly than we did, and we all congregated in the street, nervous but not panicked. This was the first earthquake I'd ever been in. Quickly the roaring and shaking stopped, and with nervous laughs, we all went back to what we had been doing.

The earth may growl, but the Turks then all seemed friendly. Actually, too friendly. I'll explain. We decided to take a shared taxi to Mugla, a city distinguished by its lack of distinction—no pristine beaches (it was an hour or so inland), no tourist sites, no ancient ruins. Just Turks. We could see what they were like, untainted by the tourist. Arriving, we got a hotel for about a dollar a night, and went out walking. Like limpets, young boys began sticking to our heels, each one asking us in the most rudimentary English where we were from, where we were going, how long in Mugla? When I asked each how long they had been studying English, they all gave answers of several years, but had so few words of English, and we had none of Turkish, that our end of the conversations consisted of "Today Mugla, tomorrow Marmaris," words which were accompanied by gyrations of my arms to illustrate this complex idea. More and more young boys joined our procession, so we found ourselves speaking these same words and gestures over and over again—"Today Mugla, tomorrow Marmaris"—like a mantra to each new arrival, and also to some of the old ones who couldn't bear to be left out of such stimulating conversation. We couldn't just, as we wanted to do, explore the place and comment unselfconsciously to each other. If I noticed something interesting, I'd tell Joyce, and she—aware of all eyes on her—would make an exaggerated response to me. Neither of us could ignore those many prying eyes, and I understood what it must be like to be a movie star or important politician, to have to play a role to the many people watching you so you lost the feeling of unself-conscious reactions to things in public. We escaped back to our hotel for a rest from so much friendliness.

Later in the afternoon we went out again, and the same school of pilot fish attended us. We were magnets and, beginning to despair we might have no privacy at all, we thought of turning back, when we heard some music in the distance. We mimed hearing music, and the boys, collecting new ones all the time, preceded us toward those increasingly louder sounds. There was a large white-washed wall, with an opening in it, and much activity. When some adults saw us, they shouted with joy, and several people ran out of the courtyard, who also shouted with joy, and they all pulled us into the yard. Once inside, the whole yard exploded in wel-come, we were thrust down in chairs of honor, food was thrust at us, and the belly dancer, dancing alone in front of us, began dancing right at me, hips jerking my way, and all the people deliriously happy to see us. I guess they needed a foreign guest to make their party a success, and we were it.

No one seemed to speak English except for one boy of about twelve or so, and he helped with their nearly frantic hospitality. I remember being handed some meat, rather too rare for me, and by gesture invited to munch away. I tasted some, but felt I might throw it up, it being so unappetizing to me. Joyce also was offered portions of food, surrounded by these generous hosts. The belly dancer invited me up to dance with her, and I did so, doing a version of "the frug" and shaking my hips, and the crowd went nuts. Then they pushed Joyce up to dance with her after I sat down, and Joyce went up and did it too, and the crowd went nut-ser. This just a few minutes after coming into this courtyard, we were both performing for this extremely enthusiastic bunch of wild sweating happy Turks! Wonderful!

A bit later the dancing got more Turkish, and many of the men including me got up and did a circling dance, while the women and the other men watched. The dance was like the Greek dances (but don't tell the Turks that). The Turks and Greeks hate each other, for good historical reasons. The same coffee is Greek coffee in Greece and Turkish coffee in Turkey, and it pays not to confuse them, although they seem the same. While the men and I danced, one drunk man, his arm over my shoulders, kept leaning over and saying softly to me, "I love you." I smiled back. What could I say? (What did he mean?) Later the women got up to dance, with Joyce included, but not with any men. This party was very exciting, and when I asked the boy who spoke English, what was this party for, he said, "a boy." I told Joyce and we asked if we could see him. The host, hostess, and a few others took us into a room. Now we had expected that a boy had just been born, and so were expecting to see the mother in bed nursing the infant. Nope. Instead we saw a very unhappy looking boy of about thirteen lying in bed. I thought, "Oh, no. He's dying. Just like an *angelito* in Mexico, a little dead boy." Wrong again. With a prideful flourish, the mother whips back the covers and we see he's just been circumcised, the newly crowned red member certifying his manhood de-hooded and bloody. We all gaze in pride while he lay there miserable. A circumcision party. We all went back to the rest in the courtyard to eat and drink and dance some more, till we said we had to leave to go back to our hotel.

They wouldn't hear of it. Turkish hospitality demanded they load us into a jeep, roar back to our hotel, get our luggage (two backpacks) together, and roar off to the apartment of the boy who spoke English to spend the night there with his family. We had paid for the hotel in advance, so there went our one dollar. Ah, well. The next day after a breakfast filled with smiles and nods of friendship, we were taken around the town by the boy to visit all of the relatives of this family, and have tea and coca cola with every single one, each visit accompanied by smiles, nods, laughs, and an increasingly bloated stomach. We begged off another night at his place because we said we must get back to Rhodes tonight. My cheeks ached from smiling so much, and we were desperate for some privacy and rest. Back to Greece and being mostly ignored. Too much friendliness in Turkey.

In 1978 I was heading through Turkey overland toward India, traveling with four English people, and we had been warned about eastern Turkey, how if you run over someone or someone's sheep, you had better drive as quickly as you could because you would be chased and killed. None of this "turn you over to the police" business. We were nervous, but wandering around Ezurum where we would spend the night, we ran into very friendly people, glad to share cigarettes with us. Traveling, one meets only individuals, and most, when met as individuals, are quite decent. Whole peoples can only be generalities by definition, and although most stereotypes I have heard of about nations and groups seem to be substantially true, beware of assuming any particular person fits the stereotype. However, beware even more of assuming stereotypes are substantially not true.

Istambul was very interesting, not quite as exotic as Morocco, but not Brussels either. The huge interior space of the Aghia Sophia, the Blue Mosque, Topkapi Palace, the Archeological Museum, the streets of the Sultanhamet district right behind Aghia Sophia where the four English (one woman, Kathy, among them), another American and I stayed jammed into one room at the Gungor Hotel, and the real Turkish Bath where we got sweated and pounded and soaped and sweated and rinsed and sweated and released. Good food here too, sitting in tiny restaurants with be-Fezed gentlemen smoking water-pipes and looking like nothing could bother or surprise them.

One night some of us went to a sound-and-light production at the Blue Mosque, and I wrote:

NIGHT LIGHT AT THE BLUE MOSQUE:

"The light flushed the night away from Istambul's Blue Mosque. We rustled on our lines of seats. Now the light show changes once again as taped Turkish voices turn fierce. Red light—war, passion, drama. Lights out. Then blue a corner. Night. Romance. We know the code dimly, spurred by music and voice. Then with history's rounded dome illuminated as they would have us see it, light stopped. As we rose to leave after short shower of applause, a scimitar of Turkish moon, unchanging for us, sliced slowly through the untouristed night."

The shape of a curved sharp Turkish scimitar is the same as the wide-open U of a smile. The Armenians didn't confuse the two after the First World War, nor do the Kurds now. I found the Turks very friendly, but I know of their frighteningly sharp edge. Their wide smile has teeth to it.

IRAN:

Crossing the border from Turkey to Iran in August of 1978 was not easy. Our Turkish bus from Ezurum had to wait at customs for three hours at the border, taking off all the luggage from the top of the bus, having it inspected, and tying the luggage back on the top of the bus, then being ordered to take it off again for more inspection, all the while we roasted in the sun as (according to one Turk) the customs officials waited for their bribe to expedite matters. I was with my four Brits——Tony and Kathy, Brian and Keith (who like any good Cockney toff pronounced his name "Keiff")—whom I had met when we were all dumped off by the Magic Bus in the middle of the night about 19 kilometers outside Thessaloniki,

Greece, and we decided to travel together. From such accidents come the roads you travel and whom you travel with.

The Iranian customs were meant to intimidate you. On the way in to the customs shed, you pass

displays of where people hid their heroin—in car bodies, in tires, sewn into clothing—and were found out. Very stiff penalties. Big anti-drug message here. Lots of uniformed guards. Finally our bus passed into Iran and on to Teheran, where all my journal said was "traffic terrible." Besides buying a ticket to the east to Mashhad from Teheran, I remember we lay around on some grassy spot for three hours, all of us exhausted by the heat and travel, having no desire to stick around, or even to see anything, in this big fume-filled city.

On the road I wrote BUS TO MASHHAD:

"On the road in western Iran, the bus pulled off, stopped sputtering, and the passengers stirred into motion toward cups of tea. I skirted the dark pools of oil toward darker darkness to take a leak. Calmed, I thought of my other desert leaks and dreamed backwards till I saw a star slide down the sky with the same trajectory as my piss. Smiling, I shook it, zipped, and strolled back, satisfied.

Desert in Iran like brown paper bags, heat-crinkled, carrying nothing, no one. Then glimpse a bird flying to a phone wire, a wing iridescent from 15th century Persian manuscript."

The route to Mashhad was, according to my rather skimpy journal, "through beautiful mountain passes, arid country, with houses and towns shaded by trees up the mountains." I remember every meal we stopped for in Iran was *chello kabab* (slabs of sliced meat) on top of white rice, with big pats of butter. Plus tea (*chai*), of course. Vegetables? No way. August of 1978 was that year the month-long Ramadan period (the Iranians pronounced it "Ramzan") during which no proper Muslim ate or drank during daylight hours, except travelers got a dispensation, and most Iranians we traveled with on the buses indulged in eating whenever we stopped. Besides *chello kabab*, we could also find "egg or meat sandwiches, plus lots of pepsi and orange soda." Plus lots of friendly helpfulness from several people. "Spent an afternoon with Hussein, and then Massoud took me all over town [Mashhad, the "second holiest city of Islam," with the tomb of the 8th Immam, Reza]. Valli I saw in Mohammad's carpet shop, but he was busy and had to leave." What was refreshing about the Iranians is that they would help you, go way out of their way for you, without trying also to sell you something, a huge contrast with so many of the people in northern India, whose surface friendship masked a very commercial purpose. The Iranians were great.

Such friendliness might be a surprise because several months after I went through Iran, their revolution happened, the pro-American Shah was deposed, the anti-American mullahs took over, and the chants of "Death to America" started. Standing outside a particularly holy mosque, one cloaked older woman began yelling at us, and I have a photo of me against the mosque with a smile and one arm up, shrugging off this angry woman behind me. Everyone else seemed pleased that we were there.

But the revolution was bubbling underneath. "All the women [in Mashhad] wear long shawls covering their whole body and head, and often hold their shawls in their teeth to keep people from seeing their faces. Many, though, have their faces (but not their heads) uncovered." The revolutionary mullahs' strict dress code was not too far from what most of the women were wearing in Mashhad before the revolution. During the three or four days I was in Mashhad, I heard that there were riots in Shiraz and Isfahan, and in Mashhad itself an army officer killed the military chief of the city.

The same day of that assassination, while walking with an Iranian, the Brits and I saw a police jeep tear down our side street, and two cops leap out of the car as it slid to a stop. Every Iranian took off, including the guy we were with who just said to us, "Run!" as he did. I spread my arms out and stepped back, pressing the Brits against the wall, and told them not to move, just watch, it's not our fight. So we watched as the two cops grabbed one guy—it looked like they knew exactly who they were after—

and began swatting him over the head with truncheons, and dragged him screaming back to their jeep, and off they drove, with him in the jeep. The Iranians filtered back into the street, including our friend, talking in a subdued way. He then took me to meet with a group of his friends, all of whom he told us were very much anti-Shah and pro-Khomeini, who at that time was still in exile in Paris, but who they hoped to bring back to depose the Shah. Our friend, in answer to my question, about what the police might do to the man they picked up, said they'd probably keep him in jail for a while, "and every day give him breakfast, you know." I asked what that meant, and he mimed a beating with truncheons. He also told me that SAVAK, the Shah's secret police, was ubiquitous, that "everyone worked for them." Then how can you trust the people in this room? They're O.K., he said. How can you trust me? I asked. My country is solidly behind the Shah. He said, "I trust you." Now in the year 2000, twenty-two years later, I wonder what has become of all of the men in that room, whether they survived the Iran-Iraq War, and life in revolutionary Iran, and whether they still love the revolution as once they tried to bring it about.

I bought a carpet from Mohammad Saberhoseyni of Nomadic Carpet, near the Shah Mosque in Mashhad, and found out from my father that the carpet, supposed to have been sent, had not arrived. I wrote to Mohammad, and he sent my father a letter (24 April 1979): "I'm sorry not to have been able to write to you sooner, but I am sure you have heard the news about Iran, the problems, a strike in post [office] and in other places for a long time. Fortunately everything is getting back to normal. All the people are very pleased with our successful Revolution. All workers are back to their places, working very hard to improve the country soon. I will try to send the chosen carpet [a marriage carpet from Baluchistan nomads, woven by a young girl for her husband-to-be to remind him what she wants from her marriage—the four birds represent four children] by your dear son Mr. Charles as soon as everything with post is O.K. There has been a great changing here....I hope America won't let Shah come to

America. We are going to bring him back to recompense because he has been too bad for Iran and Iranians. We cannot forgive him. He has destroyed our economy, our agriculture, our economy, and he has killed over 60,000 and wounded 100,000 by his dangerous secret police (SAVAK) in last year [19]78, and he has killed about 300,000 in 37 years of his dirty life. He was too ambitious and too proud....[I] hope to see you and your son again. If you or any relative come to Mashhad again, will be very welcome to my house as guest. Yours faithfully, M. Saber."

Despite the animosity that we could see on the T.V. screens night after night after they had taken the American consular staff as hostages, I still remember and treasure the decency and warmth of the Iranians I knew just before the revolution, who favored both the revolution and the very American me. And if I ever do get to Mashhad again, I certainly will look up Mohammad Saber hoseyni, and take him out for *chello kabab* and *chai.*

AFGHANISTAN:

From Mashhad in Iran, the four Brits and I took a bus to Herat, Afghanistan, on August 18, 1978. Herat now is flattened by the Russian bombing, but the Russians were several months from invading when I was there, and Herat still had the slow dusty charm of before the war, with a rather nice mosque and, on its outskirts, a crumbling sand-colored fort built by Alexander the Great when he came conquering in about 330 B.C. I have a photo of me with Keith, Tony and Kathy with this fortress behind us, some scaffolding up on one of its walled towers for repairs. Afghanistan is an arid land where war is often endemic—in 2000 there is a civil war still going on—and the past litters the land with its ancient fortresses and its modern burnt-out tanks, and litters the mind with traditional dogma and the culture of the warrior.

Yet people are very friendly—a smile from me brings out a big beaming smile in them. They seem very content and proud to be Afghanis. No truckling to the foreigner. The older men have wonderful strong faces. In my journal I wrote, "Most men in turbans wrapped around embroidered skullcaps; most women (you see very very few on the streets) wear full covering veils over their heads and faces. You can't see any of their features at all." You can't even tell that these back-draped shapeless figures are women. In Herat and Kandahar few dressed in Western clothing; only in Kabul did you see some women in dresses, with faces and hair uncovered, and men in Western clothes.

In Herat there are lots of "Chai houses," places where you can eat something and drink tea, tea which cost about five Afghanis in their currency, about 15 cents in ours. Once in another country for a while, you think in terms of their country's prices, and so in the Fariz Hotel, where three of us shared a room for 75 cents each, 25 Afghanis per person, you think of it as a modest sum, not the amazingly cheap place those prices would indicate in the USA. The bus to Kandahar, several hundred miles, cost 100 Afghanis ($3). Prices are low here, which means that many Hippies were hanging around, dressing in Afghani garb, smoking dope, and grooving with the natives. Most Hippies returning to Europe from India looked extremely unhealthy—skinny, utterly worn out. This is where I was heading?

But four of the five of us had bad diarrhea already. Only Keith could, as he put it, "fart with confidence." Toilets were our safe havens, and we tried to be aware of where the nearest one of those was at all times. Ramadan was still on, the month-long Muslim holy month where one does not eat or drink during the day, although travelers get a dispensation, but in the evening, besides the tea houses where we could find other travelers to swap tales and information, there was the circus. The circus was very unprofessional, with poor singing, clumsy acrobatics, pathetic belly-dancing, and the best of all, a clown who parodied all of the acts, and the crowd (men only) enjoying him most. We also went to hear music twice. One of the musicians gave me a tambour (like a sitar) and a drum, and I fooled around with it a bit, not well, but the watchers enjoyed my ineptitude.

Even the Army and police were friendly, though they are very tattered and no one seems to be intimidated by them. I went to an Embassy to ask about a visa, and the gate was guarded by a soldier who told me with emphatic gestures I couldn't come in. But I wanted to check on their hours, and so I put my arm around his shoulder and said, "No, it's O.K. I just want to check on something." He did not understand English, but I figured if I was friendly, had my arm over his shoulder, and was taking him with me, he wouldn't (or couldn't) very well shoot me as I walked him toward the back door of the Embassy to check on their visa section's hours. I was right.

During one day, we and several other foreigners went to the Herat Hotel to swim in their pool for a small sum. We went there in a horse-drawn buggy, a *gaudi*. The pool was dirty, and full of young Afghani males who were cooling off in the pool, but being heated up by the several European women who were swimming or lounging around in bikinis. What must these Afghanis think, coming from a society where you don't see any woman who is not in your own family, and then seeing these casual semi-naked white ladies, so at ease with their bodies and with strangers around?

Stranger than Herat was Kandahar. The bus trip there was through barren desert, with small towns circled by walls with domes set side by side, mud-brick houses, and everything dry and brown. But once again, our cheap Hotel Ahmed Shah had a nice swimming pool, with its small cluster of horny Afghani males ogling the foreign women swimmers. People here were even more friendly to us than in Herat, although one evening walking along a dark dirt road, some teenager threw a couple of rocks at us, and I looked at him, and at his smiling father, and I mimed a throat being slashed. The father continued smiling. This is a place where people do kill one another, and after, I realized it is best not to make these fierce gestures, because the Afghanis way out-fierce me. Most adults were very nice, while a lot of kids were asking for "baksheesh" and were annoying at best. And the foreign travelers were an interesting lot. Two Englishmen bicycling around the Middle East preparing to change to motorcycles when they got to India; a couple of Cambridge University students; an

Italian couple who had their baby a couple of months ago in Nepal and who had gone "Indian" in garb and attitudes—a bunch of adventurers seeing the world. My traveling companions were all teachers in England till they decided to go to Australia to work for a while.

In Kandahar there was another circus we went to, with its singing, acrobatics, etc. The circus seems to constitute much of the excitement of Afghani night life. For drinks, ice water mixed with sweet syrup is the common tipple in Kandahar. Then on to Kabul, the capital, by night bus, arriving at dawn. Most hotels I stayed in this trip so far have been foul, with all five of us crammed into one room. Great for saving money, though. Total cost of this first Sabbatical, about 14 and a half months all over the world, cost me a total of $3600 in 1978-9. Mainly it was usually just me crammed into my one hotel room.

In Kabul went to Friend's Hotel near Chicken Street, the main tourist shopping street. The Istambul Restaurant had good *mantu* (meat and onion dumplings) and *awshok* (tomato, leek, and yoghurt dumplings), though in another restaurant, popular with hippies, I got my main dish complete with a big chunk of broken green glass in its midst. Had I swallowed that, my guts would have been badly sliced up. Was this an accident? Was this like a Viet Cong punji stake, meant to harm me as a foreigner? I don't know. When in Kabul I bought a bus ticket to get to Pakistan, the man who sold me the ticket then berated me for the terrible country I belonged to. The usual left-ish diatribe in the usual left-ish language: oppressor, imperialist, blah blah. His English was pretty good, but his Marxist was even better. The newspapers in English here also had articles couched in very Communist language. More than one Afghani told us that they hated this government they felt was imposed on them by the Russians even those the Russians had not yet invaded. One man told me that they were just waiting for Ramadan to be over and then soon they'd get rid of these "Communists" running the show in Kabul.

One day walking near the Presidential Palace, re-named "The People's House" (see what I mean!), I saw a burnt-out tank left in the road near its entrance. I walked over to the gate to see if I could get in to the Palace, but an Army officer motioned for me to stay away. I waved to him, and smiling, kept coming. He unholstered his 45 caliber pistol and cocked it. I motioned to him that I was backing up, and did so. This was not the same callow private soldier that I could intimidate. This officer was nervous and therefore very dangerous to me. He must have been alerted that many Afghanis were not happy with their present government, which of course, is the general Afghani attitude toward any central government.

Besides the couple of burned out tanks near the Presidential Palace, the reminders and the fear of war were apparent. My journal: "Scads of soldiers all over the city [Kabul], and other cities too. Often fixed bayonets and at times automatic weapons, but patched and shredding uniforms." There were lots of German hippies around, and some Italians and French and English. But few Americans. Lots of these travelers had "gone native" with baggy Afghani or Indian trousers and shirts. Once I met a French girl, Brigitte, while getting my Indian visa, and later on she came to my hotel, and we ate at the Istambul Restaurant, and then went over to her hotel. In the courtyard of her hotel sat a circle of stoned Europeans, all smoking stunningly strong hash in a "chillom' (a long hash pipe), or reefers, or in a water pipe provided by the hotel's owner. It was quiet as the chillom made its circle around this group, which I joined, and after each person inhaled deeply of this hash, that person erupted into a most hacking cough, and several of us laughed, then the pipe passed to the next person—deep intent inhale, awful hacking coughing, some laughter, and then on to the next person. I did the same with the same results. My hope for some sex with Brigitte didn't pan out because she began cuddling with some French guy dressed like an Afghani. Before this cuddle, "she wrote a poem for me while we smoked and watched this nearly zero level of activity of these stoned people sitting around in a circle with us in the hotel courtyard."

Not all was zero activity of this sort. Before the four Brits I was with went off to northern Afghanistan, and I was left alone, impatient to head toward India, we all went to the early Moghul Emperor Babur's Gardens, not impressive to someone from the East Coast of America, but because there is some greenery in them, it must seem quite lush to Afghanis so steeped in things arid. I also went to an archelogical museum which then had a special exhibit of artifacts from five ancient civilizations of Afghanistan—lots of lovely sculpture, but none of these five paricular civilizations I had ever heard of. A useful reminder of my and others' vast ignorance of so much of what once was so important to many people in other parts of the world. Most of the Buddha statues in this exhibit had their faces smashed away, a reminder of the Muslim animosity and prohibition toward making human representations. Ignorance and destruction—great combination to sink the past beyond recall.

Another combination usual in traveling in the East: romance and shit. My last day and night in Kabul the manager of my hotel asked me to move into another room, to share it with a cute Spanish girl from Barcelona named Gloria. She was napping when he and I walked into her room. She looked up, looked at the manager, looked at me, grunted an assent, and went back to sleep. While she slept that afternoon I noticed two bedbugs emerge from her pillow and stroll across it.

That night,according to my journal, every hour and a half I had to squat over the extremely public toilet and disgorge my guts both below and above. The hotel was full of Pakistanis who like me were shitting and barfing all night. The sounds! The smells! But embarrassment fades under the impetus of defecation: At one point in the night I left my bed in my and Gloria's room and made it only as far as some plants in front before I was "caught short" as the British say, and, quickly stripping off my bathing suit, I defecated on the garden. All travelers on this trip felt quite open about discussing the loose state of their bowels in front of other travelers of whatever gender, soon after they first meet them. Early the next morning, without preliminaries, despite both of us being still fairly sick, we quickly made love, exchanged addresses, said "good-bye," and I headed over to get the bus to Pakistan. Traveling means lots of good-byes.

We headed east, going through the Khyber Pass, old forts topping several of the cliffs. Passed Shabi Fort, home of the "Khyber Rifles" and understood why the British forces, traveling through this intricately gullied place, so feared the ambushes that often came. At the Afghanistan-Pakistan border, the customs didn't even bother to open my luggage once he heard I was an American, but did catch one young European carrying hash, and took him back into Afghanistan. At one point I started to kid around with some other travelers, and the customs man, who had not bothered to check my luggage earlier, told me to take off my shoe. Which one? I asked. That one. I did, and he felt around inside it, handed it back to me, and said it is O.K. He didn't bother with my other shoe. I think he thought I started to joke around because the tension of me smuggling in something was relieved when he didn't check my luggage. I was just relieved because I was getting closer to India and not having had to shit in my pants so far on the bus trip.

Adventureous Afghanistan inspired a poem:

"Along with the spices wafts the shit down the street. Grey dust and brown smell in this Afghani town of Kandahar swipe at my American nose. Romance? Sure. Men in turbans with guns, women in robes. Mosques. Grapes, purple and royal, sold by candlelight. Under the turbans a shaved scabrous scalp. Sooty fingers paw a vendor's damp glass. The pitch-pipe of flies coats the grapes. Romance needs a washing, but is still romance. But leaky bowels trumpet an ironic blare. Right hand eats chello kebab, left hand wipes my ass."

So many many nations have fought over Afghanistan. Good luck.

PAKISTAN:

I spent only a couple of days in Pakistan, but they sometimes felt like too many.

From Kabul in Afghanistan I took a bus through the Khyber Pass into Peshawar, Pakistan. It was late August and blazingly hot. Peshawar had lovely suburbs on the way in, but I stayed in the center of the city at

Green's Hotel, where I shared a room with Margot, a 22-year-old Australian physiotherapist who had been traveling for seven months east of Afghanistan, and now was heading home. We had met at the border, talked a bit, and I suggested we share a room. Sharing a room with a pretty woman was great for a number of reasons. One, you can present it as a frugal measure, and since many travelers were living on tiny budgets, and even if you had money, it was a point of honor and competition to get the best (for which read the cheapest) prices for things. Two, you could share insights, information, and woes. Three, you might be able to have sex with them. I was pleased because she was pretty.

In our double room, we moved the two beds together till they touched each other's so we could both lie under the one large ceiling fan. Our room was on the roof of the hotel, with a toilet and shower in a small hut outside on the roof. We showered (not together), and then went out to shop, sightsee, and buy bus tickets for Lahore for the following night. Peshawar's market was fascinating, bustling and hectic, exotic turbans and robes galore worn by craggy-looking men, spices and odd smells, the usual and exciting exotic mix.

The next morning we gave each other massages, and went to explore some of Peshawar. We had to go to eleven banks before we found one that would change Margot's American Express traveler's cheques. That's not like it's an unknown bank! That took a lot of time, which was helpful preparation for the rest of my stint in the Indian sub-continent, where banking takes lots longer than in the USA. We also bought *sherbat*, a sweet mixed-fruit syrup, which we took back to the hotel, got drinking water from them, and mixed the water and syrup and drank ourselves silly. Muslims get *sherbat* in heaven; we tried it out here. Not that it is so tasty, but Peshawar was so hot in late August 1978, that even my legs were sweating just sitting around quietly, and drinking even luke-warm anything feels wonderful. I noted in my journal, two specimen of graffiti in a toilet in Green's Hotel: "Shop——store, Aberdeen, South Dakota," and "A man without a woman is like a fish without a bicycle" (a common aphorism, common to both genders, but this was the first place I had ever seen or heard it).

That night, we took the bus to Lahore. We were the only Westerners on this packed bus, but when the soldiers stopped our bus four or five times that night to search for guns and contraband, they ignored us in their search. Ali Bhutto, the ex-Prime Minister, had been put in jail and was going to be executed, so the Army, according to a couple of people on our bus, was afraid of a coup or a revolt by Bhutto's supporters, and soldiers patroling along the roads were seizing any weapons they could find. They would have several people come off the bus, search them, and then the passengers would get back on and we would proceed. Once, they stopped us and took off the bus one of the few women passengers on it, a woman totally covered in black veils and cloak. When she got back on the bus, she said something and everyone laughed. I asked someone what she had said: she had given the soldiers 50 rupees [$5] as "baksheesh" and they let her go without searching her. Had I been in command of the soldiers I would have them even more thoroughly search anyone who would offer money for not searching them! However, this was Pakistan where the soldiers are poor, there is immense and nearly socially acceptable corruption endemic, and Muslim women are creatures whose modesty is deemed sacrosant. The Pakistani soldiers look tough and proud. I wouldn't have been so proud to be among their ranks.

Several times that night I had to throw up, either out of the bus window or when we had stopped. My Afghanistan belly still was not cured. But it was not my belly that was the main problem that night on the bus. It was Margot's body. It proved a powerful magnet for the hands of several Pakistanis on the bus. The first time, Margot turned around and yelled at one of the three men sitting in the seat behind us. In the space between the backrest and the seat, there had been inserted a Pakistani hand which grabbed Margot's bottom. She explained this to me, and then I turned to the Pakistani who had done this and told him this time Margot had yelled at him, but the next time I would deal with him. A warning. Later on that night, Margot yelped again, and turned around and slapped at the men. I turned around and dragged the man over the seat toward me who I had warned before and started screaming at him never to touch "my woman" again. Margot said, "No, it's not him this time. It's this other one!" and so I dropped the first, and grabbed the second one, dragging him over the seat and began screaming at him. At this point naturally the whole bus was in an uproar, the man I grabbed was screaming in panic because I really was furious at him, dragged him about and ripped his shirt a bit, and everyone was trying to make peace. Two different Pakistanis help up their hands and said, "Five fingers." I asked what they meant, and they said, "each is a finger, but each finger is different. Don't blame all Pakistanis for what this man did." But two out of the three in the seat behind me seemed to me and Margot as a plurality. However, I dropped the man back into his seat, figuring that now the whole bus knew of their sins, and they would keep their hands to themselves. Not that Margot was dressed provocatively, but in a society where, as in Afghanistan, most women on the streets are completely covered in fabric, the sight of what is unequivocally a woman can be too enticing for the average guy.

The quiet guy at the end of our seat had gotten off the bus during the night, and so Margot stretched out on her back, lying against my chest, trying to get some sleep. Later I noticed that the third guy behind us, the only one of the three who had not felt her up, now had his head leaning against his arms on the back of our seat, one hand dangling down, circling around toward her breast. I grabbed his hand and sharply pushed it back over the seat. He looked up at me, a little dazed, and slumped back down in his seat. Three out of three. So much for five different fingers.

I began to feel that the middle finger was the way I was feeling about this country.

But the worst was yet to come. We arrived in Lahore about 6 a.m., exhausted, but watching the many cooking fires of people living on the streets, a completely naked bearded holy man strolling along, cattle ambling free, here in the city of Kipling's Kim. At the bus station, there were several men who met the bus who told us that if we wanted to get to India, that at this early hour the border was closed, but at their hotel we could shower, eat breakfast, and then they would get us to the bus for the border. All this for free. We were too tired to be too suspicious of this offer, so we went along with it, and taxied to their hotel with them. Going up the steps to the hotel, there were a lot of men standing on the steps and I got a bad feeling that this is a kidnapping and robbery, Once in the hotel, however, I felt better because there were several other Westerners who didn't look kidnapped.

The spiel was enticing. "The greasy staff made us breakfast, and offered free rubdowns with special oil to take against malaria (horseshit!). Margot and I declined. The idea is to get to massage bodies, and to get people out of their rooms or clothes so as to steal stuff. One Dane [a woman] had $50 in rupees stolen from her passport pouch when she turned her head for two minutes while she was being massaged. Another girl from Iceland told me she had $150 stolen, but probably by an Australian guy who offered to hold it for her." I found these stories out on the train in India while traveling with some others I met at this hotel. But by then we were over the Indian border and so couldn't return to the hotel in Lahore in Pakistan to get the stuff back. The police, I was told, are likely in on this swindle, and so would be worse than useless, just a waste of time. Margot wanted a shower, so I sat in a room with her stuff and my stuff, watching it carefully. I didn't trust these people, even before I heard these stories. After passing through Pakistani customs later that morning, I walked into India, and was so happy to get there, I shared my cookies with the two soldiers guarding their border.

Talking to other travelers throughout my trip, the place most of them disliked the most was Pakistan. I saw why.

INDIA1: KASHMIR, DELHI, AGRA:
Coming overland through Turkey and Iran and Afghanistan and Pakistan, I finally reached India at the end of August 1978 with great

relief. Train to Jammu, then a terrifying 10-hour bus trip (all the Indians and I pleading with the driver to go slower around these mountain bends) to Srinagar, the capital of Kashmir. My first impression? "India seems more familiar to me and sympathetic than does Afghanistan or Iran, although the water buffalo, the saddhus [wandering holy men], beggars, etc. are so different from home and my experience!" Now in 2000, traveling to exotic lands is bound to feel much less exotic than travel in previous centuries. So many photos, films, documentaries, T.V. programs have brought the farthest corners of the world into the center of our living rooms. How strange can anything be since everything in the world is available to us in living color? Surprise is banished by photo-full guide books. No wonder I felt India was familiar. No need to trot out a New-Ager's fantasies that I was a Maharajah in a past life.

In Kashmir, however, I did sample a bit of that maharajah's life. "I rented a houseboat ("B" category) from the Badyeri people. Sixty rupees ($7.50) a day including two meals (whatever I choose to have) and a servant or two. My houseboat is the "Kenya" near Dal Gate on Dal Lake, but it's off on a sluggish branch of the lake. My servant is Bashir." My four-person houseboat was all to myself, with a bedroom, living room, and best of all, a top sundeck where I could (and did) write and watch the lake life of the Kashmiris. The Kashmiris, even then in 1978, hated the Indians, and never felt they themselves were or should be a part of India.

Once, at the Dal Gate where you rowed to on a shikara, the small native paddleboat, to get to land from your houseboat, several of the boatmen were arguing with three older Indians, with a young Israeli girl standing by watching. I asked what was the problem, and the boatmen told me that they would not rent to or take an Indian man to a houseboat with a young foreign girl, because "she would be raped, see." This Israeli girl, Yaeli, had struck up a conversation on a train on the way to Srinagar with these three men and they suggested sharing a houseboat with her to save money. One of these Indians, a chubby inoffensive-looking small man with spectacles, told me he was a doctor, and that sexual molestation was the thing furthest from his mind, but the Kashmiris were adamant. I suggested that she could stay with me, that I had an extra bed on my houseboat. Yaeli said O.K., and one Kashmiri boatman told me he knew that Europeans (all white Americans are often thought of and begin to think of themselves as European after a while out here) could share rooms with the opposite sex and not have sex. I was less certain than he was, but I rowed back with the girl to my houseboat, while the three Indians stood there, very angry, but could do nothing against the prejudices of the boatmen. In my journal, I noted, "Nice! But no sex at all. No attempts." It's not easy to live up to others' high expectations of one.

Dal Lake with its houseboats was one of the classic British summer resorts during the British Raj. Now the British are mostly gone, and this summer of 1978 the monsoon was so bad that much of north India was flooded, and so travel to Kashmir was difficult, therefore making it a very bad season for the houseboat owners with no one to rent them. So for me, the posh life of a "pukka sahib." (Note the slang of the Raj.) My journal of August 31 notes, "Went with Subhan, Bashir's father, by shikara (one other man rowing) around Dal Lake to Nageen Lake and back—five-hour trip (35 rupees counting baksheesh [tip]). Watching women gather the lotus flowers while I lolled about on an overstuffed couch, feeling like a lord among peasants. They all call me "sahib" (pronounced "saab"). Relaxing, writing letters, poetry, journal." Life felt so easy after the overland trip to India.

But dystentery is very common living on Dal Lake. Our dishes and clothing were all washed in the lake, which was filthy. So, along with the posh, the poop—and the "shits" came back. "The ducks creak and dip on Dal Lake in Kashmir. They'll eat anything. Here in this packaged paradise, the lotus spreads its multifoliate pinkish thighs while a scarf of toilet paper twines debonairly round its stem. A shikara comes alongside my houseboat and a shrunken face offers to sell me a lotus. Behold the jewel. I decline. Dal Lake is sluggish. Cascades of water flow only from household toilets. Two men fish from the neighboring houseboat. There is something

here. I drop a poetic line into this lake and a turd nuzzles it and nibbles."
Disgusting words? You should see the water.

Disgust often differs from culture to culture. In southern India you eat
with your fingers, but don't try it at "The Four Seasons." In Puri in Orissa
state, fisherman all defecate openly on the beach as people amble by.
Disgust can be muted and transmuted by good humor: "The sun should
be going down soon, as I see from the roof-sundeck of my houseboat, and
the cooking fires and toilets pour out their redolent funes, the ducks gaggle and the hawkers haggle (I traded my Navy khaki jacket, a sweater, and
40 rupees for a hand-embroidered, flowered, dark green Kashmiri jacket
yesterday." I needed to lighten my pack, and so trading and giving away
stuff was helpful.

Getting rid of stuff, but piling up new sights and experiences.
"Yesterday I joined hundreds of Muslims (at the invitation of one) in long
lines of prayer at Hazaratbal, a white mosque containing a hair from the
beard of the Prophet Mohammed. It was the sacred last Friday of
Ramadan. This fellow took me with him in one of the many lines of
devout men as we all bowed and prayed for an hour to the recited prayers
outside the mosque on the grass. Exciting! Then I got into the mosque,
but one person was offended by my immodest shorts, so I left. No animosity, but some suspicion and curiosity at an infidel being there." As far
as I could tell, I was the only non-Muslim or European there. To this day,
I regret that when all these long lines of hundreds of devout men bowed
down in prayer, I remained in this line not bowing. Later on, in a mosque
on the island of Lombok, Indonesia, when I was in a prayer line, I remembered this, and bowed with the rest.

Kashmir is very Muslim, which is the main reason they don't feel
Indian. They also don't look Indian: "Kashmiri men often have Hitlerian
mustaches, like hair running out of their noses. Not as smiling or as
openly friendly as Afghanis. Men often have thin, axe-like faces, which are
emphasized by their narrow mustaches." I did go to the ruins of an
ancient Buddhist temple, but my best times were traveling on these lakes

in Mogul and Muslim Srinagar, where the call of a muezzin to prayer penetrated my houseboat's walls several times a day.

The Moguls, the conquerors of India before the British, were originally from Afghanistan, and like all desert people, loved the sound and smell of water flowing, and loved gardens, and in Srinagar on Dal Lake there are islands with gardens on them. After a day alone and paddling my own shikara, I wrote REFLECTIONS ON WATER IN KASHMIR.

I

"As I step into my shikara, it wobbles on the water.
I stand straddle-footed and steady it, then sit,
then paddle straight along Dal Gate
around other houseboats stuffy with comfort,
stuffed with last year's things, solid, grave stuff.
You can sink in these chairs like a stone.
Shikaras pass all day, and the houseboats never shiver.
When I shift my weight, my shikara lurches, leans.

II

The sun can spread its arms wide here on the open
lake. Too wide. I pull the bill of my cap lower and squint.
Nothing close to help my words bounce back with a softer
answer. Space stretches his feet to the mountains.
The mountains stretch over the skin of the lake
along with clouds, single trees, a houseboat, me. Here the water's depth
may be ten feet. Weeds wiggle and twist in brownish Dal
Lake. But the water's height is in miles! Mountains, clouds.
The cloud's height seems easier to measure than the lake's bed.
A fish quivers easefully through these mountains
as though they were water. My paddle's smack would show
that these mountains are not real. I drop my paddle
through the lake's skin, dig up spilling water, and paddle on.

III

After Nishat Bagh, the Gardens of Pleasure, comes

Shalimar Bagh, built by a Mogul emperor, who
like all Arabs loved the sound of water clapping hands. Huge sums
of money here ran like water through his fingers. Unfocused dew
is innocent, ignorant, but here worldly water is put through her paces,
channeled, quantified, made to answer to man's desires.
Dew comes and goes before we know it, but this garden channel traces
linear beauty, and before the uncurved answer tires,
the Mogul had fountains made, with spider webs of water
curving with an atom's penumbra, balancing the straight with curved.
All planned—answers suited to desert desire. The spider web of
spray caught
a comfortable answer about wet. Even water in shallow cement beds
served
to reflect God's mountains and man's desire, but it's stiff underneath
the shimmer.
Order's good in a disordered world. And vice versa. Learn to be a deep-
water swimmer.

IV

It's cool and calm at the Shalimar Gardens, but the dropping sun
demands
a move. I paddle out on the lake that mirrors what it has to,
cross under bridges, slide down channels to Nageen Lake. Slicing
its mirror to the center, I dive off my shikara. Weeds way under
touch me tentatively. The water is brown. I keep
my eyes closed. My lungs tell me where the surface is. I shatter
the lake as I come up to where I breathe and live, but
the lake soon grows a new skin of shimmering mountains and trees.
I dive again and again, in all directions, and the lake grows itself again
each time. Paddling off, I control my shikara's path on the lake's
unmarked face
which, like a poem about it, closes unscarred, unseamed, after the pad-
dler has gone."

My journal of that same day adds detail about the places and activities, but subtracts much of the significance. "Sept. 2[1978]— Paddled off in my own shikara around Dal Lake to the island with the 4 chenar trees— dull, dry, sleazy island—and had my tea and bread there. Then on to the Nishat Gardens planted by the moguls (Arab rulers) of 100 years ago. Invited to hit a few balls at Cricket by some Indians practising. Managed to knock a few around. [I remember that hitting balls with a cricket bat was harder than it looked.] Then off to Nageen Lake where I swam [off my shikara], had a beer [on the lawn] at the "elite" Nageen Club (2 rupees temp. membership), and then paddled home. [I remember they sold beer there only to Europeans, because it was then illegal to sell alcoholic beverages to locals, so I was told, this being a Muslim state.] 10 hours! My ass hurt from the hard seat [on my shikara], lots of sunburn, and a bit sore from paddling."

Poem, journal entries, and memory shuffle together to approach what this day was about. I just wrote, "what this day was all about," but then deleted the word "all" because the smells of the dusty trees on the chenar island, the flavors of the warm tea and crusty bread, the sun blaring down on the dry grassy lawn of the Club—all these are absent, and even if the words were there, the thing itself is too evanescent and fragile to wrap up in words. We do what we can with the things and experiences themselves translated into the foreign language of mere language.

Arabs of the desert overestimate the delights of Kashmir because here is abundant water, and in their deserts there is little. But to someone who lives in the wet northeast of the USA, the gardens here seemed less lush than damp, even after the monsoon rains had hit. In another place I mention the Shalimar Bagh more admiringly: "long rows of flowers, flowers in niches under the waterfall."

But mostly I remember the sound of water flowing, so delicious to the desert dweller's soul.

I climbed the high Satyrachaya hill from which I could see all of Dal Lake and my smidgen of a houseboat and the town of Srinagar and the tiny tree-topped island isolated in the center of the lake, itself backed by high hills. A photo I took supplies me now with details. Dal was not the only lake in the area. I took a local bus to Mansbal Lake nearby, and had an interesting conversation there with the top Police Inspector and the Examining Magistrate of the district who walked up to me while I was having a drink at the Mansbal Rest House and looking over the lake. After asking me where I was from—the usual question in India ("Tell me, what is your country?")—the second question they asked me was "Tell me, is it true that the Jews run America?" This led to an interesting discussion (my short answer was "No") and from there we went on to American corruption and judicial methods. They were both very well educated and seemed like decent men, but this was a Muslim state, and the animosity that Muslims feel for Jews nowadays is not confined to the Middle East.

The Kashmiris, though they disliked Indians and did not consider themselves Indians as several of them told me, seemed friendly toward me. Several wished that the British still ran India, one reason for which was that the British vacationed in Kashmir more than did the Indians, and so their houseboats were rented more often. Very much business people here. Fending off sellers, I wandered around in the town of Srinagar, though mostly I stayed on my houseboat, reading, writing, and relaxing. Once I went off by bicycle with Subhan, Bashir's father, around to one arm of the lake—almost a river because here the water in the lake flows—where all the British houseboats used to be before 1947 and India's independence from Britain. Not much of a view from here, but a pleasant spot.

I had heard that Gulmarg in Kashmir had good hiking in beautiful alpine scenery, so set off by bus to see. It was a touristy place, with lots of people trying to rent you horses to carry you up on the mountain trails. One of them was so persistent and kept blocking me with his horse from getting to one of the very small hotels while he reeled off his spiel, that I told him I would drag him off his horse if he kept getting in my way.

Grumbling, he left. After getting a very no-frills room in this chilly place (and at night it felt freezing here with not enough blankets), I started up one of the small mountains on foot. In a meadow, enclosed by pine trees, with the sound of horse's bells and shouts way off in the distance, I had a spiritual epiphany. Sitting in the meadow, alone, just being there, I felt that when I die, if nature here continues going its own natural way, my death and everyone else's death is not bad. Death itself is not bad. It was not a depressing feeling at all. All of nature seemed fine and right as it was.

I tried to capture some of this in a poem called ABOUT A MEADOW IN GULMARG:

I

"Hearing: bees and flies mixed, crow caws and croaks, a little wind beneath, silence beneath that, and above all.

Poem: the above words read (even read well) disappearing into a less resonant silence.

II

"Smelling: pine the way it always smells and with its smells the other places it smelled like this. Pine and some grasses, some horse dung from the path, and dust. And some flowers, but I'm not certain.

Poem: some paper does smell and some ink, but not this.

III

Seeing: greens, from light-struck green to blackened green, a beige path with brownish-green droppings on it, some orange and fewer bits of purple-blue of forget-me-nots or bluebells (it doesn't matter here), grey cloud blotch on blue sky, darker grey rock and one tree changing to yellow (it's fall but it doesn't matter here) off-center.

Poem: rows of black words on squared white paper.

IV

Feeling: sun on face as hot, rough stump rasp on ass and legs.

Poem: words don't braille on smooth paper.

V

Tasting: nothing to do with this meadow on a mountain.

Poem: nothing to do with this meadow on a mountain."

And another poem, IN A MOUNTAIN MEADOW IN GULMARG, KASHMIR:

"Why does this silence here say more than other silences? Even punctuated by crow croaks and bees, this silence flows full. Silence told me nothing matters, especially me. I sat in this mountain meadow happy, listening long." This silence helped me hear the world, and I was grateful for this absence which allowed me into the presence. Religious thoughts sometimes come on tiptoe.

My houseboat servant Bashir and I sauntered off to the ruins of an ancient Buddhist temple and then "walked back along a lovely stream-cum-culvert for irrigation water." I remember the walk because Bashir told me he was unmarried, but of course when his father and elder brother chose a wife for him, he would marry her. He liked that arrangement more than he would of choosing a bride for himself. He felt that a marriage arranged by his family was preferable, because they were older, therefore wiser than he is. And maybe he's right. About three weeks on this houseboat was enough. I was rested and since the floods in India were draining, I thought I'd head down to New Delhi.

By bus down to Jammu, and then with two Italian girls, Agneli and Gabriella, by overnight train to Delhi, "sleeping in the luggage racks because we couldn't find the rail car with our reserved sleepers." Ended up in a cheap hotel (30 rupees per night) near Connaught Place or Circus, the central tourist area of New Delhi, with streets radiating out from it as from a wheel's hub. Plunged into big-city life, with hamburgers and "2 chocolate shakes at The Parlour (good) and next day, steak and veg there." Were the steaks beef from a sacred cow? Haven't a clue. Met a psychiatrist from Maui in Hawaii, who was here "to study sexy Tantric philosophy of guru Raj Neesh in Poona." Little did I think that I would end up for two and a half months at his ashram also.

The next day I went on a day tour of Delhi. Usually this is a good way to get a feel for the sights in general and which are worth going back to for a longer stop. We saw the Red Fort, and I wrote, "The guidebooks say that Shah Jahan built this seraglio with this water course, mosaics and mirrors. But his hand touched no brick nor mortar. Men the color of brick and mortar built it, whose names are buried under the tile. Little is left of the inlaid mosaics, the color of what they once were. Fewer mirrors, small, inlaid, and diamond-shaped, reflecting the Shah's pleasure in his building, remain. The rest a blank brick wall. This wall, this building, this poem. All also mirrors."

I was in India for about about five and a half months in 1978 and 1979, and for long visits also in 1982 and 1993-4. Absolutely exotic and absolutely annoying. In 1993 all the rug merchants from Kashmir had congregated down in Delhi near Connaught Circus. No tourist would go to Kashmir because India was fighting to keep Muslim Kashmir as a part of Hindu India. So the rug merchants came to Delhi to sell rugs. Constantly was I being asked if I'd like to buy a Kashmiri carpet till if you see someone approach you with a carpet over their soulder, you shout out, "NO!" and turn out of their path.

But most of the beautiful buildings and monuments of northern India are Mogul and therefore Muslim. The Red Fort itself. In 1982, I wrote of a mosque here: WASPS AND WORDS:

"Behind the curlicue paths of the Arabic script on the sunstripped front of this mosque in Delhi are the scalloped indentations inside the inside arch, like teethmarks in a ripe pear, and pendant from these indentations are nests of wasps, teeming, slowly filling the arches, ignoring the words of love.

Pigeons, urban doves, dung from the ledges of the cathedral in Firenze. Heroes on horseback, bronze, brass, are made fearful pale by these plucky doves less than interested in talk of Christian love."

Indian Delhi and Italian Florence, Muslim and Christian, words of love and religion too rarely dilute the disdain, even hatred, one group feels for another. In this big mosque in Delhi, you can climb up the minaret and on some of the high levels you can walk around the minaret outside on sloping slippery red sandstone—no railing to keep you from slipping and shattering on the courtyard below. In 1978 I walked around it without too much fear. In 1993 I remember feeling very scared to do it. It seemed so exposed. I did it anyway because I thought if I didn't I would feel a coward. Once again, machismo triumphs over good sense.

Delhi also has the very high Quntab Minir, a large minaret standing solo and isolated, and to give the Hindus their due, the Birla Hindu Temple among many others. The cremation sites of Gandhi and of Nerhu, and "the Mogul tomb which is like the Taj Mahal except it's reddish." All things we see are compared with something else so we can connect the world to what we already know.

In 1993 almost as soon as I got to Delhi, I got diarrhea and felt in general awful and weak. This on top of the monsoon rains which flooded the streets and greyed the skies. This on top of the airport official money-changer who tried to give me the wrong number of rupees for my dollars. My plane had arrived very late at night, and all the passengers were exhausted. His receipt was accurate for me (because I changed a one hundred dollar bill, which made the math pretty easy), but the actual cash given me was wrong, so I counted the money out carefully in front of him, handed him back the wrong amount he had given me, and told him to give me the correct amount. This I had to do three times! The man in front of me told me he didn't even count the money given him. Weariness, dealing with a different currency, worried over baggage and hotels and transport—these would let this cheating moneychanger rake in the rupees for himself. Bad first impression of India for the tired tourist.

First impressions may be even more shocking. Leaving out the obvious shock of the poverty and the beggars, there are also the betel-nut chewers. I wrote in 1978, "At first I thought they were bloodstains in the street. Traffic is worse than I thought, I thought. Or murders. Delhi's crime rate was soaring. T.B. perhaps. Non-pasturized milk. I grew suspicious of what I put in my tea. But no, it was just spittings from this red betel nut everyone chews till their teeth look like cannibals' and the streets look like war. This stuff is wrapped in a green leaf and can be mixed to your taste. Sweet or sour, or in between. It reminds me of death, of life." I've tried chewing betel nut mixed with lime and ash— once, one guy mixed some for me, and a whole crowd and he were laughing as I screwed up my face in total distaste, and kept spitting till finally out came the whole leaf, and still I kept spitting. A great hit with the crowd.

Being the center of a crowd in India happens all the time, and generally is very annoying. There's almost never any privacy for a foreigner in India. You are the circus come to town! In 1978, I wrote, "Just by stopping, I collect a crowd in India or Nepal. So this is what fame is? My concentration leaks away through their eye holes, ear holes. They all ask me the same questions: how is it to be you? I feel I'm in a zoo. (Ambiguous.)" It's the same in China. If you ever thought it would be wonderful to be famous, go to India and you'll probably find that you do what many celebrities here in the USA do: wear sunglasses to get some privacy, and often flee your fans.

Most celebrated is the Taj Mahal south in Agra. Coming upon it after walking up some steps, I could only utter, "Wow!" I worried that my reaction would be: "Oh, just like its photos." But it is gorgeous, although in the years from 1978 till 1993 it developed a brownish tinge in places where once it had been so clean and white. In 1978 I wrote TAJ MAHAL:

"Needlemarks in night's sheet prick me toward poems about this light building. Taj Mahal. White shining. No moon but night vision spurred by stars that flashlights stab at and confuse. I stumble after the attendant shined at my shoes, shut his light. Star vision is low but never shut. The Taj is dead love living.

Down in the basement the real bodies lie. Nothing is dead in the cenotaphs upstairs where tourists still go. Shining. Outside in the garden (the world writes poems too) fireflies twinkle, star tourists come down to this world's star."

Another time at the Taj, I tried to tie together some of the ugliness and beauty of India together, prompted by the very human cough of the guard of all this exquisite place. THE COUGH:

"In the mausoleum of the Taj Mahal the guard coughs and the cough resonates like a leopard's purr, an organ, the sound opening, continuing, a note aloft, profound.

From Agra to Jaipur the train is trailed by fireflies speckling all our clothes with black dots. The sparks from the coal-burning engine.

Rajastani peasants, faces of mud, clothing color of spices, smelling of spices, smelling of mud, mud in the cracks of their heels, cracks like lightning bolts connecting ground and sky.

The strong sweep of the vulture circling, the energy of the vulture dining. A bit of dead buffalo like an opera cloak: black outside, sharp red silk inside.

By the graves of the lovers Shah Jahan and Mumtaz Begum the guard coughs and the sound fills the dome like water running, fading, indivisible."

I stayed at the Taj the whole day, except for a short break to see Agra's Red Fort, also lovely with its audience halls and small marble mosques, and the chambers where Shah Jahan, the Mogul builder of the Taj, was imprisoned but could see out across the Jamuna River to his wife's white Taj tomb. In 1978 there were thousands of folks wandering around the gardens at the Taj, and because it is such a wonder, it's no wonder. Truly a marvel.

In July 1993, I also spend a couple of days here, and noticed some other things.

TODAY'S TAJ:

"The hawks sweep over the Taj Mahal
while the rickshaw drivers circle round
the tourist. The hawk seems more noble
though need is naked in both.
Brown drivers stick fast, beak with sounds.

Innards of red sandstone hide behind
white marble on two top turrets.
White marble is grey, beige, brown.
As feet wear down the flooring
small stones emerge from the marble.

Around the frames of doorways words
in Arabic flow and sweep in a design.
Bright red sarees stain the photos of tourists.
Birds too poise, preen, and warble.
What one calls love, another calls whoring.

One bird tocks like the hours marking.
The vulture shows us the meat
we're made of, the red beneath
the white. The rickshaws and the birds
wheel around the Taj with insistent calls."

Insistent are the rickshaw wallahs, desperate to get your custom. In Agra they are all desperate to to take you to the marble factories, because, as one admitted to me, they get a kickback for every tourist they snare. My journal of 1978 notes, "They take you even if you say "no." I got out of several rickshaws when this happened."

That is not only scam in Agra. In 1993 I stayed in a nice hotel for several days, and as I usually do, gave my valuables (passport, money, traveler's cheques, and credit cards) to the manager to hold in his safe. I always get a detailed receipt, but while you can count cash and cheques, you cannot count if your credit card has been used. Your passport and other cheques have your signature, and someone at my hotel forged my name and charged me for $225 U.S as the hotel's bill, although I had paid them in cash. By the time I had gotten home almost a year later and found this debit, it was too late to appeal. My broker sent three letters to the Indian

bank that cashed the cheque to see the signature, but no answer from
them. I became suspicious when I took my valuables out out the manager's safe to change some money, and found some slight alteration from
my habit of putting things back in the pouch the same way always. I mentioned it to the manager and he denied several times that anyone had
touched them, until I insisted and then he said, "Oh, yes, it must have
been the other manager who needed to inventory all valuables when he
took over the duty." To both the managers I had blabbed that I would be
away from home for a year, and so they figured it would be too late to
catch the forgery then. One rickshaw driver had told me that the manager
was bad at this hotel, but everyone seemed so friendly, I chalked up his
comment to perhaps low kickbacks from the hotel. He was right. Now I
feel I cannot entrust my credit cards to the manager's safe. Too unsafe.
$225 per lesson in distrust. But this was the only time in all my travels
that this scam happened. Do not trust The President Hotel, Fatehabad
Road, in Agra!

Touristed India is more full of pleading, and Agra is its heart. In 1978,
I wrote, "Sahib, hello.Come and see some rugs. Some wooden carvings.
Some paper mache. Costs you nothing to look. Come see the factory
where they're made. Beautiful paper mache. Objects of paper mache."

"Sahib, baksheesh." The motion of putting food in the mouth. Tilt of
head, scrunch of mouth. Give. But it costs you nothing to look. He holds
up a twisted hand. He points to no feet. Something for me to buy. In
India see the factory where they're made."

India produces this poverty, where some poor parents deliberately
deform their child, because at least a badly crippled beggar can more likely
get money from a horrified and pitying Indian. But India produced other
objects of horror and pity and beauty. Fatehpur Sikri is an old abandoned
Mogul city near Agra, an empty red sandstone city with few tourists walking its hot open courtyards. Horror and pity at all the work done by so
many over-worked underfed people for such a short time for this city to be
lived in. Barren and beautiful, a reminder of how the powerful Moguls are

now gone. It makes you think in such cliches. India demands big generalizations, but with now a billion pople, anything you say about it, has some truth to it. What a confusing hectic place!

INDIA 2: VARANASI, BOMBAY, CALCUTTA:

On the way from Agra to Varanasi, once known as Benares, I took a train to Jhansi, then bus to Chatapur. All Indian trains were steam-driven, and so at the end of each train trip, you were covered with little black dots of greasy ash, which, when you brushed yourself off, left long adherent smears of black on your clothes and face. The black smoke coated your clothing and your lungs. At Chatapur, I was walking around with two Tasmanian guys when suddenly I felt like someone had held a lighted cigarette to the back of my hand. It was the painful bite of a blister fly, and it looked and felt just like a burn.

Lust is supposed to burn, and the archeological center of Hindu lust is at Khajuraho, where Asoka built many temples famous for their erotic sculptures. My journal of October 1978, however, noted that these "erotic scenes are in the minority." The hottest thing here was the weather. I remember the blistering sun made walking around a hardship, but like a good dutiful traveler and tourist, I trudged along these "elaborately carved medieval sculptures" while a photo of me shows my shirt all drenched in sweat.In many temples in Nepal, the gods and mortals are copulating and/or performing intricate oral sex, in order, so I've read, to show the human connecting physically and therefore symbolically and spiritually with the divine, or because (I've heard this too) the god of lightning is upset by all this hard-core porn and so stays away from and won't strike any temple with such immodest carvings.

From Khajuraho, I went to Mohola, but couldn't get the train because it was "jammed solid with people going to a festival (the roof of each train car was lined solid with people on top.)" Finally a later train and a bus and I arrived in Varanasi, now traveling with a Chinese guy, Robert, from Hong Kong. We stayed in the New Imperial Hotel, its name belieing its

cheap price of 7 ½ rupees per night. We were in the section most packed
with people, like rush hour in a geriatric facility where everyone is on
amphetamines. "Bustling" doesn't do the energy there justice. Almost hysterical it seemed. There were Krishna effigies up in the streets, musicians
playing, cows and beggars laying, purposeful bicyclists with great loads on
their bikes, and unpurposeful cows, usually relaxed and bovinely looking
for fruit peels underfoot or fruit in vendors' carts, but at times swinging
their heads dangerously, knocking into people and being smacked back.
Cows are sacred in India, but they still get poked and hit hard when they
try to swipe bananas. No problem about recycling here: I got used to
throwing away paper food wrappings into the street because very soon
along came a cow or a dog or a water buffalo to eat it.

Red betel juice stained many men's mouths—these *paan* shops are all over
India, selling this custom-made sweet or sour mixture wrapped in a green leaf
and inserted into the mouth. When I inserted one of these into my mouth, I
finally had to spit it all out. Phooey—too sour! "Lots of rickshaws—few cars.
Men wear straight pigtail of long hairs at the back of their heads to show
they're religious Hindus," notes my journal. "A pushy place." Someone told
me the pigtail was so that the gods can pull you up to heaven by it. You
always hear many different reasons for any one custom.

Life is harsh in Varanasi. I wrote, "In Varanasi, India's holiest city, I
took a bicycle rickshaw. The driver has elephantiasis of one leg. He needs
me to exploit his need. At the station in Mohoba, there is a shoeshine man
who only has one leg." Bizarre. Ironic. The worst is it's true.

One afternoon, Robert and I were resting in our hotel beds when came
a knock at our door. Two men, well-dressed, asked us for our passports
and visas. I had heard of so many scams, and fake policemen, that I asked
them for their identification. They smiled and said they didn't have any on
them. I said, "I'll show you my identification when you show me yours."
They said they'd be back. Later, there was another knock on the door.
There they were again. They presented their I.D.s and asked me to come
down to the lobby with them. I went down, and saw there were several

burly men, all much better dressed than I was, watching me. Their leader, clearly an important man based on their deference to him, asked me for my passport. I asked him for his I.D. first. He smiled and produced it. I then produced my passport—my visa had not been overstayed. Their hopes were dashed. I told the leader of this group that ordinarily I'd show my passport to anyone in the street, but not to anyone who demanded it without identification himself. We ended this session with great joviality and friendliness all around. I was being proper and adhering to the rules; they understood and respected that.

"Everyone wants to show you to a factory or store where you can buy brocade or silk or a sitar.

We met two Indians who seemed very friendly, and we were surprised they invited us to tea later on without trying to sell us anything. Our faith in India was redeemed! We [Robert Chu and I] showed up at the address, and it turned out to be a carpet shop where they started to make their pitch. We looked at each and smiled. Friendship without salesmanship? No hope here." I also went to "one of the corniest movies ever in Hindi about 2 lost brothers, buried treasure, singing and dancing, etc." After having been to several other Hindi movies, their depths of corniness can not be imagined by someone in the West. It embarrassed me to be sitting in the movie theatre where a little wink or an over-acted lasciviously bulging eye can reduce the theatre's patrons to a roar of delighted hysteria.

One of the main embarrassments of traveling in India, or Asia generally, is having diarhhea. At this point I had the industrial-strength professional type—amoebic dystentery. In Varanasi "I went to Dr. Chowdery and got a prescription for Terramycin which killed the things that had kept me shitting for 2 months. I had Leyden crystals in my stool which meant I had had amoebic dystentery." Besides the antibiotics, Doctor Chowdery (who charged me $1.25 for the complete visit) told me that for a while I should just eat curd and tea. Curd is yoghurt, and a common food in India. I used to eat in the Aces New Deal Natural Food Restaurant. There were often cows hanging out by its door, so it must be natural. A bovine truck stop. Milk, when it is drunk by itself, is almost always served boiling to kill the germs or T.B.

Many Indians, especially in Varanasi, instead of boiling water for purifying it, simply take a healthy slug of the Ganges (*Ganga*) River as an early morning eye-opener. The most touristic places in Varanasi are the Bathing Ghats and the Burning Ghats. These Bathing Ghats (wide steps down to the Ganges) are where the living and devout men and women bath each day, brush their teeth, gargle, and splash about. The Burning Ghats are where they cremate the dead, and dump the ashes into Mother Ganges. Infants, particularly holy people, and some others are dropped into the river without being burnt. So bits of bodies, garbage, dead dogs, etc. go into the water just a short few yards from where people are rinsing their mouths. Gargling with someone's Aunt Arsha doesn't sound like fun to me. Neither time I was in Varanasi did I bathe in holy Ganga although it is usual for me to dip into some of the local customs.

Varanasi is the ideal city for a Hindu to die in. Lots of merit. Lots of temples. The Durga (Monkey) Temple has scads of monkeys scampering around it, and one of them whipped my cap off my head and scurried up to the temple roof. A man who worked there went up and retrieved it for me, and I tipped him. It could well be a business between man and monkey. Wonder how they split the tip? "Also saw Sri Annapurna Temple— incredible—scholars and holy men reading their scriptures, pilgrims ringing bells to summon the gods, and throwing water or sweets or money at gods' statues." It all looks and sounds like chaos, but all are working toward many individual purposes. "Indians can say "yes" when "yes" doesn't answer the question, and can indicate direction by a vague wave which indicates 180 degrees of direction." To say nothing of that side-to-side head waggle which looks like a "no" to us, but means "yes."

But there's no doubt about what happens at VARANASI'S BURNING GHATS:

"This is where all the bodies are brought. White wraps male, and red female. Holy men, children, people with diseases cannot be burnt, but must be dropped into the Ganges tied to a stone. But these are for burning.

They lie, stretched out, the only quiet things in this fire-flickering scene. Even the Ganges breathes more. And while Untouchables build the wood criss-cross, and the family buys some sacred flame, they wait, tense is it, or stretching as they awaken is it?

When they're put on their pyre, logs are put on them, wooden weight that only burning will free them from. They burn like logs, charring and reducing to this flame that enlightens this city.

One pyre was too short, and while a worker was poking an adjacent pyre, he almost stepped on a foot, only a little burnt (the legs and the rest were close to cinders), a corpse foot pressed to the ground, and sometimes tapping—impatiently was it, trying to push off was it, or trying to keep some physical connection with the earth was it? (I think it was successful.)"

The families of the corpses stand around and watch the cremations, while we tourists have to be on the river to watch the bathing and the burning, although "guides" will, naturally for a price, take you up to above the ghats where you can watch and smell the cremations. I was told that the corpse's eldest son is supposed to break the corpse's skull once much of the burning is done, both to free his father's spirit from its earthly confine, and to spare people the sight and sound of the boiling skull bursting brains all over the onlookers.

In 1993 I eased myself into the hurly-burly of Varanasi by staying at a quiet tourist hotel in the outskirts, and taking the tourist row at dawn on the river to watch the bathing. Even wandering around by myself around the ghats and in the city it seemed calmer in 1993 than in 1978. The beggars still lined the approaches to the ghats, their pleadings still with the same stylized gestures of outstretched arms and agonized faces. You either give to all or to none, which may prevent envy and riots. I discovered, though you can't do it at these too-public places, that the best way to give to beggars in a city you may stay some time in, is to give only to blind beggars. They don't know who you are, and so cannot rush at you for alms the next time they see you.

Varanasi, the holy Hindu city of death, will never run out of customers.

Bombay, another great Indian city, had less attraction for me. The first time I got there in February 1979, "I left there immediately for Lonavla, where the Karla Caves are. Hewn out of solid rock, carved with Buddhist bas-reliefs. Spent the night in Lonavla." Ho-hum, another Buddhist ruin. However, not all was mere tourism. "Spent evening with Connie, a very pretty German girl. Had shoes and sneakers fixed by shoemanker. Sold my duty-free whiskey and cigarettes (paid $9.50 and got back 180 rupees)." Indian shoemakers can do anything with old shoes, and while a shoemaker in New York City charges only a little less than an orthopedic surgeon, those shoemakers in India are amazingly cheap. I've several times over the years sat under a tree while a shirtless old dhoti-dressed man, sitting also under this tree—everything here in in the open—works away sedulously over my worn-out sneaker. And as far as selling the whiskey and cigarettes, this is common practice among travelers by plane into Burma and India. Most of India was "dry" in a liquor sense, but many richer people wanted your duty-free stuff only obtainable from travelers who act like semi-smugglers. You can ask a rickshaw man to help you sell it; once in Patna, coming down from Nepal, I just drove around with the cigarettes and whiskey on my lap in the open rickshaw, and a man in a car asked if he could buy it. If people want something, prohibitions on it only raise its price.

In June I spent some more time in big Bombay, going to movies and eating Chinese food as a vacation from the Indian variety (or lack of variety). I stayed in an ashram's boarding house, in tiny cubicles, but was with foreigners and it was cheap in this expensive city. I learned of this boarding place when I proposed to an Australian doctor soon after meeting her that we find a hotel and go and make love. She agreed, and knew of this place. She was flying back to Australia late that night but we had several hours together trying to be quiet in our little cubicle. Life and sex were quite casual on this Asian trip before the terror of AIDS.

Besides movies (many) and sex (less), there are always museums.

IN THE BOMBAY MUSEUM:

"Downstairs in the Gents', I saw a rat and a roach fight, or rather the roach ran, the rat attached to his leg. The rat was tiny and the roach was big for a roach. But it seemed so improbable, we all forgot our bowels and watched this struggle, our money on the rat.

In the Bombay museum upstairs, in the Tibetan section, there were aprons and skullcaps of human bones. From another room, Durga, Hindu earth mother, glares at another of her skewered victims. From top to bottom, through all the shades of the real, in this museum the persistence of our dust." All religions are grounded on the fact of our deaths.

In 1979, going up from Bombay to the famous caves of Ellora, like the Karla Caves carved by hand out of solid rock except much more ornate, with Hindu, Buddhist and Jain carvings, reliefs and statues, and then to the Ajanta rock-caves with their paintings from 2nd century B.C. to 7th century A.D., I wrote also of the Muslim Moguls: BIBI KA MAQBARA:

"A tour of Aurangabad and Ellora's rock-cut cave
takes in the Bibi ka Maqbara, designed to imitate
Taj Mahal, and built, by Aurangzeb's son, for his mother.
The Taj Mahal, also for love, of a king for his wife.
Love. Ah, love. After a death, to authenticate
your love with beauty. Like Michaelangelo's slave,
the temples in Ellora struggle out of solid stone
for love of god. And for beauty. One follows the other
as did these Mogul emperors, as death follows life,
as did these loves, one for a lover, one for a crone,
follow. Our tour bus follows beauty.
We're here out of love, boredom, curiosity, duty,
to see that with even love and beauty we cannot save."

The reason I made this trip to these caves in June 1979 was I couldn't get an Egypt Air flight, for which I had bought a ticket in Bangkok, out to Egypt for three weeks, so how to spend these weeks? These caves, and then back to the Raj Neesh ashram, and maybe some few more days in Bombay going to films and eating Chinese food sounded good for these weeks of delayed flying. For a few days after I heard of the flight unavailability, I hung around Bombay trying to get a stand-by, but then realized I could use these three weeks for someting better than being on the phone or on line every day. Same thing happened in Belo Horizonte, Brasil, in 1987— no bus up north for ten days, so went somewhere I could get a ticket for rather than hanging aound a big tiresome city.

Near Aurangabad, northeast of Bombay a couple of hundred kilometers, is "Daulatabad Fort, the most brilliantly defended fortress I've ever seen or heard of. Hate like Hell to have to capture it (the only way was through seige, which did work)."

Easier to try to capture it in words: DAULATABAD FORT:
"At the top of Daulatabad Fort, Aurangzeb took his summer pleasure,
his cool sherbat defended by hard rock and cold steel,
his rich silk robe waved by the breeze far above the hot still plain.
No enemy could take this fort. He took precautions without measure:
Seven walls, snake-filled moat, poison nails
in a dark passage (but the wheel
of time rolled on and flattened him,
through thick walls as though up a broad lane,
through the dark to light-hearted emperor
steady coming, his war drum unerring,
beating steady, timed in a measure slowly increasing
to match faster throb of Aurangzeb's blood.
One attacker, two futile assaults gaining only death,
enlisted time to help in his seige,
whose rattle of bones against the skin on the drum
breached the walls, and Aurangzeb, hearing,

admitted defeat, his palace of white marble melting
to his tomb beneath "a heap of mud"
where this, the greatest of the Mogul emperors,
his fort and he admitting time as his leige.
All that he with moats and smoke and fire
and seven heavy stone walls defended,
time just watched, and certain, steady, marched
on and seized it all without a shot,
slowly waiting time rock crumbled, blood slowed,
and just the drum of death spoke loud.
And not just mighty Auranzeb, but you too
and me, our high deeds up-ended,
end up at the bottom, all our fancies buried
beneath the plain
    fact we rot,
and whatever brave colors we wave as our flag,
times fades all to grey. Over the fort waves a shroud."

Since I turned 18 years old, the sense of time passing has wafted over me, and in the past couple of decades, so has the sense of death. Not a terribly depressing or obsessional thought, just a thought which, whenever I write poetry, re-occurs in my work. Wherever you travel, you bring yourself and your usual preoccupations. Time, death, and sex are typical of mine.

Time and death are associated by many people with Calcutta. Filthy, hectic, with grinding poverty. Many families live in the streets, like the ones clustered under cloth lean-tos near the YMCA where I stayed for a few days in 1978, the families cooking and washing, children playing and begging and skylarking, men shaving and chatting, making the street their own living room, kitchen and bedroom. On the huge open field of the Maidan in the center of Calcutta in 1978, Indians in whites are playing cricket, people are strolling, kids are kite-flying or kicking a ball, and on one corner, passed by many who look on with pity, but continue walking, as I too did, lies a woman of maybe 35 or 40 years, on her back, one breast exposed, open-mouthed, dying of something. We all walk on. In late December 1993 in Calcutta I met several Westerners who were there to work for Mother Teresa for a while to help the poor and dying of Calcutta, but then would also walk on. Merry Christmas!

In Calcutta death is many people's preoccupation and occupation, like in Varanasi. In 1978 I wrote: "Only optimists bother with shoeshines in Calcutta. Dust to dust. The people know it. A dead dog remains on the sidewalk for days. Grey dust, like illness, pales the leather's glow. Darkness brings out decay's phosphorescence like wisdom's lamp."

And again, "All the earth speaks for us in its fashion, its tones taken and mistaken. The banyan tree in Calcutta's Botanical Gardens had its trunk destroyed; each root now tries to be that trunk, penetrates the paradox of the many and the one. My body speaks while writing, right leg crossed over and foot behind left, arms crossed on chest, back bent as though stomach struck, contorted by the pen's pressure to connect only right moments to this moment lost. Some right few of the many. Banyan tree twists around it vines, crossing each other (itself) like bandages, like bonds, like arms, like gems, like snakes." I note imagery here not only of the poet and the banyan tree twisted, but of the ways some impoverished children's limbs in India were twisted to make their begging more pitiful and therefore more profitable, and also imagery of pain, of manic reproduction and replication, of desperation in flora as well as fauna.

You can get numb from all the desperation around you in Calcutta. There I wrote something called NOT STIRRING ENOUGH:

"Calcutta's late afternoon shoves toward me ingredients for a poem: the white marble Victoria Memorial. Signs asking you to keep off the grass. Two kids whack at plants with sticks and yells. Police stroll casually with rigid laithi sticks. Sun setting red behind Victoria Memorial. Lots of small black ravens whip and curl around it. Half moon pale and weak behind it in blue sky. Follow the colors. Follow the numbers. Follow the notes. The packaged poem. For you to assemble it, all you have to do is stir." How can you stir people to do something to help the dying woman on the Maidan at the other end of which is the gorgeous Victoria Memorial? No wonder Hinduism and Buddhism look upon this world as illusion, and try to escape its pain of life and death.

In Calcutta you can also escape bureaucracy and laws. My travel agent, a Mr. Singh (all Sikhs have this name which means "lion" which sounds like "lying"), was able to help me out of a tight spot. He got me a flight to Rangoon and Bangkok, but to leave the country I needed a cholera shot, and the time was too short. So Mr. Singh got me a faked cholera-shot record, all authenticated with the right stamps and signatures, right before I left for the airport. Pay a little money in Calcutta, you get whatever you want. I enjoyed the fine Buddhist sculpture in the Indian museum, the doll museum illustrating the story of the Hindu epic, the Ramayana, saw the garish Jain temple with its scads of mirrors, its gold and silver, entered the Hindu saint's temple of Ramakrishna, watched the women putting butter on the god Shiva's lingam in the Kali temple for fertility and for keeping their men's sexual prowess, ogled the Indian classical dancers in their performance at the Oberoi Grand Hotel, and ate in the Omar Khayam Restaurant and the Waldorf Chinese Restaurant. A diverse city, Calcutta. The beggars and slums were not as bad as I had feared, but I noted that the dogs are skinnier and mangier than elsewhere in India.

Calcutta still had two-wheeled rickshaw pullers on foot. The rest of India had motorized or the bicycle rickshaws used as taxis. Calcutta had those too, but many of the poorest rickshaw-wallahs could not afford to buy or rent one with a bicycle. So you still see in 1978 and in 1994 skinny men, wearing no shirt, only a dhoti around their waist, and running through the streets carrying behind them on their two-wheeled rickshaw people and their goods. I remember a pencil-thin black old man, white-ish hair, struggling up the camber of a small bridge over a canal, hauling three fat Indians—a corpulent couple and their fat kid—they not thinking to get off to make it easier. Calcutta. All life is sacred except human life.

INDIA 3: ASHRAM:

Coming home in the evening, wrapped in my own thoughts and a shawl, a man driving a bullock cart flicked his whip across my shoulders. It didn't hurt nor was it meant to. It was just a light insult. Startled, I roared at him and ran at the cart. He whipped it up and the oxen started to speed up. I went for the driver, but the wheels of the cart would have crushed me had I tried to grab him as he stood at the front, so I went around the cart to the back. Several men lying in the back of the cart quickly scrambled to the front, but not before I grabbed one of them, a teenager squealing with fear. I pulled him off the cart by one leg and threw him down, but realizing that he hadn't done anything to me, I let him go and he took off running for the cart which was going faster with the oxen now running, the driver standing and whipping them hard. I shouted, "Come on back, you fucking chickenshit bastard!" "Really angry. But then I felt O.K.; my anger was spent in that drag-off and that yell. Felt great! No tension of anger lingering, because I just blew it all out in the moment! Eureka!"

These notes from my journal of February to April 1979 show not only my own emotional exultation in these exclamations and exclamation-point-rich sentences and hair-trigger responses, but also the animosity that many Indians had toward this ashram—the Raj Neesh Ashram in Poona, India, where I went for an afternoon and ended up staying for two and a half months in early 1979. Another example was a bicyclist with a buddy on the bike's back passing me while in the evening I was walking along a road in the rural outskirts of Poona. The boy on the bike's back gently slapped me on the head, just a little insult to the orange-clad foreign ashram-ites of Raj Neesh. I took off after the bike, and despite the cyclist peddling standing up and hard, I caught them. Dumping them off the bike, I grabbed one of them and screamed, "Why do you slap me? Why insult me?" A crowd gathered as I held and shook the young man and screamed at him. He gibbered in fear and distress, and then I just let him go, turning to the crowd and telling them we do nothing to provoke such insults, so why slap us just when we are walking around minding our own business? Then I walked off, annoyed. In India, if you want to be left alone to burrow into your own psyche or to meditate on the meaning of life, buy a plane ticket back to New York where you can be left alone. Not in India. A more commercial nation you could not find.

But the Raj Neesh Ashram is not quite India. You can be left alone, or you can ask for and get hugs from strangers. From my letters to my father, describing the place: "Most of the things in the ashram are free. Kind of a spiritual summer camp, this. India with its noise where I live [in a tiny roof-top room at a hotel near the railway station], and then over to the quietude of the ashram. I'm enjoying the contrasts!" Daily activities are listening to Raj Neesh's lectures in wide-open concrete Buddha Hall. Dancing in the evenings to wonderfully repetitive hypnotic music, where most poeple move to the music in their own twirling or weaving ways. "Sufi dancing" in the afternoons, sort of the Catskills meets the Ganges, chanting affirmations to each other, holding hands and sweating gloriously on each other. "Today we did a Chassidic hora!" There are meditations of breathing and sitting quietly. There's a garden to sit and write in, which I used a great deal. CIRCUS IN THE GARDEN: "Amarylis, barker, blares through red throat that frangipani will juggle smells with sharp young blades of grass, the marigolds will cartwheel, ants will drag several times their own weight (watch them!) And sunlight slides along a spider's strand and never falls all day. Nature, surefooted, spectacular. Only one thin time. And worth every penny."

Poetry and ideas seemed to pour into me there. The sanyasins, his disciples, wore orange. "I bought some orange clothes and had some of mine dyed orange. I fit right in! Orange is the color to remind you to be your authentic self, a laudatory aim, although other people's authentic selves are (I hope!) not mine. But it's a bright color and feels good....this year away is the best time to experiment."

ORANGE IS THE ASHRAM'S COLOR:

"Green is banished, Black is banned, Blue slinks off to familiar sea. They live across the rainbow's tracks, distant cousins of the long blood lines of sun. The partial prism's friends are like Brother Sun and Sister Moon, Orange and its cohorts, Red and bright Yellow, light's one-sided legions reminding us of ourselves and of all light.

You must dye in order to be re-born. I had a perfectly good green shirt, turning orange now when I wash it with my other orange clothes. The dye is not colorfast. Is what's happening to me colorfast? Everything's turning the color of orange as I clean off my old sweat and dirt, staining me the sun's jaundice, orange at dusk dying, orange our morning drink against our common cold.

I often wanted a whole new wardrobe, and daydreamt fire burnt all my clothes and so I'd get a chance to choose again. Here all the colors of clothes are burning without smoke, without ash, warmly burning. If this color can take to my own clothes, I can keep them, dyed like the old self burning." Would I be able to travel into a new me? Would I want to?"

"Tonight I start on a group called "Intensive Enlightenment" (chuckle) in which for 3 days we do nothing but answer the question "Who am I?" Some good insights should crop up!"And insights did. For three days I had 40 minutes with one person, then switched to another person, each time asking the other, "Tell me who you are" and then listening for five minutes while that person told me, and then they would ask me, "Tell me who you are" and I would expatiate. Now after a short while, you went through all the obvious curriculum vitae stuff—man, professor of literature, divorced, 39 years old, et al—and then you begin to say things like, "I'm hungry!" or "My ass hurts from sitting on concrete, and I'm angry!" and so it goes. You find the "you" is a whole bunch of discordant and ephemeral things too besides those on your resume. Also, in these three days, everything you do is considered a meditation, where you are to approach it concentrating only on it and yourself. "O.K., now it's time for shower meditation" and off you go to shower communially together,

expected to ignore the fact that lots of beautiful naked women are showering next to you, trying to ignore dozens of lovely breasts, and at the same
time guiltily to sneak a peek at those same lovely breasts boobling bob-
bling two feet away. "Time for eating meditation!" and you are given toast,
peanut butter, an apple and a banana, and you eat them slowly, medita-
tively, ignoring the others all lost in their own thoughts too. Slowly chewing the food, concentrating on the texture and the flavors, made for a
wonderful meal. Since I saved the banana for later, though I craved it first,
I learned something about the general way I run my life—save the reward
for later, but do your duty first. So I decided to use the phrase "Eat the
banana first" to remind me of this insight—do the things you want to
before you do your duty. Of course, now in 2000 at age sixty, I still do my
duty first. But at least I figured it out even if I don't live this insight.

There were very few Indians in this ashram. Indians as a race got
thrown out of Sufi Dancing while I was there because they could not stop
trying to feel up the women while dancing, and Raj Neesh, though himself an Indian, banished them. The ashram was more Californian than
Indian. Anything goes—almost anything— when you're not in some
group activity.

In the group "Centering" we had an exercise to substitute "he" and "his"
for "I" or "me" or "mine" in all conversation, to distance oneself from one's
personality. When you are angry, but say "he is angry because Jack screamed
at him" this makes it easier for you not to scream back at Jack.

I did the "awareness walk" in which you repeat the sentence "Now I am
aware of ——" and wait till after this pause to see what actually swims
into your consciousness, then saying what that is. You are utterly in the
present moment then. An interesting useful group, if only to show me that
I am too rarely centered.

A couple of groups seemed silly and pretentiously "New-Age" to me,
like "Mysterium" where you breathe, make sounds, and make arm and
body movements. Rather than put me in touch with my mysterious inner
spaces, it put me more in touch with my aching bony butt and with the

heat that as February slid into March and April toward the hottest part of the Indian year, the pre-monsoon spring, built up all around us.

The best group I did in the ashram was the two-week Primal Encounter Group. From a letter to my father of April 4, 1979: "For the last ten days (and for the next four), I've been in isolation and silence except when I'm in this "Primal" group where we explore feelings now and in our past. It has been proably the most amazing, weepy, angry, sad, and blissful ten days I've ever had! I've been in pillow fights, sprained both thumbs, cracked a couple of ribs, had bruises and teeth marks all over. A couple of fights have been with women. There are 12 of us and 3 therapists, and everyone including therapists get into everything. A letter cannot do justice to these experiences."

Nor is it fully the place to do so here in this book of my travels. The therapists pushed us to fight with pillows with each other to explore our anger and act on it rather than surpressing it. Go fully into your emotion, and only in that way can you rise above it.

Once, in a fight with one young Italian woman, after knocking the pillow out of her hands, I stopped hitting at her, and picked up her pillow and handed to her. One of the therapists grabbed me from behind and wrestled me to the floor. "Come on, Charles is too much of a gentleman to fight. Anyone can hit him who wants to. Anyone want to?" The woman I had been fighting with can over and whacked me a few times. I couldn't move because Akasha, our American therapist, had my arms pinned to the floor. Then a big German guy came over and hit me so hard that he cracked my ribs. Akasha let me up after no one else was willing to hit me, and I promptly picked up a pillow and slammed it twice into this big German guy who was cowering away from me against the wall. "You're gutless, you big bastard! But I don't have a problem with you." I hit him again. "She's my problem." And I went after the woman I'd been fighting with. I knocked her pillow out of her hands, she burst into tears, and instead of comforting her, the way I've always acted before, I hit her again, at which point several of the men jumped on me and pulled me down, and stopped me from attacking again. After this fight, the group broke for lunch, and I went out and ate, alone, like an animal, making noises, smacking lips, moaning in bliss not so much at the food, but at the full- ness of going into and thereby transcending my anger. Something like when I screamed at the ox cart man who whipped me.

The next group after this wild two weeks of "Primal" was the Tantra group, three days of sharing energy, often by having sex. But here after two weeks I had just gotten fully into my anger at the power women had over me, when the next day in the same room (they did change the pillow covers though) I was supposed to have sex and be loving with them. I was not ready. I should have had a week alone to deal with all these negative feelings. In the Tantra group, we all started by taking our clothes off and getting acquainted. First time I'd ever hugged a naked man. One of the women started playfully swatting at me with a pillow as we walked from person to person, trying to start a little friendly tussle and wrestle with me. I turned around and with my pillow knocked her off her feet. She screamed and I realized I was still operat- ing in the anger of the previous group dynamic rather than in this loving one. So I told her I had just come from Primal, I had nothing against her and I was sorry, and then proceeded to slam my pillow against the wall as hard as I could, screaming at each slam, "I don't need your f———— c———— any more!" They stood around and watched, appalled, and rightly so, at my explosive fury. Afterwards, I was able to be tender and loving and sexual over the next couple of days. In these groups and in this ashram, the traveling was back into your own past and into the muck of yourself and all sorts of your trou- bling emotions.

Every day for two and a half months early each morning I went from my little hotel room to the more expansive ashram and spent all day there. LIFE IN THE ASHRAM:

"The sign says, "Please leave your shoes and minds outside." As we passed in, two young ladies sniffed us to see if we smelt of anything. I did- n't. And so I passed in, shoeless, smell-less. Bhagwan Raj Neesh spoke in

Hindi. When I got outside, someone had taken my shoes, my new blue thongs, and left another pair, not far away, of blue thongs.

I'll trade you a bit of my mind (certified grade A) for a bit of your mind (certified non-existent). How about some of my stability for your dizziness in dance? If I give you my hard-earned adulthood you'd sacrifice it for a kid? (Remember the Bible?) Am I nuts to trade in all of me for just a little you hanging beneath my heart?

That hand is only flesh, and sweats. That only flesh is handled here and flesh is handled here on spirit's impulse too to quiver into flesh which hopes to fondle spirit too. It's all mixed up, the two of them, and all are all mixed up in Bhagwan too. Too bad? Not to me. He says he's just a man. And I agree.

Today I helped clean strawberries for the kitchen. Leafy top in one bowl, mushy part for jam in another, firm red part in another. Later in the garden, an ant was dragging a part of a bug across a flagstone. The two of us helping out.

If all that lives is holy, what about the cat who kills birds in this garden?

In Nadabrahma meditation, we hum for forty minutes each time we exhale. It is like star sound, white noise, the resonant buzz of God. In the men's urinal, later, I heard it again, God buzz, the exhaust fans.

On the way home from the ashram, there's a beggar who always sings out, "Blind one paise, Babaji. Hungry paise, Babaji. Blind one paise, Babaji. Hungry paise, Babaji." Catchy tune, that.

I found myself singing it all the way home."

The ashram was hermetic, without any necessary connection with the India outside it. Many people came straight from Europe or America to the ashram, lived in it, and never wanted to be in the swirl of Indian life, and I often felt like that. Every long-term traveler needs to get back home even if that home means a strawberry ice cream soda in Nirula's restaurant in Delhi. The ashram was European, the language was English, the faces were almost all white.

Outside there was the weepy beggar, always holding his infant, and rushing after me for the full two months I was there because my first day in Poona, I gave him a wad of rupees to buy medicine for his sick child. Then of course I was his patron and every day he saw me he brought me his open needs and expected me to fill them with my rupees and paise. There also was one young and spectacularly twisted individual, his legs like thin sticks shaped into the intricate pretzel an inept apprentice baker might make. He begged, but without obvious despair. He smiled some, and you could have a conversation with him. He was a person, not just a begging machine who shows you only his agony and after your give him something he skips off happy, although this crippled fellow could never skip off anywhere. One paise is 1/100 of a rupee. The beggar in my poem didn't want or need much to live. In India, in Jaipur, you see lepers begging without fingers to catch the coins, just with rags around their stumps, and these lepers beg in groups. Misery here is vast, but not all beggars are miserable. All here have their lives. It's a hot climate, and one doesn't really need much to live on. I found it only pays to give to blind beggars—they don't know who gave, and so they won't bother you when they see you next time, because they can't see.

Outside the ashrams were also the entrepeneurs. One woman started with absolutely nothing, just enough to get some bananas. She sold them, bought more bananas, sold them, and when I knew her she had two carts on which were piled oranges, and she made juice from them which she sold. A couple of people now worked for her at these carts. I would have several glasses of juice each day from her. She worked, saved, and now she had a business. In India if you have a blanket and some fruit, you've got a business. She was aiming for lots more carts to sell juice all over town. She deserves to grow rich.

From a letter of June 7, 1979, in Poona: "The monsoon is about to start; today looks grim and threatening. (Just heard a band outside—a wedding procession, but a small one. Saw two in Bombay with the groom on horseback. Wow! Like a maharajah!)" Bombay is big bucks, Poona is small potatoes. The rumble of thunder, the boom of a drum. The world like the rain growls outside the ashram, which then was emptier because of the monsoon when I returned there after being in Sri Lanka and south India for a month and a half. Earlier, a letter from Rameswaram, just three hours away from Sri Lanka by ferry, at the end of April, shows the effect the real Indian world had on me once plunged into it again: "But one week away [from the ashram] in south India, and I'm back to my own grumpy sullen self (too much being stared at, being begged from, and line-standing-on gets that self rolling). So don't expect an Enlightened Being. Marvelous moments, even hours, at the ashram, but serenity seems rather beyond my physiology."

The monsoon finally hit, and much in India was washed away, including some of the heat. Tried to wash some of my anger and worries and tensions away, but that didn't work for long.

"The current slides back up toward its source in some green spring of far-off hills, and becomes our past while movement's current keeps our pace when we walk or sleep, or sit or ride, and every stone we toss to test this only river's different depths splashes silver nipples on spreading circles, mandalas of concentric breasts now spreading back and out and forward too, a nourishing of now through then as we're down the river born again." I was not born again at this ashram, or if so, slid back into the familiar grooves and the deltas of one's quotidian life.

At the ashram, most everyone had long hair. One day I decided for the first time in my life to get my head shaved. Not cropped close as in the Navy. But shaved bare bald.

ON HAVING MY HEAD SHAVED:
"Mongols and Turkish wrestlers are my brothers.
My head feels like sandpaper to my hand.
Cleaning, clearing off. Building a home
on land where no secrets can hide. Hair.
Dead skin near the roots where never light lurked.
Here in the ashram everyone is hairy.

Sages' beards droop from the armpits of women.
Leg fuzz flares up over ankles. Many
men from behind seemed women till long beard
balanced long hair. Is to shave rebellion?
Is it violence to myself? Does it repudiate
sexuality? Does it like a rock show stubborn mind?
Or like a rock, like granite, show constituents clear, clean?
A woman felt my head, said it feels like velvet."

My head as sandpaper and then as velvet. Appropriate for my time at
this ashram in Poona.

INDIA 4— SOUTH INDIA IN 1979:

The 24-hour train trip to Madras in southeast India was not so bad.
The usual jostle of too many people crammed in with me in the second-
class bare benches, the little black spots of coal dust that stipple everyone
which when brushed off leave a greasy smear on your clothes and face, the
big irregular bundles of stuff underfoot, the bits of smoked-out bidis,
orange peels, and dropped food, the red spittings of betel juice, the peanut
shells, all crunched under your feet, the noise and head-wagglings of conversations in several languages (English is usually the language in common
between people of the south and north here), the blind musicians and
beggars who get on at one station and get off at the next, petitioning you
for money, the uniformed conductors checking your ticket and the passengers who sidle into your space or who stretch out on a couple of seats
and refuse to be awakened, the curious children or adults who, while I was
writing a poem, actually put their head under my writing arm to see what
I was writing—in short, the usual steam-engine train ride through India.

Ready for a rest after this 24-hour ride, I found that all hotels in this big
city were occupied because of the all-India teachers conference there. I
asked several people at the station where I might get any hotel, and they all
said "full up." So I walked out of the station, saw several Indian travelers
with their luggage asleep on a construction-site sand pile, and figured I'd

sleep in the station. Finding a space between other sleepers in the main hall, I lay down on my pack and managed to sleep some. In Indian railways stations there are often whole families camping out, some who are not even waiting for a train—their encampments look semi-permanent, which in India may mean permanent. Cordoning themselves and their sleeping mats off from other families with worn-out grey fabric and boxes, the poor go on about their business and lives without privacy but with acceptance. I, however, wanted to leave Madras station, so next morning, stiff from the hard floor, I caught the bus south.

My letter of 22 April, 1979, says, "Tomorrow, not for the last time, but for the first time in 3 months, I leave India. Next stop, Sri Lanka (or Ceylon as it was known till 1972). Rameswaram is at the bottom of India at the closest point to Sri Lanka, and is a bit of a primitive hole. The electricity keeps going out, then the fans and water stop. But for 6 rupees (75 cents), what can one expect? I've been on route about a week...buses to Kanjipuram, Mahabalipuram, Thanjuvar, Pondicherry, Madurai. At most of these places, magnificent and huge Pallava or Chola temples, ornately carved in stone, at times even temple caves carved right out of the rock. But...the heat (great) and the crowds (very) make one week of temple watching enough for a time." As in Italy after a certain number of churches, so in India, the mind and eyes so stuffed with beautiful things, a mental indigestion occurs from overdoing. Aldous Huxley said that "one should not blunt the edge of seldom pleasure." In other words, anything done too much is not good, whether food or sex or looking at Indian temples. Also, late April and May is the hottest time in India, especially in the pre-monsoon south. One almost literally wilts in the sun.

But on to the traveler's duty: to see. In Kanjipuram, there are lots of Dravidian-style temples, high tapering stepped pyramidal shapes, almost like a intricately carved stone spearhead thrust against the sky. SACRED ANIMALS GIVEN TO GOD:

"At Kanjipuram's Vishnu temples, the priests all look like women.

The front part of their scalp is shaved, going Florentine Rennaissance ladies
one better, and their back hair is done up in a bun. In one ear,
they sport an erring, a diamond in one priest's ear. They seem to simper,
and walk delicately, their brown bodies thin above their white lungis.
In these temples to Vishnu, there are sacred elephants and white horses.
One elephant, with the white semicircle and red bar inside it
of the Vishnu devotee on his forehead, was taking coins with his trunk,
passing them to his keeper, and patting the head of the giver gently
in blessing. The elephant's trunk was warm, fumbling, curious.
In another temple, the white horse had a raven standing on his neck.
At a sacred 3,500-year-old mango tree in the center of a temple, two priests
told me of its connection with Shiva, and daubed my forehead with
sacred white ash."

There are many other temples to Hinduism's many gods. SHIVA
TEMPLE:

"The lingam and the yoni: this temple is Shiva's.
Effeminate priests moisten the lingam's tip
and women drape over it flowers and oil.
All things are born from the dance of Shiva.
(Here he sports a stone halo of yoni, thus
generating generations.) His many arms moving
are the flurry of Indian cities, Hindu
hurly-burly in his dance. But here he is, still, lingam
and yoni, no more personal than unshaped rock.
Shiva and Parvati, lovers, stare into each other's eyes,
even in stone, movement before and after this stone moment,
but here generation is all. No need for eyes
or mouth or movement, for here in stone
is Shiva stuck and still, in sex still stuck
though a god, like Zeus, all gods, we all."

From Kanjipuram by bus to Mahabalipuram, and more temples, one right on the shore of the Bay of Bengal. "Maha" is right—it means "big" as in Taj Mahal (big Taj). The most unusual sight for me here (I even bought a postcard of it which I kept) is a single huge rock with many carvings called "Arjuna's Penance"—gods, men, houses, and two large elephants cut into the rock. The long nights of old time have worn down some of these bas reliefs, and worn down the carvings of the five Rathas, looking like big tombs in the shapes of small temples, with separate stones carved into an elephant and a lion. Postcards or photos must remind me of what they were. Names and memories fade much much faster than do rocks.

Then on to Pondicherry, with its French presence still lingering, and with its Sri Aurobindo Ashram still drawing the devout. I noticed in Tamil Nadu state here in the south, the Indians call all white men "master," not as they do elsewhere, Sahib or Baba. Being called "master" makes me particularly uncomfortable, and seems a sad holdover from the racist colonizing era. But two of the British I traveled with through Turkey and Iran and Afghanistan, accepted it as their due that the "natives" ("wogs" and "gollies" are what they called them) should make way for the white man. Both of these fellows were of working-class backgrounds, so I suppose this was their way of being the "pukka sahib," the ruler of the darker races, having no doubt been below the salt, being Cockneys, in their native England. One fellow, also of working-class background, I met in Cambridge, England, told me there that the one time he had been in India for a couple of weeks he was treated with so much more deference than had ever happened in his life before. In the Navy I was used to deference, but this was excessive.

But in Pondicherry at this ashram, deference is demanded. I wrote then, "At the ashram, the tomb is all they have to show. Sri Aurobindo and The Mother buried, are buried now under flowers, arranged by sober ladies watched by other ladies, spaced neatly in front of their doors in the courtyard. Language on the posters in Reception is also neat, with the most proper mystic love-bloat. Sri Aurobindo himself has a bit of old bloat in the 1920's-style photos around, but it lends him majesty. The Mother [his mother] looks cancer-struck, shriveled in her old age. The soul cannot tailor-make its body.

The sun bakes Pondicherry into an Indian shape, blurring the French names of streets, and with its so much sky squashing the town, a fallen *souffle*. The Hotel de Ville, the statue of Jeanne d'Arc, the hats on the police like Paris *flics*—all bake in a sun hotter than Provence. The French evaporate, leaving an Indian chappaty, browner, flatter, plainer. While I was at the tomb at the ashram, crowded with ladies arranging flowers or praying, two ravens right over the tomb started a fight, dislodging leaves and flowers."

Further south in Madurai, there's the Meenakshi Temple, with its elongated spear-headed Dravidian temple, typical of the south, but here superb and stately, with its thousand-pillar hall with statutes of elephant-headed Ganesh and of big-bosomed slim-waisted women dancing, and with relief carvings on the pillars themselves. "At Madurai's famous temple, a brown devotee kneels, supplicating. Less than ten yards away, a banded brown squirrel stands in a similar position.One is eating now. The other hopes for later. So much for animals and men!" The world keeps presenting me with ingredients for poems. There's a vast tank, or bathing place, in the temple itself, with its still and not very clean, but holy, water. Sort of a "Ganges south." I did not bathe in it, but did continue south till the three-hour ferry plus the customs hassles of getting cross the narrow strait to Sri Lanka.

On the way back from Sri Lanka, several weeks later, I went north up the other side of the India, the western side on the Arabian Sea. I had been quite ill in Sri Lanka and weighed about 105 pounds, and I needed a rest, and the best place to rest for me is on a beach. A few days on the beach in Trivandrum, "then up through Kerala province to Goa, where I spent five days on that beach, eating vast amounts to get back my strength (I did!). Traveling all the way by bus—very draining, dirty, hassled. Feeling rested and fine now, except for the omnipresent "shits."When I returned home I thought of organizing tours for people to lose weight on—Dr. Stickney's Miracle Weight-Loss Tour—just follow me, live where I live, eat what I eat, and you won't need liposuction ever again!

Using a central metaphor of food, I wrote, "While traveling, usually time is overstuffed, crammed with odds and bits, hung with the hook of the strange to catch in your eye. Off Kovalam Beach though, near Trivandrum, blackened men in lungis [sarongs] row black boats with upswept bows and sterns, or put up black shark-fin-shaped sails that look like antiquity, and are. These sails that sail so slowly, time forgets its passing, men who pass so quickly, turning on earth's spit in time's fire that they blacken into night and melt into the mind we have and had." Food and cooking on the mind of a semi-starved and skinny man translated into words. On this beach I also was MELANCHOLY: "The monsoon at Kovalam washed away my defenses. Grey sea swept in over me, filming like fish's eye a world and plans gone grey, glazing a wobbly mirror, unsure of why to bother. Rain at the beach, the sun whited out, the air full of the water we feel, this inside grey, these colors sapped, the sun's promise a grey memory." In my tiny room in a fisherman's hut on the beach, feeling worn out and depressed under the sad weepy skies, this day was a low point.

But up through the canals of Kerala and on up north, things were looking and feeling better

until I arrived in the town of Panaji in Goa late one night. What I first noticed was that there were a lot of drunk men lurching around. In India you'd never see drunks in the streets in 1978 and 1979, but here it looked like just after pub-closing in Scotland. Looking for signs for hotels, I had to trudge up stairways to find the "hotel" to be a shut door that would open cautiously and partially after I knocked and tell me there were no rooms available, meanwhile the glimpse I had of the dim lobby inside with lots of men milling around and shouting, make me a little glad they didn't have room. In the street, the drunks looked aggressive, and I was still very weak from the amoebic dystentery and the Sri Lankan flu and being still so very malnourished. Finally I spied a neon sign for a big hotel up one of the roads, and found they did have room. One room only, smirked the desk clerk. The Bridal Suite. It was grossly overpriced for me—maybe ten dollars. I thought for a few seconds, then figured what the hell! I took it. What a wonderful night's rest that was.

The next day I headed for one of Goa's famous beaches, Colva, where I got a dorm room, with no one else in the dorm, and headed out to swim and walk. "Under the stars, a starfish travels a sensible pace and leaves a track, wave wiped, but not sky black so soon. I stalk time, tracked in sand, where even the puffball, white froth, slowly smalls from is to nothing, in time. Twig feet of the crab, V of seagull toes, show from here to there, walking with time past stillness, while the waves' engines gun, and creatures move, and I get older and old." Being weak, I thought of the weakness of age. The world always filters through the writer's mood.

"There was this dead dog on Goa's Colva Beach. Just like all the other Indian dogs—mangy, scabrous, skinny. But what a change Death did! A red flower blooms from his mouth, and he's never been fatter, puffed up the way the rich in India aspire to be." Time passing, death, weariness, I felt enveloped by these thoughts then.

But there was one high point here, the time I got my pants ripped off. I was sitting at a small beachfront restaurant talking to a couple I had met and waiting for our food. An argument between several Goanese fishermen and three people at a table suddenly got very loud. I looked over and saw a woman, the only European person at the table, throw the water in a glass at one of the standing fishermen. I excused myself from my friends and went over to see if I could calm everyone down, which I seem always to take as my job. The anger and yelling was at a high pitch when pleasantly and calmly I asked them what was the trouble. One of the fishermen looked quickly at me, then grabbed my trousers and ripped them right off. I was wearing no shoes, no shirt nor underpants, and my drawstring pants were light and flimsy. Very flimsy. So there I was two seconds after I walked over to help, and I'm standing buck naked except for my shredded pants around my ankles. I turned to the guy who ripped my pants, and sticking a finger in his face I

said, "you owe me a pair of pants," and he said something which meant "no"
and all the fishermen turned to me and started to argue with me, leaving the
three people at the table alone. Not one of the fishermen paid any attention
to my being utterly naked, and I was so caught up with the arguing, I just
stood there and argued back. Finally the argument ended when I said I had
to go and get some pants on, and walked off back to my dorm room, my
ripped trousers wrapped around my waist. Coming back from my room, new
trousers on, the fisherman who ripped my pants was waiting for me. "Do you
have any problem with me?" he asked me, somewhat truculently. I, who had
realized how funny it all was, smiled and told him no. Going back to my seat
in the restaurant, my woman friend said that they had turned back when the
noise at the table grew even louder, and she asked, "Where's Chuck?" not seeing me. Then she realized the naked white guy arguing with the big fishermen was me. We laughed, and I kept giggling over it the whole evening. P.S.
Our waiter offered to mend my trousers free for me because I had stopped a
possible big fight, and the next day, after presenting me with my mended
trousers, I gave them back to him as a gift. More than a week late, I was at the
Bombay Post Office and this English woman, whose party had departed the
restaurant during my picking up of my second pair of trousers in the dorm,
came over to me, and thanked me profusely, saying no one else seemed to
want to help them, and invited me back home to meet her Indian husband
and their daughter who had also been at that table. Before they thanked me,
my lesson was "Keep out of fights that are not yours." After they thanked me,
I reverted to type, intervening and trying to stop fights. Lessons!

After Goa, back to Poona and Bombay, and then flew off to Egypt.
That was in 1979. In 1993 my other Indian beach was on the east coast
below Calcutta. From Bubaneswar with its temples I went on to Puri, and
stayed there relaxing from November 17 till December 27 in a hotel right
on the beach. Long walks every day down the beach, to the left passing a
very poor fishing village, where the men openly defecate on the beach
below low tide so the shit is removed twice a day by the ocean, which
sometimes floats the turds down to where we bathe in the water. Once

past the fishing village there is almost no one there, just ocean, sand, and wind. Walks to the right go past the main part of the town, with crowds of Indians on vacation bathing, splashing, staring at me, and having religious ceremonies at the shore, till past the town to inlets and the green forest closing in on the beach.

In "Xanadu."one of my favorite restaurants—great prawn masala—one morning after a long morning walk down the beach, I wrote, ON THE BAY OF BENGAL:

I

"It really doesn't matter.
Which dog is top dog on the beach in Puri,
who gets first crack at discarded fish in the water
before the crows take over and then the flies and crabs;
the fishermen argue, the children batter
small pufferfish or dogs. It really doesn't matter.

II

Soft silver swords of dead fish swirl
in brown woven baskets. Sellers and buyers swirl
around them. Washing all, the batter and mutter
of waves, the swirl and white wash of the sea.
The Bay of Bengal drowns hobbled dogs and men
and plastic water bottles. It really doesn't matter.

III

The fishermen haul their nets up toward the beach,
dying fish patter, sand and water spatter.
Between sailings, the fishing fates fix their nets,
weaving close, closing holes, repairing tatters,
so the deadly air pours in, and out goes the breathable sea.
Drown in air or water? It really doesn't matter.

IV

The silver sides of fish mirror the ocean
with the 10 a.m. sun scrolling the water

silver or gold. This precious light glares,
aches the eyes. Do we see what we should?
On the sea the light coinage sinks as waves scatter
the silver or gold. Which? It really doesn't matter.
V
Widows set sail leafy boats with sparklers or candles
on them, like human lives. A wave hits. They go out.
The widows return up the beach to build on Bengali Bay
wet sand lingams inside sand sketchings of a house:
their families, alive and dead, they wish to serve and save.
Lingam? Effigy? Grave mound? It really doesn't matter.
VI
The tide, every six hours, changes the water,
cleans the beach, and starts again its oceanic
breathing. Love notes, names, drawings of divinities
are lines forgotten; writ in sand is writ in water.
Fishermen scoop sand with their feet to catch crabs for bait.
Lines of words? Of nets? The former or the latter? It doesn't really matter."

Puri also has the famous Jagannath Temple—our word "juggernaut"
comes from it—where devotees of Krishna used to throw themselves
under the wheels of the large wagon bearing his image. I saw this temple
from the outside, but as I remember I was not allowed in. Some days after
I saw the temple, the news had an item about many worshippers getting trampled in the temple when someone panicked and ran. At Konark
near Puri I stayed in a tent for two days to see classical dances at a festival
near the Sun Temple. "Right now picking coconut meat from between my
teeth as I study the erotic and divine carvings at the temple." But mostly I
stayed on the emptier beach at Puri.

But nowhere is very safe. The fishermen's catch is interesting to show
you what you swim with.

Sharks of several kinds, including hammerheads. Highly poisonous sea snakes, yellow and black. Evil-looking eels. And little round fish with an erectile spine at their top. Once on a date with a young German girl, we walked way down the beach to the right to be able to swim and relax away from, as she put it, "all those Indians who stand behind you and watch you as you lie in the sun." We crossed the inlet, and lay down in this deserted area. The heat was brutal, so I went in the water and stepped on a fish with a sharp spine. I couldn't tell what kind of fish it was because the water was too stirred up. But I thought it might be very poisonous.

I told the German about the puncture wound, and told her to stay here while I went to get some medicine for it. The truth is I didn't want her around in case I had to scream in pain. The pain was bad, a dull unrelenting pain, and the worst was I didn't know if I might die from it. Our private little picnic place had been chosen so nobody was around, so I had to walk for more than an hour to get near anyone for help. I saw two fishermen walking and showed them my puncture, but they couldn't help and so I walked on, panting with pain. I began to realize I would probably live, but the pain forced me to lie down a couple of times. Finally I saw a rickshaw man on the road nearby, and got him to take me to a hospital

He took me to an ayurvedic hospital where we found a doctor who asked me about it, looked at it finally when I had to lie down on the floor because of the pain, and gave me a prescription for pain medication to be filled at a chemist's. He seemed uninterested, so by now I assumed it was not fatal. By rickshaw to the chemist's, and I popped a couple of the pills despite being told to take only one. Not helping my agony was been stared at sitting in front of the chemist's, writhing in pain. When the rickshaw man took me back to my hotel, he asked for such an outrageous price that I got angry enough to forget my pain for a while. Anger as analgesic— another lesson. We arrived at a fair price, mediated by the manager of my hotel, and I went up to try to sleep. I took another pill, and tried to soak my wounded foot in a wastebasket of hot water but was still in pain and couldn't sit still. A neighbor from an island off Vancouver next to me gave me some tylanol and a big shot of vodka, "the cowboy's pain killer." That finally put me out, and next morning 1 didn't have pain except when I walked on the puncture which now was a small black hole in my instep. The black spot of the poison lasted for a few weeks, and so did some of the swelling.Hobbling down the beach a couple of days later I noticed a small round fish with a long spike sticking out of its back. That's most likely the one, I felt. When I was in Singapore several months later I saw a picture of a fish just like this in an exhibit on poisonous fish. It was called, embarrassingly enough, a rabbit fish. I knew of the lion fish, the scorpion fish, but—the rabbit fish! However, in the description of it, its jab is "rarely fatal, but it causes almost unbearable pain." So I could now hold up my head as a tough man. (But still—rabbit fish!) The ocean off Puri, the Bay of Bengal, is dangerous.

"Sunlight streams on the sea's skin,
bright like urine after too much vitamin B.
My eyes slit against the light.
But light, like gold, is beaten very thin
and barely covers the dangerous stone
fish or whatever's poisonous spine or spike
I stepped on near Puri in the Bay of Bengal.
Limping, staggering, nothing friendly heard my moan
which harmonized with the spent waves' hiss.

Orissa fishers get under the skin and the fishes'
Fates, weave a casual and an airy death
for friendly mackeral and tuna, and dishes
more forbidding like the brassy hammer-head
and the regular sharks, six feet of deep-death
with stone-dead eyes, and nine-foot snakey eels, all fed
on each other and on men, their wishes vicious
as men's who hunt them. Washing at ashram,

metal dishes clatter silence like holy cymbals.

What then does the silence say? What the wave's whisper?
Cone-shaped snail shells at the ocean's edge
trace their daily journeys in curlicue Orissan writing,
but not their purpose. But purpose, as we know: to live.
To swim on the skin, but to press out to the ledge
with snorkel to see the dark deep where we can't see,
yet know it's not just nails they're biting.
I killed on Puri Beach a small black and yellow sea snake,
deadly. Despite the golden light, more golden just before the dark,
I smashed it, smashed, all we three trapped in the same sieve.
Today I shit in the sea. Yellow sea snakes of my own devising surround me."

INDIA 5:RAJAHSTAN:

The sand on the east Indian beaches of Puri is different from the sand
of the Thar Desert of Rajahstan. I was first in Rajahstan in the summer of
1982, and then in 1993. More hotels to stay in in 1993—more tourists,
more pricey, more comfortable, less exotic. What is only to be expected.
Anyone who wants places very different from the urban West better get a
move on and get there fast. It is so easy and cheap to travel now, and everyone does it.

Rajahstan is desert country, quite empty except for in the cities, and the
people with their saris and turbans are among India's most colorful. Jaipur,
with its intricately carved pinkish stone buildings, is lovely. In 1982, after
some time in Nepal where I met Kiki, a German girl, I rendezvoused with
her in Jaipur at a hotel for budget travelers, and spent several days there,
mostly following her around to shops where we priced fabrics, looked at rugs,
drank much tea. I was bored by this, not wanting to buy anything, but she
said that shopping around gave us an excuse to talk to people, and that interested her more than did the buying. I was more interested in her. Too often

especially in my earlier travels looking for women superseded most any other interest. Age (and enough experiences) usually modifies that.

Jaipur in 1993 seemed more crowded. I stayed in the same hotel I had in 1982, but now the swimming pool was drained and the hippie travelers seemed more sedate. One woman was with her two very young daughters, and writing a book about it, feeling that women alone traveling with their children was a guide-book niche which hadn't been enough explored. While we discussed this, I had to excuse myself several times and grit my teeth and struggle up to my room to get to the toilet. She understood. She had had to excuse herself often too. Bowels dominate, providing an embarrassing perpetual undercurrent to your days wandering the cities' sights. Above the city is the Amber Fort, where you can take an elephant ride for the short ride to its gates. I love elephants and riding on their backs, but this was a rip-off for too short a ride. I walked. I beat the elephants to the top.

Dry Jaipur is pretty, but so is wet Udaipur, with its palace (now a hotel and a scene for the James Bond film, "Octopussy") out in the middle of Lake Pichola. All sorts of palaces in this city, many now restaurants, hotels, and museums. In 1993 I stayed in Udaipur for seven days in August and went out on a boat on the lake, but couldn't get into its famous lake hotel to look around. I heard you can have dinner there one day a week, and that you would be segregated in a separate room from the other hotel guests. I suppose if you are paying vast sums to stay there you don't want the cheap hoi palloi like me to dilute your pricey digs.

One thing in Asia that is useful about being an older white Westerner is that you can wander around many of the fanciest of hotels almost with impunity. After all, despite your casual or even shabby dress, you may just be a guest. I use this privilege often to taste the luxurious surroundings I rarely have in my own hotels. You have to choose your price. Pay a lot, and the trip doesn't take its price so much out of your body. My 1978-79 trip, 14 months of it, including airfare, cost me about $3600. But returning from it, I looked like I had just spent a year in Auschwitz, having lost about 50 pounds and having gained hepatitis. My 1993-94 trip, including everything, and going in a bit more luxurious style (I tried to always if possible have my own bathroom), all 15 months of it, cost me about $8600. Some spend that for a few weeks vacation. Choose your price.

Pushkar in the desert also has a lake, but it's much smaller than the one in Udaipur, and Pushkar's lake is holy. I had been there in 1982 and there were many fewer motorcycles and bicycles then. As people get richer, they go from walking to bikes to motorbikes to cars, and each step smells and sounds worse, and is more dangerous to others. The price of progress. The holiness of Pushkar's lake brings the Hindu pilgrims, and the Western tourists too come for its comparative calm. Here I wrote BLUE:

"Blue is often the color of Brahmans' houses,
and the god Krishna, beloved on bank calendars, is blue
too, and not just the sea and sky in India only,
but the blue shirt I bought bleeding blue on my trousers
so I'm all over blue, like Jodhpur's houses of every hue
of this color. But I'm not blue, I'm not lonely
or sad, though alone.

I'm pleased at being in Pushkar
by the holy Hindu lake eating ice cream and chow mein
when it suits my appetite, but deploring in vain
certain modern inroads. Camels share with cars,
and practising for Pakistan, army jets circle like vultures
but with more noise. Water pumps thump more than bubble,
and generators illuminate the scene with sound.
Selling *puja*, worship, at the lake is another racket,
giving flowers, sweets, and a red cord bound
around the wrist, demanding 200 rupees for the packet.
Trucks bless all with blue fumes. The incense is in trouble.

I can smell the herbs cut by the squatting women,

I can see the blue kingfishers flash off the phonelines,
I can hear Hindu prayers magnified on speakers.
Worshippers bathe in the holy lake, are bathed by the blue
of T.V. sets in *paan* shops. Among the fumes I smell a lemon.
Like most tourists and most Indians, I'm of two minds
about this clash of two cultures; we as true-blue seekers
of the exotic also want lots of the familiar. All too
true, pros and cons, both this and that. All too true.
The child Krishna, bitten by poisonous snakes, turned his beloved blue."

There are lots of animals in the streets of Pushkar. Cows wandering, trying to filch fruits from open-air market stalls. Dogs trotting or lying around, trying to find some shade to sleep in. Each competing to live in this harsh desert land, just as we humans do. I walked out into the surrounding desert often to think and observe. There's a high hill overlooking the town, with a small temple at the top, and a very long stepped-path to get to it. It's a holy trudge, harder in this heat, often at 120 degrees, but old and sometimes fat Indians manage it. (I've noticed over the years that the handsomest Indians are often the poor, and the middle and upper classes are soft and fat and the men somewhat epicene.) Birds can get to this temple the easiest, and scout for crumbs of bread or cake to eat. Men and beasts and birds all competing. I wrote ANIMALS IN PUSHKAR:

"In the rain-pitted desert near Pushkar there are these hieroglyphic lines, usually straight, Nazca lines miniaturized, made by the feet of ants. Ant feet repeated, patter of tiny feet erases the patter of rain, darker brown dots on the dry desert. Tracks looking like a treadless bike had passed. The ants flow like black blood corpuscles in a vein. Strange so many bodies in a path so neat.

"The animals are enlisted in the people's army. Even cows who flop down in front of cars on the road, drop their cow flop down for fuel, for fly-proof floors their urine. That banana peel, that sweet-stained newspaper page, all are grist for milk, urban grass. But so are apples from a vendor's cart, bananas meant for monkeys at the bathing ghats. The monkeys fight back, slapping the cow's nose, grabbing the giving man's trousers with man-like hands, frantic as the fruit sellers.

Millet and corn flung out by pilgrims at the ghats are mopped up by pigeons and goats, not gods. *Puja*, worship, is taught and sold by young swaggerers, aping the worst of the West. Several magpies swoop down on a *pakora* stand, scattering what they can't grab as the owner aims his stick at them. Sparrows pluck twigs from a broom for their nests at Brahma Temple. Gods and animals connive at mirroring man. Water buffalo stare at us as though they were Indians. Dogs will nuzzle you, then run to attack another dog, their doggy hierarchies to maintain.

All paths lead to food or power, as we enlist in the army of animals. Peacocks, resplendent in green and blue, cry their strident cat call; cats, in heat, yowl theirs; the disco blares down the road; a parrot parrots the green leaves, but brighter; a dead green snake, foot and a half long, is eaten by ants. Yellow wasps enjoy a swimming pool. Wisdom, dead or alive, is a trodden path,with prints of ants and birds and men. When electricity fails here, candles light up our past as well as our path. Villagers shit in the dry river bed leading to holy Pushkar Lake. When the rains come, all we hoped to leave for the pigs to eat comes streaming down to stain us. Brahma, in his temple, has four faces in a two-faced world. Rain under florescent lights makes muddy puddles flash and glitter and shimmer, reflecting the restaurant, pretty colors, thin wet layer over mud."

In 1982 I spent about a week in Pushcar; in 1993 I spent two weeks there, hiking, writing, reading, drinking orange and pomagranate juices at the juice wagons on the street. In 1993 I first took a room in a private house, overlooking the lake and the bathing ghats. However, the toilet was down a couple of outside staircases on the outside wall, and the family also used it so it wasn't private, and the monkeys who clustered around the walls could enter my window and steal stuff. After a day there, I got a large room, private bathroom and terrace overlooking a garden, including noisy peacocks, in a state-run guesthouse. Pretty cheap, with room to write, room to relax away from everyone.

More away from everyone is Jaisalmer, far out in the Thar Desert. In 1982 there were many fewer people. I hunted around to do a camel safari with a young English couple, and finally found someone who could take us. Three camels—the other two had riders sitting behind them to control their camels. I insisted I would ride alone, so my camel guide stayed home. We just went for one night out. Camping on someone's roof was at first wonderful—the stars were within your grasp. Then it rained—so we went below and slept in the crowded rooms with the family and the guides.

Next morning, back to Jaisalmer.

In 1993, the camel safaris found you. Lots more hotels built, and every one could have a camel safari arranged for you. A big business now. "Two days, three days, five days—whatever you wish!" I wished for three days, and got it. There were five of us and three guides. One of the women, French, couldn't eat anything, and kept throwing up and fainting, but we made it back all right. Riding a jeep out to connect with the camel drivers, we stopped at a tiny village which had a festival of swinging. A swing was attached to a tree branch and the villagers were flying way up and back, taking turns. I got a turn and pumped it way up till it almost fell back instead of swinging. Just showing off. Lots of delight and friendliness there. Then on to rendezvous with the camels at the edge of a Sahara-like area of sand dunes. Most of the Thar that I saw was like the northern Arizona desert—dust rather than sand, rocky, with a few scrubby plants. Where we met them was like deep northern Africa Sahara. We had an hour or so to wander these dunes, and I walked off on them alone to imagine what a few hundred miles of these ahead of you on a safari might be like. Daunting! This was now late afternoon, my shadow was immense lying across the high curved dunes, and we set up camp for the night. The stars that night were bright and piercing, and the whole sky was lit up with just background starlight. I watched the stars from my pallet till I fell asleep.

Next day, I helped collect the camels. They had been hobbled, but could slowly move to graze.

The second day I was told to find my camel and bring him in. I found him over a hill, walked up, patted his neck, and bent over to pat the back of his knees to get him to raise his feet so I could remove the hobbling rope, then looped the rope over his neck as a lead and walked toward the camp. He obediently followed, to my relief. Camels are big, strong, and often hard to control, and will bite and kick you. When one tried to bite me, I slapped him in the neck and gave him the "don't try that again" look. It works usually with horses, and it worked with this camel. They have one hump which the wooden saddle, with a hole in its middle, is put over, and then comes the blankets and more blankets. In Rajahstan the camel blankets are of very coarse wool. Very coarse. After a couple of days riding a camel, your bottom is shredded raw. I suggest either getting the camel drivers to get you a smooth blacket, or to take a smooth cover for theirs. All of us had raw buttocks after this trip, and a few of the travelers walked beside their camels the last day. I didn't—I paid for the damn camel, I'll ride on him!

Camels are controlled by their reins being run through the inside of their nostrils, so any tug will be extremely painful to resist. How else to control such a large recalcitrant beast? The ropes to hobble them are also used as leads and as stirrups so you can shift your weight to stand up in the "saddle" to relieve your butt. The weather on this trip was brutally hot, but at one point where was a small shallow lake and we bathed in it. The reason there was water in it was that there had been a huge downpour just before we got to Jaisalmer, and the rivers flooding kept anyone from getting to or out of the city for a few days. We were the first people to get in. Our bus couldn't do it and told us to get back in, we were going back to Jodhpur. In a pig's eye, sez I. Several other bus passengers also rebelled, and we found a 4-wheel-drive jeep that would try to get across the flooded river. The road had been washed out, but the water was way down. We drove through the flooded wash, got stuck, piled out and pushed, shoveled and shoved, and finally cleared it. And then off to Jaisalmer. We saw a big crane trying to right a overturned slightly crushed bus, which later we heard had tried to ford the river, been moved to the side by the water, started to overturn, and two people in panic tried to escape by going through their windows, and were crushed and killed when the bus turned over on them. One man was Indian, and the other, a woman, was English and on her vacation. Suddenly you're dead. She was with some friends and now she's gone. Happy trails!

In Jaisalmer several old houses had collapsed because of the rain, and one old woman was crushed beneath one. Walking along to pick up some rice, crash—you're history. They hadn't yet cleared the fallen stones from this collapse up in the ancient golden fort of Jaisalmer, and I was reminded of a fellow I had met in Prague on this trip, and of his story. So I wrote EDDY:

"I met an Englishman named Chris, with earring and tattoo,
who moved away from England to live in Amsterdam, and who,
when needing extra cash, would drive from here to there
whatever goods needed moving. Staying still was more than he could bear.
Chris loved to travel, and once he ended up in Sumatra
on a river as rough as roads are there, jounce and
jog, lurch, the ruts all filled with water, the sand
and gravel slipping. So on this river, three friends and Chris
went past some rapids and then were snagged by an eddy,
going round to nowhere else, with a slap and a hiss.
Paddling hard they tried to break out of this undulating ellipse,
but failed. Tried again. Harder. Again failed. "O.K. Now ready.
Pull!" Failed again to break out. The eddy hissed its mantra.
For two hours till arms were weak and fear was getting
stronger, they knew the eddy would calmly stay the same,
and they could end up starved to death, or with despair's eclipse
of reason could leap and try to swim. Doomed. So heading
nowhere, they readied for just one last push, draining despair
into propulsion. "Push!" Whines in their throats, teeth set,

they paddled to their bodies' edges, and just then
.   broke free.
The eddy still whispered, but now further away,
            each stroke
into currents new and strange. They now knew
            that Nature doesn't let
desire nor desperate need swerve her current laws;
            no prayer
but doing only, springs you from when you need
            a pattern broken,
some monotonous regularity of eddy in life
            or river or rhyme."

Jaisalmer once had a pattern of *sati or suttee* where the widows would throw themselves on their husband's funeral pyre. On a hill near the town, there are many cenotaphs of dead rajahs and important people of the town, and there are carvings on these tombs showing the numbers of wives who sacrificed themselves in this way. If they were reluctant to throw themselves on the pyre, then their fathers or brothers would throw them on, to keep the family from dishonor. In 1993 during the August heat, I thought and wrote a lot about death. UNDER THE BODHI:

"The Buddha said the earth is burning. Get out. Withdraw.
The body wants its sex and chocolate. The soul wants more.
Today's Fire Sermon: quick nuclear war, slow burn of decay.
The body overshadows us; the bodhi tree illumines the core
of what mere body and what pure soul. Or so they say.

On pillars in the Pearl Mosque, Red Fort, Delhi,
a vegetation motif looks like flames, like waves.
In an old and ruined Delhi fortress, a dying kitten's belly
had bright red spots on it, the scum in the well bright greens.

A blue-winged kingfisher bird, sudden flashing out, saves us and preens.

On the way to Jaisalmer an English girl was crushed and drowned
in a bus upset by a flood. In a tank of rainwater held by a mound
of earth a young boy cracked his head and drowned.
Each man's death **increases** me. To my stories, a little spice.
Which bus rolls over, which die? Whose number comes up on the dice?

The fragile dew weds the green with the light.
Both blood and flame are red, red even a sore.
Warmth drinks the dew. Green bills make hot the whore.
Death adds color and dash. The body has the soul bound tight.
The stars are like salt, so appetizing, on the night."

A young French guy and I had hiked a bit in the desert, and we stopped
at this small pond near the town where many young boys and men were
diving off a rock and swimming. We were invited to join them, but the
water was so sandy that you couldn't see what was under it, and so we both
declined. The next day, passing this pond again, I heard screams and
found people very distraught and milling around and shouting. A boy had
dived into the pond and broken his neck by landing head-first on the
cloudy shallow bottom. Just another reminder of death unexpected.
    Walking around in this ancient hilltop fortress and town, narrow streets
and few crowds here, but in the new town surrounding this hill, more
crowds, hassles, hotels, motorbikes, camels and donkeys. And around this
town too is a poor mud-brick village where you can if you wish bargain for
a camel trip or some crafts or food. This is where I learned that camel
urine on the floor and walls keep the ubiquitous pesky flies away. This is
where and how most Rajahstanis live. In the newer richer town there are
rooftop tourist restaurants and leather shops where I bought a round
backpack made from camel hide. Riding a camel scrapped my hide badly;
now I literally have his hide on my back. Speaking of hides (in two senses),

once in 1982 I got a room with a very young English girl, Katie, in the fancy Jailsalmer Hotel up in the town. We got a good deal on it and so splurged. Giving her a massage one evening, and nuzzling at her breasts, she suddenly leaped up and screamed. I looked to my right and saw an eye peering at us through a hole in the wall. In many places in India and Sri Lanka, holes are made in the walls so that the staff can ogle the naked women in their rooms or while showering. It is fairly common in the hotels I stayed at. I whipped on my shorts and chased him outside, but couldn't get him. Next day, she headed off to her trip and I went down to cheaper rooms (a room on a roof) down the hill. We took a camel trip for an afternoon, and saw one evening a famous and rarely seen green flash at sunset from our room—the green lasted for almost half a minute. The beauty and the squalor mixed.

In 1993 in August, I had a lot of time to hike, but usually waited till 2 or 3 p.m. to go for my afternoon hike into the desert because the heat (120 degrees) was so intense. I wrote:

"The wind walks like the Japanese, scuffing the stone
of the church in Telc [Czech Republic], scuffing the headstones' names
and messages, driving complex flesh out of remembrance.
The dead are now just names, evoke sadness for ourselves
only at the wind's blowing. The wind rubs, time embraces, polishes.
In Rajahstan this process quickens. You can watch the sand
wash out your prints. Sand and water hitch up with wind
on time's team to polish up our livings' pride,
to wear down all thought of the dead, of all who pass.
"The sandstone in the desert near Jaisalmer weathers like charred books,
all books, no matter how hard, made of just sand.
Monsoon puddles, dried, flake leaves of mud, sun- and time-curled.
One low tree, comforting in the sand, smells like lemon tea,
while the rest smell of wind and silence, of heat and absence.
Plants string out like spiders, hugging the dunes for dear life.

A thorn went through my shod sole an inch, long, impressive, like
viper's fang.
What lives and moves leaves its mark impressed in sand.
The camel's splat of foot, the lizard's skittery jittery print,
the spread-tines forks of birds, the prod of goats, the wide brush
strokes of the desert vipers, and my distinct and foreign lattice,
unnatural, shod. Walking back an hour later, all tracks are blurred,
my foot's impressive power gone while the wind blows loud and blurs.
There is one desert bush, fern-like, low, that scribbles on a dune
with fingers of branch and wind. The whoo-who of the wind swishes
chaotic messages or self-expression, worm trails, of desert
calligraphy which the bush, sun-burning, god's casual hand,
impresses on my mind, and hard, before tree and wind wipe them out."

Before time erased my memories, in November 1993, in Puri, India, I
wrote of places I'd gone to so far on my Sabbatical trip—what I liked, what I
didn't. Here's a chunk of that. First, the great moments: OH, WOW!
"Oh, wow! The moon over Prague Castle;
Oh, wow! Krumlov Castle, the painted ballroom, the view from the
covered bridge of the roofs of the town, the old oaks of the castle park, the
sun-speared woods, the cobbled square, the luscious chocolate sundaes;
Oh, wow! Telc with its wide old-fashioned square and houses;
Oh, wow! Slicing tthe scroll of the Duna, the Danube, by boat, the
round Hungarian rolling hills rolling back;
Oh, wow! India! Amber Fort defending now the barren hills above
Jaipur, the Maharajah's Palace now museum;
Oh, wow! Taj Mahal—maha, maha, maha, mahal! Sweaty and airless
below with the real sarcophagus above ground; Taj white marble now
browner and greyer under the changing light and sky; Agra's Red Fort and
its cool white mosque, so cool to bare feet, and fountains;
Oh, wow! Views of Lake Pichola from the Maharajah of Udaipur's palace;
the funny New Zealander Brice and how many uses can we squeeze out of

the name of the food "Idilly," and our rickshaw trip to the top of the Monsoon Palace hill and the views, and that strange tame gazelle-like creature by the side of the road and its licking our arms for salt;

Oh, wow! Jaisalmer on the Thar Desert—the color of the turbans and the sarees and the bravo mustaches of these sun-blackened people; the camel safari and the solitary walk on the dunes at sunset, and the whole sky at night more full of stars than I've ever seen it, stars even seen in the empty places of the night sky; and two days later the yellow fort of Jaisalmer on the horizon; the full moon later on and the quiet dog-haunted and cow-full streets of the fort—quiet, ancient, sleeping; the chicken jalfrezi at the Trio Restaurant just over the maharajah's palace; the little Hindu temples—the birth of Krishna celebrated by the henna-haired old man and his harmonium; the singing through of the text of a whole holy book in the hot Shiva temple with the flies singing over the butter-soaked lingam; the Jain temple so intricately carved and their priest so greedy and pushy; just me, the priest, and Durga in the tiny private temple just near the jail by the fort; the views over the desert and the cool breeze from the fort's battlements; the long walks in the afternoons to the far hill and past, in the desert with its wind and then silences, its dunes and tracks and shrubs, and only in the distance a camel or sheep or man or cow, and then returning toward the town on its mesa, passing the old golden stone cenotaphs and red memorials of Rajput royalty; the fresh orange juice and the choco-pops and fresh lime sodas to tame the scorching heat; Oh, wow! Varanasi—the river and the bathing ghats thronged at daybreak, the orange ball ascending, the smoke ascending from the cremation pyres, life and death ascending; Oh, wow! Puri—the long beach, the fishing village, the sun and moon taking their share of time; the prawn masala at Xanadu Restaurant, the fish battering the air drowning...."

There are more of these "oh, wow!' moments in the section on Nepal, but all these moments must be balanced by the inevitable frustrations and pains of traveling. I did so by writing BLOODY:

"Bloddy Prague street numbers—late at night, trying to find my designated lodging in Caroly Square, feeling that Kafka is not fiction, not finding the numbered building; Czech language is too foreign for me;

Bloody Hungarian train conductor—trying to charge me more for the trip to Bratislava because we were more in Hungary than in the Czech Republic than my ticket seemed to show (I didn't pay extra);

Bloody money-changer at the bank in Delhi Airport who tried to cheat me of 500 rupees (didn't succeed); Bloody "Delhi Belly" knockout from eating at several of the Nirula restaurants, and then when sick, feeling "Why did I come to India again?" while outside the monsoon rains flooded Delhi streets;

Bloody beggars and salemen everywhere, their pitches thrust at you with the glue of persistence—hoping to wear you down with patter like the monsoon drops;

Bloody rickshaw-wallahs everywhere, lying about distances and prices and hotels, only anxious to get as many commissions as possible;

Bloody touts everywhere, bombarding you with true and false information about everything; Bloody fevers, the pain of stepping on a poisonous fish, the "shits," the long lines at banks and railway offices, where the lines are burgeoning at the front with new arrivals who let the patient "tail" of the line wither with neglect or explode with anger;

Bloody traffic in India—no sidewalks, except to lay out your work or stuff to sell on, so no one can walk on them; the buses and trucks driving in the center of the road, and many of them still trying to pass each other; the constant struggle for right of way so that the person who sees the traffic behind you has to step out toward it;

Bloody people of Puri beach who will not take "no!" for an answer about selling you their massage, peanuts, post cards, getting from you a school pen or money, and who force you literally in some cases to pick them up and deposit them away from you;

Bloody friendliness that won't leave you alone or in peace—"Tell me, what is your country?"

My country is not here!
My country is not here!
My country is not here!"

And yet on balance, when I am balanced, India is worth going to again. And I will.

SRI LANKA:

Sri Lanka started out great. After the short crowded ferry ride from Rameswaram at the southern tip of India, got to the calm uncrowded ruins of Anaradapura. Bicycled alone around these ancient temples and palaces, with the few Sinhalese I saw all so friendly—big wave, big smile. "Good morning!" I shouted to them, feeling wonderful and free. From the beach in Hikaduwa one week later, I wrote in a letter of April 28, 1979, "The people here are very sweet, compared especially with most of the Indians, who seem more aggressive and hustling." But the heat now before the monsoon was murderous: "this room is like a wet oven, or a barbecue pit still working under a lake. Hot and moist." Sri Lanka, once known as Ceylon, and also known as the land of Serendip, felt fortunately arrived at.

Part of the reason for my delight was Sabine. I was thirty nine; she was nineteen and very pretty, a German girl traveling alone, and now with me. Casually while traveling, you hook up with another person traveling in the same direction, share a room to save money or for companionship, which can lead to sex or good friendships. I had just come from the Raj Neesh Ashram, so I was used to both easy and casual sex on this trip and also to easily accessed and expressed emotion. First came the casual sex. In Hikaduwa I wrote SIMILARITIES:

"I looked up, hearing the wind in the palms, but then remembered the surf.

Somewhere on this beach in Hikaduwa a wave is always breaking,
breaking pouring into my ear along with the swish of, same
swish as wind. And I've seen earth red too as fire. And no one could tell

in the tangle of wet, hot and pubic hair which is Sabine's and which is mine.

Today a grey-fisted cloud clamped down on the sun and the whole sea greyed its green, and the thunder stepped in its boots, loud like the surf."

While lying on the beach with Sabine in Hikaduwa, a European man ran over to me and asked me very politely if I could swim well. I said yes, and he asked me, very politely, if I could help rescue his wife, because he couldn't swim well, and his wife could not get back to shore past the breakers. I ran off and helped her in. She had not been drowning, but the waves seemed too big to ride in. I loved these big waves—great body-surfing! But I knew how easily a lazy day at the beach on vacation could kill someone.

In Colombo for a few days. Most impressed by their zoo "with superb botanical stuff. Vegetation like the jungle, with jungle animals—in cages, true, but well-arranged." Danger and wildness, but tamed for our ease and pleasure. Jungle shaped for our own human paths.But brutally hot."Wll go up to the hills soon to get away from the heat (they have hill stations high up with a climate like England...)"

From hot to cold. Not just the weather, but my emotions too. On May 6 I wrote, "Life with Sabine, my German girl was fine for a week, but when we were traveling for 2 days to get to Numara Eliya (pronounced "New Aurelia"), it got too sticky. She was snappy, so I displaced my anger onto the poor peasants who stared at us like freaks, and escaped into reading. Then I realized: why take shit? So for a day, I went my own way, and when she was with me I walked around this beautiful garden deliberately at my own pace and my own pauses. No compromises. For a night, I took a double room, but just for me, while she (to save money) stayed in a dormitory. Next day I left. She came out of her room to see me off, and she cried, and we hugged. She was hurt, but I was pleased, relieved, a bit lonely and sad and horny. [Later on, I got a note in the mail from her— "How did it go wrong?" I wrote back, and tried to explain. She's German, and so likes to plan everything meticulously and was so decisive that I felt crushed by her.] But—no need for me to take shit! How good it feels! Nuwara Eliya is tea-growing hill country (6182 feet up) and is rainy and cold at night. What a change from the heat a few bus-hours away!"

From hot to cold. The country as backdrop to our emotional tangles. One problem with traveling with Sabine was the difference in our ages. Not a problem between the two of us, but with every Sinhalese we'd meet, from waiters to hotel clerks to ordinary folk. "Is she your daughter?" was their common question. Once I said she was not, they stared and grinned and made obviously salacious comments to each other, and it felt humiliating. I remember one restaurant where several waiters after we ordered food, simply stood very close to our table and were commenting and laughing at us, till, finally I stood up and pushed them all gently over to the other side of the room. In our bathrooms, we found several "spy holes" where the staff would observe their guests at their toilets. My feelings about the Sri Lankans in my letters show increasingly diminished respect and affection. Part of this is because of traveling with a lovely but much younger woman. It happened before, in India and elsewhere.

Once in Puri, India, I was asked by a very young and pretty English woman if she could travel with me down south—she was about 19, I was just 54. She was very sweet, but I knew I wouldn't be able to sleep in the same room as she was without getting very sexually frustrated, and even if we did have sex, I remembered my annoyance with the Sri Lankans drooling over Sabine, and I said sorry, but no. This young girl and I went in to the surf once after she had put on a tee shirt over her bikini, then removed her bikini top underneath the shirt. Once in the chilly water, her nipples stuck out under the cold wet shirt and I remarked on this and told her that this was sexier than if she just had her bikini top on. She said she knew this but—and raising her shirt a little—said she could stand not for Indians to see her very white belly. (It was very white and seemed very private.) As we stood there, suddenly into the surf came charging several young Indian men right for us, so we waded back on to the beach, I acting as a blocker for her. She said this happened all the time to her, and she was really hating the Indians for it. A neighbor of mine in my hotel, traveling with her boyfriend, had been pursued while on her bike by several Indians, and decided to go back to Canada early to get away from the "damn Indians."

The Sri Lankans seemed not so different to me as my month here went on. Of course, about one third of the people in Sri Lanka are of Indian origin, mostly from Tamil Nadu, and many of these Indians wanted independence from the majority Sinhalese and the Sri Lankan government. Even back in 1979, there were fights and killings between the Sinhalese and the Indians resident in the country, as I was told by a Sinhalese in Trincomalee. He said some Sinhalese were massacred by Indians up north, but the Sinhalese will take revenge soon. (And they have.) On April 18 in Negombo, a city near Colombo, the capital, I wrote, "Ceylon is getting (and has been getting) much too much. I'd love to miss this place! For example. Last night the mosquitoes kept me up till 4 a.m.; some imbecile has to ask me the same f——— questions ("Where is your country?" "What is your name?") that everyone else always does even when all I want to do is sit and eat my dinner in peace; now some employee of my hotel has to take me out to eat (and sit, and wait, and blow smoke in my face)—they just can't give me instructions (down a straight road), but must hang about while I eat. This place is on my nerves! Also, I've just had one week of being really faint, and the "shits," etc. feeling **awful**, but now after a doctor (and then another) and a bit of good food last night at Colombo's Ceylon International Hotel (American style), I feel human again."

So it's not really fair to talk of Sri Lanka as a pain. The pains were often more in me. Being very sick with, as one doctor put it, "malnutrition, amoebic dystentery, and a virus that's being going around in Sri Lanka lately" was more my problem than was the country. When I arrived in Trincomalee on the west coast, sans Sabine, I met a woman on the bus who, a week or so before when she asked me where she could get a shell necklace like the one I was wearing, I took mine off and gave it to her. She remembered this, and once we arrived, asked me to come with her to share a room at some cheap place on the shore. I was passing a hotel which looked pretty good, but when she said that it seemed too expensive for her, I decided we should part company. She was cute and nice, but I was feeling the need for a big rest and a bigger respite from other people. Especially from women. I got a room in my hotel and collapsed.

Literally collapsed. I would struggle out of bed to the toilet or shower, and would faint. I had no appetite for any of the food here (which was not as good as Indian food), but I did have a recurring daydream about food: I conjured up a soft-salami sandwich with Gulden's mustard on rye bread with caraway seeds in it. Why this specific food? Because it is quintessentially Brooklyn, I grew up in Brooklyn, Brooklyn meant my old home, and my old home meant my mother and Dad, and they meant I would be taken care of! I weighed less than 105 pounds after this week-long seige of illness, and felt lonely although I did want to be alone. This sick and weak week cast an unfair pall over the whole month-long stay in Ceylon.

The temples in Anaradapura and in Polonnaruwa were interesting, especially the beautiful reclining buddha and the statue next to him of Ananda Gal Vihare (I've a postcard to remind me of these statues). The Rock Temple with its many golden buddhas and carved and painted ceilings cut from the rock in Damballa was stunning. Hikaduwa's waves and Colombo's zoo were very fine. But the most amazing sight was Sigiriya Rock. Two huge lion's paws straddle the entrance to the stairway, which then turns into a narrow pathway along the few-hundred-feet-high rock face along which I got to the summit. Great views from the top and great topless great-big-bosomed painted figures of women holding jewels and lotus flowers. The combination of this religious and sensual art enhances this natural dominant upthrust of Sagiriya Rock, one of the grandest sights here.

Another lovely spot? "Bus to Kandy, and a sweet place it is! Beautiful lake with the famous Temple of the Tooth on its marge. I went there twice for the drums and (a sort of) flute playing, and viewing of the sacred place—gold and jewel-encrusted—where a tooth of Gautama Buddha is laid. (The Portuguese said they destroyed the tooth when they were in their "only Christian things are good" phase, but the Ceylonese say that they only destroyed a replica. Who knows?) Marvelous botanical gardens in a nearby town. Spent all day at them. Wrote two poems there, and one in my room this morning. This after a non-creative few weeks. Feels good to have the muse back again. I missed her." I also missed sex with Sabine, but didn't miss her as a person much.

The sexual and parasitic images of this poem I wrote in Kandy fit my mind's underlying ambivalence with Sabine (and with many many other women).

BOTANICAL GARDENS NEAR KANDY, SRI LANKA:

"Like some delirious packing clerk, like a boatswain with amnesia, Nature ties her trees with creepers up till vines can winding no more find, parasite not belly-room to lie and prey, so entangled, dangled they are, the trunk's not seen or parts seem wholes or holes in lines of vines that hang till tree gives up, and passes life to parasitic snakes that suck, like rococo obscuring lines the life from some great simple truth which lies there wooden, thick, and straight till wind's whim and seed's weight start the spiral in time up tree, and we can grasp these vines as they do tree and climb up top or like Tarzan swing free from crisis claw to stable truth on— oh, say—Pegasusean wings of poetry."

My desire to fly off and away emerges also from another poem on these gardens:
"In the Botanical Garden near Kandy, there's a road
runs round a circle where all the world
leaders have planted trees. Sianouk late of Cambodia,
U Thant of Burma, Tito still alive and rooted.
A thicker firmer tree was in 1891 planted
by the late Czar of Russia. In it, ravens romp,
beaking in a patty of cow shit or in grass as here,
or in eyes at Austerlitz—it's all the same

food, and appetite the same. A mahogany tree
on this circle has many branches which rise
looking like trunks from the base. I too try to rise
like a raven from the base I need to the air
I want. Even the local sports wear thick-bottomed shoes.
Time that fed these trees planted these men
who planted them and now nourish other
trees or grass or men. The road runs round,
and people walk, trees grow, and ravens, ravens romp."

The sense of everything being food and prey for something else, whether plants or animals or men, is easy to arrive at in poor and sometimes desperate Asia. When this intellectual premise is combined with one's own hunger and dysentery, body and bowels and mind agree, and out popped and pooped a poem:

"Kandy's artificial lake is natural enough. Real fish feed and carp about the sewage pipe that pours their daily bread upon the waters. You can see them nibbling air not only for practice, while waiting. Augustine says we are born between the piss and the shit. Anatomically speaking. I too hang around the sewage pipe, nibbling, for practice, at airy sexy vision or at hairy fishy flesh. I do not always want to want what I want. On Kandy Lake a white blossom sails taut, quick, looking ambitious, will-less across the willing water."

At that fancy Ceylon International Hotel in Colombo, when I so needed food after being so sick in Trincomalee, I sat down in their air-conditioned coffee shop, very much like one in a five-star hotel in America, and ordered a Salad Nicoise. A chilled salad, lettuce and tomato, with a scoop of tuna fish in the center. Followed by a big vanilla milk shake. Fish. Milk. Women. Delicious.

After eating, I went back to my cheap hotel where I had to yell to stop one of the staff from climbing up to look in at my transom while I was lying in bed. After a month here, I was very willing to sail through the air back to India.

NEPAL1: KATHMANDU:

Before 1954 Westerners weren't allowed into Nepal, but by the 1970's it was easy to get there. Easy if you flew, that is. My summer trip of 1982 started with a flight to Delhi and the next morning, a flight to Kathmandu. Fast and easy. But my trip in October 1978 was overland, and neither simple nor comfortable.

In early October, after spending the night in Patna, India, I started for Kathmandu. Went across the Ganges River by crowded ferry, then with two French guys and one French woman, got a jeep-taxi toward the border. After a couple of flat tires and some sharp frustration, I saw a man walking his water buffalo along the road, and asked him, pointing to his buffalo, "Raxaul?" which was the town at the India/Nepal border. He didn't understand. I said it again, and pointed to his still moving buffalo. Ah, yes! He nodded, and I climbed on the buffalo's back, which did not bother the buffalo much—they are usually very phlegmatic—and which delighted everyone except the jeep driver, and I proceeded to shout, "To Raxaul!" and goad on the buffalo. After some time, further down the road, I dismounted, thanked the grinning buffalo owner, patted the buffalo on his huge black back, and went back to where the driver still worked on his flat tire.

Eventually got to where we could get a bus. Problem is, like in so many poor countries, the bus was jammed. Not just inside, but outside as well. The roof was chock full of people and their possessions, but we all wanted to get on, so we all did. At first, I rode on top just over the cab, but there was nothing to hold on to, and the curved camber of the cab meant every time the bus turned to the left you slid to the right, and vice versa, the roof being simply smooth shiny metal, and there was nothing between you and the ground but air. I was the only one foolish enough to be on top of the cab, and I realized I could slip off and be killed very easily. So soon I crept toward the rest of the people crowded around their luggage, which area at least had maybe a foot and a half fencing around the edge of that part of the roof. Now while it was harder to fall off this part, being so intertwined with everyone else, you could still be swept off whenever the bus went underneath the branches of a tree, which it did frequently. You had to face forward into the wind, and when a low-hanging branch came at you at 40 miles an hour, you had to duck and pull others down as well. All the passengers seemed to take this as a game, and laughed despite the dangers.

Finally "we got to Raxaul, then crossed the border with lots of stops to Birganj on the Nepalese side. Suddenly the electricity wasn't there. Kerosine lamps or candles lit up the small shops. Primitive and dirty (even compared with India)." So I noted in a journal. "Stayed in a room in Birganj with the 3 French, 2 Dutch, 2 Swiss and their child. Next day by 10-hours-or-so bus through great rolling hills and rice paddies to Kathmandu, there the French and I went to the Maha Laxmi Guest House (a single room on the roof, sharing it with the water tank, cost 15 rupees—12 Nepali rupees = $1)." It felt like a long trip.

In 1993 I took a long-distance bus from Delhi to Kathmandi, the bus filled mostly with Tibetans returning from an audience with the Dalhi Lama in India, and it took three and a half days to get to the Nepalese capital. No room in the seats, so I rode up in the driver's cab, along with two other tourists, plus about three or four of the driver's assistants. We were sleeping all over each other, in amongst the gear shift, water bottles, propane canisters, and tools. An ordeal, but the driver was the only one who drove, so all was on his schedule—when he was tired, he stopped, when he was ready, he drove, when he didn't have to take a meal or a leak or a dump, no one else did either. He drove in the day and often through the night when the traffic was less. We wasted almost a day at the Customs because they suspected the Tibetans of smuggling stuff in—they had massive and intricately tied-up bundles of electronics gear and clothing, all of which had to be undone and pawed and argued over interminably. Who knows what bribes passed hands before the customs inspectors let us through, too late to cross the border into Nepal that night. We slept in the diver's cab, interlaced with the driver's crew. No much sleep. Car-sick, diarrhea, hungry, the usual.

The most interesting time in Kathmandu was certainly the earliest, in October 1978. When I first arrived, everything was closed for the Durga Puja festival. Durga is the goddess of, among other things, death, and there were parades through the streets honoring her and a vegetation deity and other gods, and the King of Nepal himself presided over a public ceremony of decapitation of goats and water buffalo, with all the military big-wigs there, and the Chinese and U.S. embassy staffs sitting side by side but not mixing, just viewing. Maybe 20 or 30 goats and 20 or 30 buffalo were slaughtered, and even after their heads were laid in a row, their eyes would roll, mouths would open and shut, and ears would wag. These movements didn't last long.

My movements did (not bowel, but by foot and by bike). Kathmandu combined the very primitive—customs, architecture, clothing, streets, temples—with being able to eat a most contemporary lemon meringue pie or Mexican food or a peanut-butter sandwich. Crossing Asia the travelers, starved for non-Asian food, often talked of Kathmandu and its food. Since 1978, the choices of cuisine have grown even more. And not just food. Even in 1978, native Nepali culture was changing. I wrote (Dec.4, '78), "Two Nepali girls, dressed all in the Western mode, stroll through Hanuman Dhoka, arms linked. They have shed their bare feet. They have dropped their nose rings. They circle around the statue of Hanuman, hooded, stained red, mysterious monkey god, dip their fingers, nails polished and stained in the Western mode, into the blood on the stone and touch their foreheads." When I came back from trekking and Pokhara to Kathmandu again in late November 1978, I wrote, "my room's window overlooks Swayambunath Temple up on the hill. With some bargaining, the room costs me 20 rupees ($1.80) per day. Now if the lights wouldn't keep burning out in this part of town, it would be a terrific area. It's right between two tourist areas, but is real Nepali (which translates to [cow and human] shit in the streets and lots of barefoot nose-ringed people carrying enormous loads on their heads, and lots of noise, but quite friendly and easy-going).”

Swayambunath Temple is wonderful. You climb straight up a long steep staircase, with packs of monkeys chattering at you, and clambering all over. Then at the top there is a round series of big drumwheels with prayers on them that you push to turn round, each turn sending up prayers to the gods. There's also a temple with Tibetan monks often chanting in their amazingly deep monotones. The view over the city is instructive, because you can see where the city ends and the rural takes over, the rural farm life that is the basic Nepal. From my room I wrote LOOKING AT SWAYAMBUNATH'S HILL: “Reality is thick, surely thicker than paper. There's a mile and a half of it, between here and that hill. All full of air if of nothing else. Air and distance, both real. All too thick to paste in a scrapbook or hang on a wall. Or pare down to paper, onionskin at bottom only more onion, until finally there's nothing, only air.” How to transfer the smells, the rich and myriad details of that scene to paper or to a photo? Poor pale paper and words!

The food left for the gods in the many temples will rot more quickly than the acid in this paper will dissolve both paper and thought written on it. There's a temple in Patan, a town close to Kathmandu, which has another way of dealing with the food for the gods. “Food and flowers for the god were laid before the priest who placed them on the altar. The Nepali woman watched, placid, as the rats nibbled her sweets. Rats all over the altar, crawling over the god, the food! I wanted to tell the priest of the golden temple of Patan about the rats, but he knew what they were there for.” Rats to the devout Hindus of Kathmandu are just another animal, another sentient being, and the food was to be eaten by them in honor of the gods. Even gods like the food in Kathmandu.

The great stupa of Bodanath, with its huge painted eyes staring out from all four sides to see what is going on in the world, is crowded with Tibetan exiles. The last time, 1993, I was there they had carpet and antiquities shops surrounding the lavishly whitewashed stupa. In 1982 I got there just as a ceremony in honor of the birthday of the Dali Lama was underway, and I joined in, following the maroon-draped monks walking while chanting and tossing white flour to the wind around the circular sides of the stupa. They then had for several days a festival of Tibetan dancing and poetry reading and speeches nearby, they all in Tibetan clothing, drinking yak-butter tea and some things more inebriating than tea, very friendly to me, looking very tough and weather-beaten.

Past Bodanath stupa, once I rode with two American friends (one I had met in Kabul, the other, a psychiatrist from Maui I had met in Delhi—all travelers constantly running into one another on the roads around Asia) by bike to a 4th-century monastery named Changu Narayan, having to wade a river of chilly water above our knees and then a nice hike. Then back through the roads and streets in the dark, a darkness that we in the West don't often see. There were few lights, and they tiny and candles, and I vividly and fearfully remember the trucks and buses roaring over a bridge where I had to hold the bike very steady on a muddy slippery surface to avoid sliding under their wheels.I still sweat thinking about it. Don't ride your bike at night on roads around Kathmandu!

The temples all over Kathmandu in 1978 were very busy and almost ubiquitous, from the temples in Durbar Square, all touristed, to the small Tibetan temple down an alley. Late at night things are different. I wrote, "Late at night, the cows take over. Like bone on bone, the hooves puncture the quiet left in Durbar Square when the hawkers leave. The few Nepalis crossing now carefully skirt the restless circling clattering cows who, in the day, like self-absorbed saddhus, are merely bovine. Now two of them square off, while another mounts a fourth. I walk close, but wary. I know people like this at this hour." "Hawkers" is meant as a pun, meaning people who sell kukri knives and Tibetan woven belts and buddhas, as well as people who hawk and spit more loudly and liquidly that you could believe or bear. "The sound of the East" I thought of it, although in 1993 there seems to be less hawking and spitting. It's so disgusting you sometimes have to laugh at it. The Chinese were the same in 1984. In the USA we'd be appalled to hear such sounds. There, it's just part of the background noise, like traffic.

It's easy to get disgusted too by the animal parts you see for sale in the markets. No Saran wrap here. Just buzzing flys to coat your steak, often with the black hide still on it. Death is no secret here. No euphemisms on the Nepali streets. After ordering a chicken chow mein dish, the waiter went out and grabbed a chicken and killed it for my dish. I could hear the panicky bird from my table. My desire to eat got that particular chicken killed. So I wrote THE RELUCTANT VEGETARIAN: "Suddenly something on my plate cleared its throat and clucked. Clucked at me for eating it. Clucked the death rattle of all the chickens fearful at the moment. (I just ate the vegetables that day.) Next day the cow mood hit me. So I ordered steak. From the kitchen came a moo, a shreik. A waiter staggered out, spattered with blood. Not so rare, I said. Tomorrow lamb curry will render me sheepish at meal time; the ham in my sandwich will "oink" when asked why. Such noise, such sights on my sacrificial table. In Kathmandu the King of Nepal put his hands in freshly decapitated bulls' blood and put his handprints on his regiments' flags to bless them. I saw it. I crumple my napkin up after I use it. A potato may well protest too, but I never learned how to speak Potato."

I never learned to speak Nepali either. English, luckily for me, is the lingua franca out here among all the Western tourists, and the Nepalis who have cause to deal with foreigners learn it. Nepalis are less business-y than are the northern Indians, although in 1982 and even more so in 1993 Indians seemed to be taking over many of the shops, especially in Pokhara. Indians I was told were able to move up to Nepal freely and legally to open businesses there. There goes the neighborhood! More hustling and hassling, more entreaties to "come into my shop, please. No need to buy!" The same with Tibetan women selling their goods. They'd come into a restuarant and sit down at your table while you're eating to try to sell you woven belts or jackets. In 1978 Nepalis left you alone, no sales pressure. Most foreign travelers I met preferred it that way.

So there were changes from 1978 in Nepal and Kathmandu. In 1982, as soon as I got to Kathmandu in early June, I tried for a flight out to Lukla so I could hike in to Everest Base Camp by myself and then return alone, walking back to Kathmandu. It would take me about five weeks I figured, walking through very wet monsoon jungle with lots of leeches, but I was ready. The flight to Lukla was ready too. We were on the runway, the plane's engines were at take-off revolutions, and all the pilot had to do was release the brake and we were off. Then the heightened revs were diminished, and we taxied back to the gate. Rain and fog closed in the airstrip at Lukla, and it at the best of times is a dangerous airstrip, so the flight was cancelled till tomorrow. I talked to the personnel in the weather center and they said the monsoon is coming and they may not be able to fly there. Come see tomorrow. So tomorrow I came again, waited with the other passengers, and the flight was cancelled again.

The other passengers were all Sherpas from the Everest region who were going home now that the trekking season was over. No other tourists or trekkers. I had let a couple of them use part of my baggage allowance for their stuff, and got friendly with them. Their leader told me that trekking through some of the Nepali villages was very dangerous, and that he himself would not go through them alone (as I was intending to do). They'll kill you for your boots, he told me. I just had sneakers, I said. No matter. Too dangerous, he told me. He talked to one of his men, and said that this other guy would accompany me toward the base camp of Everest because it was on his way. But they were heading home, anxious to see their families. I had heard several stories of trekkers being robbed and sometimes killed. Still I would do it.

The third day the flight was again cancelled due to rain. The guys at the airline said it looked like the monsoon rains had arrrived, and that there would probably be no more flights. The Sherpas told me that it the flight was cancelled tomorrow for the fourth time, they would catch a bus to as far as the road went (not far) and trek in the rest of the way. I decided that the third cancellation was it for me, so I cancelled my ticket, went back into Kathmandu and sold my sleeping bag, the one I had since college and used for all my hitchhiking trips. Suddenly I had five or six weeks empty of plans. So I stayed in Kathmandu and hung around.

A couple of weeks later at my hotel, the famous and comfortable Kathmandu Guest House, two men showed up who were part of an expedition to climb Everest. One of them, Al Burgess, I later heard, made it to the top. They were both very strong climbing professionals. We became friendly and after a few days, they invited me to come along with them to the base camp. They were going to hike in early with a few of their Sherpas and help prepare for the expedition. Very tempting for me, except by then I had the usual Nepal bowel problems, could not eat much, and was feeling rather weak, too weak I thought for a three-week hike with world-class climbers. And then I'd have to walk back alone, another few weeks with the monsoon in full pour. I declined their offer with both regret and relief. I did end up agreeing to meet the girlfriend of the Al Burgess (who climbed Everest) in Jaipur in India later on in the summer. (She was a nice but steep climb too.)

I did see Everest. In 1978 I went up with three friends to Nagarkot for the night—"to see the sunset and sunrise—and Mt. Everest, a little nubbin off one other mountain. Lovely, the panorama." But just a little nubbin far in the distance. Never did get much closer.

In 1993 Kathmandu had changed a lot. The tourist areas were larger, many more hotels and restaurants, much too many more cars and motorcycles. Walking over the river to the city of Patan and under an underpass, the fumes from the cars and trucks almost made me faint. Then on to the nearby city of Bhaktapur with lovely bronzes in the museum, and the central Durbar Square is wonderful, mostly unclogged by tourist shops, except for one rather picturesque restaurant. The sunlight in this square over the years seems brighter than anywhere else in Nepal. Every time I'm there I can barely squint, the light's so painful. Seems lately like a calmer

Kathmandu, more like the place I knew in 1978. In 1993 they charge tourists fifty rupees to enter the city, in order to keep the old temples and squares preserved. I applaud the idea. Next time I'm in Nepal, I'll likely stay in Bhaktapur more than in Kathmandu.

In 1993 Kathmandu was disappointing. The traffic of cars and trucks and people drowned out the old slower street life. An American who had lived there for many years said that now, instead of being out in the street, everyone was at home watching television. When I went out to eat, I often chose the restaurant because of what movie they were showing on video, and I was not the only one. Technology had arrived. One Nepali in 1982 told me he was saddened by the changes in his own people, who now were thinking much more about money than they had. Once, he took me and his son to a temple outside of town for a festival where they had the usual animal sacrifices and ceremonies. Old Kathmandu was filthy and exotic, full of human shit and animal blood. I liked it that way.

NEPAL2: JOURNAL OF MY TREK TO ANNAPURNA BASE CAMP:

October 16, 1978: Last night in Kathmandu—met Carlos and Herman (Mexican musicians) who took me to Pashupatinath Temple. Watched burning of corpses from across river. Smoked dope. Went to Practice Restaurant off Freak Street. Talked about spirit, death, circle we all are.

Oct. 17: Bus from 7:40 a.m. to 3 p.m. or so to get to Pokhara, then taxi to Phewa "Lakeside." Stayed with Robert, [Hong Kong] Chinese guy [I had traveled with to Varanasi], in farmhouse masquerading as a hotel (4 rupees per person). [1 Nepali rupee= 8 cents]. Met Efrat, Israeli girl who was to trek with Robert. Diarrhea fairly bad with me. Pokhara city crummy, but Phewa Lake lovely, Hawaii-esque hills surrounding it.

Oct. 18: Left Pokhara by bus for outskirts of town with Robert and Efrat, who were trekking to Jomosom, while I was going to Annapurna Sanctuary alone. Met on bus Matt and Graham, 2 brothers from Canada, also going up to Annapurna, so joined forces. Efrat at last minute decided to trek with me. Walked to Suikot [Tibetan camp with many weavers of carpets], ate, then up the side of the valley and a couple of hours walk to Dhampus on the ridge. Rained. Rice and wheat fields on the way. Lots of leeches! My feet were bitten and bloody. 6 ½ hours of walking, excluding sitting around or eating. Pretty tough hike, especially climbing up to Astam. One rupee per bed. Rained after we got there—hard!

[My sneakers were white, but when I took them off in Dhampus, they were completely red with my blood. The leeches were small, maybe an inch or so long, but there were so many of them, coming out in force during the rainy season, which was supposed to be just about over now, but wasn't. We met a Nepali, bare-legged, coming down from Dhampus, and he said he put salt on his legs, like many Nepalis, to keep off the leeches. Yet he had a leech on his thigh, with a long streak of his blood running down to his knee. (Also, often if you eat in these little "teahouse—hotels" you can sleep on mats or upstairs from the family for free.) On that first day with leeches, Graham, a Canadian doctor, started to panic—"get those damn things off of me!!!"—so we tried to, but they would slide in the openings for our shoelaces, onto our hands as we brushed aside the tall grass, down our socks. This first day was our worst for leeches, but we didn't know that. I was afraid Graham might panic and turn back. My last day on the trail, traveling alone, after defecating off the trail and wiping myself with some leaves, I noticed blood running down my hand. A leech had fastened itself to the webbing between my fingers. When I think of where that leech could have fastened, I feel grateful it was only on my hand!]

In Chomrong, after my Annapurna trek, I wrote: LEECHES:
"They move just like inchworms, curling into half a bow,
then uncurling, or else beckoning like fingers curling
to any flesh or blood on the path to Dhampus
to come closer, to offer itself (myself) to
these leeches, to accept the beckoning fingers
on ferns and grass and stones on you (me)."
I also wrote of that first grey wet evening :
"Around both sides of the ridge of Dhampus, Nepali village,

vapory hands closed. Then the hands poked out gently
our eyes and rained. We're losing the world to this
fog. From Dhampus, we will trek higher to Landrung,
to Gandrung, to Chomrong, and then to
Annapurna, the Nepali for Durga, earth goddess.
But the earth fades more each night as we climb
into the clouds, and life totals just climbing and clouds,
as like a teacher erasing a lesson, it greys out hills and valleys."

Oct. 19: From Dhampus, walked to Landrung, 5 ½ hours hike through rain forest, mostly on the ridge, then down, then across to Landrung. Ate "dahlbat"—rice and dahl and a few fried vegetables (4 rupees—32 cents), the Nepali hill diet. Got the shits—using the fields of wheat or rice as toilet. Then down to the Modi Khola River (rapids) where we crossed on a wooden bridge, then

UP for 2 hours to Gandrung on the other side of the valley from Landrung. [Frustrating to see across a narrow steep-sided valley a town so close as the crow flies, and to realize, not being a crow, you have to make a steep descent and then a steep ascent for hours before you can reach it. Typical in Nepalese trekking!] Magnificent views of terraced rice fields, houses perched on hillsides, grey clouds overhanging the tops of the hills. Stayed in Fishtail Lodge on the floor with a bunch of other trekkers and family. Ate Vegetable Chow Mein plus 3 chapatis [tortillas] smeared with peanut butter, plus milk tea—glass after glass. [Peanut butter from the West has become a staple in some villages—good energy in a small jar. I developed a liking for it for the first time in my life in Nepal.] Chilly weather, cloudy. Just one piece of a view of high Himalayas—Machupuchere Peak riding high still in sun while the valleys were night-full.

Oct. 20: Walked up from Gandrung to a teahouse/hotel overlooking the next valley, then steeply down crossing a river, then up to a ridge from which we saw Chomro ("Chomrung" on the sign here), then down to Chomrung. Stayed at hotel— 5 rupees for eating; sleeping free on floor-mats. Low rain clouds hide the top of hills, except for moments when the

Annapurna massif appears, then disappears. From Gandrung in a.m., saw great views of the whole Annapurna and Machupuchere mountains. Lots of people coming down or going up to Annapurna Sanctuary and base camp—French expedition to climb Tent Peak in the massif; 3 German women and 2 porters returning. A "3-shit night" during which I saw the high Himalayas clear in the moonlight. [A woman's expedition to climb Annapurna was up there then, and several women we passed had tee-shirts on which read, "A woman's place is on the top."]

Oct. 21: Walked from Chomrung to Hinko Cave where we slept. We were now in the main valley leading to the Annapurna Sanctuary [a cirque around which are several peaks of over 26,000 feet elevation]. This valley has steep jungley sides—cliffs, waterfalls, bamboo thickets, much mud—and at the bottom pours the Modi Khola, full of rapids and falls, roaring continuously. Before we got to Hinko Cave [just that—a cave], we found a small tea-house just being built, and there we ate "chow chow"—Tibetan noodle vegetable dish like Chinese Chow Mein at hotel in Chomrung—4 or 5 rupees for chow chow; lodging on the floor on mats is free.

At Hinko Cave very chilly, and had trouble starting a fire, till helped by porters of this German trekker—3 helpers for one guy!—who had carried dry wood up from below. Hinko Cave's about at 10,000 feet.

[We were tired, and began to withdraw into ourselves. I wrote, "Let the chatter stop. Birds chirp the only song they know, the song that's them. Our Tin Pan Alley talk is clatter, clutter, clanging, clash. Hot air to blow up my self's balloon. So blow it up then! Make a hole of silence, a cave where self can cower alone and watch the sun at spirit's noon sear sheer the shadows, in lobotomy of light." I wanted more sun than clouds on this hike, and didn't get it.]

Oct. 22: From Hinko, walked up to Machupuchere Base Camp—tough walk. Elevation starting to be felt, packs weighing on us. From M. Base Camp, could see Machupuchere Peak, steep and looming. Then 1 ½ hours walk through easy up-sloping meadows, Scottish moors nearly, with fog all around. [I was walking and puffing, and I thought to breathe as

though I were trotting, which made this day easier.] Quiet except for the
stream. Clouds obscuring the mountains all day. At Annapurna Base
Camp, altitude of 13,800 feet, a French climber read off 4330 meters
(approx. 14,200 feet) on his altimeter.A French climbing party up there
already, were joined by another French group, but plenty of room up here.
We (Matt, Graham, and Efrat and I) slept under a rock cleft with our tarp
over part of it—but COLD! At night, I had a 4-shit night and so was up
often—from 10:30 p.m. on, the mountains appeared clear in the half-
moon light. [I remember squatting by some rock, my butt freezing, my
stomach clenched, but in awe of the moon-lit peaks finally cloudless and
fully seen. I was actually grateful for diarrhea then, because it got me up
and out of our rock-cleft often that cold night to see Annapurna above me
as bare as my butt.] Occasional avalanches, but a clear and windless night.

Oct. 23: Awoke before dawn and climbed part way up a ridge and
watched the sun come up slowly over the shoulder of Machupuchere [a
peak, called Fishtail, too sacred for anyone to get permission from the
Nepal government to climb], and watched the sunlight work its way down
from the top of the peaks of Annapurna I, Annapurna III, Annapurna
South, Huinchuli, Fang (although we weren't always certain which peaks
were which). Surrounding our camp were these major Himalayan peaks,
and we were actually on the ridge leading to Huinchuli. Took several photos. About 9:30 or 10 a.m. clouds and fog came rolling up the valley
below till it obscured the peaks. Magnificent views before that! While I
was climbing above the base camp, a helicopter flew in ; it seems the fem-
inist American Woman's Expedition is lost, and no one knows where they
are. They are climbing Annapurna I. It took us about 4 ½ days from
Pokhara to Annapurna Base Camp. Pretty good! We left the camp at
11:30 a.m. and got down to the new teahouse 2 hours below Hinko Cave
at late dusk, where we ate dahlbat and tea, and some whiskey in honor of
Gunther's 30th birthday. Lots of mud below Hinko Cave. Started taking
Efrat's anti-dystentery pills (Flagyl) (2 pills 3 times a day for 15 days).

[Gunther must have been the German we met in Hinko Cave. I learned from a Swiss guy with the French expedition that some women were "lost" and at that time I didn't realize he meant killed on the mountain. Two women who fell died on this expedition.]

After this trek I wrote SIMPLE MOVEMENT:
"A new dawn is a new chance in the Himalayas
because all that matters is a good view and warmth.
The in and out of breathing, the clamp of muscles
in the thighs climbing, the jolt of thighs going down
is what matters. The sun here first lights the peak,
then works its way down Annapurna to spill
like yellowed dishwater below base camp.

Chugging up the mountains to Annapurna Base Camp,
I moved quickly, puffing, pushing, steeply climbing
or going down, things in motion remaining in motion,
only the hills at rest, though moving by me
at my same speed. That was then. By Pokhara's Lake,
movement slowed, the steam escaped, the shush
of water softened speed, the slide to the side
started, I slowed, I tired. Stopped. A thing at rest."

[From Chomrong, the other three left for another short trek, and I was ready to relax now.]

Oct. 24: Walked down to Chomrong, had chow chow for lunch, then up, down, then up to Annapurna Lodge in the saddle of a ridge above Gandrung. Rained a bit, as it did yesterday, but it was an easy trip compared with most days. Guess I'm getting fit! [The year before, 1977, I ran the New York City Marathon—4 hours, 3 minutes—which reminds you there's a lot more stamina in you than you think.] Cold at night as usual, but no getting up for a shit in the cold all night. Hooray!

Oct. 25: Morning at Annapurna Lodge; slept on the floor on a mat. Then down to Himalaya Lodge in Gandrung (where I'm writing this journal of the past 3 days). I "did" Annapurna Base Camp in late October with sneakers (not boots), a nylon sleeping bag (not down), no tent, no porters or guide (just a map), one tiny short-sleeve sweater, one thicker sweater, one nylon rain jacket, no down jacket. Hot stuff! "Unprepared" Stickney, Mr. Travel-Light, still brings it off! Spent the whole day sitting around eating and drinking, and hoping for a view of the mountains. No luck.

Oct.26: Saw the peaks Machupuchere and Annapurna South from Gandrung. Washed clothes and me. [Freezing water pouring from a pipe made this a grim business.]

Oct. 27: Walked with Brian and Fran, a Canadian doctor and his wife, down, then up to Chandracot.

Oct.28: Stayed at the tree overlooking the valley in Chandracot. Beautiful and clear views all around, and of Annapurna too. [As the fall turns to winter, there is less rain and fog, and the views are much better. That day I wrote a poem, watching the water buffalo strolling past and ogling the sunlight.]

"Slippy with sun, my body can't remember
the grey cold of Annapurna, nor then
could it recall heat. Climbing out of the valley
to Chandracot, I remember back to Hinko
Cave where in October there's still a snowbank
left over from past winters. Two winters to be precise;
a diagonal line lies between two sorts of snow,
a line that summer's warmth did draw, though none
of summer's warmth remains recorded there.
Sides melt to scalloped edges, reminding me of
Moorish Spanish ceilings, reminder of Arab conquests.
And so lines drawn in history books joggle memory
to warmth and recall, or else cut clean between
the smooth drop down of time and what
occurred. So this snow bank made clear
winters passed with scalloped edges has all

its center melted, like the body's memory of real
hawks sliding stiff through the tangible air,
of duck quack and wood smoke and flies,
of wind waft cool from Himalayas of past feeling."

Oct.29: Walked by myself through Naudanda and down to Phewa
Lake at Pokhara. Got lost at the end, but bushwacked and scrambled
down and made it. When I got back [after two weeks], stayed at Lake Side
Lodge (10 rupees per day). Ate for 5 ½ hours acres of food!

A wonderful trek then. In 1993 I heard there were two or three tea-
house/hotels right up in Annapurna Sanctuary. More crowds and more
comfort now. But the same clouds.

NEPAL3—POKHARA AND CHITAWAN:

Coming back down from my trek to Annapurna Base Camp to
Pokhara was a "high." First of all, I did it and made it back alive and
unfrostbitten. Second, Pokhara by Phewa Lake in late October 1978 felt
perfect. All sorts of food, not just the boring dahlbat (rice and lentils) of
the Nepali villages in the mountains, and both food and lodging were
amazingly cheap. Lots of travelers, friendly and relaxed, from all over the
world. Gorgeous scenery—the clear lake mirroring the high Himalayas,
yet with a gentle warm climate. It felt Edenic.

So I wrote THE LOTUS EATERS: "It's perfect. The grass here grows
on trees, and any restaurant will serve you magic mushrooms in either
soup or mushroom omlette (tomato and onion extra). I had one (with
onion and tomato) and joined the lotus eaters, leaving the rest behind on
the same shore. I did not intend to travel by this conveyance nor with this
crew, but here I go, sailing with Greg and Sandy down the road to the
totally unravelled rocks on the far side of Hip, washed by Zappa, van-voy-
aging East. Words buoy up, then sink under laugh ripples. Hours sink in
the glistening water. I follow. And when I wash up again on Pokhara's

shore, it is lotus land still. A belt of restaurants hangs loosely around the lake; we stuff ourselves on pies and buffalo steak, sixty cents for steak and fries (tomato and onion included) at Baba's. Then to the lake to watch the sun blaze purple and the peaks of Annapurna and Machupuchere. You can get closer to the mountains by hiking up from this lake, this town, but why bother (though I did) with bother? In Kashmir I once ate real lotus. It was stringy, an inferior vegetable. I'll stay in Pokhara a while."

And I did. Several weeks in 1978. In 1993, from October 2 till November 10. But 1978 was the best. The magic mushrooms were a revelation—no hallucinations, just a yellowish tinge to whatever I saw, but the feeling was of delight and awe about all I saw. A bus going by, the swelling veins in a man's forearm, the glistening water, the smiling friends—all seemed magnified and enrapturing. According to my journal, I "took magic mushrooms 4 times—10 [mushrooms] first and last, 15 second, 22 [mushrooms] third." Essentially you are poisoning yourself with these mushrooms. After eating them, you become nauseated, and have to keep from throwing up. The magic mushrooms in Bali, which caused strong hallucinations, are quite different, but also nauseate you. I took the ones in Pokhara with a few other folks, and we eat them and then wait, watching ourselves and each other for symptoms.

Pokhara by the lake in 1978 was full of hippie dopers. Grass and hash were passed around freely at all the restaurants, and nearly all partook. For many, this was their central purpose. Not mine, though I dabbled, often taking a hit from the chilloms (pipes) of hash passed around. Once I sat at a table in the open air at one of the many restaurants by the lake. Nearly everyone at this table was a hippie drug dealer, a thoroughly friendly and unthreatening bunch, and they passed around their cigarettes of grass and hash, special mixtures. "Try this one—it's some Afghani mixed with some great shit from Manali." I tried it all. Soon I couldn't even keep my head up. Earlier, I had ordered some food and as always it took about an hour to arrive. When it did, I could only raise my head from my arms folded on the tabletop, look at the food, moan a "no" and drop my head to the table again. The dope dealers laughed, the waiter went away. At one point I sat up, turning to one dealer, gripped his arm for support, turned and threw up behind my chair, then put my head back on my arms on the table. Everyone laughed. Great sport. That evening stopped my toking anyone's chillom for quite a while. The drug scene was wide open here, but never obnoxious, always gentle and friendly.

Eating here was central. "Eating went on for hours [in 1978]—waiting for food to be brought, ordering 3 main dishes and 2 desserts was common. The bill never came to more than $2, and usually it was $1.50 for huge meals." While eating, we talked about our travels, exchanging the names of good hotels in Bangkok or Herat, Bali or Hikkadewa, what brand of cigarettes you should smuggle into Rangoon, what scams to watch out for in Lahore. Information about the road. Many hippies here had traveled all over Asia, and for many of them this sort of travel was their life. They might work in England or Australia for six months, and then on their savings, would live for a year and a half in a hill town in India or on a beach in Thailand.

The disdain that travelers felt for conventional and comfortable tourists I wrote of in 1978:

"The Land Rover drove over to Pokhara's lake and five people got out. Four were Japanese tourists, and all immediately looked to set their cameras up in order and , side by side, aimed and fired at the view. Their Sherpa and the mountains were umimpressed. Concerned with beauty's rigor, they framed and focused carefully. They didn't seem to look beyond the cameras and their laws. Framing. Focusing. The feeling of a good shot at your object feels better than your feeling of that object. Hey, you! Now I'm talking to you, poet even of love lyrics!" Turning these jagged mountains into a shaped photo or turning a love affair and a lover's breasts into a shapely two-stanza-ed sonnet forces feeling into distancing words. As Cyrano de Bergerac noted, "sometimes the heart sickens at pretty words." Sometimes making art from something great feels like cheapening the actual experience. But it can also help us hold on to that experience.

In Pokhara in 1978 I did have a surreptitious affair with Jean, an English woman traveling with her boyfriend, Paul. She wanted to enlarge her life, though traveling was both of their lives for the past seven years (she was 25). We went running at 7 a.m. every day for a week, and grabbed some very quick sex in my room or off the road among the trees before she went back to Paul. Part of what makes a love affair so sweet is that it is doomed and of a short and poignant duration. Same thing about life. But in 1978, at age 38, thoughts of sex filtered into most of my writing and thinking. In BY POKHARA'S LAKE, what I saw I coupled with sexual imagery: "By Pokhara's lake, beside the Hindu temple, white puffs float with seeds of green down from the trees onto lake or land. Our needs need land us on each other. But the outside, not the inside, the silk, not seed, decides. One sees what there is to see....The women I do meet may put the lid on meeting others I might have chosen....Why stop? A calf's curve or a circle of lips may close tighter than a bear trap.And perhaps I'll see my single face doubled by her eyes....The body is lace to pretty up the dining table. These are metaphors for sex. And when that lace is stripped away, what then? Beneath the teats, what heart? What thoughts to nibble on with bright sharp teeth? In Pokhara—anywhere—fresh green salads can give you the "shits." One never knows. Butterflies flex their wings like biceps. One never knows the dark beneath the water's glint"

I also notice the metaphors of food here about the dangers and delights of sex. Whatever you see and wherever you go, the world is a mirror of your self. Its colors are your own. I wrote WATER IN THE METAL CUP: "Here's the lake. Thin skinned mirror. Here's my cup. Silver skin smalling me, misting me, me all prints, cup cuts creasing. I dip my cup in the lake of larger vision and my reflection quivers, then steadies again. Throwing my head back to drink, I see only sky, not me. I feel only cool water within, without. I drop a libation from my cup from the lake. I give some up. Here's the mirror, my mirror, shattered, rocking. I have just to wait."

Wait and listen till the mirror steadies and I can see who I really am. What the world really is.

"I thought that snow was white. Usually it is, but here in sunsetting Pokhara from the lake with Antonella paddling (we don't know the name of the bougainvilla-colored flower in her hair, either in Italian, Nepali or in English, but it is a shape of bright against the greens and rice yellows and water colors) it isn't. At first it is white, but then the sliding sun drapes gold, then reddish purple, then grey on the Annapurna massif. Now if life can change so quickly from what it's supposed to be…(I meant "light")." Not only does the light change, but so does the lake. In 1978 the lake was clear, good enough in its center to drink from. I took off my clothes (Antonella shyly refused to) and dove into the lake and swam around the boat for a bit. In 1993 the lake was full of shit and garbage. A Nepali who knew the lake from his childhood more than sixty years ago said it then was pure enough to drink from, and had the best water. Not now, he noted. Food, sex, shit, all part of this colorful mix of lake water and words.

On October 19, 1993, I wrote: "Things sometimes say things, and animals too say things; things say themselves.…Walking 'round Phewa Lake I saw huge spider webs connecting light and phone wires, themselves twisted rubber coils. Cicadas in the hills sound like the humming of electrical wires. But the spider webs say, regardless of wires and our conversations, "give us life from food." The flies that batten on our shit in the path betake themselves to the spiders. Yellow butterflies flutter about this buffalo or that human turd, casual and teeming, at the side of the rice paddy, the turd not meant as defiance or marker of territory, but just as its steaming self, the result of appetite and rumination. Pigs batten on our yesterday's food. And half a million plastic water bottles a year are discarded in the Annapurna region by trekkers. But the earth can also use these to make the place uninhabitable by us, and so get us off her back. Pretty useful that dumping too. Those clear plastic bottles have a message in them, clear, clear. The spider webs, gauzy, vague, also say we've caught you, we've caught you."

Both the world and I had grown older by 1993, and Pokhara mirrored my mood. Colors darken. The rainbow may end in an ash heap. Every day I went paddling on the lake for a few hours early in the morning, and when the

wind picked up later on, I had to fight to bring the boat back to the shore
where my boat's owner waited. The lake was a rippled mirror of change, and
so was a waterfall on the outskirts of the town. DEVI'S FALLS:
  "Shafts and sprays of water plunge
  down Devi's Fall to a dark narrow slot,
  the shafts of green whipped white
  at the edges by the brown
  rocks till shafts of water turn sprays
  of white and white noise
  and crash, shatter, splatter
  in mist which turns the brown rocks more green.
  On some maps Devi's Falls is David's or Devin's
  Falls. *Devi* means divine in Hindi;
  David's just an easy name for tourists
  to remember. From the divine to the human.
  We always need to force the world to mean.
  In Devi's Falls there is a rainbow's arch
  for as long as the sun will shine,
  just as God's covenant with Noah
  said the shafts and sprays of another flood
  will never plunge the earth in water.
  The rainbow contains in it all the colors
  but really is just wet air. The green water
  is whipped to white despite it's solid water.
  Long or short waves of light, short or long ways of life?
  We always need to force the world to mean.
  But the greater the plunge, the less the light?
  And where is the rainbow during the night?"
The dark slot of Devi's Falls and the water pouring down into its darkness was an intimation of good things inexorably vanishing, but was so
beautiful too, its cool water above the falls good for pulling the noon heat
from your body. That mix of bright and sad was also in the change of col-

ors in the jungle on the uninhabited side, the King's own side of the lake.
GREEN NEPAL:

"At first I thought they were parrots,
green flashing in dark green morning woods,
but there was yellow and black, and a different head;
the two nameless birds slide through the branches
while I drifted past in my red and blue boat.
While I drifted, an iridescent green dragonfly paused
on my paddle. Greens! The word is a sheet
under which and out from which the motley actuals fly.
Rice paddies layer the hills, the woods wrap them
in other greens, the chill morning lake, white
mist obscuring the green water reflecting green woods.
It's almost November. Crinkled brown leaves, clenched
fists, tick down to the water, rolled parchment
stating the time. The brown lake bottom unrolls
below me, stones, mud, moss, wood, water.
Two weeks ago, I saw a green and red snake—
"could send to the hospital for a week" said a Nepali—
curving through the water, and it would stop
as I got near, and start when I paddled ahead.
It slid, finally, into the woods. I had got close,
but not too close. The red on his back scared me.
Against the far shore of one inlet are murky curves
of brown, a wave, an elongated S of tendrils
of shit, wiggling and whirling, as my paddle
stirs the still chill early morning water.
Just inside the shore, the King of Nepal had put
a barbed wire fence, to keep the woods his.
The wire is mostly moss-green, old as the grey
wood boards it runs between. Scape the moss
off that wire it's the brown and red of rust.

Brown follows green as the year unrolls, unravels.
Green follows brown as the next monsoon drowns
the woods, from skies grey as the weathered boards
that turn blue like the kingfisher home to his woods."

A colorful place, this Phewa Lake near Pokhara. At night, the electricty
often goes off, and we sit in the dark till the staff at the restaurant or at the
hotel brings us candles. I was reading Dickens' "Pickwick Papers" and the
lights would go off, and so I would continue reading by candlelight, the
way Dickens was originally read at night in England. In Nepal it very
often was not in the twentieth century whatever your calendar said. Every
day paddling on the lake was wonderful—so much of the present could
slide away on this empty water with the woods around it. I wrote in 1993,

"In Pokhara I caught a dose of Buddhistic compassion,
so I started rescuing things drowning in the lake.
A butterfly was easy: yellow, black, pretty. I upended it
with my paddle, as it weakly whacked water shivering
around it, as if it cared. Good signal for fish feeding.
It dropped off my paddle twice before I put it on one
of the seats, but it had stopped bashing the water
just before. I got it in a dry spot and steered
the boat to where it was sunned on. Nothing happened
for a while till I tested it with a finger. It fluttered a bit away.
It was just one of the souls I saved over the next few days
from the green-rounded lake. A half-winged butterfly could fly
to shore; several dragonflies iridescent green or blue,
long skinny stems straight; I could pet their wings,
both flies and dragonflies. Love toward all creatures
and they accept it, return it. I even rescued a wasp,
yellow and black like the butterfly. He recovered soon
and flew off. (Little obvious gratitude, but we were both busy.)
Following the indentations of the lake, the shady passages,

I tried to read the braille, the stumps, as the sun
slithered through the morning jungle, the green wood, that brown.
I tried to read me: the compassion was real.
But also real was the anger that aimed my arm
at flies around my bed in Puri, intent
as everything always is on feeding itself more.
I find I can more easily love a wasp
than an Indian rickshaw driver or salesman,
love a tree with real leeches under it than
a young beggar girl, crippled, insistent."

The more sentient a being, the more my compassion for it? No way. Often I was disgusted with people on my travels, and it could warp my perceptions. On Phewa Lake once in 1993 I saw this misperception clearly:
"I saw what I thought was a cheeseball bag,
red, gaudy, marring the forest-skinned water,
and so paddled over to unstick it from the breast of the lake.
Why this litter, making ugly the sky-mirroring lake?
It was a red flower—grand, vivid, smooth,
lovely. The same thing. A square of silver
foil from a chocolate bar winks light flashes.
Silver foil: the backing of all mirrors. The mind."
We see outside what is in us. In 1993 I saw more brown and dark than I had in 1978.

A few times I hiked up into the hills surrounding Pokhara, and spent the night in different lodges there. Better views of the Annapurna peaks from up top, but in so many villages in Nepal, all the kids want fountain pens or some rupees or want you to subscribe to a fund to re-build their schoolhouse, that it was not fun. So many kids in the villages of Nepal are essentially beggars whenever they see a foreigner, and if you don't give them something, they often will throw rocks at you. Not fun.

A couple of times I also got down to the south of Nepal, to Chitawan National Park. In 1982 I spent a few days there, going out to look for rhinos on elephant back, once with a couple of tourists with me on a howdah, a box we sat in, our legs dangling, as the elephant ponderously maneuvered into the grasslands. We saw several rhinos, all quite exciting. Another time I went out alone on an elephant, with his mahout (driver) sitting on his neck, and me clinging to a bellyband around the elephant, my feet under the armpits of the mahout. At one point, the mahout had to get off the elephant to make a toilet stop, and he dismounted, while I sat atop the beast who began wandering off to graze. A nervous few moments there. But the mahout remounted, and we went off to find rhinos, and did so, finding several deep in the grass, which was taller than they were, so it would be very easy to come upon them without warning. They tend to charge and gore, and had done so to several tourists recently, killing a couple. The ones we came upon, first started toward my elephant, then thought better of it, and took off when my mahout got the elephant to charge them. We had the weight and height advantage. People on foot don't.

On a few-hour walk with a guide in 1982, we came suddenly upon a rhino wallowing, but he, startled, snorted, and ran off. There were lots of rhinos easily found then. Once I heard a coughing growl, and we stopped and crouched down, and I asked the guide what that was. "A tiger," he whispered. I waved him to get closer, and he shook his head, no." We saw in the early morning a leopard's paw prints outside a Tharu village. In their village we saw there were no windows. Who needs a leopard to enter your hut and carry off your child? Sensible reason not to have windows. In 1982 I stayed in a tiny hut just outside the park, with the field behind the hut as toilet. I knew of the tigers, leopards, cobras, et al. But the bowels trump fear. So out I went more than once in the rain that night, hoping I would be alone.

For one night in 1982 I arranged to sleep out in an observation hut up a tree near a small pond in the park. A ranger carried out my mattress and warned me to stay in the hut because of the tigers and leopards. He also told me to put my bed over the trapdoor so no animal could get into the hut and eat me. I did as he suggested. He left, and I was alone. Dusk came and so did lots of chitral, and a gaur, and one big rhino to drink at the pond. He put his head deep under the water and began blowing bubbles. He also farted, so there were bubbles coming out of each end. He was playing, so it seemed to me, because there were a lot more bubbles coming out of his mouth that he would be producing by merely drinking. Amazing sight, to watch a playful rhino. In the morning the ranger came and got me, and we warily crossed the fields, watching out for non-playful rhinos and tigers. Soon after this, they stopped letting people sleep out in these observation huts because some had been killed and eaten, so I was told.

In 1993, there had been a recent flood, which drowned many animals and some Tharu, the indigenous people in the area. On one long 6 ½ hour hike in the grasslands we saw only one lone rhino, which we followed. On a jeep drive we saw some few animals but from quite far away. Both in 1982 and in 1993 I took a short dugout boat ride on the river, looking for caimans, small crocodiles. Didn't see much of anything on the river, but lots of birds above it and us. Chitawan is an exciting nature park, but don't go when there have been floods. In 1993, a bit of a wash-out.

In 1982 and in 1993 I also went rafting on two white water rivers which were thrilling, though not in the same class as the Colorado River which I once spent ten days on going through the Grand Canyon. In one trip on the Trisuli River we were paddling through one rapid and I got flipped out of the boat. I had on a life jacket, but as I caught the back of the raft and was hauling myself up on the raft I felt big rocks sliding under my feet, and so, not wanting to get caught between the rocks and the boat, pushed off from the boat. I then realized the rapids were pulling me a little too far from the boat, and also one of my river shoes was hanging by one strap. If I kicked to get closer to the raft, I'd likely lose that shoe, so I drifted behind the boat and breast-stroked, using that leg gently, and was finally back on board. Startled to so suddenly be in the water, but every little bit of adventure counts. Camping on the banks of a swiftly flowing river is always magical to me.

In a summary of the best moments of my 1993-4 trip around the world, Nepal ranks toward the top. "Oh, wow! Nepal—cool and bright morning at Swayambunath in Kathmandu; first meal after traveling solid for four days—Helena's for Salad Nicoise and lemon merengue pie; the smell of incense and blood as headless goats bleed for Durga in a sacrificial slaughter at a temple; the Tibetans, clockwise trudgers around the shrines; sitting watching Durbar Square from a stepped pagoda; the old squares and temples of Patan and Bakhtapur; Bakhtapur—ancient, dirty, untraf-fic-ed, life still old-fashioned and plain; Kathmandu— Mexican cheese-bean burritos and videos, pizza and videos, no native dahlbat in sight;

Oh, wow! The three days rafting on the Trisuli River—the mountains and the paddy fields, cliffs and rapids unreeling toward and then behind you, the noise and jolts and splash of the rapids, the quiet looking between; Oh, wow! The few days in Chitawan, the birds and the long six and a half hours hiking in the jungle and grasslands finally paying off with a rhino followed to his wallow, and I went closer than the rest to watch him, keeping my eye out for a tree to quickly climb, the danger as part of the tang; feeding the [tame] elephants grass and then the big-leaf packets of grain and sugar, their trunks hard and delicate, their size masterful and tame; the dances and songs at the lodge that we were roped into doing too; and then the ride through the canyons to Pokhara; Oh, wow! Pokhara—the chunk of topmost peak of Machupuchere from my win-dow, more and more of it as the monsoon lessened; the almost daily soli-tary boat rides—7 a.m. mist off Phewa Lake, the sun rays poking through the jungle, the monkeys bending the branches down in a "shush" of leaves so they could drink from the lake from their trees; the little white house on stilts that I could judge my progress to the other side of the lake by; the red and green water snake, the water buffalo, the flocks of parrots, the other green birds, the backside-bobbing bird often by the lake's edge; the spaciousness of the air and light and the high mountains beyond Sarankot and Nagdanda on the ridge above the town; the *momo* [dumplings] at the Tibetan restaurant, the "heavy trekker's breakfast" at the place on the edge of town, the long talks over food; the overnights at Sarankot and Nagdanda; the stream above Devi's falls and the falls themselves; the prayers at Tashi-ling [a Tibetan settlement just out of town] and after them, the head Tibetan lama smashing heads with me in blessing, and then after I had my head and beard shaved I did it back to him, holding his bald head between my palms and butting his forehead with mine in a restaurant by the lake, and how he and his monks all laughed when I did it, me rubbing my shaved head just like his; and the long walks by the lake past rice paddies and villages and small boys minding goats or water buffalo; the view from outside my room on the roof of the lake and the green and brown paddies; the goat and chicken sacrifices to Durga at the main temple, the bodies thrown to one side, the heads nearby; the sense of time stretching its arms in all directions...."

Cruelty, beauty, repetition and change, Nepal and I changing as time flows and circles, Nepal less primitive and more comfortable now than it was in 1978. Not sure I can say the same for me.

BURMA:

When I asked one man in Rangoon for directions to the Shwe Dagon Pagoda, he took my hand and took me there. Walking down the street with this middle-aged man holding my hand, I felt embarrassed and strange. Men in my country don't hold hands. (In the future I'd see in China they did, and there were the Sudanese in Cairo who held my hands while we talked in the street. But this was in December 1978 and I was not quite ready for this cultural upset.) My three friends, two English and a New Zealander, walking behind me told me that when he held my hand, my back went up very straight and I was walking rather stiffly. Uncomfortable it was.

Another element of discomfort was the staring and the giggling. I felt as though I were in a zoo, and I was the animal. The young men all giggle like pre-pubescent girls if you ask them a question, and I noticed that they often, when walking past, suddenly will veer and gently bump you, perhaps to see if you are real. Many of the men here seem almost feminine and delicate, even in their mannerisms. But all here seem very polite and friendly and helpful. There is no big hard-sell at stores and stalls, which is so different from pushy India. You were only allowed a one-week visa in 1978, and there were no extensions. Few tourists around in Rangoon. Perhaps your rarity makes you special.

Your money makes you special to the Burmese government. When you first arrive at the Rangoon Airport (and you could get into the country only by flying in, which lets the government control things tightly), you have to change money at the official rate, which then was 6.46 kyats to the dollar. The black-market rate was about 15 kyats to the dollar. So why not hold off changing money till you hit the street? The Burmese government insists that before you leave you have to account to Customs for all money spent in the country, and so you get a record sheet. If, for example, you spend 4000 kyat, but only changed 2000 kyat officially, they know you used the black market, and they can give you grief. But the official rate is less than half the real rate, so you feel cheated (and are cheated) if you do everything the official way. What to do?

Smuggle in duty-free scotch whiskey and Salem or 555 cigarettes, then go to the cafeteria at the YMCA and wait till a Burmese walks over to you and you both settle on a price for them. He gives you the money (I got 220 kyat) and leaves, you wait a few minutes, then you walk out into the garden, someone walks out from behind a tree, you give him the cigarettes and whiskey, he vanishes, and you go back into the cafeteria. This smuggling is mentioned in the Lonely Planet Guidebook, and must be condoned by the authorities because everyone does it. It's like Prohibition or hard drugs in the USA. If people want something, they'll get it. If you forbid it, it only raises its price. And what a status symbol! Foreign whiskey. Foreign cigarettes. It's the same in India, where I easily sold my duty-free stuff in Patna after coming from Nepal by plane.

In Burma many adults smoke, not cigarettes (nor small hand-rolled bidis as in India), but cheroots. Women as well as men smoke these, whose distinctive smell permeates the air. This was the first country I'd been to on my 1978 Sabbatical trip where the race of the people was "Oriental," quite distinct from the Bengalis in India. And everyone wore "lungis," a sarong which all were forever tying and re-tying. If they wore trousers, they could increase the country's productivity by about 30% because they wouldn't have to keep stopping what they were doing, and using both hands to re-tie their lungis. But being productive doesn't seem to be a virtue in backward Burma. All the guidebooks say, and all the travelers repeat like a litany: Burma is backward. Nothing works well. Time stopped here after the British moved out. Could be. If you expect something, you will often find and see it.

Most travelers and tourists flew off to see Mandalay and the ruined temples of Pagan, but I was weary of travel, and just wanted to hang around Rangoon, and copy out the poetry I had written over the past months. After my first night in the dorm at the YMCA trying to sleep on a wooden bedframe with no mattress or sheet on it, I got a single room there there for 14 kyats, much more comfortable, with a table I could write on and a mattress I could sleep on.

During the day I explored Rangoon. At the Zoo, I fed the crocodiles with some fish the keepers handed me, and noticed that the Burmese do not tease the animals as they do in many other countries (Turkey, for example, seems the worst country for this). There's lovely gold filagree work in the National Museum. But for gold in abundance, there's Shwe Dagon Pagoda—thick gold covers the tower, with lots of temples around its base. As in Thailand, you can buy small and inexpensive very thin squares of pure gold which you then press onto a statue of the Buddha as a sign of respect. So many have been pressed onto some Buddhas that the Buddha's features are almost completely "gold-ed over" and erased.

One night, I went to a local festival featuring puppet shows, the grounds crowded and the people friendly, and then to Botataring Pagoda, about which I wrote, "faceted mirrors all along the inside corridor create a dream-like fun-house illusion. This is also suposed to have a hair of the Buddha, but it was too thin to see in its gold frame." At Sule Pagoda, I noted, "around Buddha's head are neon rings going on and off to form a multi-colored halo—not quite as un-religious and schlock as its seemingly bad taste would imply." Light and color can symbolize spiritual power. Certainly gold does in Burma.

The women here to look golden. Many put a grainy yellow powder on their faces and arms; they told me it was to keep them cool. But the golden color couldn't hurt. Several people surreptitiously tried to sell me rubies, but they were illegal to buy on the street and anyway I was not interested. Gold jewelry is not expensive here. But I was not interested.

I was interested in the Burmese dancing, and got in to a dance school one day to see some. Lovely hand twists and tilts, very feminine and delicate. Like the Buddha's hair in its frame.

Like so many of its people. I did do some singing here, but it was at a pre-Christmas service and in English. At the YMCA the Burmese and a few tourists and I sang Christmas carols, and after each was a commentary in Burmese. It felt strange to be singing these winter carols in that hot sticky Rangoon night.

One day, a Friday, I took a bus to Pegu, 50 miles northwest of Rangoon. Here, atop a high wide staircase was the Shwe Maw Daw pagoda, 318 feet tall, looking like the Shwe Dagon Pagoda, but more impressive because standing solitary in the countryside. There's also an impressive reclining Buddha, the longest in the world. But size is not everything, despite what some women say. This reclining Buddha had, as I noted in a journal, a "pretty tacky paint job—[his] smile is a little foolish." The countryside on the way to Pegu felt timeless. But at this Buddha you couldn't help but notice time's claws.

Many Burmese in 1978 noticed the human claws of the government and of the Shan and other guerrillas. One man I met who cooked wonderful Burmese food at a stall in the YMCA cafeteria told me he had written a novel, but naturally couldn't publish it in Burma. In it, he described life in a small village which both the guerrillas and the government were fighting over, and in the literal fighting, the village and its inhabitants were destroyed. He said it was based on a true story. Most people here, he said, just want to live their lives in their own, and often old, ways, and resent the politics that doesn't let them do it. I think most people in the world are like this.

Eating in the markets is fine here. I was at a small market restaurant, and one of us wanted to have a soda. We all sat down and were all given tea. I told the waiterress that only one of us wanted anything, but she said, that tea is always free here in Burma. No resentment that only one of us wanted anything, and the manager too came over and said to please have our tea. Free. No hassle. Just smiles and pleasure to welcome you. Nice place. Nice people.

Same in the markets. In the big Bagyoke Market, I bought a short Burmese jacket and two shoulder bags from Shan state, that mountainous part of Burma that is usually in revolt against the government. This sort of bag is carried by many of the Burmese. These bags have words woven and stitched onto them in the distinctive Burmese characters. One side of one of my bags (I got them translated) has the words "Nan Kam,"which is a city in Shan state where the bag was made. On the other side is the word, "cooperation." Not with the government, I take it.

And not the government with the tourists either. At the Rangoon airport, our seven-day visas expired, our Thai Airways plane delayed in Calcutta because of a storm, we were not allowed to go back into town to get a hotel, but had to remain for 24 hours penned up in the airport. When I mentioned to the airline people that they should open up the VIP Lounge to make our stay a little more comfortable, they said no way. A few free meals, and no leaving the building. So much for cooperation. The Burmese people deserved a better government, and still do.

SPIRITUAL: INTIMATIONS OF GODS:

A student once asked me, "How long can a grammatically correct sentence be?" So in early November 1979, with memories still fresh, in one very long grammatically correct sentence, I wrote about some of the spiritual and religious experiences during my 1978-9 Sabbatical trip around the world. (The "he" is really me.) For this reprise, take a deep breath:

"He, remembering that August in Mashhad when the Iranians were reving up for revolution, Mashhad, the second holiest city in Islam, during Ramzan—no one calls it Ramadan—when no one eats or drinks during daylight and everyone lies around doing nothing but waiting, especially in the afternoon blaze when the heat seems solid and you glide from stripe of shadow to shadow as though the sun were an enemy who would blast you with his sunray gun, and waiting for the muezzin to cry out "Allah akbar" and chow call at the dusty reddish relief of dusk, during the day that the head of the military in Mashhad was assassinated by some junior officer and the helmets appeared on the streets and he saw two policemen screech down a street in a jeep, then explode out and tear down the street after one screaming man, all others on that dusty street shooting off like a pack of motley marbles struck by a big one-thumb-shot hard, and he, holding his English friends still while an Iranian friend, Massoud, shouted "run!" and ran, watched as the banging of shoes and boots melted together into one scuffling sound as the two policemen and the running man melted into one Laocoon statue of three entwined and the grey truncheons, flexible, flew about the man's head and body, and he was dragged off by his hair, he leaning back and they forward, like a V, into the jeep and they drove off, and then that tense night, walking with Keith and Brian, this black-wrapped crone came screeching over and words high-pitched like a dentist's drill, poured out words batted at him with wrigglings and swipings of her arm, a thin black wrap draped over it, drooping, until moved, and then it fluttered, like laundry, a butterfly's wing under water from her weaving arm, and her words soaring beyond him to snatch at other passersby and swivel their heads, dark and not smiling, at them, white and European and, as he felt, American and so, they might think, backing the Shah, and therefore aiding SAVAK, the secret ubiquitous police, men responsible for just such things as that man today getting truncheoned, and now they had an American right there by their most holy Islamic place, their mosque, forbidden to the infidel, the burial place of Reza, the eighth Imam, and this American had been looking down the walkways into the holy places, although he had been told to leave and that he was not allowed in the mosque by both guards and ordinary worshippers, and even though no one had seemed particularly angry or hostile, he knew there was no welcoming in that Muslim turmoil, and here was this possibly mad and certainly angry woman directing all heads toward him, and all he could understand of her words was the tone, the anger, the hectoring around the bright-lit walls of the sanctuary within which their, not his if indeed there is a his, god lived or came to visit and which was made to be his home, and here was this woman, crevices in her face deep enough to fall into and be smashed, and here were her words flung at his head and aimed to hurt and him not sure of the crowd, whether they were sympathetic toward him because she was mad, or maybe since this was god's ostensible place, sympathetic towards her because the daft are supposed to be touched by god and she seemed to have been poked hard by god and now was poking at him, but finally by dint of smiling and shrugging and assuring her that they did not understand a word, although you did not need to know words to hear her drift, they ambled on around this holy place, kept out by their different clothes and color, the Iranians dark-brown and sand-gritted, unlike the paler softer moister Burmese they were, and he also different from them, and their clothing different, Iranian, Burmese, American, yet the Burmese seemed more friendly and more like him, less primitive though further from the white cleaner Europe he saw as the limits of the really civilized, as in Pegu, a couple of hours outside Rangoon, there was certainly a great civilization, Buddha rather than Allah, calm and renunciating rather than fierce, and in Pegu this reclining Buddha, the largest in the world, more

than three hundred feet long, reposes out of the sun and wet under this
rusting metal roof, lies smiling foolishly and simple-mindedly, newly
painted, with no trace of spirit save that of innocence so pure it is stupidity, and in this Buddha shed lean and loll teenagers who wander over to
peer at the foreigner and the book he reads till their shadow blackens the
page , and then they'll say something in Burmese or even in English, but it
will make them giggle just to be talking to a foreigner, their giggles like
pre-pubescent girls', these teenage boys wearing shirt-like lungis like all
Burmese, hand over the mouth and brownish faces turned to each other
like mirrors reflecting more giggles, golden mirrors less opaque than the
inscrutable pure gold squares they press on the statues of the buddhas,
sometimes obliterating all features in this coating of riches, the little
squares so thin they waggle in the slightest movement of air, such a heavy
metal yet so thin it crumbles on his fingers, are like the small pale Burmese
woman selling drinks nearby with lines and smears of yellow powder on
faces and arms, makeup to protect them from the sun's heat, making them
look like gritty golden dolls, overlaid like the buddhas with what the culture deems is prettier than pale flesh, or hard stone, or a naked god, as
does the Thai culture further to the east, toward the rising sun which yellows after its rising like a bloody bruise but beautiful, the clarity of an
hour after sunrise less golden than the gold leaf pasted on the buddhas by
the people, gagging their mouths and blinding their eyes with the thin
gold leaf fluttering in the incensed air like a flag or garment enveloping
the wind, and the golden filigree work on the dragon snakes, the nagas, or
the curved heads of stylized antelope that mount the tops of temples like
those of Chiang Mai, where behind one temple, Wat Jedi Luang, being
painted and repaired, the sound of hammers thumping like a clock's tocks,
stands or squats a ruined chedi, an old holy place sliced diagonally down
like a wedding cake or a wheel of cheese or a cropped photo by an earthquake in 1459, a chedi brown with green tangles of grass shouldering
apart cracked bricks and butterflies fluttering by, crinkling dots of yellow
whirling against the quivering grasses and the still brown bricks, the black

cracks between, the chedi calling out the spirit as the newer temple could not, the plain weary brick sighing "old" when the wind brushed by late in the afternoon, so soft where once the ancient fist of god showed his earthquaking time-crumbling might, and the newer golden temple showing thin and brittle and gaudy against the simple brown and broken brick, and he had felt it, that power, power tingling in his mind and chest, also in Ceylon, Sri Lanka, in Anaradhapura, in the pyramids of greying white rocks and the sharp sunlight as he bicycled through the clear green countryside on the charcoal grey road, stopping for a coconut with its sweet milk and its thick white meat, near an ancient pool with carved steps and watching a snake S its way across it and then getting another coconut while three old women stopped with their baskets on their heads to watch him drink, coconut milk spilling out of the hole and threading through and off his beard, and paid two rupees and resumed cycling toward these white towers which could still break through the membrane of the sky into the spirit which could then thread down like milk through the holes these pyramids pricked, pouring down a clear rainbow of earth's water, not with the earthbound pattering splatting from the garden hose onto the garden earth in the ashram in Poona (Pune) in India, with white frangipani flowers, odorous trumpets, visible and scented signs of ripeness whose smell is beyond the power of rot, speckling the ground, the white touched with brown at the bottom after hours on the ground, and the sannyasins (disciples) at the ashram, orange draped, bright, almost artificial yet like real flowers, so bright and simple and free-flowing like water, so different from the grey stone of Polinarua in Sri Lanka, empty and heavy, rock figures carved and now left to the fondling jungle, grey temples empty of spirit, heavy and worn, unlike the light colors, the colors of light, of sun, of fire, of the air's gold worn lightly by sannyasins at the ashram, flapping at a Sufi dance like a large hawk soaring, so high slow undulations are all that's needed for flight, or walking in a breeze, their robes quick flicking like flame, or seated on the concrete floor of the main hall in a meditation where for forty minutes he breathed in, following the breath, and then on each exhalation, letting the breath out through the nose with a humming sound made in the chest or the throat, feeling in his chest the humming made by all the others in the hall, feeling the sound vibrating in his chest like the hum of the planets moving, like the humming of god, the sound of the stillness behind all sound and this the sound that stillness makes, and he could plug his sound into all other sounds and fuse with them into an IT and yet still vary his pitch and hear himself as separate if he wished he were, and all that day he heard that humming sound, the water flowing through the pipes and the exhaust fan in the toilet also humming, no place left out of that god sound, and he floated, his chest a balloon of breath cradling him high, flying him high to the spirit's Himalayas, and he remembered, cradled by Pokhara's lake watched over by Machupuchere, unclimbed peak, and the Annapurna himal high above, where he had spent two weeks trekking, how the real Himalayas were, lovely but not easy, and that yearning for the valley and the lake pulled him eventually down, down to one of the eating places, draped like a loose belt around Phewa Tal, the lake, where he ate mushroom omlette, magic mushrooms picked fresh and dew-damp from the forst floor by a small boy and delivered to a small three-sided wood hut and then chopped up with onions, and cooked and served—he had fifteen mushrooms—to him and Greg and Sandy and Jean, and then they waited till the sunlight turned more yellow than the day could furnish, and the veins in the French hippie's arm seemed like tree roots and everything seemed friendly and funny and pleasureably acceptable, in an ultimate sense, even when the king of Nepal, together with his guest, the Prime Minister of Sri Lanka, drove down the one road in Pokhara from the King's residence, and still floating from the mushrooms, he waved both arms above his head in sincere arcs like a car's windshield wipers at the royal duo who waved back, the Prime Minister seeming delighted to see himself evoke this foreign white man's pleasure, and the King seeming more sardonic about this bearded professorial hippie, so happy to see them, their royal highnesses not quite at the highness he himself was as the mushrooms swelled his soul with delight at all that happened, acceptance quite total, an uproarious stoicism or Buddhism, wherein his arms could certainly open wide enough to embrace both mountains and those huge spiders that hung like pendants on webs between the trees, both this tough chubby king and the village children who each had half an inch of snot, like a jade nose ring or a green Hindu caste mark, below one nostril, and then the festival in Kathmandu in Nepal, that combination of blood and shit and god worship, during the Durga Puja in early October, Durga, the goddess mother of all and the goddess who, as Kali, kills, Durga who presided over that ceremony in the Army barracks courtyard when maybe twenty cows and as many goats were decapitated, their eyes rolling, mouths opening, and ears waggling even after their heads were laid alongside one another's in a line and their blood collected in a basin wherein the king's hands were dipped, and then the king pressed his bloody hands on the battle flags of his Gurung regiments which held his handprints of previous years, brown and crusty, with the new prints as bright as his own blood when in the trek toward Annapurna base camp, the leeches sacrificed him to their gods of survival, and he watched his grey sneakers turn red as he pressed through the grass in the fog and rain, with leeches beckoning like tiny fingers from the grass blades, bright blood bright as the torches and lanterns in the streets the night of the procession, the cymbals and flutes and two drums furious, drunk with rhythm, not for Durga but for some vegetation god or goddess who was bourne upon some platform held aloft by eight strong men, one man twirling over the goddess's head her umbrella, symbol of royalty or divinity in the East, and he for some five rupees in cigarette money for the bearers got to carry the umbrella for a while, sweating under its weight and the effort of twirling and running to keep up with the procession bourne along by the speed of the cymbals and drums and the excitement of the Nepali crowd, and he caught the umbrella on the electric wires that ran across this dirt street, dogs and human shit and fruit peels underfoot, and it almost went down and his muscles strained and he disengaged it from the wires and ran off to twirl it again over the goddess,

and then he gave the umbrella back to a short, young and powerful Nepali
and took off the special belt with a socket for holding the umbrella staff
and could breathe again and got some sacred rice from one of the bearers
and handed some to a mother and her daughter, all of them sweaty giggles
and grins and grime, and then the procession, which had been under a
balcony waiting to get the garlands of fruit and flowers handed down and
draped carefully around the goddess, started off with renewed shouts and
faster drumbeats till the next balcony hung with flowers waiting for the
goddess, and he took the place of one of the bearers but was too tall and
his shoulders too tender so he held his share of the weight in the crook of
his arms and ran sideways out of breath, the loud speedy music making
him breathe even harder, the yells of the Nepalis, the strangeness, the
unsure footing, the lanterns and the torches and their smoke up these narrow dirt streets, and the roars of delight when they saw him, a stranger,
white, Western, not a kid any more, carrying the litter of their goddess,
made him almost drunk with excitement despite the ache in his arms and
shoulders and in his chest, the ache almost adding to his pleasure at being
there with them all in this harvesting festival, he too busy to be aware of
the god who reconciles inward with outward, the feeling with the ceremony, himself with all others and all else, as once he had gone with two
Mexican musicians to the river running through Kathmandu—was it the
Pashnupati?—and sat on a terrace looking over at the Hindu temple too
sacred for non-Hindus to visit, and the three of them and some young
Hindu saddhu, a groovy smoke-and-sun-blackened monk, smoked some
marvelous dope and watched the bodies being burned on the far bank of
the river, and the whole scene looked like some movie set, so perfect in in
condensation of scenes of life and death, of him and them and god, that it
stayed in his memory like some full-felt abstraction, like these other
scenes, remembered, remembered."

A cluster of many examples of gods and spiritual and religious intimations from many times and countries all in one sentence. Yet these here are

translated into mere words, exhalations from our perishing mouths. Once, in the ashram in Poona, I was IN BUDDHA HALL, WAITING FOR BHAGWAN SRI RAN NEESH'S TAPED DISCOURSE:

"The canopy ripples like a sea of snow, and the wind asks for quiet while she shoos all the leaves in to listen. I hear their frantic footsteps on the floor and on the soft cloth above I see their shadows, cinders, like liver spots on old skin, taped words to mind you of spring and wet. The white cloth billows with the wind, alongside the words, silibant, salivating. The cloth billows down, a white breast for us all lying on the floor, drinking in the words. The cloth then stretches up, taut, like a sail to ship us out, shanghai us, past the Straits of Familiar, where all charts are in Sanscrit. The cloth stretching skyward is now a breast to suckle our spirits hovering in the air above that is our expectant breath and earth wind together, while we are bourne up within this breast which is ours, however strange, and is warm, however white." Words can bridge.

THAILAND 1: CHIANG MAI AND TREKS:

Traveling back in time is easy in northern Thailand. Just walk to small tribal villages in the jungle. This is changing quickly—the clothing, hand-woven, which many of the women still wear is being replaced by the ubiquitous tee shirt. But at the end of 1978 it felt pretty "primitive" in some of the villages.

I was traveling with Denise, a New Zealander, and Ashley and Sally, from England, whom I met in Burma. From Chiang Mai, the main city in the north, "on Dec. 29, [we] went by bus to Fang (3 hours), then by bus to Tha Ton on the Mae Kok [*Mae* is Thai for "river"] near the Golden Triangle [where Thailand, Burma, and Laos meet, and famous for growing opium]. Pick-up truck taxi to Ban Mai, then an hour on foot to Maung Nyam, a Karen hill tribe village where we stayed for 2 days and nights with Panga, his beautiful wife, and their 6 small boys. Next day went to Lisu village where I smoked 2 pipes of opium (50 cents for both) with some character. Then up a mountain (great views) to another Lisu village

where Sally was bitten by a dog, so we left. That night stayed up till midnight to welcome in the New Year with Panga. Bought a bottle of Fang
whiskey (60 cents)—tasted like strong sake; also made from rice. Rained
that night & early next day. We left for Ban Mai on foot, then got a river
boat [on the Mai Kok] for Chiang Rai. Panga's cost 5 Baht for a meal plus
5 Baht to sleep: 4 meals of rice, vegetables, 2 eggs, meat, and more rice,
plus two night's lodging [wrapped in a blanket on a mat] cost $1.50 total.
Rained on the 3-hour boat trip, so we got under the floor mats, then the
boat stopped for a bit till the rain let up a little. Jungle, mountains, a few
small rapids—great boat trip! Got me interested in a boating vacation
again. Stayed at Chiang Rai overnight...."

My first trek in northern Thailand cut short by a dog bite. At Chiang
Rai we got to a hospital and they started on the series of anti-rabies shots
for Sally. Sally and Ashley had been traveling together for quite a while,
but Ashley never made any sexual passes at her, and Sally was rather disappointed in him. Sally herself was always upset that things on her trip in
Asia were not more as they were in England. She felt she never got a
"proper" English breakfast. After a while, her use of the word "proper"
began to annoy me. "It's another damn country!" I felt like shouting. I was
interested in her sexually, and since the four of us would usually share a
room, the temptation was in my face. But her "proper" complaining
diminished my desire. The dog bite and the need to travel only in the cool
of the night to keep the anti-rabies serum cool and therefore effective
changed our trip and I stayed with the three of them till we reached the
south of Thailand.

Smoking opium in the Lisu village was interesting. As we approached
the village, a man in traditional Lisu dress came out to greet us, and asked
if we'd like to smoke. I was the only one who did, and we all went to his
hut, and he and I lay down side by side, our heads on a wooden beam, and
he prepared the pipes. This little blackish ball, which he, with a needle,
melted and smeared into a hole in a pipe, was the goods! I didn't quite
know how to smoke it, so he showed me. After two pipes, which we

shared, I started to feel high, but realized that here in the Golden Triangle is not a safe place to lose one's marbles, even temporarily, so I paid him for what I had smoked, and we left the village. There were a lot of bandits holding up people here—when I got back to Bangkok, one guy told me that of four guided treks recently up north, three of them had been robbed, and everything was taken, including some of their clothing— and there were also Communist insurgents up there as well, and several Kuomingtang villages, where Chinese opposed to Communism moved to after 1949 when Mao took over China. We four foreigners had gone off walking with a very rudimentary map and a well-developed sense of naive security. A dangerous place at the best of times, and in 1979 all of Thailand including the south was politically unstable and perilous. We were perhaps lucky to escape with only a dog bite.

In the summer of 1989, I was also trekking in northern Thailand. It was a three-day affair out of Chiang Mai, and this time I went with a guide, a porter, and several others, including two Swiss guys just finished with their Army service, who were off to see the world. The young porter was an opium addict, and every time we stopped for lunch or tea or a rest, he lit up his opium pipe. His complexion was yellowish and sick, but he could and carry a huge load on his back. In Bolivia in the high (no pun intended) Andes, everyone including me chewed coca leaves which was supposed to give you energy and diminish the exhausting effects of the 12,000 foot altitude. Who knows? Our guide was originally from Burma, from Shan state in the north, and he hated the Burmese government. He once asked me seriously if he could buy an atomic bomb from the U.S. government. I told him I doubted it, but what did he want one for? He's drop it on Rangoon and wipe out the whole government, he said. He also told me if I wanted to go into Burma with the Shan guerrillas, he could get me in. Other travellers had done it, he said. One group was caught in a firefight between the guerrillas and the government troops but no foreigner got killed, he assured me. I actually considered it for a short while. A little bit of combat experience. What a great story, if I live to tell about it.

On this trek we'd spend the night in little tribal villages to the southeast of Chiang Mai, around Mae Cham. Wrapped up shivering in a blanket on the hard wooden porch of some hut, up a ladder so that the village pigs and the cobras and kraits wouldn't get at you, listening one night to the loud ravings of someone in a bad opium dream, waiting for the sun to come up to get warm, wondering if you should get up and brave the night to go out in a field near the hut to take a leak or a dump, wondering if you would have a choice (everyone had the "shits"), realizing how soft is our life and our beds in the USA compared with village life here—so went the nights. In the day, one of the Swiss soldiers said that the pigs followed him out to the field to wait for their meal of his defecation. They circled him as he crouched down to shit, and he worried they would not wait till he had finished producing their meal, but would attack his bottom before he was finished. He had another gripping spasm, and laughed that the pigs seemed now to be waiting for their "dessert." After he woke up that morning, he said that now that the sun was up he could get some rest. The nights here in the hills of the northern Thai villages, whether in the winter of 1978 or the summer of 1989 were very chilly and uncomfortable.

The nights on my third trek there in the winter of 1994 were also cold and uncomfortable. But a little less uncomfortable than before. As more people trekked, more villages had facilities for the trekkers. In Chiang Mai now there were scads of shops with windows full of possibilities, illustrated by photos and promises to get you to nearly "unexplored" villages full of oddly dressed tribes and to include elephant rides and rafting down rivers. I chose a three-day trek after canvassing the shops. After a long van ride stopping at a small town for lunch and shopping (I bought some extra socks at a market), we begin to hike. Sweating, slipping on the muddy trails, trying to take in the scenery despite having to pay very close attention to the trail, we work our way up to a village as the afternoon light waned, dump our gear in a long room in a wood-and-thatch hut, and go out to meet the villagers and eat. Most villagers were shy here, the kids as usual the exceptions who gape at us as we gape at them. While washing in the evening down at the stream, and using my knife to cut holes in the sides of my sneakers so my bunions wouldn't scape and blister, I sliced a finger open. Another trekker had bandages and helped close the cut. Cuts gotten in any jungle need to be kept clean or they'll easily get infected. Note to all trekkers: take band-aids, extra socks, disinfectant, local currency in small bills to pay for lodging (if you go on your own) and souvenirs and opium-smoking (if you want to try the stuff—one afternoon in 1989 we stopped at a village celebration of something or other and the opium and whiskey, food, dancing and drumming was free and lavish—for a small village) and remember, as your mother always told you—dress warm! Hot during the day, but the nighttime chill will make it to your bones.

The second day, several of the trekkers in 1994 decided to go back to Chiang Mai. The cold night and the hot trek was too much. A French couple and I and our guide continued on to an Akha village, whereupon our guide left us in a long room with a concrete floor and mats to sleep on, and (gasp! wonder of wonders!) a squat toilet in a room next to the one for sleeping. No need now to go out into the fields or jungles at night when your bowels or bladder wakes you up. This small hut was the ultimate in luxury for village life.

The Akha women crowded around us trying to sell us bracelets and shoulder bags they had woven, clearly used to dealing with trekkers. After this initial flurry of bargaining, they left us alone, and the woman who owned our hut started cooking some rice and vegetable for supper, and we rested. I wandered off to explore the village, and have foot races with the kids, me making car and airplane noises as we swooped around each other, they giggling and making extravagant gestures which I would imitate, and they would imitate me, making even more extravagant gestures. Village life settled down soon. The boys endlessly pushed a small wheel on a stick or a small 4-wheeled cart on a string back and forth down the dirt street bisecting the village. Nothing wheeled could get to these hilltop villages—all goods were carried on the backs of people or animals, but the wheeled toys were the preoccupation of the very young. A man came back from hunting with a old single-shot shotgun. A retarded older boy, naked and drooling and grinning good-naturedly, came up to me and patted my shoulder in a friendly way. One woman invited me to have tea on her porch and, flirting, eventually sold me an Akha seed-bracelet which she tied on my wrist. We didn't understand each other's words, but we understood each other.

As it began to get dark, the French couple and I ate, and then the kids came and sat around us and, pointing to things, seemed to ask us what they were. So English, French, Thai and Akha words were exchanged, and then so were songs. The kids sang their songs, we sang ours, and everyone was quite enchanted with one another. The kids seemed happy and reasonably well-nourished, and were not begging, a far cry from Nepal where all kids seem to beg from foreigners. The village went quiet after we all stopped singing, and we slept as well as we could (not too well) in the chill air and on the hard hut floor.

The best elephant ride on a trek I had was when the mahout, the elephant driver, asked me if I could drive the elephant myself, and I said "sure" (though I was not quite). He instructed me to put my feet behind the elephant's ears, my legs being draped around the elephant's neck, and push against the ears giving a sharp "HUH! HUH!" whenever I wanted him to move. The mahout, handing me his iron-tipped prod, one end of which also had a curved and sharp hook on it to use if the elephant was really reluctant to do what I wanted, got off the big beast and walked in front of him, and I was now in charge. When the elephant grabbed some branches to snack on, sometimes I would let him feed for a bit, then "HUH! HUH!" went I, my feet poking his ears, and off he went down the trail. I felt wonderful! I love elephants, and this was my first time in control of one down this slippery jungle trail. Elephants walk very cautiously, especially when they are going downhill and the trail is muddy. They are sometimes quite delicate and precise in their movements. The guide and the porter at the end of the trek and the elephant ride usually cut down some bamboo saplings and quickly make a raft from them that you climb on and float down whatever little river you end up near. This happened on two treks of mine, and others have said that this is the usual three-day multi-purpose all-adventures-included trek in the north of Thailand. Then we all go back to Chiang Mai, Thailand's second biggest city.

Much has changed here from my first trip in the winter of 1978-9. Chiang Mai then was smaller, calmer, less touristy, and much less noisy than it was in 1994. In late December, I saw all the spots that every tourist should: the temples ("Wat" means temple in Thai) Wat Phra Singha, Wat Jedi Luang, my favorite, with a large chedi near it, Wat Chiang Man, Wat Suan Dork with its chedi having mortar elephants as though holding up its top, Doi Suthep at the top of a mountain with a great view and with a stairway up to it lined by beautiful tiled dragons at either side, each dragon (*naga* or snake) having four heads at the bottom of the stairs. Spectacular golden chedi of Wat Phra That at the top of Doi Suthep.

Seeing all these ancient temples first in 1979, I thought then of time passing, and wrote TIME AND TIME AGAIN: "Chiang Mai touts, through microphones, the primitive hill tribes—tours available, see real jungle, real primitive people. At Wat Jedi Luang, there is a chedi, wreaked by an earthquake in 1545, where the butterflies now swarm and conquer. The newer Wat is being restored with all the palette's colors. The chedi is left brown brick, sliced like a birthday cake by the quake. Behind it, I heard a hammering like a primitive dance beat. Someone was repairing or destroying something. I don't know which. The butterflies flitter, fritter. My heartbeat slowed, but not enough." Ancient places exacerbate my obsession with the movement of time.

There I also wrote TIME TRAVELING:
"However far you travel, time travels too.
You just make the train. Time's already settled in.
Your local bus is crowded and dirty. Time took a cab.
For a while you don't notice him in all that din,
but then in every town and station and hotel, you do.
Finally you nod, maybe say "hello." Friends—no. He looks too drab.

I see time's toothmarks on old temple walls.
He can digest grass and flesh like rock.
He runs his nails digging grooves in my forehead.
How to fight him? Poke him hard with balls and cock
and have kids? He'll have them too. So cock and balls
won't do. Write? We'll only be alive if we're read?

But acid is in the paper. Books like brains will rot.
Feet will trip and hands will cramp. Nor body nor mind
can stop him, but can only stop. Time will gnaw
all. In Thailand I saw a mother-of-pearl dragon's tail combined
fire with water, waves looked like flames. This work was not
signed. Time didn't eat it, just licked it. Time sticks in my craw."

In 1978 all travelers seemed to gravitate to the peaceful Thai-German
Guest House and Dairy, but the plethora of guest houses and the big new
hotels in 1994, the restaurants with videos, the Baskin-Robbins Ice Cream
stand, all the new money and new cars in 1994 made Chiang Mai much
more comfortable and much less calm and quiet. The way of the newly-
Westerized world now. More places look like America these days, which
most everyone seems to want. Even some tourists who go to a foreign
place, but don't want things getting too foreign and unfamiliar. I understand and sometimes share, though I also deplore, this attitude. In
Ayutthaya in Thailand, I confess when I saw a 7 /11 store, I first deplored
its vularity amidst the ancient ruins, and then went in and got a hot dog
with mustard to go.

In 1994, after arriving on the night train up from Bangkok, and having
gotten a hotel but having to wait till the person vacated the room, I wandered around Chiang Mai soon after dawn. At a small temple compound,
I stood looking at it while the two temple dogs ran at me and barked. A
short shaven-headed monk in orange robes came over to talk, and after a
few minutes, invited me to stay at the temple with my own room and

bathroom for as long as I'd like. No cost. Sounds good, so I went and retrieved my pack from the hotel, and moved in.

This monk was the abbot in charge of the temple, Wat Ou Sai Kam. He was studying English at the Buddhist University there, so I helped him with that, though when he once asked me to do his English homework for him, I asked him what Lord Gautema Buddha would say about his request. He still wanted me to do it for him, but I gently refused. He was also teaching English at a school, and several times I accompanied him and helped teach, and gave talks and answered his students' questions. Once he had me as one of the judges for who could give the best speech in English at the school, and I gave out the prizes.

As head of the temple, he had responsibility for several other monks and novices, and for the upkeep of the buildings. Before I left, I asked him what gift I could give him and the temple. Finally he said that it would be very kind if I could pay his monthly electric bill, and so I did. As a monk, he was not supposed to handle money, yet he of course had to, though when I was around I could take it from a donor, and then hold it to pass it on to him later. I became his *hai yum*, as he laughingly put it, which was his novice-servant, the one who carried his shopping bags, his pail to collect the donations that devout Buddhists give to their mendicant monks, and his umbrella to keep off the rain or the sun. He was about 39, I was then 54.

I was also his confessor. He could complain to me that the duties of an abbot were very wearing, and he often wished to go off into the forest to be a simple monk to concentrate on his own salvation. He had to attend many funerals and ceremonies, and often preside over them, and I would go along with him to these events. At a huge cremation ceremony for a very venerated monk, I along with about 100 others, pulled through the streets of Chiang Mai his funeral cortege by hand, one hand on the rope pulling the coffin, the other holding the umbrella over my abbot's head. At the burning of the venerable monk's body, which had been en-coffined in a temple for one full year, I was the only non-monk and foreigner in the stands amongst hundred of orange-robed monks. It was thrilling, but not very spiritual. Sometimes we would get into a theological discussion, but he seemed not to be terribly interested in theology. Once, speaking to the head of the Buddhist University, I asked a theological question, and the Principal told me the whole gist of Buddhism lay in reducing the pain of living in the world. That's it, he said. End of theological discussion.

Once I went with two of the other young monks of Wat Ou Sai Kam to see a very old and revered monk living way out of town. We got there by local bus, everyone being very solicitous and respectful to these monks on the way. One monk had failed in his business, and so was taking a couple of years out to be a monk. The other was in between things in his life, and was being a monk for a while. Both were quite religious and decent, but it was not the kind of religion where you renounced the world forever, or had to take vows for the rest of your life. A great many young Thai boys become monks for a while, and then continue on with their civilian non-religious careers. I stayed in Chiang Mai in 1994 at Wat Ou Sai Kam for a month. Kind of like "monk for a month." Then I too left the temple, and resumed my journey in Thailand. The abbot told me to come back any time, and I could stay there again. Maybe some time.

THAILAND2: BANGKOK & AYUTTHAYA:

In Bangkok in December 1978, travelers congregated around the Hualampong Station in the center of town, and many ate at the nearby Thai Song Greet Restaurant. Upstairs from the restaurant was a whorehouse, and the girls who worked there also ate at the restaurant, but there seemed to be little sex going on between them and the travelers. All dishes here were cooked up by one guy, a handful of this, a handful of that, some oil in the wok, and done. Good and cheap, the central criteria for travelers. And amongst other travelers too, where you could get the straight and current scoop on where to trek, what beaches were laid-back, what scams to avoid. Great stories.

When I first arrived, Ashley and Sally, Denise and I shared a room (for $1.50 each) in the Hualampong Station Hotel. Bangkok was known then, and still is, for cheap plane fares, so I bought a one-way ticket to Bombay, Cairo, and Athens here, not to be used for months yet. Bangkok was also known as a place where you could mail off goods and letters securely, without having to worry about the postmen steaming off your stamps to sell them again, as is a practice in Nepal, Brasil, Burma, India, etc. I sent off sweaters and other cold-weather gear I wouldn't be needing (3 kilos weight) at the main post office where they have a wonderful quick service to take care of customs inspection, packing it in a box, and sending it off. In Kathmandu it may take six or seven hours; here it took 20 minutes. How nice to be in a place with efficiency!

How nice also to be in place where you can get a Coca Cola or a 7-Up. In India and Nepal, because Coke wouldn't share their secret formula with them, the Indians devised their own version of Coke—Campa Cola. It doesn't come close, nor is it nearly as good. So another thrill about being here is that there are Western products to soothe the home-sick soul. One negative difference is that there are no cows wandering the streets to eat up the garbage. I was so used to being in India where when I finished eating a banana, I just tossed the banana peel on the street, assuming a cow would be along directly to clean up. In Bangkok, I dropped the banana peel, and then remembered that there seemed to be no cows ambling around. Whoops! I picked up the peel and looked for a bin.

Lots of Chinese people and restaurants in Bangkok in 1978. Some of the dishes are oddly translated into English. I noted several and wrote: "What if the menu means what it says? "Steamed rice and crap meat." Could be truer than the crab the Chinese offer at the restaurant near Hualampong Station. Also: "Fired Grab." Crabs do that, so it is descriptive. All meat here is "fired" (as the translator should be) which is also true. Freudian slips? No. On the menu is also "Sea Death." I don't understand that one. (And I'm afraid to ask.)" But the food in Bangkok seemed much healthier than in India and Nepal, if by healthier you mean less likely to give you diarrhea. People here do not stare at you as they do in India. Being here is much less stressful. Except for the noise. I wrote my father:

"Bangkok is the noisiest city I've ever been to—no mufflers on any motor-bike, etc." Lots of revving and banging in the streets day and night.

And speaking of "banging," Bangkok was and is still known as Sin City, a place for sex tours.

Once I went off to walk along Pat Pong Road, the center of the sex trade. Walked into one bar, and the girls made a bee-line (B stands for Baht) for me, the fresh fish. It so reminded me of my time spent in bars in Japan in the Navy: the girls' understandable rapacity, the pathetic loneliness of the whole enterprise, the falseness of the music and the lights. I had a fast beer, told the girls I wasn't interested, and left. I walked up one staircase to a club, saw the show was a guy copulating on top of a woman, and was so put off I left the area. There were signs outside the clubs— "See pussy smoke. See pussy eat ping pong ball." I'll stick to regular menus at restaurants, thanks!

Returning to Bangkok (appropriate name for a sex city) by myself, in January 1979, I got a room for the night at the Thai Song Greet Hotel which doubled as a whorehouse. All night, girls popped by my room, knocked, and asked if I wanted them. No thanks, but thanks anyway. They were friendly about it. No hard feelings (in several senses).

Bangkok is known not only for gold-diggers, but for gold. Marvelous temples here—I noted, "Twice saw Wat Phra Keo at the Royal Palace, its treasury of jewels and coins, the Wat Po with its reclining Buddha (golden, of course) with a more intelligent facial expression than the one in Pegu in Burma, and the Wat Trimitur...[its main Buddha] wasn't that expressive in its cramped setting, its skin too shiny to feel like real gold." But it wasn't the faces of the other buddhas here that were interesting, but rather their overlay. My poem: "The Buddha is solid gold. Five and a half tons worth in Bangkok's Wat Trimitr. It was under cement or stucco covering to hide it from Burmese invaders. But now, palm upward in lotus position, Buddha smiles. Other buddhas in the temple have gold leaf squares put on by the worshipful over the buddhas' faces. Over the eyes, choking the mouths. Cemented on with love and awe. Buddhas like blindfolded prisoners of war." Solid gold here in abundance as in Burma. Then there's the Chapel of the Emerald Buddha, though it is really made of jade. Lots of tourists, foreign and domestic and local. The Royal Palace alone with its many gorgeous temples and buildings is worth the trip to Thailand.

But there's lots more than the Palace to see. "Went on a 2 ½ hour boat ride through the klongs (canals) of Bangkok (really of Thon Buri across the river). Part of it real canal life, part tourist shops with very high prices. The ladies with their squat lampshade hats selling vegetables or tourist stuff. We stopped at Wat Arun (temple of the Dawn), across the river, which is covered with porcelain and ceramic and glass, different from other temples. Climbed up the very steep outside staircase. Great views of the city." Another place to get great views of the city is to take a local river ferry—see the boat life of Bangkok and spare yourself the stinking traffic on the streets.

Another way to escape Bangkok by boat or by bus is to take a trip to Ayutthaya, an ancient city with lots of fine ruins. It's a calm place. No one bothers you as you walk the spare streets. People are friendly. In 1979, I "went to Ayutthaya, the old capital of Thailand, and saw ruins of "golden mountain" temple—a huge white-ish stone sharp-topped ruin with a long staircase going up it; 3 chedis [where Buddhist relics or sacred scriptures are placed]; and Wat Magol. Nothing too exciting. Went back by boat to Bang Pa-in, a royal summer palace with pavilions in a lake—also not too great."

In 1994 I went again to Ayutthaya, and liked it much more. The calmness (and perhaps the ancient-ness too) fit my mood (and my age) more. I had a skimpy little room right on the river, and one night and one day it rained fiercely, the rain pounding on the tin roof, but the loud noise of this rain pleased me more than did the loud traffic noises of Bangkok. When it wasn't raining, I walked the quiet spacious streets and prowled the many ruins. Like Antigua in Guatemala, destroyed by an earthquake and left mostly in ruins, so Ayutthaya, destroyed by time, its ruins a reminder of time passing, of the vanity of human efforts, was a serene place.

Now Ayutthaya in 1994 did have a 7-11 with its hot dogs and American products, with the Thai staff in American 7-11 uniforms speaking pretty good English. But across from that store was a typical Thai market alongside the river, selling fruits we don't have in the USA, and snacks and meals utterly Thai. Nice combination here in Ayutthaya.

In Bangkok in 1989 and 1994, the hippie travelers went right away to the Khao San Road area for lodging, airline tickets, and banana shakes and burgers for the homesick. I checked out the old Thai Song Greet restaurant and hotel as soon as I got there in 1989. No longer there. So I went to the Khao San Road and got a place to stay. Same in 1994. When I first flew into Bangkok, I quickly caught the first train to Chiang Mai, figuring on getting to Bangkok later. Night trains and night buses are convenient, and you arrive early in the morning with the full day ahead of you. In Chiang Mai I got there very early, went for a walk, and was invited to stay with the abbot of a temple. In Bangkok, coming back, I got to Khao San Road too early to get a room, and so sleepily hunched over a breakfast and hot chocolate while time passed. There's the Mango Guest House, the Merry V. Guest House, lots of places to rest up in in this travelers' ghetto. It's fairly close to the Grand Palace, the wonderful National Museum, and parks where you can get fried grasshoppers. I shared a big batch of these with a young woman I shared my room with, because there were no more rooms available. We wandered around the city, snacking on chocolate milk, noddles, and the above-mentioned grasshoppers. I started off eating the whole hopper, legs and all. Later on, when I began to tire of this greasy but not unpleasant snack, I spat out the legs.

When I began to tire of greasy, noisy, but not unpleasant Bangkok, I'd head south for the beauty of beaches. And so I did.

THAILAND3: BEACHES OF THE SOUTH:
Most beaches are pretty much the same all over the world. The sand may be powdery or coarse, the people may be sweet or coarse, the surf may be gentle or rough (the people also), the beach narrow or wide, long or

cramped, crowded or empty. Early in January of 1979 I wrote my Dad, "Right now I'm sitting on a beach on Phuket island down in the in the southeast of Thailand's tail tailing into Malaysia. I may be here for a month on this beach—very few people on it, long & curving & clean, the water turquoise and clear, beautiful. Kata Beach is its name, about 16 kilometers out of the town of Phuket. Got here yesterday, and tomorrow's my 39th birthday. So the time goes. Sounds so cold in Europe now (and the US I guess), and here it's so hot. (I can't complain, now that I got a mosquito net this morning). I'm in a lttle bungalow of woven bamboo and straw (cost, by the week, 75 cents per day). Kerosine lamp for reading. Walked along the beach this morning and ran back. I'll start running and swimming. And writing."

The emptiness of beaches makes me want to get more empty, to strip down my life as well as my body. Whether on Fire Island near New York City or a beach in Thailand, the stripped-down simplicity of the sand and water stirs me to do the same with myself, and often I write about this desire and process. The absence of outside distractions throws me more into the gooey gooney lagoon of my own mind, and I paddle around and snorkel in it, looking for something of interest. On Phuket island I wrote, "What grows on Kata Noi beach to write on? Sand irritates me into cultured pearls. The ocean waves rafts of notes. Nipples of women are felt tipped pens. And other poet when known begin to mushroom in my hair, blow across like old newspapers the streets of my steps." And elsewhere, "I use whatever comes to hand: an arm, a palm tree, a temple, light. All ideas we ever get—love, death, the ways we resemble things—wrap up with different colors, coded to where they come from. Granite headlands or electric lights show power. Rain is life to the dry, death to those who've slogged through mud. What parts lock in significance depends on what you stumble on, what your eye takes in. Death sees itself mirrored in a lake or in the road's dust. I've seen it in both. I've traveled." If you are obsessed with an idea, all you see will be tinged with the color of that obsession.

Using imagery from this particular beach and sea I wrote SEA IN MY MIND:

"The grids of a fishnet slide toward the bottom and so out of sight. Some fish eat men, some fish are eaten by men. Logic. I think of sharks. (Ill logic.) Fish is brain food, I was told. Down among the brain coral, fish flutter and slip. Brain coral is built up slowly of dead animals, dead incidents. Divers cut their feet on it. Fish nets are torn on it. It is very hard. (I am talking of secrets, of brains. Of my past.)

Under which incident, which phrase is the hole to empty the chilling sea? Dislodge it, dislodge it! Empty me out and start over.

Sunset on this Thai beach today is mauve, pink, gorgeous. Greens and blues turn feminine, and dark niches pock the waves. The jellyfish here are jello, stingless top hats. Pulled by a cord of appetite tied to my leg, the shark? Not yet. Not likely, according to locals. So why this gunmetal blue, this gunslinger's eye mirrored in the sea? I"ve snorkeled and seen angel fish here. Why do sharks follow me on land?

I've had good experiences. People have been good to me. I like my job. Why can't I then pluck up the dead fish that rots the catch? I can smell it. I may even know what killed it or hurt it into rotting. (I swim among my fellows hoping that the smell's not me.)

If the phrases linked together make a net, and the fish that I've eaten make a life, why not then cut it up, spew it out? Why not? Then. Dynamite the coral. Find the hole, let out the water blue and green and mauve. (What if I get sucked down in the hole and never see daylight again?) I see on the salt flats a man flipping about. Is it ecstasy or thirst? The reef shattered, all the fish swim in. All the fish. The restaurant down the beach serves shark. Smaller fish too. There's a choice. (Have something different tonight.)" In my journal I note, "Ate the usual "sweet and sour shark," ovaltine, rice and coke at Ling's, the tiny restaurant one kilometer away at the other end of the beach." No huts or anything between my hut and that restaurant. In a letter, "Last night and tonight, I ate shark (tasty)! Better me the shark than vice versa. At first I though they said the fish was "cha." Then I realized. Delicious!" How to understand what you see or hear or feel.

I wrote WALKING ON A BEACH IN THAILAND:

"Wet sand is like pudding to walk on, a desert where, shod with sand, the sun on your shoulders weighs you down like the many moments of dried habits. Waves thump and crabs scatter. The treadmill unwinds past troops of sand and sea, all brothers, on a closed loop of sand.

Hell is the burning of garbage. Last night, fires stained the hill at the end of Kata Beach, grey and red background to three palm trees. Limbs of palms, papers, whatever can't be used is burnt. Last week I thought my bungalow was on fire, a red hole in green jungle. Running from the beach I saw it was garbage. So last night I knew the red was no danger. A car slowing on the road, braking around the corner, shone redder than the fire, flashing red against the flame. No danger here. (Like hell!)

Walking on the beach at sunset, I admire the light dragging through ever more weights of air as it sinks. The deeper, the redder it gets. Every evening. It's a habit. Walking down the beach, the off-shore island shifts and boats move past my eye into memory. But the sun stays at the same angle, only lower. It tells me that at any time I can just walk away from my old life."

Walk away from my old life? My old, and older, self? Fat chance. We are born to be bent like bonsai trees, and the pruning hands are our culture and parents and our own experiences and how we see those experiences, and those can make us more handsome and yet somewhat crippled. Travel at least give you some fresh air and other foreign things to incorporate into yourself, even though we make (may indeed need to make) the foreign familiar. Like the Cockneys who changed the foreign Spanish of the Infanta of Castile into the understandable the Elephant and Castle.

To make more understandable the above allusion about the danger of the red lights of a car slowing down near the beach, I'll tell you what happened one night. I had just eaten my usual shark at Ling's Restarant, and headed back down the beach the kilometer to my hut. A couple of minutes after I left, a couple left and also walked down the beach. A couple of minutes after they left, a New Zealander, Bruce, his wife Margaret, and their three young kids, did the same, and down the beach they came upon that first couple, the woman hysterical, and the man lying on the sand with his throat cut. Bruce walked the guy down the beach to where he could phone for help, all the while holding shut the guy's cut throat to keep him from bleeding to death. I found this out from Bruce, who with his family, had just moved into a hut near me. He saved the guy's life. I met the woman from that couple and she told me that a bunch of Thai men suddenly rushed at them from behind some trees, and hit them both with a board with nails driven in it, then stepped up and cut the man's throat. Nothing was said. No one tried to rob them. Just wanted to hurt and kill.

During this January 1979, all over Thailand, there was a great deal of turmoil. In Phuket town I heard from a local that there were one or two murders a day. In my journal: "Thailand has too many bandits. The buses to Hat Yi get robbed nearly every day by gangs with guns. Three out of four groups got robbed up north in the hill tribe area, the Golden Triangle, where I had just trekked. Back to hustling India!" Elsewhere, "Lots of hold-ups with guns or knives, and one beating—Europeans are really jumped on at Kata Beach." I had planned to go down to Malaysia and Singapore after Thailand, but Hat Yi was on the way there, and I didn't feel like taking a chance with the bandits. I had been warned about the Thais—that they are very polite and often sweet, but mess with them and they may kill you. After this episode of throat-cutting, there were some soldiers carrying rifles on bicycles patrolling the road behind the beach for a few days, but then that stopped. I still would walk down the beach most every night to eat sweet and sour shark at Ling's, but I was now more careful, watched the shadows by the tree line for movement rather than watching the calm star-lit sea, and was ready to rush into the water at the first sign of movement, to take my chances with the sharks rather than with the Thais. This was nerve-racking. Here I was in this seemingly peaceful uncrowded beach, exquisite, Edenic, but lurking among the trees was something quite deadly.

Now on the beach and in the Indian Ocean beside it were also deadly creatures besides sharks, appropriately enough in this Eden, venomous snakes. My mullings over where to go with my life, and now also where to go after Phuket island, incorporated what I saw in my everyday walks into my written DIRECTIONS: "Scars on the beach, before they vanish tide-ily, show me lives moving in time. Worm curvings often spiral, twist and go nowhere in particular. Hermit crabs foot it on either side of dragging shell, but go slow straighter, further. Snakes will often strike right out for or from the sun. Today near Kata Beach I saw the jumping fish, nearly eel-like, hanging on rocks where the sea just put them. Then they wriggled further. Today at Kata Beach I saw a green and broke-back sea snake, dead, with thrashed and foolish patterns like a halo around it. We do the best we can."

However and wherever we go, the bitter comes with the better, the shit with the stars. One evening, after a meal at Ling's, I wrote, "It reminded me of Nepal. That dropping in the bowels, that strangled gurgling as of drowning, that gripping, that chill along the arms. So I excused myself from the table and walked slowly (false calm), stiff-legged, looking like Charlie Chaplin, out to the beach. There, the dark blanket of night pulled over my head, I shit on the sand. Then shit again in the sea. The stars were far away. But wiping myself in the water, I stirred up (beauty even here, even now) phosphorescence, the shit sequined and glittered." Amoebic dystentery, while awful, in rural Asia can get you outside to see, while crapping, the moonlit Himalayas in Nepal and the phosphorescence of the Thailand nighttime sea. The shit and the stars.

And the stars don't care. That thought can appall or comfort. I wrote, "When I woke up from napping on the beach, the sea didn't even notice. No one was collecting tickets for its show, and the hermit crab was just interested in enough sand to scoot across.

The party went on, and when the astronomers and poets pleaded previous engagements, or got drunk and incoherent and had to leave, the stars
stayed and talked intensely way past sunrise to each other."

How to speak stars and sea? How to hear what you really are? Listen
quietly. A beach is a good place for that. It's also good just to be a physical
being. "Jan. 26—walked over to Kata Noi [another beach] and met Steve
(1/2 Chinese Australian) and his Aussie wife Ceilly. Played frisbee and
swam. Great to be nude and active among friends! Then walked back to
Kata over the rocky headland and met Neville, the older Aussie, and 2
others, and went snorkeling. Angel fish and fish like Op Art!" I then wrote
a poem: "It was one of the nicest days, naked to the sea. Ceilly put oil on
Steve, then she put oil on me. We glistened like fish. After the frisbee tossing, I spurted into the sea, and after lolling, licked by the water, I stood up
in the center of an oil slick. It radiated from me, an iridescent halo. So this
pleasure of mine calmed all seas to my seeming."

On Phuket, you can be alone or with friends, but the world can intrude
with a nail-embedded stick or with a sharp voice. "Jan. 17—a bunch of
Australians moved into my "set' of huts—loud raspy girls. Obnoxious. I
(and they) ignored each other almost totally....Jan. 20—Walked to Karon
Beach, Karon Noi, then to Patong Beach. Jungle trails overlooking the
water. I thought of Kathy [a girl friend] and how great it would be (and
was) to hike with her and how much she would enjoy it. Patong is a
resort—soft-drink stands galore, beach chairs and umbrellas. Glad I'm at
Kata!" Usually while traveling, I had wanted to meet people, especially
women. This time I was glad to be alone. One note: I heard that now on
Kata Beach, that uncrowded un-built-up strip of sand, has now a Club
Med resort on it. Farewell, tranquillity! Whenever you discover a beautiful
place that no one knows about, know that they soon will, and there goes
the neighborhood. Of course, that's what the people who got there before
you said when you showed up.

One gorgeous place near Phuket that was well known before I showed
up was Phang Nga [pronounced "fang nah"] Bay. I went on a boat tour of

it, ate lunch in a very touristy "sea gypsy" village on stilts, and stopped off at "James Bond Island" (its Thai name is Khao Pinggun). It was here they filmed some sequences from "The Man With the Golden Gun." It's the same karst limestone shapes—separate tall prongs of jagged limestone—as you get in Guilin, China, and in classic Chinese landscape paintings. Here, they form separate islands. Marvelous and steep, other-worldly. While there I asked if I could swim around a tall prong of limestone just off-shore, known as Ko [island] Tapu. The guide said something about sharks. But I swam out alone and went round it, a tall steep spurt of stone out in the bay. A very thrilling place, Phang Nga Bay.

Lots of different islands in Thailand. In the summer of 1989, I was in Bangkok with about a week before I was to catch a plane home, and so went off to a beach a few hours south of the capital, not too far from the coast of Cambodia. It was on a rather arid island, Ko Samet. There was so little fresh water, that I washed myself in the ocean rather than with fresh water—after several days, my hair and body were matted and grimy with salt. There were several beaches all along the length of the island, and lots of travelers. Lots of topless beaches, which was an incentive to walk them all. Walking, lazing in the gentle warm water, eating *pad thai* for breakfast and lunch, and off to another restaurant to meet some new friends for my favorite dinner here of squid with garlic sauce. "Restaurant" is perhaps not the right word. These places were often just a couple of rustic tables on the sand, a generator loudly powering the couple of electric bulbs that acted as a magnet for insects, a flimsy roof, and a cook with his wok. That was enough. The friends were travelers, usually much younger than I was, one fellow from Canada who was teaching English in Japan, another couple going round the world, hippies, the usual interesting bunch.

Much talk in the evenings, the days spent mostly alone, and pleased usually with that, though at times lonely. About this island, I wrote, "Watching the wall where the lizard waits for flies. Outside the hut, I hold loosely the frangipani flower twirling like propeller in the wind from the sea. Sprawling squids of banana peels fester in the village, starfish rot on the beach. Tonight, the starring Dipper pouring out water over the ocean, or scooping it up from the ocean, a balance forever, just above us, going on, and tomorrow watching the wall where the lizard waits for flies." Lots of lizards, the cute geckos, who walk the walls of the rooms, hunting insects, bobbing up and down on their front legs, doing push-ups, and saying, "Gek—ko" to remind you that they're there.

In February 1994, I went off to Ko Samui, an island off the opposite coast, the east coast, of the Isthmus of Kra from Phuket in the south. A couple of weeks relaxing, seeing my cousin Anna who married a Thai and who both run a scuba-diving outfit on Chaweng Beach. Chaweng is quite a busy place, with many tourists and lots of places to stay. I wrote, "The monkey enjoyed dropping on my head from his branch, and the very young elephant bathing in the sea liked holding my forearm with his trunk while he submerged. The other animals on the beach today preen and perch on chairs, or loll, bosoms flat, on their mats frying in the Thai sun. The tide nibbles the beach till the bay's beach too is a wide white smile with seaweed and dead fish caught in its teeth. The smile narrows as the tide floods, but the smile never stops." Both the monkey and young elephant were tame, pets, easy around people. A nice narrow strip of sand with a few too many people on it.

I went off then for a week to Ko Phangnan, a smaller and less touristed island, famous for its full-moon orgies of dope, booze, sex, and dancing. Sounds great! But as much Dengue Fever there as Saturday Night Fever, and I had a look when I arrived at the sort of sordid travelers gearing up for this full-moon party, and decided to pass it up. Went off the other way to a calm beach, which unfortunately was rocky, with sharp coral chunks, and shallow, so not so good for swimming. Walked the dirt roads and along the shore to other beaches, and explored. One day, having run out of anything to read, begged for anything in English, and it was a Jackie Susann novel. I was that desperate! Read all 500 pages that afternoon. The stuff was just like water—you don't need to pause and think about what you've read. A lot less thick than the sea water, but not very potable. Ko Phangnan was a little too calm for me.

Then at the very end of February 1994 back to Ko Samui, though this time to a different beach—Lamai. Much less crowded than Chaweng Beach, wider, longer, altogether more to my liking. Spent a month on Lamai—every day walking the beach from one end to the other in the un-peopled mornings for a couple of hours, running for a mile or so and then sprinting, feeling in great shape, swimming in the warm and gentle water, watching lots of videos at restaurants along the beach, discovering in one the red "Thai savory curry" with chicken or shrimp that each time I'd take my first bite I would literally moan with pleasure. I wrote my ex-wife Joyce, saying, "This is the easiest place of this year, which has been the eas-iest year of my life [my 1993-4 Sabbatical year]!" I found a fine English bookstore in the town where I could rent or buy books, and scarfed them up with almost as much zest as I did that Thai savory curry. A wonderful month here. Every morning I would climb up the Grandpa rock at one end of the beach, from which I could see the entire length of the beach, the palms and jungle and hills inland to my left, and the sea off to my right. Felt little need to go into town except for books, and little need to talk to anyone.

Once, two pretty young European women came over to my table and told me they had seen me sprinting down the beach that morning. They asked me my age. Fifty four, I said. Wow, they said, "you're in great shape. We are going out to have some drinks and go dancing.. Want to come with us when you're done with dinner?" I said I'd think about it. They went back to their table. Then I thought about it. All my life I wanted this sort of thing to happen, and rarely would have turned down such an invitation. Pretty women! But I did want to see this video, didn't feel like going out drinking and dancing, and didn't feel like starting anything with anyone, even with one of them. So I walked over to their table, and politely told them I wanted to see this video, so I'd have to decline their invitation. I felt so powerful—not ruled by lust, at least for this one evening.

Lots of people in the town were ruled by lust it seemed. Many bars and bar girls. Many couples of older white guys, with quite young little Thai mistresses, often hired up in Bangkok for a week of vacation down here. It felt sad to me for everyone involved. Walking the beach once, before noon, I saw a couple—he English, she Thai, neither very young, both clearly had been up all night and drinking a lot, and looking very wobbley and frazzled—having an argument in which he was saying "no" and she was pleading with him. Paying little attention to them, I continued walking. Later on, walking back along the beach, I saw her in the surf, crying and yelling at him, and now he was the one pleading. A drunken whore-ish battle, thought I. The hell with them. But as I walked past, I saw her being battered by the waves, lying boneless and unresisting the surf, and he

up to his calves in the water, unable to go further. "She's trying to drown herself," I thought, and raced into the surf, grabbed her, got knocked down by a wave, swallowed water, lost my John Jay College cap, and dragged her out onto the beach. She was just dead weight, and she was hard to move. Her boy friend was no help at all, but finally I got her above the waterline, and started to press water out of her. No sign from her that she was alive for a few minutes, though I knew she was. Finally, a cough, and water out of her mouth. Her boy friend told me he had no strength to fight her after he had told her he was going back to Britain alone, and she said she'd kill herself if he did. He thanked me again and again for saving her life. Then I noticed I had lost my hat, went looking for it, but no luck there. He said he'd buy me another one. She just lay there on her stomach, saying nothing, just dripping and breathing. I told him, don't worry about the hat, just good luck, fella. I walked back to my hut, feeling a bit heroic.

This incident may have been part of the reason I pulled together these observations:

"People cling to each other, but also they let go. Barnacles cling to anything, and stick fast. Barnacles cling to florescent bulbs (to the poet meaning light and truth, technology, the unnatural). Barnacles cling to coconut oil bottles (meaning our obsessions with tanning? The powers of darkness? Whatever). Barnacles cling to shells—meaning like attaches to like? Some analogy, some cliche like that. This is like that: the core of all intellection. Metaphor and simile. We need to find meaning, to mean, meaning we need to recognize the stolid dumb world."

The beaches of southern Thailand are stolid and dumb, but other times discourse most powerfully to the attentive ear. The beaches are usually beautiful. Sometimes what they say is that we do not really matter. And that can actually be a comfort to me.

MALAYSIA:

Like Julius Caesar's Gaul, Malaysia can be divided into three parts—the urban west coast, the rural east coast, and the jungled central highlands. In 1989 I went along the west coast, and in 1994 I circled the country, including the central highlands. But the west coast has most of the exciting sights, and Penang Island is one of the best.

Georgetown is the main city on Penang, with a heavy Chinese influence, which seemed diminished from 1989 to 1994. Things became more modern in those few years. But even in 1989 there was the Komtar, this tall kelidoscope of a building, with its Mall featuring Western clothing shops and McDonald's, the one real aberration on the Penang skyline, yet a popular place to hang out for tourists missing their American fast-food—the vanilla frozen milkshake felt soooo good after so long on the Asian road—and the many young people who are so anxious to suck up things Western, and therefore things powerful and contemporary.

The Botanical Garden is best for its packs of semi-wild monkeys, who freely roam among the exotic plants and trees. The monkeys were more easily approached in 1989 than later because they were later becoming a nuisance, and some were killed, making the rest of them rather skittish about people getting near them. I'd go into the modestly jungled parts of the Gardens, and once as I got near one pack, three of its males stalked toward me as protectors for the group. I backed off after they showed their teeth, I looking down in a submissive and non-threatening posture. After the males went back into the pack, I just stayed nearby, getting them used to me, and slowly moved right up to them. They're fascinating to watch, and although they were still nervous about me, and would look up at me apprehensively as they darted right by my feet, the aggressive males left me alone to watch them.

In another group I saw one monkey assiduously rubbing one rock against another, using both his hands on the one rock, then looking underneath it every so often, then scrapping it again hard. There seemed to be nothing between the rocks or under the rock he held. Pointless? He wasn't trying to break open a nut. I could see no purpose except the delight in the activity, yet he did keep checking the underside of the rock he held. Making a tool for some simian purpose? Seeing what would happen to the rock if he kept scrapping it? He seemed to be evolving into homo sapiens as I watched. Monkeys are more like us. The males are more aggressive than are the females. I think the Feminists did get that one right.

Another time in the Botanical Garden, several monkeys were jumping into the water and playing by a bridge in a populous section of the park. As I got close, the alpha male came at me baring his teeth and staring me down. I moved closer, eyeballing him. He moved closer to me, and seemed ready to attack me. I blinked, backed off, and watched from further away. He and his group went back to jumping off the bridge and splashing in the water like kids. Monkeys are very strong, many have very large teeth, and can act as an aggressive group. You have to decide how serious they are to keep you in your place, away from them. They can change moods quickly.

But the most frightening creature I saw in Penang is the bamboo viper. Lots of them, and all in the famous Snake Temple elsewhere on the island. I had read about it, so I thought I was prepared. But when I walked into it, seeing highly venomous vipers on the floor of the temple, on platforms in front of the altars, and draped on what looked like coat racks, my heart constricted. Taking extreme care not to step on one, watching the floor and sides for any surface that might harbor a serpent, I sidled up to the front of the temple. There was one attendant there who I saw was picking up the snakes from the floor with a long stick, and putting them on these coat racks, but the things were all over. I remember the terror I was feeling as I looked at the altar—a typical Chinese temple, lots of garish colors, demons and high-foreheaded wise men and gods—because right behind me, about three feet away, on a platform level with my upper back, was this pit viper, alive and moving. It made it difficult to concentrate on the altar. The snakes are supposed never to have bitten anyone in this temple for the reason, some say, that the gods keep them tame and good, and others say, it is the heavy incense which keeps them semi-drugged and unaggressive.

Soon I moved into the next room where they had these pit vipers, fangs and poison sacs extracted, and painted with red on their heads to let you know which was not dangerous, available to pick up and have your picture taken with them around your neck. I stood around and finally picked one up—I like holding snakes if I know they're used to people and not poisonous—but having a pit viper with its triangular head weaving around a foot from my face was too much for me. Once again, I had that terror and peculiar constriction, and so I put him down and left the temple. My chest had felt like someone was literally squeezing my heart. That's raw fear.

In the Cameron Highlands the jungle walks were not so fearsome. Well-marked trails are easy to follow and I hiked mostly by myself there for three days. There were wild monkeys, and years ago a guy named Thompson disappeared on one of these trails, and the best guess is that a tiger killed and ate him. They never found the body, so it was a mystery. But the town itself—even the name—feels fairly European. Tidy little trimmed gardens for strolling. Little tea shoppes. The place I stayed in was called Twin Pines Chalet, filled with European travelers in dorm rooms. And in the nights, the damp chill of Scotland or of an Indian hill station. Up in the hills are several tea plantations, and you can watch the tea being picked in huge hillside fields, and then sorted from the finest to the stuff they sweep up from the floors.

In 1994 I wanted to spend some time at a beach, and so chose Pangor Island off the west coast, where I spent more than a week in a place up a hill behind Bogak Beach, a small sickle-shaped beach. I hooked up with two young German girls who I had met near one of the tea plantations in the highlands, and spent the week or so with them hiking around the island, sun-bathing, playing squash (against two very good Malaysian players, both police officers), swimming, and by myself a couple of times paddling off in a rented kyack around a small island off the beach which had on it a fancy tourist resort, but its back parts were totally un-peopled. You felt you were far away from everyone. Once when one of the women and I were going to go for a swim, we noticed that there was a sea snake lazing in the water right at the shore. We moved down the beach, and there was another poisonous one. We continued walking, and decided against a swim for a while.

In Kuala Lampur, Malaysia's capital, the poison I noticed was between the Chinese and the Malays. One Chinese merchant told me that he, as a Chinese-Malaysian, had to pay higher taxes, higher government fees, higher tuition at schools, etc. because he's not of the Malay race. Very angry about that, felt it was not fair. Malays I've met, and read of, said that those of Chinese ancestry in Malaysia controlled most of its wealth, and that most Malays, who were the original people of this peninsula, were poor. They felt that that was not fair. In Bali and in Lombok, both in Indonesia, I've heard from people who've killed Chinese people there for just that reason, and in Lombok, one man told me that people of Chinese ancestry better not go into this neighborhood because "we'd kill them." This animosity is strong in places. Envy is universal.

Kuala Lampur is modern and crowded, but there are still small exotic neighborhoods, mostly Chinese and bustling with business. In Melacca (or Melaka), also on the west coast, it's much less crowded and much more historic and touristic. In 1989 a bicycle-trishaw (there they call them "samlors" I think) man named either Ling or Lem (I must rely on fallible memory rather than a journal here) asked me at the bus station if I would stay at his "pension." I did, along with other travelers, and it was very funky and noisy and friendly. The town also is open and friendly. There's an old Portuguese stone gateway, leading up to an old ruin of a church on a hill overlooking the sea, and an old Dutch graveyard, all of these places part of Malacca's colonial past. There's a small museum in an old wooden mansion, the Sultan's Palace. In 1994 it's all still there, and still charming. A pretty town, especially near the old Portuguese Gate, historic with all the sadness of history, old things which exemplify decay and long time passing.

On the other side, the eastern side, of the Malay peninsula, the passage of time feels different. You don't notice the old things so much because the whole place feels more timeless. It's the more rural, less Westernized, less modern part of the country. And the more Malay part. There are fewer "tourist sights" and sites. Going up the eastern coast by local bus, shared taxi (a cheaper way to go, because the driver picks up people on the way till the car is packed, but I still had to bargain every time for the fare), and even hitchhiking (you are often asked to pay something here too, which is fair), I got to Kuala Terengganu and the beaches nearby where , if you get the season right, and I did, you can see the large sea turtles laying their eggs on the beach. I got a place to stay on a beach and waited till the word was out that there were turtles laying. Finally came that word, and several of us scurried down the beach with our flashlights. We were not alone. Other tourists and locals came running too. We—there were perhaps 15 of us European (by which I mean white) tourists— were not allowed to approach too closely to the single turtle. While two or three local fellows stood by the poor laboring turtle, we could barely make out which was the turtle and which was the sand pile he had made by digging. We were not supposed to shine our flashlights, and the locals were chary of bothering the turtle. It was all mysterious, and began to get boring, this standing quiet and tense in the almost complete dark, and being able to see so little. After almost an hour, I turned around and went back to my room on the beach and got some sleep.

Melacca's my favorite place in Malaysia, and Malaysia is fine. You can get into its mosques, and the folks are friendly. It still is in places quite exotic. And the A&W Root Beer Stand in the old railroad station in Kuala Lampur should not be missed.

SINGAPORE:

Talk about a time warp. The old buildings that symbolized Singapore for generations of movie fans—the classic Chinese shop on the bottom floor, the shopowner's family's lodgings on the second floor, and no third floor at all—in 1994 only seemed to exist on the outskirts of Singapore island. Taking a local bus to get to the outskirts of Singapore so I could walk across the causeway into Malaysia also in 1989 showed me the disappearing old Singapore. Singapore anyway is really a small island, just the tip of Malaysia, a miniature country, but one that consciously attempts to be as contemporarily "Western" as any in Europe, yet with three basic peoples living in it: Chinese who make up the majority and run it; Indians; Malays. Add in many European businessmen, and you've got the modern Singapore, Inc.

It's a great place to dine. Many multi-ethnic food courts, usually downstairs off the main avenues, solve the problem of dining with friends if all want different sorts of food. Not just the universal "Chinese" food, either. Hainan chicken, Shanghai-nese sea cucumber, Szechuan shredded pork, Hong Kong dim sum, Yunnan mushrooms and chicken, stuff from places in China you didn't even know of, and of course the famed Singapore rice noodles— and all their little food kiosks are cheek by jowl with one another down off the main drags, surrounding a bunch of tables and chairs, common to all these kiosks.

One common trait among people of Singapore is that they are clean and neat. Tickets on the spot for jay-walking. Cross the street only on the green light. No spitting (and for Chinese spitting, at least in mainland China in 1984, is a national pastime and passion. The sound of hawking is heard in the land! But not in Singapore). Foreign travelers are warned to clean up their looks and acts. It used to be that grubby hippies were turned back at the border, or had to submit to an impromptu haircut by the border police. Or so the word went in the 1970s. However, I noticed that Singaporeans did sometimes cross against the lights, while we timid and informed white foreigners stood there waiting, more law-abiding even than native Canadians, while there might not have been a car coming for three blocks. Scare stories abounded about public canings for minor infractions, but the people here didn't seem cowed law-abiding robots at all. Singapore did feel very safe, unlike parts of Thailand. A benevolent semi-despotic democracy. Good for business. Good to live in, when you compare what other countries are around.

Shopping is central here. Huge international department stores. Highest quality. Thoroughly "Western." And very high prices. The first time I was in Singapore, I slept over in the airport because I had a flight out to Jakarta in the morning, and I had heard horror stories about how costly it was to do anything in this place. The next time I was there I found a section where there were cheap hotel rooms and dormitories, where all the travelers went (The Lonely Planet Guidebooks are the best for these kind of places and information). The last time I was there in 1994, that cheap section had mostly been torn down for urban renewal, but there were still some few cheap places, one of which was way up, 20th floor or so, in a high-rise building, and I got a room there.

I was sharing a tiny cubicle with a double bunk and a small sink. I got the upper bunk; a taxi driver who'd come from China had the lower bunk. He worked in his taxi all night, and would arrive home before dawn, crawl into the upper bunk after washing some clothes and hanging them on the twine attached to the sink and to the stained wall. He barely spoke English, and we exchanged very few words between us. The only problem in our relationship was that sometimes he or I had to move the other person's laundry so we could wash and dry our own. One door of the room led to another room, where a scruffy and loud young European couple were staying. When they wanted to leave their room for the toilet or whatever, they had to come through our room, and they liked to have the later-night life, so I was awakened several times a night by them wandering right past my head, and usually talking. The other door led to the "break-fast room" where we all, for our Singaporean pittance, could get tea and bread and marmelade, and watch the soccer matches on the TV. A few nights of this was enough.

A few days in Singapore also was enough. The wonderful Zoo was worth a day. There are some few historical streets kept intact to show how the rich "Straits Chinese" once lived ("Straits" from the Straits of Malacca between Malaysia and Sumatra). But these serene old-fashioned low-lying streets are dwarfed by the new buildings quickly being erected all around them. Walking around one day near the docks, I met a Chinese woman who struck up a conversation with me, and took me back to her place to show me her old-fashioned apartment. It was spare, with a few old Chinese scrolls and some heavy old furniture. It was quite roomy, and sev-eral members of her family lived in it. She told me such buildings are get-ting demolished and new high-rise apartments are being put up to accommodate the increasing population on what is really just a small island, dignified though it may be with the status of a separate nation. She seemed sorry about these changes in housing, but change comes fast in this rabidly capitalist city.

One place that was very recently renovated at great expense to be as it once was long ago is the Raffles Hotel. One of the great hotels in the world, it has a wide courtyard where you can get a drink or eat a barbecue dinner in luxury, lovely expensive exclusive shops in the hotel itself, and fine public spaces. A perk of being "European" (white) and of a certain age (middle-age) is that you can wander around it freely. Just look like you belong and are confident—difficult to do when you're wearing a torn tee shirt, so it's better to wear your best, though when I travel I usually take my oldest most battered stuff, wear it till it's worn out or given away, and then get new stuff wherever I happen to be. Sitting in the lobby or the garden of the Raffles as though I may be waiting for someone is a pleasant way to get a whiff of the luxury that I won't have when I return to my upper bunk in that stifling cubicle shared with the taxi driver.

These contrasts between rich and poor are perhaps being eliminated by the Singaporean government and by its economy. Maybe one day everyone can afford to stay at the Raffles. A lot of people here are trying for exactly that.

INDONESIA:

Mount Bromo just before dawn glows redder than will the sun. Inside the heart of the crater of this active volcano, bright red and yellow magma and the stench of sulphur draws your eye and grasps your nose as you and the many other tourists wait for dawn. Indonesians and foreigners stand around the crater, some in a party mood, others, usually the Europeans, more reverently. From the little Javanese town that abuts on the wide and flat dark grey ash field that you cross in the dark, many flashlights flickering, then climb a long and steep stairway to the top, it's not far to the crater. Once at the top, most cluster around the wider flat area near the stairs— but I walked along the rim to get away from the noise and people. I'm almost always more moved by beautiful natural sights when I'm alone. After dawn, most left, and I walked around the whole crater. You need good shoes to avoid slipping which could be dangerous. The red glow from the magma in the center now is not longer visible. The sun's light blots it out. But the sulphur smell still wafts over the crater, and is still nauseating. Mt. Bromo is still an active volcano.

More delightful are the smells and sights of lively Yogyakarta (pronounced "Jogjakarta"), the main cultural city of the crowded main island of Java in Indonesia. Indonesia is nothing but islands, many of which have their own languages and customs, and so sometimes holding them together as one nation requires a heavy hand. Now in 2000 there is sectarian fighting between Christians and the majority Muslims on several islands, and in northern Sumatra there is an attempt to set up a separate Muslim state. East Timor has already been given independence, and other islands and groups are wanting the same. But when I was on Java, both in the summer of 1989 and in 1994, things were quiet. Kind of like Mt. Bromo.

Yogjakarta has great open-air markets on the main street, smelling of nuts and spices. One spice, however, I got almost disgusted by was cloves. A wonderful smell, but in Indonesia it is associated to me with cigarettes. Clove cigarettes are almost universally smoked, especially by men, and on the long-distance buses, with everyone smoking, the buses whipping around corners, and the smell of low-octane gasoline permeating the coach, it can be as nearly as nauseating to me as the suphur on Mt. Bromo.

At the end of the main shopping street in Yogyakarta is a lttle open grassy park and past that is the Sultan's palace, where you can wander around. Once I saw a dance recital in one of the main open pavilions. A postcard I bought there reminds me one dance was the "Golek dance" with beautifully costumed and trained dancers. All very impressive. There are dance emsembles all over the city, but one I went to in the evening a couple of times, with changing programs all based on the Ramayama, the great ancient Hindu epic of the lovers Rama and Sita, the monkey god Hanuman, and the evil Rahwana, was out of the center of the city at Pura Wisata, a small outdoor concrete-seated stadium. Athletically danced, these sections of the Ramayama bring the Hindu myths and literature of India to the Muslim Javanese. I met one of the dancers, a beautiful young woman named Entam, and spent an afternoon with her, eating and shopping (she helped me get a good pair of sandals, after the ones I had bought in the street a day before fell apart). I paid for our modest lunch, and while several people insulted her with words like "whore" as we walked the streets of the city, we neither slept together nor did I give her money. She gave me her photo, and enjoyed practising her English. She was supporting her small child, as I remember, with her dancing, and often worked during the day in an office. Life was hard, but she loved to dance.

In one fancy hotel on the main street, late every afternoon, there was a gamalan ensemble playing in the lobby. I'd drop in, often being the only one sitting and listening to these xylophone-like instruments, these gongs, these clattering though soothing sounds. It was meant to be an ethnic musical background for the goings-on and people waiting in the lobby. A great appetizer for the evening's dance recital, and the walk along the busy main streets. The hotels I stayed in in Yogyakarta were way down the social and financial scale, down the smaller streets but near the centers of interest.

One Australian guest in my small hotel, a businessman, told me that since he carried large amounts of cash with him for purchasing stuff, and some locals knew about it, one time he was robbed rather ingeniously. During the night, they pumped in to his room some sleeping gas which knocked him out, and then they entered the room and robbed him of it all. Just part of the game, he felt. One caution that guidebooks and other travelers warn you about is not to accept any food or drink from anyone on a train or bus. One fellow told me he drank something offered him, and the next thing he knew he woke up groggy on an empty train, with his passport and valuables, his luggage, and even some clothes he was wearing—all gone. Drugged. Even if they open a bottle of beer or a soft drink for you, they can slip a pill into it as the cap comes off. People have been robbed and killed this way. Thailand is supposed to be the worst place for this. I have accepted food and drink from other local people on trains there, but don't recommend it.

Highly recommended, though, on Java is the great Buddhist temple of Borobudur. It is a series of rising terraces, the first few levels square, with marvelous bas reliefs of ordinary and of royal life, of dancers and musicians, of courtesans and craftsmen, carved in blocks of stone all around the terraces. Despite the heat, you circle the whole terrace, then mount up the stairs to the next terrace, and so on. After the top square terrace, there are three terraces which are circular. These top terraces have bell-like stupas arranged in a circle, within which stupas used to be stone statues of the Buddha, but now only a few open ones have Buddhas remaining. At the very top of Borobudur is a larger bell-shaped stupa. None of these stupas have carvings on them. The square terraces with their carvings are sup-

posed to represent the earth and its life. The stupas at the top represent the
Buddhist heaven of the spirit. Intricately carved is earthly; the heavenly is
empty, with the Buddha contemplating that wondrous emptiness of
Nirvana. I've been to Borobudur a few times, A marvel.

Near Borobudur are several other temples, more difficult to get to.
Little local pickup-truck-taxis or vans which you flag down and negotiate
a price, can get you to the Hindu temple of Prambanan, with its statue of
Ganesha, elephant-headed Hindu god of good luck, and its southern
Indian carved stupa-like form. I also saw the Buddhist temples of Mendut,
Plaosan, and Kalasan, all of them close to Borobudur. Borobudur is
Buddhist from the 8th century, Prambanan is Hindu from the 9th cen-
tury. Java now is Muslim, yet these ruins remind the traveler that other
countries and civilizations had colonized these islands long ago. Northern
India is now Hindu, but their Mogul monuments like the Taj Mahal were
Muslim. Now only in Bali is there a living Hindu presence in Indonesia.

Java is to the west of Bali. Lombok is the island to the east in that long
tail of islands making up the Indonesian archipelago. Lombok is much less
touristy than is Bali. It's primarily Muslim, but it has a large native Sasak
population, mostly in the less populous north of the island, and to see
them I went up there in 1989. I had read of a schoolteacher who lets travelers stay in his house, and walking up toward his village, I asked directions of a man in the village of Bayan. He spoke some English, was the
Vice-Mayor of the place, and invited me to stay at his place. He was talking to one of the scariest looking guys I'd seen, with absolutely cold "killer
eyes." I passed up that invitation. The Vice-Mayor then invited me to see
a Sasak traditional "stick fighting" ceremonial combat of men from different Sasak villages, who later that afternoon were going to coverge near
Senaru. I got directions, and told him I'd see him later.

After I settled my stuff in the shoolteacher's house, I walked way up the
hill where the battles were to be. Lots of people were already there, the
men smoking and laughing, with small groups of them preparing for the
fights. The Vice-Mayor, named Radan Gedary (as best I can make out

from his handwriting), was the referee of the fights. He nodded and smiled at me, and I joined the crowd around the open dusty area where the fights were to be. Everyone leaned on each other. Some old Sasak draped his hands around my shoulders and neck, and when I looked back at him, he looked surprised and then burst out laughing, and kept his hands on my shoulders. This was not the subway in New York City where people try to avoid touching each other. I figured, what the hell—and I leaned on the guy in front of me who took no notice. There was, as I remember, only one other foreigner there, a woman, and she was also sitting in the crowd.

The individual fights began, a guy from a village pitted against someone from another village, and each had their partisans. The "sticks" they used to hit each other with were really long limber whips, and each man had a shield to defend himself against his opponent's blows. When one got in a really nasty lick, he strutted, boasted loudly, and preened around to the cheers of his village. The one who got the hard end of the stick would often also strut around to show everyone that that particular blow was nothing, and he was going to win on the next exchange. One fellow stuck his butt out at his opponent and wiggled it to show his disdain, a primitive "mooning." The crowd loved it. The frightening fellow with the "killer eyes" was one of the fighters. He advanced on his opponent, slightly crouching, like a leopard hunting, never taking his eyes off his opponent's face, then launching his quick attack with the stick. On one of his attacks, he whipped his stick into the other's face, drawing a lot of blood. The referee stopped the fight, and a man with a syringe gave the wounded man a shot, probably tetanus. One time, between fights, the referee Radan looked at me, and waved me in to fight. I shook my head with a smile, and he laughed. The individual fights continued long after that.

I left before the end, and was followed down to my village by scads of kids who, as I tried to walk so quickly that they couldn't keep up, began running alongside me, with whoops and shouts, as they stared at foreign me and tried to keep up without tripping on a rock. After about twenty

minutes, seeing I was not slowling down, they left me. The next day I
went up to a waterfall just off this road with three other travelers, and we
took turns standing under the falls. The falls were very narrow, with little
water running over them, but the height was high enough that the water
could knock you down. It felt like a cool beating. More pleasant than the
sticks of yesterday.

A fine place for other water sports was on Gili Air, one of a small group of
islands off Lombok. *Gili* means island in Sasak, and *Air* means I think "hot"
in Bahasa Indonesian, a Malay language spoken all over Indonesia. On this
island in 1989, which you can get to by small fishing boat, the big attraction
is snorkeling and scuba diving. There were only a few places to stay here, and
I chose one that seemed simple. Kerosine lamps at night lit the tables where
several other travelers—an English couple and an Aussie couple— and I and
the staff sat till late talking. Calm nights, good and simple food, and long hot
days snorkeling on the reef watching the amazingly colored fish dart underneath you. Snorkeling reminds you that the surface of the ocean is so dull and
empty compared to the life that lives beneath it.

One day I walked around the small island, and was followed by a large
deer. He never got close, but when I moved he did, and kept me in sight.
Someone from the mainland had bought him over, and now he just was
on his own, going wherever he felt like. Either that evening or the next
evening, I don't remember which, I was sitting down on a part of the
island to watch the sunset over the sea—as the sun went down, the full
moon came up, so both were in the sky nearly simultaneously. I was sitting
near several other travelers, all sitting quietly, solemnly taking in this natural wonder, when the deer who had followed me earlier walked out of the
woods, walked right over to me, lay down in front of me, and leaned its
neck back against my lap so I could stroke the underside of his throat. As
though he were my household pet. The others were in awe, and I was too,
how this animal, I suppose recognizing me, trusted me so completely as to
offer up its throat to my hands. Naturally I patted and scratched and

stroked the deer, as I contined to watch the sunset and moonrise, and to feel so blessed by the natural world.

The human world is often more trustworthy that one might think. In Lubuhan on the far east coast of Lombok, I walked past a small mosque and I was invited in for prayers. Since I was wearing shorts, one man offered me a lungi (sarong) to wrap around my legs, and another man offered me his Muslim skullcap while he wore my baseball cap. I went in, and prayed with them after several of them explained to me what to do, and to follow their leads. After the payers were over a young man invited me to his house nearly. He introduced me to his family, and the women served me tea and flirtatious laughter. He was the only one who spoke any English at all, and his wasn't very good, but we all communicated rather well. He suggested that his very pretty young sister would make a great wife for me. She was aware of what was going on, and we both smiled at each other, she rather more shyly than me. I was 49 years old, and she was very early 20s. Everyone was laughing as he explained to his family what he was telling me. Of course, he could have been talking about "this old goat" but his tone and their laughter didn't seem tinged with acid. The young man, named Andi Abu Azis, told me he was of the Bugis people, many of who lived on Lombok and other islands. The Bugis are notorious pirates, some of the most feared pirates in history. The terrifying spectre of our childhoods was the "boogy man," right? This spectre's name was a linguistic corruption of the "Bugis man," a real terror to any seafarer. This family of Bugis were sweet charmers. (Of course, we were on land, not at sea.)

Crossing further to the east through the Java Sea lies the island of Sumbawa, a romantic name if ever I heard one. But my Indonesian visa would not continue forever (two months was the extent of it, and afterwards you had to leave the country to get it renewed), and I wanted to spend a lot of time in Bali (this was in the summer of 1994), so getting to the easternmost point on this island, at the town of Bima I stopped heading east. Also, the bus rides with their clove-cigarette smokers was wearing down both my lungs and my patience. The countryside is fairly empty and pretty, a lot of it uncultivated it seemed, but not distinguished by much that is special. The people in this town, getting relatively few tourists, were very friendly, everyone wanting to practise their English, but coming over to you shyly and asking gently, rather than as in India where they descend on you like the waterfall near Senaru with precipitate glee and intrusive demands. You sit on the sidewalk or at a outdoor table eating chicken sate (*sate ayam*) and young men will tell you of their delight in Michael Jackson's music and the latest Hollywood film which they saw on a video pirated from Hong Kong. Bima was fine for a short time, but boring compared to all the things and places there are in Bali.

Bali is the jewel of Indonesia. It's Hindu, rather than Muslim like the islands all around it. Very pretty countryside—rice terraces, volcanos, towns and temples—and lots for the tourist to see and do. Shopping is great, if you want stuff (I don't)—some towns here specialize in gold and silver jewelry like Celuk, stone carvings like Batubulan, wood carvings and furniture like Mas, paintings like Ubud, batik wall-hangings and clothing all over—pick your desire and find the town that specializes in that. I saw one town where they were carving elephant ivory, but they told me that it is forbidden to import it into many countries (USA among them), so that hurts their business, I am delighted to say. Beautiful traditional crafts, and not too much purely tourist crap.

For some purely tourist crap, go to Kuta Beach. It's the main beach town right near the airport, with the best beaches on the island—wide, white, soft, with good waves for surfing. It's filled with Aussies on cheap holidays who just want cheap beer and food, and a beach to loll on. I should not be so dismissive of them. I quite like Australians and have had them as good traveling companions.

The streets at Kuta are also filled, the last time I was there in 1994, with Javanese men selling cheap watches. Walking on the narrow sidewalks was difficult because every few paces a Javanese would proffer to you his briefcase which he then would flip open to reveal the same cheap watches that you had just turned down four times in the last hundred yards. Then you could choose to avoid them by stepping out in traffic and get run over, or you could (my favorite method) gently put your hands on their shoulders or their briefcases and gently move them back against the stores so you could pass. Several Balinese told me that they didn't like the Javanese coming to Bali for business, but Indonesia is one country, so they can't stop them. Bahasa Indonesian is the country's language, but Balinese and Javanese are also two separate languages too. Their dances are different, their religions are too, and so is their gamelan music. Javanese is calmer, while Balinese has sudden loud changes in the middle with very speeded-up tempos. But you don't get much traditional Balinese gamelan music in Kuta Beach. Westernized rock is more like it.

Disgusted, I wrote KUTA BEACH, BALI 1994: "Too many Balinese now for their land so now plow tourists as their dirt; like planting rice shoots, each individual tourist is picked by hand and mouth, to buy the watches, rings, tee shirts and wooden statues we and they become, unreal, as masks in their dances represent beasts or gods, so we and they lose ourselves and only represent the dollar or annoyance. The beggars and watch-hawkers buzz and we bark back. The open jaws of valises of watches gape for us. On this scimitar of Kuta Beach, by all the sewage rivers draining the land, pale green bubbles looking like foam, are infant crabs climbing over each other, clouds, clumps, shoals of them, moving like bubbles breaking, shifting as the sewage and the tide flow, appetite, appetite, appetite and its dirt everywhere."

But you can walk along the beach, past the small streams of raw sewage and the crabs that feed on it, and if you do this for an hour or so, you get to where there are few tourists or locals. I wrote to my ex-wife Joyce on 18 May '94, "5 ½ hour walk on Kuta Beach is pretty much a daily thing these past 5 days. Lots of hiking lately—climbing Mt. Batur volcano, hiking trails in Tetebatu on Lombok." But I especially love the beachcomber life. If you go far enough down Kuta Beach, there is a beach where the hardiest of surfers stay. At Kuta itself, the waves are sometimes dangerous—I got into a pickle once with a strong undertow, and large waves coming hard

one right after the next. I was over my head in depth, and with the waves
banging me toward the beach and the undertow dragging me away from
the beach, there were some scary moments, but once I gave up on trying
to ride the waves there (no one else was swimming where I was standing,
which should have told me something, but I wasn't listening), I swam in,
having swallowed some water and some pride. A couple of people told me
about a Japanese guy recently swimming at Kuta who died when he was
bitten by a poisonous sea snake, so that also added to the anxiety.

Speaking of death, one Balinese ceremony that many tourists try to get
to see is a cremation. I saw an organized tourist tour waiting for a cremation—many Balinese don't seem to mind strangers at such a cremony,
though I've also met some who told me they much prefer it to be private—and so I tagged along. This cremation was held in an open place in
a wooded area. There were wooden pyres, but under the wood were large
propane gas burners. The tourists stayed back and snapped photos as the
family and workers prepared the pyres. I wrote:

"Corpse meat is no nation's national dish,
yet cremation is a shocking waste of meat.
After the Bali street procession, several bodies burned,
and after the skull of one was, to free the soul, broken,
and the clothing was burnt off, I watched sizzling
fat all down his legs, proper barbecue for the gods.
Recognizable knees, legs, the feet
already charred stubs. Soon the flesh charred,
and then just bones. But before, human and mere meat.
Once in Varanasi, on the Ganges' banks, at the Burning
Ghats, I saw the cremating body's feet
suddenly jiggle, move, trying to escape
from his blackening meat. The tender of the fire
shoved roughly with an iron bar the feet to the flame.
Well done, this body too. Not even food. Just meat.
It's a rare beach holiday we don't brown and bake."

Burning to a tan on Kuta Beach is a pleasant progress in one's life toward that ultimate heat.

The most pleasant place to pass time in Bali for me is Ubud. In 1989 and in 1994 I spent time there, and in that space of five years many more hotels and restaurants had been built. The Monkey Forest Road in 1989 was fairly rural, but in 1994 almost all of both of its sides were full of new hotels and shops. I stayed in one of them. The managers were easy-going, the breakfasts of fruit and scrambled eggs were delicious, and I managed to borrow the complete works of Shakespeare and re-read 15 of his plays on my sun-streaked leaf-shaded verandah over the few weeks I stayed in Ubud. A bit of England in old Bali.

In Ubud the old Bali is still around, despite being somewhat tatted-up and touristed-up for us multi-cultural culture vultures. Every night I would go to the old temple, the Legong Kraton, on the main road to the dance concert. On an old ticket I've kept, I have some of the dances named: Panyembrama, Baris, Legong (the welcome dance, war dance, palace dance), etc. Every night of the week at 7:30 the dances change, and then the next week the same series begins again. Some nights, buses will take you to certain towns for their particular famous dance, like the Kecak Dance, where dancers dressed in black-and-white-checkered lungis, with red flowers in their hair, enact the chattering of monkeys, and later one does a fire dance, scuffling barefoot through burning coconut husks. In Ubud kids roam the streets all day selling tickets to these dances. Very well worthwhile. I went in 1989 and 1994 every night, every week.

The locals also have their own ceremonies, with masks and costumes, more lewd and much more interactive with the audience than the tourist ones at the Kraton. Nice to get all sweaty with the locals, almost all quite friendly, even at their own local ceremonies. Even the traditional cock fights in local villages are fairly welcoming—really, the locals are so intent on betting and on grooming the roosters that they ignore you, which is how I like it. Let me be a fly on the wall in these things.

Another favorite place to be for me is at the Monkey Forest itself. In 1994 I had to pay a fee to get in; not so in 1989. The fee helps pay for the keepers and feeders who feed the monkeys and also protect visitors from the sometimes-aggressive primates. I'd go most every day, and the keepers who knew me would give me the fruit and the knives to cut it up with so I could feed the animals. Some aggressive animals went right for the fruit in my hand, but I would pull it away from them. Calm and unafraid—that's the best attitude here. The large alpha male of the troupe would see me, come over, and hold on to my lungi while I cut up fruit and handed it to him. When he would yawn—I think to show me his very impressive teeth to remind me who's the boss—I might get nervous, but try to project calm to him, and not look him in the eyes because they take this, as would any New Yorker, as a challenge. When I figured he had had his share, I would turn away and pull my lungi out of his paws gently so as not to startle or challenge him. Usually it worked. If he insisted on more fruit, I would give him another piece and try turning away again. I wanted to show him that I was the boss over what food I gave out.

Sometimes a monkey would be on my lap and, while I fed him, he'd look up at me, catch my eye, and bare his teeth. Sometimes then I would bare my teeth at him, leap up, and glare at him. He would leave, back down, because I did have the size and weight on him. I would not try this with the biggest animals. Once a monkey scrambled up on a woman's shoulder and neck and began grabbing at the peanuts she had bought to feed them. She started to scream, and I swatted the monkey off her shoulder, and he turned and confronted me. I gave him my"how dare you, you little sumbitch!" look, did my monkey imitation of glaring, baring my teeth, and advancing on him. He skeddadled, for which I'm grateful. If the whole troupe got involved in that fight, I'm finished. I had essentially to become part of the monkey troupe and establish my position of dominance too. Once I was in a rice paddy field with a woman who had her bag of peanuts plucked from her by a wild monkey, and when I tried to get it back for her, several wild monkeys came toward me very menacingly. I backed off. They can be dangerous. With the ones from Monkey Forest you can follow them up into the forest and see them doing what comes naturally with humans not around.

In 1989 I did just that. The male protectors were elsewhere, and there were maybe eight monkeys, mostly females, several with their infants, in a small woodsy clearing. I had established a feeding relationship with one big monkey, and I fed her (or him) nuts, and when I ran out of them I looked for what the other monkeys were eating—seeds from the trees— and got some and continued feeding the monkey. She was on my lap, we holding each other's arms and shoulders, wonderfully casual with each other, and she at one point noticed that I had chest hair coming out of the top of my tee shirt. She fingered this, and then reached down into my shirt and started to climb into the top of my shirt, ending up with her tail and butt in my face and her body down my shirt. Curiosity, or maybe a realization that I was rather like one of them, all hairy. The other monkeys in the clearing ignored me, just eating and playing with their infants. Later on, my monkey climbed up on the back of my neck and began scratching my head with her fingernails. First, I got nervous. Then I realized she, in return for me feeding her, was now grooming me, looking for fleas and making nice. I realized I was accepted by her as another member of her monkey troupe. A wonderful moment for me!

I had moments like this in the Zoo in Bandung, Java. Several monkeys in their cages, after being picked on by the usual local louts poking and shouting and teasing them (no difference between Javanese and our own local American louts) were first angry and spitting at me too, but I got the confidence of a couple of them, and later on could scratch their backs, as they leaned against the cage, and when I took my hands away, they'd look over their shoulders with a "why'd you stop?" look, and press their backs against he cage bars again for me to scratch them again.

The elephants used for tourist rides in the zoo were feeding on hay, and I asked some keepers if I could feed them. They said "yes" and I went in the elephant pen and began feeding one. They each had one leg chained, and so I got a handful of hay and handed it to the big grey beast. I saw him swatting my handful of hay against his knees before he placed it with his trunk into his mouth, so I thought to save him the trouble, and the next batch of hay I swatted against my knees to get some of the seeds off. After I did this a few times, he would bring his trunk up and open his mouth, and I'd step in close under his head to put the hay directly into his open mouth. He trusted my hay-swatting now. He would also at times put his trunk over my arm and face and breathe out of it onto me, which was playful and friendly and accepting. I was a little anxious to be standing right under him, even right under his legs which were huge. There were several elephants in the pen, and one which kept moving back and forth restlessly and agitatedly and sometimes trumpeting was one I was afraid to go near. The one I fed though was a sweetheart, trusting and gentle.

The highlight of this day at the Zoo in Bandung in Java was my hour and a half or so with an orang-utan. He was caged, but I sat on the outside railing with my legs toward him, and though we still had bars between us, we were physically very close. Once he was used to me, which happened quickly, he would put out his reddish arm and I would take it in my hands and groom and scratch it. When he would grip my arm with his hand (paw seems too non-human for this great ape), I would soon remove his grip gently by turning away from his thumb, all the while keeping hold of his arm with the hand he had gripped to show him I was friendly and did not want to break contact. He would sometimes turn his back to me to have it scratched and if I would stop, he would jiggle it against the bars to get me to scratch and groom him again. Now bear in mind (I certainly did) that he was a huge male orang-utan (in Malay this means man of the forest), his massive round jowls making his face almost square and his larger size differentiating the male from the female. Other zoo visitors came over and would give me food to feed him, which I did. He liked to push out his lips after I gave him food and I brushed my palm against his lips which he got me to repeat, seeming to like me to flap his lips. He also liked to take his huge hand and drop it on the top of my head with a resounding slap. It didn't hurt, but it made me nervous because they can crush a man's skull, and I heard of one guy who was bitten by an orangutan in the woods who offered the man his hand, and when the man took it, the orang-utan raised it to his lips and bit down hard on it. I was hoping that this primate facing me was not of that betraying sort.

We would look into each other's eyes without causing either of us to feel challenged, a rarity among primates. ("Who the hell you think you're looking at, buddy?" is the reaction among my own primate group.) He was very big and very ugly, but we kept physical contact with each other for about an hour and a half, with no keeper coming by to tell me to leave. Once, he unintentionally scratched my shin and caused it to bleed. I looked at my shin, got some of the blood on a finger, and showed it to him. He took my hand, looked and then sniffed the finger, then licked it, and handed it back. He knew what he had done, but there was no malice in it. Finally I felt the time had come to go. I was getting nervous at his delight in dropping his hand on my head, and also was tired of grooming him. I left him with, I'm certain, some regret on both sides. But I did not want to push my luck. He was not tame, though he was so far with me.

Back to Ubud in Bali now, and away too from its Monkey Forest. Getting out of Ubud is easy, and there are many villages along dirt roads bordered by rice paddies and fields, often with flocks of domesticated ducks feeding in the paddies. Every house has its own little temple shrine, and every house doorway in the morning has a little bit of burning incense in front of it with a bit of fruit as a god-offering in this Hindu land. Temples are open to anyone, but to enter many of them, you have to wear a lungi or long trousers, and often also a shirt to cover your arms. In some small villages away from the main towns you might find a woman, bare-breasted as once all the Balinese women were, washing by a fountain or in a irrigation canal. Now the women who are bare-breasted in Bali are some of the old women, keeping the traditonal customs, and the young European women on Kuta Beach, with their newer traditions of the French Riviera. When Muslims from Java come onto Kuta Beach the men frantically shoot photos of the bare-breasted white women, while their own Muslim women, swathed from top of head hiding their hair to their ankles, giggle and peep decorously at the whites, and play in the water fully clothed and even more decorously.

Besides the house-temples and morning incense at each gate, there are also often dogs. Very territorial, these dogs, who bark at you and move closer to bite if you don't leave. Picking up a rock, or even looking like you are bending down to pick up a rock, usually gets them to back off, without however stopping barking. Late at night in Ubud large packs of dogs roam the rutted dirt streets and can be aggressive and frightening. Hiking from Ubud, you can see the famous shrine, the Goa Gajah, the Elephant Cave, which has frightening carvings of demons and animals on the rock on the front of this rock cave. Inside it, carved deep into the rock, is a small room, black and hot and airless, with a couple of candles guttering for light, containing, as I remember, a rock statue of Ganesha, the Hindu god of good luck with his elephant head. You can't stay in this cave long, as the heat is crushing. When I got out, the great heat of the tropical summer in Bali seemed like a cool breath of air after that stifling cave.

Bali is not a large island, but you can't walk its length easily. Instead, you can take these little vans. Just flag one down, tell him your destination, he tells you the price, you get in or if the price is too high (you get the right price from the locals or a good guidebook like the Lonely Planet ones), you name your price. If he says no to it, you either let him go on (and often he'll stop further on and beep his horn for you if he was just bluffing and will accept your offered price), or you negotiate. But it's easy to get around on Bali this way. I wrote to my friends James and Dena on 16 June '94: "Beautiful island, getting chock-a-block with tourists in Ubud, but 10 miles away walking the rural rice-felded roads almost no Western faces, a still very rural island, doing its own things at its ancient farmer's pace." Still using water buffalo for plowing the paddies, still sticking the rice seedlings in by hand. Still believing in the old Hindu gods and rituals.

The north coast of Bali has pretty poor beaches, filled with coral rocks which sliced up my feet badly. One slice at the bottom of my foot got infected, and I began limping painfully. I soaked the foot in hot water stuffed with laundry detergent for a few hours and the deep infected cut opened, the scab came off, and the infection was gone. Better than antibiotics. At one place near Lovina, I tried the magic mushrooms, very hallucinogenic, quite different in their effects from the magic mushrooms of Pokhara in Nepal. The Balinese ones made me see brightly colored Nagas, the dragon-snakes, and made luminous the stars over the beach where I lay with two young Dutch women, who also tried the mushrooms with me, and with the young Balinese fellow who got the mushrooms. "I've never seen such bright stars!" I remember gasping out to them in awe. But the number of mushrooms I took was too many, and I could barely stand up, and could barely stand it. What made it more comfortable for me was that I knew it would be over once my body processed the mushrooms. These very rare forays into psychotropic natural foods are always interesting, and often a bit too much for me. Worth a trip, but only once.

Same for the north coast in general. There are some intriguing temple carvings near the town of Singaraja, but the towns on the southern coast have in them more to see. The small beach at Candi Dasa is pretty, but I couldn't see much of an attraction to this newly "hot" (in 1994) resort, except that from it you can get the road inland to the very old indigenous Balinese village of Tenganan. There in this somnolent place, you can look over at a few men preparing palm-leaf books writing them out with ancient script, glad to show them to you in the hope you'll buy one.

There's also the town of Klungkung where I stayed one night, with its ancient open small wooden courthouse of justice with its marvelous paintings on the underside of its roof. From Klungkung, I hopped a public van up to the mother temple of Bali, the Pura Besakih, at the foot of Mt. Agung, a big volcano. The soft vocanic stone wears away easily in the rain, but it's rather easy to carve, being so soft. In the temple near Ubud, I talked to one fellow who was repairing a carving of a demon's image. He worked and lived now in Denpasar, the crowded and noisy capital of Bali, but whenever they had a festival in his native village, in his case one near Ubud, he left his work to work on the temple there. He told me that he takes care of his temple, and works for its festival, so the natives of his village will take care of him or his family if they need help. A great many men and women were carving or weaving grass into mats or baskets or preparing food for the festival, and I could be there to see it if I wore a lungi. One man tied my bandana in the Balinese style instead of my usual pirate-style, which made me even more proper. Nevertheless, at one point the head of the village asked any tourists to please leave, and we all did. Some things were private to the villagers themselves.

Tanah Lot is a tiny temple on a tiny island some few yards off the south coast, west of Kuta Beach. You can walk up to it at low tide; at high tide, the sea washes around it. I was standing waiting for a van-taxi, when a man pulled over on his motorcycle and said he'd take me to Tanah Lot. I climbed on the back of his motorcycle and we were off. He, Katut Suada, was a guide and spoke English, and lived with his family near the temple. He put me up for the night, unasked, at his family compound, even evicting his brother so I'd have a room to myself. I shared their small dinner of rice and nuts and some vegetables—they didn't have much to eat— and later went over to the village's fountain for a wash. The men bathed on one side of the waist-high wall, the women on the other. I tried to be modest and discreet about washing my body, as did we all, men and women. Thrilling to be part of the real village life! A gentle pace about life here, everyone going to bed early, no T.V., no phones, few distractions from the basics of living.

Earlier that day, I had seen a procession along the road, and got off the bus I was on to follow it. I struck up a conversation, very easy to do here with these friendly people, with one young man traditionally and very elegantly dressed in lungi and headcloth, but he and his fellow young men also had on bright red lipstick and brightly rouged cheeks. It was to pay homage to someone recently cremated, he told me as we marched, and for his "tooth cutting ceremony."After the homage to the dead person, he and his fellows submitted to a painful filing down of their front teeth so that they would be straight across. Each boy lay down in turn and the elders filed away. Straight teeth mean beauty and harmony, he explained before it was his turn. The ceremony was, as all are here, accompanied by women carrying huge piles of artfully arranged fruit on their heads as gifts to the gods and to their neighbors.

Bali is a rich and fertile island, with sinuously curved rice paddies carved over centuries by hand out of the hills, with the color of the new rice the most shimmering and radiant green. Much of its fertile soil comes from the volcanos on the island, and the most interesting of these volcanos is Mt. Batur in the center of Bali. You can either stay at the chilly and cloudy top of the wide caldera at Kintamani, or if you are sane and I was, wend your way down by road into the caldera by the lake where it is warmer, calmer, prettier, and friendlier. Once in 1989 I walked down and got a little room in a hotel near the lake. In 1994 I took the offer of a man who said he'd take me to the town of Air Panas, the hot springs, for a bungalow. The price was right. Hotel touts can be useful. So I got aboard his motorcycle and down we drove. The bungalows were named by its owner "Under the Volcano." Apt as hell. And I liked the literary as well as the geological allusion. From my own inexpensive bungalow swooping up above me was the still active volcano Mt. Batur.

Some of that thermal activity went into keeping the springs hot down by the chilly lake that gave this town its name. I stayed there a few days, and every evening the townsfolk and some tourists went down to bathe at the hot springs. Soaping up, never naked in front of others but sometimes bosoms bared, we all luxuriated in our communal hot bath, a bit like in Japan, except there you don't soap up in the bath, but do all that before you get in the *atsui furo*. Here, soap scum floated in the water. If you wanted a cold plunge to close up your pores, you just stepped over the rocks that kept the hot springs from leaking into the lake. Some enterprising souls had built a separate fancy bathing place for tourists nearby, for which you were charged a fee, but no one was using it whenever I went by. Perhaps the gaggle of horny young men stationed on its steps kept tourists away. The communal bath, free of charge, and with locals and elders bathing too, would prevent any shenanigans by the rowdy youths.

I went over to the cemetery on the lake in 1989 with a guided tour. This is an area controlled by the natives of Trunyan, people with a culture different from the Balinese. They neither bury nor burn their dead, but lay them out unwrapped in a loosely woven open-worked basket to keep the animals from getting at them. But the flies make it through. There were some fresh bodies in the cemetery, and the many touts from Trunyan herded us over to see them. I kept thinking that this is sombody's Grandma, but the locals seemed to be only interested in how much money we'd tip them all, or how much we'd leave on a corpse so they could divide it after we had left. They got hostile when we wouldn't leave more money than we thought was right. I have at least as much ghoulish curiosity about dead people as any other red-blooded American, but these locals were more off-putting and nasty than the corpses.

In 1994 I rented a small boat and paddled across the lake, warned by both a guidebook and the boat owner, to watch for the wind. It picks up quickly and strongly in the afternoons, and can maroon you in the middle of the lake no matter how hard you paddle. I figured I had time, and paddled over to the graveyard, thinking I'd stop in for a quick gander at the newly dead. A local on the shore near the cemetery waved me over and named an outrageous price to see the cemetery. I refused, tried to bargain, but the price was still too steep, and so I waved him away and pushed off to paddle along the shore. Later on, coming back he yelled out and offered to me to see it for free, but I thought of the hassle and exploitation, and shouted "No thanks." I had seen it once and was disgusted, not with the dead but with the living in that cemetery. I did have trouble fighting the stiff wind getting to the opposite shore to bring back my boat, but I made it. Seeing the volcano rising above this lake, the vista so wide and beautiful and empty, was stunning.

Both in 1989 and in 1994 when I climbed Mt. Batur, I did it without a guide. It is difficult to get to the base of the mountain over the deeply fissured black lava flows, but eventually I made it. The trail up is very steep and I needed to stop several times to catch my breath, my calves aching from the climb. At the top there was a tiny hut and a boy selling sodas who pursued me part way as I walked carefully around the whole rim of the crater. With my sneakers worn down, I slipped a lot, which here can get you killed. There were wisps of smoke coming from this crater with the attendant smell of sulphur, known also as the devilish brimstone. This was less active than was Mt. Bromo on Java, itself more active in 1994 than when I first saw it in 1989.

But Mt. Batur sat right in the center of the caldera that once upon a time had blown itself up, creating the hole for the lake and all of the cultivated land around, and Batur now was just the latest building up again of the volcano which someday will explode again. Kind of like the volitile politics of Indonesia itself—internal wars for independence or against the resident Chinese or another religion. But for now, sliding and slipping on the way down from the top of this mountain, I was ready to bathe my sore muscles and abraded hands in the comfort of the hot springs.

I'll be back.

CHINA1: HONG KONG AND MACAU:

Flew into Hong Kong the first time with the U. S. Marines. It was at the end of August 1962, I was a Navy officer stationed on a ship in Iwakuni, Japan, and this flight was for R&R, Rest and Recreation, not an invasion. We were met at the airport, not by troops firing at us from their bunkers, but by tailors' representatives, trying to get us to buy tailor-made clothes. One very persistent fellow, to our every question about if a suit could be made quickly, answered "no sweat, no sweat!" He had dealt with so many U.S. military people, that he sounded like one of us. Hong Kong in 1962 was where people bought cheap suits.

It was a poor "country." I wrote to my parents on September 3, 1962: "Terrible poverty and crowded condtions in H.K. and Kowloon [the city across from Hong Kong island]." I remember walking along Queens Road Central, a bright busy bustling street, and then going up one side street and walking along that—a street that had people living in cardboard cartons, stinking of garbage and shit, dark and dead, one block from the brightness. I was sharing a room in a Kowloon hotel with Rocky, a "mustang" officer who had risen from the enlisted ranks, and during the day, after getting measured for our bespoke suits, we did the usual tourist route: the absurdly garish Tiger Balm Gardens, the racetrack and the temples, Victoria Peak, from the top of which the harbor lay vast and ship-full, one of the grandest views in the world. We ate in the Tai Pak Restaurant in the sampan-clogged Aberdeen harbor at the other side of the peak, and saw the beach at Repulse Bay. In the evening, being proper Navy people, Rocky and I went drinking. We wandered around the Wanchai district, a tough sailor's area, looking for our own Susie Wong. Bar girls were always coming over to our table and hoping we'd buy them drinks, but Rocky was married, and I was too fastidious, but when Catherine and another girl came over, I couldn't say no. I kept buying her drinks, but Rocky told me he couldn't keep up with this, and so let his girl leave. Catherine saw that I was running out of money (she was drinking tea masquerading as expensive whiskey), and she told me I could meet her when the bar closed, and till then she'd get some other sucker to buy her drinks. I met her when the bar closed and went home with her. On her night table she had a photo of her boyfriend, a U.S. Navy Lieutenant junior grade (one rank above me). She showed me a photo of her as a semi-finalist in the "Miss Hong Kong" contest. She was beautiful and rather sweet, and worked during the day as a businessman's secretary and at night as a bar girl. Typical Hong Konger—holding down two jobs, going for the money, working hard, using whatever advantage she could find, her beauty being one. The next day I bought her some perfume and left it with her after I learned we had to leave quickly because Typhoon Wanda was blowing onto Hong Kong.

"Left here [Iwakuni, Japan] Weds. morning and got there [H.K.] in the afternoon. Planned to leave Sat.morning, but Typhoon Wanda forced the Marine flight I was on to hurredly leave Fri. night in a flurry of good-byes, picking up suits, packing, tipping (an abominable practice still very rare in Japan)....The typhoon killed at least 39 people in Hong Kong, flooded the area. Usually dry (worst drought in 50 years here. Water hours about 4 hours out of 24, and between these hours no water even for toilets). A cholera area (I had to get shots)." My two suits were ready for me,but they were given to me in the elevator on the way out of my hotel to catch our flight. Talk about close. Two Marines we couldn't contact, so we had to fly without them. Flying out, I went up to the cockpit with the pilots, and they ran the radar out to its maximum range so I could see this huge tight spiral of the typhoon. Only two days in Hong Kong, a whirlwind.

Hong Kong in 1962 felt quite British. I noted, "British undercurrents in H.K. life—driving on wrong [left] side of the street as in Japan; the signs and the names of roads; the British and Aussie soldiers and sailors." Rocky and I and a bunch of our Marines went up on one hill in a tour of the New Territories, land ceded by China near the border between Hong Kong and the People's Republic of China, and from this hill looked out over the P.R.C. In 1962 Americans couldn't get in there, and I, with my top-secret and top-secret cryptographic clearance from the Navy, would never be allowed near it.

China seemed from this hill to be very quiet, no farmers walking around in the fields. There was a severe famine in China then, many millions starving to death, but it was a secretive land, and all I knew was it was my nation's enemy. We stared at it, trying to see and grasp it. But it was just an empty sere patch of winter land, chill and brown.

The next time I was in Hong Kong was in late January 1984, 22 years later, and I was on my way to work in China for a year as the graduate professor of British and American Literature in Kunming in Yunnan Province. I had crossed the International Date Line on January 25, 1984, and arrived in Korea and Hong Kong on January 26. Never had a January

25. Another slippage of time. The view from Victoria Peak was not quite the same. Many more skyscrapers were down in the city, and the paths at the top of the peak were better paved. This time I stayed in the Fortuna Court Hotel on Chi Wo Street, one block off the main shopping street, Nathan Road in Kowloon. Bought a couple of shirts and a sweater in a open-air market in Stanley, ate in the Jumbo Floating Restaurant in the harbor of Aberdeen after renting a sampan for a half-hour ride around. Lots of sampans moored here on which the families live. Ate several times in dim sum joints down by the Hong Kong harbor. An afternoon trip again to the New Territories, much more crowded now than in 1962. I noted, "Squatter shanties dotting bare land, near tall shafts of apartment buildings, ultra-modern, 30 stories or so each." Still contrasts.

Hong Kong is a picturesque ride by the Star Ferry across from Kowloon on the mainland, and there are other islands, also part of Hong Kong, an island-country as small and special as Singapore. Lantau island, with Silvermine Bay and Tai O fishing village and Po Lin Buddhist Monastery, is one hour away by ferry. On Lantau, I wrote, "where the water channels and erodes the hills, it is just in these eroded gullies that the plant life is the thickest. Life to the plants, death to the eroding hills." All things change.

Still lacking the language, when I ordered things in a restaurant, even after the waiter tells me what the food is, it's still not quite clear. Pre-verbal understandings, intuition, taste buds—and the nose knows. It's like Eden before Adam named things, except not quite as warm in January Hong Kong as in Eden. And the serpent? "The Hong Kong Metro is a long snake of a train, open so you can see the curve, open like one long subway car, and you can see see way back and forward through all the cars." In 1984 Hong Kong was grown up and rich, everyone worked very hard, but it was post-Eden. I also noted, "On Argyle Street, there is a Public Hygiene (V.D.) Clinic. The V.D. in parenthesis was so as not to mislead you to think of the place as one where you get a vaccination for your toddler. So why bother with the euphemism?"

In 1984 one afternoon I met ten H.K. high school students, all 17-year-olds, boys and girls, who attached themselves to me on the top of Victoria Peak, and we explored the paths there, with pausing-places for the views, trees all around, then went down to the city and we ate dinner—a hot-pot where you cook your own food in boiling water at your table—from a street-stall restaurant in one of the side streets. Very nice kids. They were worried about their future in Hong Kong because several other places now—Taiwan, Singapore, Korea—could produce quality goods in Asia cheaper than they could. How to keep Hong Kong the best of Asia's tigers?

If it's not skill but luck that can keep you on top, then Macau, the old Portuguese colony across the water from Hong Kong, is the place where many Chinese go. On January 31, I took the hydrofoil to Macau. Gambling, a traditional Chinese vice, was outlawed in Hong Kong and also in Mao's China. But in Macau they can gamble. Some notes: "Floating Casino—all customers Chinese, many workers with grime still on them, almost all very young men." I went to this casino with a pretty young American, Lisa Wilde, studying Chinese in Shanghai whom I had met in the Bela Vista Hotel where I stayed. The Bela Vista was on Rua do Comendador Kou Ho Neng (talk about an address that is multi-cultural), an old faded-elegance ramshakle place where the omelet I had ordered in the hotel restaurant was so bad, and so was her dish, that we became instant friends and went out to explore the fleshpots of Macau together. Macau had a reputation in the 1920s and 30s as a dangerous place filled with smugglers, white slavers, Peter Lorre and Sidney Greenstreet. Not so in 1984. The fleshpots are pretty much vegetarian and tame now.

The gambling here extends beyond the casinos and the domino games. Like Pascal's wager, you can bet on the gods in the temples here, and many do. My notes: "In Chinese temple (A Ma Temple—Ma Kok Miu)—smell of poured-out rice wine; red paper with gold characters on it burns in special scrolled metal cages; a woman holds burning smoking punks in her hands, palms together, moving them up and down praying." And "in Kun

Lam Temple (Kum Yam Tong), dedicated to Kue Lin, there are 3 succes-
sive altar rooms; the incense smell mixes with the smell of burning spirit-
money, gold characters on red paper; the sellers of incense and
spirit-money are blase old crocks, hawking, coughing, smoking, their
smokers' vice, Marlboro mixing with heavenly incense till the worldly
blends with the otherworldly, and all, as the sages say, is mere smoke, dis-
sipating and diluting in time's vat."

"Yellow coils of incense hang from the temple ceilings, ascending toward a
point, narrowing steadily from a wide bottom coil, like a Yeats-ian gyre. A
woman spreads out her spirit-money into an open lotus-leaf shape, then folds
it over on itself and sets it on fire from one of the candles, and drops it into
one of the stone cauldrons for burning. The lotus leaf shape is like that of the
Buddha's pedestal. Before burning the punks or money or inscriptions, her
hands go up and down a few times toward the Buddha, then the punks are
placed upright in a brass or stone cauldron and left to smoke up the
air....One old man chants a bit as he pours some rice wine out on the altar,
and some oil into the lamp suspended in front of a main statue....An old
woman holds a round case of sticks like chop sticks used for telling fortunes,
and shakes them up and down quickly, making a sound like maracas except
she steadily increases the clashing sound like silver coins shaken. Another
woman drops two halves of a round peg while on her knees praying, drops
them several times. Offerings of food—dead ducks, their necks pulled back
over their bodies, and apples and oranges. If the cut face is face down, then
good fortune, and if the cut face is up, bad fortune. Or vice versa. I'm not
sure." Neither are the gods.

"Another room in the temple has red and green memorial tablets, with
golden characters, and with photos of the dead at the top, mostly old people,
some young and not ready for death judging by the photos, a whole room
filled. Most photos are formal as though from some identity card. Some
informal, the dead caught in a smile. Most unsmiling, memorialized as still
and stiff as rigor mortis." Now in the year 2000 Hong Kong and Macau are
officially part of China. When I was living in China, some of the other for-

eign experts wanted to get out of China for their summer vacation, and chose to escape to Hong Kong. Now they have to go further afield.

"Pale green English church in Macau. Pale green old Bela Vista Hotel where I stayed in Macau. Pale green netting over the bamboo scaffolding in Guangzhou [we know this place as Canton] surrounding the buildings now being built [to protect the workers and the construction materials]. The old ways, the Chinese elements, wrapping around even the most Western-style skyscrapers."

CHINA2: KUNMING—1984:ONE YEAR:

From January 1984 till January 1985, I was in Kunming, Yunnan Province, China, as the graduate professor of British and American literature. I had seven graduate students in their last year of a three-year M.A. program, and was to supervise their Master's theses. While I did travel around China and Tibet, mostly I lived and worked in Kunming at Yunnan Teachers University. Being a worker is often different from being a traveler. The year passes and leaves time's residue.

I had studied some Mandarin Chinese language for a term at New York University, while I was teaching English Composition and Literature part-time there. I was not good at this tonal language—it was difficult to hear the subtle differences between the tones. When I got to Kunming I stopped studying the language because everyone wanted to speak English with me, and I felt too stupid mangling their words. Kunming's dialect is Mandarin, but this city has its own particular vocabulary too. *Mutter* means it's not available; *Go bi* means go away. And on an American computer there are no keys for the variety of tones to show you how to pronounce these words. Pronounce them incorrectly and you say something completely different. Too difficult for me.

Chinese characters are the same for all Chinese dialects, but each area has its own pronunciation of them. Once at a Foreign Languages Department party where each person has to do something entertaining— I generally would recite an English poem or sing "You are my sunshine"—

one of the instructors told a story in the dialect of Fujian Province on China's southeast coast. No one else knew what he was saying. Wonderful to see every Chinese person as puzzled by linquistic incomprehension as I often am here. If a Chinese person speaks to you and you tell him you don't understand, he often will sketch out on his open palm the Chinese characters for what he said. If his speech isn't understood, then his writing would be by all literate Chinese. But not by this Chinese-illiterate, me. I wrote, "Wordlessness—not knowing the language here. What parts of speechs are important? Nouns? Verbs? Copulatives and conjunctions—to connect things? Or seeing things better without or with language?" For me it is a little like Eden before Adam named the things of the world. But China is not Eden.

The Chinese language is written as ideograms—one sign placed next to each other without the explanatory connectives and transitions we're used to in English. Juxtaposition of characters with

suggestive ambiguity as to all of what they might mean. But more clear than the juxtapositions in the poetry of T.S. Eliot or of Ezra Pound. The shape of this chapter will be the shape of the events of the year of 1984— a most suggestive Orwell-ian date for living in the most populous totali-tarian country in the world. Time will shape it. Events from my calendar and observations from my letters and journals and poems will fill it. A meal of ripe cut-up 1984 dates. *Bon appetit!*

January 1984: Flew to Hong Kong. Macau. (More details in my chap-ter China1.)

February 1: On to Canton (Guangzhou) in China. Couple of days here—Chinese New Year firecrackers. Flower market I was taken to by one of my graduate students, Pan Ying Zi (or Erica as we call her), and wandered around. But not that impressive or appealing. A drabber Hong Kong. Lots of H.K. people were visiting China for the holidays.

Feb. 4: To Guelin—for some of the most spectacular scenery I've ever seen. Like Thailand's Phang Na Bay—jagged fangs of limestone erupting from the fields, like 1000s-of-feet-high canine teeth. Went on a boat trip for five hours on the Li jiang [Green River], and froze my ass off even wearing two pairs of long underwear and several sweaters. C-O-O-O-L-L-D-D! Three hours back to the town of Guelin by bus. I'd like to go back in the summer.[I did.]

Hong Kong Chinese young people on vacation taking photos of each other against the drab Guelin Airport Building while the gorgeous scenery shines on the opposite side of the airfield, unphotographed, unwatched.

Factory smokestack outside Guelin pouring out smoke which blends with mist that swirls around the jagged limestone rock outcroppings looking like molars and canines. New industrial progress mixes with the old and natural weather. Haystacks outside the villages west of Guelin look like July 4th rockets, or like phalluses. Ruins of houses outside caves in the limestone hills look like American Indian pueblo dwellings.

People's Liberation Army (PLA) soldier in uniform, a woman, wears slightly high heels. A PLA soldier, a man, wears shocking-pink long underwear under his uniform green trousers.

Spent a few days there in Guelin and then 36 hours on a sleeper-train—six bunks per open compartment on to Kunming, where at 6 a.m. I was greeted by several Deans at the Railway Station. They stood at the first-class cars awaiting me. I of course went lower-class and carried off my own luggage, a duffel bag stuffed with books for my graduate students, and a backpack for me. The peasant professor.

Feb. 8: Arrived in Kunming! My private office at the college has five desks in it. My own classroom—all spare and simple, with concrete floor (no rugs). No shower or bath at my apartment, but can take a shower across and down the street in the broken-down spider-infested (lots of webs) small hut three times a week (Mondays, Wednesdays, and Fridays, at 1 p.m. are my times) for which they heat the water for me and at other times those days for the other two foreigners here—a couple named Richard and Teri Zelenetz. My apartment has four rooms—a rudimentary kitchen with a hot plate, which I almost never used, and a single cold-water tap; a bedroom; a living room where I work; another room which I use to store my pack and bicycle. There is also a small toilet, and a nice terrace. The toilet, inside but next to the interior stairwell, is open at its very top for ventilation, and also for sounds and smells. Less privacy than an American is used to for his defecations in China. I'm on the second floor of a three-story building complex where the Deans and senior professors stay, rather than in the special housing for foreigners the other universities have. No guards at our gate, so more people feel comfortable about dropping in on you. Less surveillance. Welcoming committees descend on me and we drink tea and discuss things. The first month I'll work preparing the students for their thesis research, and check to see what books are available for them in the several universities in Kunming.

Feb. 10: Went with Deans Guo and Liu and professors Di and Tang and a few of their children to see the Stone Forest of Lunan, 75 miles away. Dark-grey rocks, limestone chemically dissolved into bizarre shapes intricately cleft and caved, are, as in any country, given names like Lotus Blossom Peak and Sword Peak Pool. All peoples try to make foreign Nature familiar and human. A good day of bonding with my colleagues!

Feb.20: Classes start. Prepare for tomorrow's class on research methods. Tell students to get me their tentative M.A. thesis prospectuses by next Tuesday. The grad students would like me to be in my apartment rather than in my college office, where other students and professors would distract me. So Mondays through Fridays, I'll be available only for grad students from 9 a.m till 12 noon. They also would like me to go with them to Beijing, Shanghai and other big cities in China to help them gather research materials. I'd love that. We'll see. Tonight my "Welcome Banquet" from the college. Everyone here is very helpful and nice to me. On sunny afternoons I sit out on my terrace shirtless and warm. Nights get cold. Kunming is about 4600 feet in elevation, and is called "Spring City" because its weather is spring-like all year round.

March 4: "Serve the People" Day! The college took me by car to the Kunming streets where I answered any questions anyone had about the English language, American political system, or anything else! All college students set up tables in the streets to answer questions, fix bikes and radios, give haircuts, etc., all free for anyone who wants it. Mostly, questions and answers were translated by my student Jem Li, but there were some few who could ask questions in halting English. Many people came over to watch and listen. The *Weiban* who take care of foreigners drove me all over the city to see students cleaning and re-painting parts of the Railway Station, sweeping the streets, etc. These students are giving back to the community. I think it is a great idea, this "Serve the people" Day.

Executions in the prison of Kunming—announce on the P.A.system his name and crime, then the volley of rifle fire, then the next prisoner to be executed is announced. There are every month or so a list of eight or nine names with their crimes posted prominently all over the city. After the execution has been carried out, there is a big red check next to the name of the executed. I did not see any public executions. In Lijiang where foreigners were not then allowed to go, we foreign experts went with the authorities, and I saw in front of a police station, a bulletin board with photos and commentary on the criminals who had been shot by a firing squad in front of a large crowd. Photos also of the criminals being tied to wooden posts prior to their execution, some with their heads down—one woman was looking down at her legs being tied—and some with their heads up, facing the squad. Then the photos of the shot criminals lying face down in the field, a long "tail" of paper or cloth down each of their bodies on which were characters which described their crimes. Always, crowds around these police bulletin boards avidly looking and reading.

In the hospitals in smaller towns, because each person can only have one child now in 1984, the doctors or nurses may do away with one of a pair of twins.

Many restaurants and individuals use rape-seed oil for their cooking. It smells like cheesy feet.

The Deans and Vice-Deans are in charge of teaching in our foreign language academic department. The Chairman or Party Secretary and Vice Chairman of each department are in charge of political and Communist

Party matters. In 1984 I was told they are of about equal importance. (As I said, rape oil smells like cheesy feet.)

Interesting story? A man may not marry a woman because they cannot get permission to get her place of residence changed to the city he was assigned to? One of the Deans in my department had to live for twenty years away from his wife because they were assigned to teach in places two days' bus ride away from each other. They saw each other usually once a year at the Chinese New Year vacation. This is not uncommon.

One of my favorite places—an old Kunming tea house. Its occupants almost all old men. One or two people in the evenings play the *er hu*, a two-stringed instrument, accompanying others singing falsetto selections from various Beijing operas. After singing, they usually hawk and spit as falsetto singing is hard on their voices. (Everyone hawks and spits a lot all over China!) Different men sing, and a woman or two who also may be in the tea house. One man usually strikes a block of wood with another stick of wood to punctuate the music of the strings. After singing, they may argue or discuss the song. Often one guy's directions rule the performances, and he stops or indicates how it should be sung. Most other people in the place ignore the singers, or sometimes listen in. The singers do it for pleasure. No one ever takes up a collection. One fellow who often is here to play the *er hu* looks like he just came out of working in the fields—dirty blue singlet, stained blue trousers. I was told that some of these singers were once professionals, and couldn't work at this art during the Cultural Revolution and so were dragooned into working as peasants in the fields. Everyone smoking bongs of cigarettes. Smoke hangs heavily in the tea house. Tea cost 5 fen per cup of tea leaves, simply thrown into the bottom of your cup by the waiter, and then all evening endless refills of hot water from a man who comes around with a steaming kettle of water. 5 fen is about 2 cents. A cheap date.

Drink beside tea available here is beer (*pi jio*)—many cities have their own local brewery, and in Kunming it is *Bai Long Tan* which naturally we Americans changed to a more familiar "Ballantine" or as Jim, an older professor from Texas teaching at the Minorities Institute would ask me as I got up to get another drink at the Green Lake Hotel, "Hey, Chuck, get me another bottle of that Panda piss, will you?" I knew what he meant. And there is soda too—*chi shuay*—often in long plastic containers looking like full condoms, sometimes left around on the streets after using, but the orgy is of drinking soda, not of sex. The local neighborhood seller of soda would often when he saw me, bang his chopsticks on the side of his wooden food container, offering me some of his food should I wish. I never took him up on it, but it was a generous and friendly gesture.

Every so often, there would be a transfer of the excrement from the neighborhood toilets to the "honey wagon" and those days were perilous. You would hear a "huh, huh, huh" from in front of you while walking down the lane in our old part of town, and see folks flattening themselves against the houses. You did the same. Around the corner came a man, a pole across his shoulders, and on each end of the pole was an open bucket of shit, splishing and splashing out of the buckets as he half-ran with it to his wagon. I was told he was paid more than the usual workers' wages and was "honored" for doing this job. The neighborhood folks had a large public lavatory, no partitions between the holes into which you crapped, but a partition between the men's and women's sides. The excrement from the "honey wagon" was parceled out to farmers who left it in large concrete circular troughs where it would ferment for weeks and then be shoveled onto the fields as fertilizer. Cheaper than artificial fertilizer, and god knows, all too readily available in China. Makes economic and ecological sense to me, but it means you had to cook everything you ate very well, including lettuce and tomatoes. No raw salads in China. Another disadvantage to these troughs of raw excrement was that on many a bike ride outside the city, along bucolic country roads, the almost overpowering stench of shit from these farms would overtake you no matter how fast you rode. Yet in China the almost ubiquitous diarrhea I was accustomed to in Asia rarely happened. My own bowels were (hate to brag about this) in great shape. No shit!

March 23: Turns out that I didn't get to Beijing with my grad students to help them in their research there. Bureaucratic problems—foreigners are more segregated there than they are here, and if they let me go then it sets a precedent for all of China. Many different reasons given, and different people tell me different "real" reasons. Who to believe? While my grad students are away I am still very busy: teaching a course in modern American poetry (and poetry in general) to the teachers of English at Kunming Teachers College, soon to gain a higher status as Yunnan Teachers University (or Yunnam Normal University). Tape-recording English language texts and stories so that my voice will be immortal (or until the tape breaks). Giving two large public lectures, open to everyone, on "The Poetry of War." Teaching a few classes of Sophs and Frosh about the English language and about life in America. Letting them listen to a "native English speaker." Available for all teachers to consult with on any subject. Directing short skits for the May 4th celebration for five different classes. Reading the literary works by, and critical works on, the seven authors the grad students will be writing their theses on. Busy. But life is not all work.

I ride my bike all around town, out to Daguan Park, the Western Hills, the temples, the zoo. Walking in the old sections of the town near my university is exciting, but they're threatening to tear down these old one- or two-story houses, for the poorly-built but more space-efficient three-story apartment buildings that make Kunming undistinguishable from other cities. Spending lots of time with the other two Americans teaching here, Richard and Teri. Reading a great deal, mostly for work. Many of the students, both grads and undergrads, are delightful, and I enjoy the Chinese Deans and professors, and the other foreign teachers who often after work congregate down at the Green Lake Hotel, drink beer, complain about their working conditions, and drink some more beer. Not for me a bad life. My cook—she cooks for the three of us foreigners at my college, and we pay each month only for the food, not for her services—is a good one. Six days a week she's on duty, and the one day she's not I go off to some noodle or a dumpling joint with dirt floor, and with my rice coupons and a little cash get a tasty and simple meal. There are other restaurants in the town, but they are longer to travel to, and often I don't bother. One nearby place is Tang's (or the Burmese place because Tang comes from the southeast near Burma) where the food is very tasty and Tang is fun to listen to. Just a few tables in a shack, but better food than most.

Was on Chinese TV when I and other foreign experts were taken by the *Weiban* to a kindergarden to celebrate Woman's Day. Lots of speeches, but mostly by men. Shots of me dancing with a kid who was dressed as a rabbit, and I wiggled my ears at him. Ah, the life of a diplomat. That's also what we are. Banquets, speeches, meetings. Their classic toast is "To the friendship between our two countries!" I'll drink to that! And I did. People here are very friendly, especially when you smile at them. They stare at me a lot, but we foreigners are odd looking to them, even when we dress, as I and they do, in olive-drab trousers and Mao jacket.

The Chinese are very open, even startingly so, with me in their criticisms of life in China. But only when they are alone with me. When they are with another Chinese person or in a group, it's all politically correct, life in China and the Party are great! Kind of like the politically correct people in 2000 in New York. Public speech and private speech differ. Many of us in both countries are afraid not to lie about the truths we may see and how we actually feel about them, and political correctness in China and the USA is very similar even in the ideological positions and attitudes it takes.

March 26: Bring in book on Modern Poems and give Freshman class their English names from the first names of famous poets. One fellow wanted to be named "River" because it's a translation of his Chinese name. My poem of March 24, 1984:

"A lake in Green Lake Park. A green willow tree
stains the murky brown blue water of Green
Lake Park with its reflection. All these colors
repeating but shifting, shimmying of the imaginative
from the more rigid real, deeper, murkier, the ideal

submerged below blue water brown with mud and bits of life."

In the pond by the temple the sky reflects itself (ideals), but sometimes a large carp or other fish breaks the water and we see what is lurking underneath this reflection of the sky. The circle of the carp's leap spreads blackness and wavering and uncertainty over this sky. In early May, there are the green water-lillies with yellow flowers poking out.

In Green Lake Park there is a man who cleans ears. Several people are watching this man clean an older man's ears with a long thin metal rod on a wooden stick. At the end of this metal rod is a tiny rounded spoon-like spatula which he manipulates in the man's ear, holding the ear and peering in. The man whose ears are being cleaned grimaces—in pain? Distaste? The cleaner shows the wax to the man when he's finished. They examine it closely. The paradox of making cleaner, hearing better, with the risk of puncturing the eardrum and becoming deaf.

In Green Lake Park there are often bouts of "cross talk." Two peasants sing in alternation, the man to the woman, then she back to him. I think it's often lewd cross-talk, causing great laughter among the listeners. One man in the crowd of listeners moves his lips to one song, so this seems perhaps a memorized exchange rather than an invented one? I laugh because the singer smiles or laughs, or sings a line more emphatically and suggestively, and the crowd laughs. I don't understand a damn word he says, but the crowd's wholehearted laughter is infectious. They are -mostly peasants who hang around the park. The authorities eventually banned "cross talk" in the Park, and a policeman told them to disperse, but everyone moved over to a vacant lot behind the Park, and continued singing. Later on in May 1984 the authorities let it happen by a little pavilion in the Park and later on the "cross talkers" sang along a path beside a main gate. In Green Lake Park there were others singing Beijing opera, or doing traditional tribal dances, mostly done by men in a circle, many of the men being very effeminate, tapping their fingers for the rhythm on round small boxes with their tops off. The words "he" and "she" are the same in Chinese—*ta*—the same sound, the same tone. Mandarin—the language, not the official—blends genders as the falsetto pitch, the sugary sway, the pursing of the face and eyes, the fruity flutterings of the fan, as the role of the woman in the opera duet in Green Lake Park is taken by a man. *Ta.* The character is not the same. (The linguistic character, not the behavioral one.) Or maybe that too. It all blends. The tone is slightly different in Scotland where "Ta" means thanks or good-bye.

Once a medical doctor asked me about homosexuality in the USA, and said he was puzzled by what homosexuals actually did sexually. I told him what I knew, and he said that that was really disgusting. He said there was almost no homosexuality in China. A doctor with so little knowledge.... Yet in China the men hold hands with each other in the streets and wrap themselves around each other, but it's affectionate and not supposed to be sexual at all. The girls and women do the same, even more so. But in 1984 in Kunming a man and woman did not hold hands or hang on each other. I told my students it was the opposite in the USA. They were quite surprised. China is on the opposite end of the world from us, in more than just geography.

If a Chinese has sex outside of marriage, he or she would at least be severely criticized by her work unit, or have her or his name written on the neighborhood "wall newspaper"—chalked up on this blackboard for all to see, or they might go to jail. Many Chinese teachers and friends in their thirties or forties, if they were still unmarried, confided in me that they were still virgins, but seemed to feel this was natural.

April 1: Go with Richard and Teri by bike to Golden Temple. Chinese roofs, especially of temples, are curved because evil spirits can only travel in straight lines, so these curves and the screens by the entranceways prevent the demons from getting into the buildings. Now in 1984 when spirits are being somewhat believed in again, the curved roof is still made as typical Chinese architecture, and firecrackers are still set off at festive occasions, festive occasions such as changing the name of our college to Yunnan Normal University. In the city of Dali, they had a tape recording of firecrackers going off, so the noise is enough, without the smoke and actual explosions. Evil spirits are easily fooled?

By the Muslim mosque near the main department store, a young Chinese man, skullcap on, is reading a Koran in Arabic. Minority beliefs, while not encouraged, are usually allowed.

On April 3, I went with the English author Jenny Cox to the bird market and to the large and deep bomb shelter under a hill which had in it room for hospitals and living quarters in the event of a conventional or nuclear attack on China. Evil spirits can be deterred by prayer perhaps, but the Chinese make non-spiritual preparations too.

April 7: Went early in the morning to the Minorities Institute for lectures. "Minorities" are tribal peoples who have their own customs, languages, and dress, and are not Han Chinese. China once tried to make them like the Han, but later on let them retain their own ways. [Tibetans are the most obvious "minority" in China now in 2000.] Yunnan Province where I live is full of tribal peoples. At the Minorities Institute I learned that Bai poetry is rhymed, Yi is the nationality with the biggest population (with three different dialects of their own), the Nasi (pronounced Nah-shi) are related to the Mongols (the Nasi men take care of the children and the women are harder working than the men). The Chinese have problems with integrating these minorities into the wider culture and I was told, to help along this integration make special places for education and jobs for these tribals, requiring less of them, lower grades and skills in English for example, than of the Han Chinese. In some small tribal villages, they may not have access to radios (TVs were still quite rare in Kunming in early 1984), and so did not hear English, and may never have met a native English speaker. Many villagers spoke their own language, and so even Chinese was not learned well enough to qualify for any kind of higher education. With their "minorities," as with the Harijans ("Untouchable" castes) in India, and here in the USA, all three countries face some of the same difficulties of integrating all peoples into one culture. Separation and autonomy? Assimilation?

Which is best for different peoples and for the culture as a whole? We're all working on it.

April 14 till April 22—an interesting trip west to see some different peoples. A letter to my friends James and Dena describes some of it: "...all us foreign experts got to go on a trip to Dali (or Tali) and Lijiang, way out west in Yunnan near the Burmese border. Lots of fascinating minorities in their tribal clothing: Bai, Nashi—got a tape of a Nashi orchestra, 15 old farts, all of them over 65 or 70; 3 over 80, who took me out to dinner with them after their practice, because I hung around them, watching and listening to them make music in the Five Phoenix Pavilion. The Nashi orchestra consisted of 2-string violins (*er hu*) played on the knee; bells; a 10-gong vertical thing tapped on, and a bell rung with the other hand; plucked 3-string banjo-like thing; bass violin with a bigger base and a deeper sound than the *er hu*, and played with a bow; 4-string guitar-like thing which was plucked. The names of the musicians and most instruments and all the players I don't know. They were all old men. When they die, these pieces and part of the Nashi culture may also die out. Only one person at their restaurant afterward knew any English, and he helped a bit. But much friendliness and much misunderstanding of each other's answers. One piece they played made me feel stoned it was so lovely and evocative.

Antique buildings and cobble-stoned streets in the old town of Lijiang are giving way quickly to 4-story apartment houses looking as exotic as Peoria. China is modernizing and is losing the lovely as well as the lousy. Yet the rhododendrons' pink blossoms in the Nashi area near Lijiang, the sheep sorrel with its reddish flowers on its desert-y bushes by the side of the road, the blue flowers in small patches in the green fields, blue as the Nashi people's tribal color. Nature is still lovely here. Saw the March Fair in Dali: selling water buffalo, woven baskets, sun glasses and hand-carved doors. Fascinating peoples.

Climbed on the flank of Jade Phoenix Peak—I got to 10,500 feet, still at the pine tree level. Hiked here with Paddy Booz, who once taught in Kunming. When we got to a good view, we contemplated it in silence, and

then I started to laugh, thinking how small and trivial we are in the face of
this huge mountain. Paddy started to laugh after I did, I think about the
same thing. We never talked about why we laughed, but we just looked up
at the peaks and chuckled for a while. Wonderful Zen-Buddhist moment!

Boated on the Er Hai Lake where there is a great old temple on land
that looks like the Scottish moors. Went to a typical Bai village. Saw three
fine tall pagodas, Freudian symbols of Mongol-influenced old China. A
long evening of marvelous minority dances—each group from all over
Yunnan in different costumes, different music. Visits to Middle Schools,
where one English teacher told me he had never spoken to a native
English speaker. Various receptions and banquets to honor us foreigners."

I wrote AT A CHINESE BANQUET IN XIA GUAN, YUNNAN
PROVINCE:

"After the sea slug, it was all downhill. The sea slug, called a sea cucumber to make it less ugly, was in a red spicy onion-garlic sauce. The jelly-like
marrow from a deer's foot was in a light beige broth. That small rarity, red
bits "from near the snail's heart" which no one knew the name for, but I
thought might be snail embryo, came next. "Many snails have to be killed
till they find one with this. Not every snail has one. It comes from near the
heart." The reasons are all there: Sacrifice. It's rare. It comes from near the
heart. The cost is counted more than the taste, the rare becomes the good.
Sam Johnson's maid may have swell-ier breasts than the duchess, but the
duchess will be more remembered. Sunrise is spurned for neon, which is
brighter. A mere roasted peanut looks like old ivory, but tastes better." At
the end of this banquet, ended up huggling all the Chinese leaders, repeating *mei guo* (America) to show them this is our hug of friendship.

And also another, about mixing more than food: "Use nothing but the
most unusual ingredients: the spice of Kathmandu, saddhus of India,
bright yellow Sikh turbans, opium from north of Chiang Rai, or else some
church in Florence. While all around simple life goes on, unpoeticized,
unwritten, barely worded. The Chinese banquets they give us are bounteous—deer marrow, sea slug, shredded fish fin, a special fish nearing

extinction, bear paw. Rarity counts more than tastiness. Ordinary Chinese grow strong on rice, a few shreds of vegetables, with salt for savor. The body makes what it needs from anything." And indeed so can the poet, when he needs to write. But traveling and then telling in exotic places—like eating exotic foods—makes the writing chewier.

In Dali there were some other foreigners there for the March Fair. The Chinese and tribals were also doing non-traditional things. Many women in hair-curlers. Acrylic and nylon trousers. Western-style apartment houses. Western-style truckers' caps, at times worn with the bill way off to the side like poor teenage Blacks in the USA do, or perhaps the style was copied from some Tibetans who wear the bills of their fur hats off to the side. I don't know. One girl with a hair style of a curled-under stiff helmet, very like a popular Black hairdo here in the States.

The brown-red clay of the fields are the same color as the houses on the way to Dali. Upturned roof eaves and sway-backed houses. In a rice paddy, two small boys walk on the raised sides of the paddy to avoid crushing the new rice plantings. Eucalyptus trees planted at the side of the roads have their bark shredded off, but it is their natural state. On the road, old people gather the buffalo and cow shit off the road into a little basket for fertilizer or for cooking fuel.

At the March Fair, held this year in April in Dali, two PLA soldiers, carrying on their backs rifles with fixed bayonets each holding one arm of a reluctant prisoner. A Tibetan boy, wearing an old fox-skin hat with the fox tail behind, eats a brightly colored ice pop. Miao tribal women have large black turban-like bands around their heads.Some hats have "danglies" pendent from them. Some men play right-angled pipes. Hats here are not gender-specific—men wear flowered very feminine hats quite unself-consciously. Two twin brothers, the blind one led by the sighted one, stroll through the fair.

Speaking of the blind, briefings by the authorities are always very quantitative—numbers of farmers, numbers of rice catties per mu (how much is produced), statistics. The quantitative gives one a sense of scientific validity, of objectivity. Quality is less easy to assess (and access). The word for "bat" is the same word as "rich" or "abundance." The Chinese use puns—bat pictures are drawn to bring abundance and riches to the house or event. Same with *yu*, the word for both happiness and for fish. So they serve fish at a banquet to bring happiness to the diners. Superstition: based on an arbitrary linguistic similarity, the two different things are profoundly connected. (Our poetry often does this too.) Statistics? Language? Lies? How can we wrest reality to our purposes? Humans keep trying.

In Lijiang, where only some foreign experts were allowed to be at this time, while I was wandering around by myself, I was invited into someone's house as I was passing by. They gave me tea and we smiled at each other, lacking any words to communicate with. The whole family and then the whole street gawked at me in the living room and through the windows. Everyone was very sweet to this so-strange *wei guo ren* (foreign country person) who was also *mei guo ren* (beautiful country person, which means here American). Smiling became strained for us all after a while, and so I left their house, with much grinning and bowing and pattings on the backs. Often in the streets anywhere in China, I was stared at, and so I walk out with lowered eyes and a preoccupied look so I would not have to connect with anyone. So often, Chinese children seeing us would raise a shout: *Wei guo ren lai luh.* "Here come the foreigners!" One of us got the idea to make up a tee shirt that had this phrase in Chinese characters and English letters, along with a big red "W" on the shirt front—sort of a Wonder-Woman symbol. The shirt amused both us and the Chinese in China, and in New York, while the shirt lasted, it was a big hit with Chinese Restaurants' delivery men, one of whom almost fell off his bike laughing.

"While the shirt lasted." My face reflected in a glass shop window, then gone as I pass. What permanence here? Or there? Or reflected in the lake? Others' poems or lives, or these exotic locales lodge in my poems, in this travel memoir—do my hikes here in foreign China make these my words any less pedestrian? I smashed a fly against my white bedroom wall. What difference the smudge on that wall, or the smudges on the paper I write on? First of all, what can last? Words? A Chinese girl told me she loves my "smelling." My deodorant? My sweat? No, she means my "smiling." My living room window is poorly made, and an imperfection in it distorts things I see outside. I can only speak here to you with words.

CHINA3: KUNMING (cont.):

When I got back to Kunming from the trip to Dali in late April 1984, I hit the ground running. I wrote to my friends James and Dena, "When I got back I had to prepare for the first anniversary keynote lecture of the Yunnan Foreign Language Association on "Confusion, Ambiguity, and Multiple Meanings in English Language and Literature" (my choice of topic) and had all of 3 ½ days to prepare it. Laid on them bits of Shakespeare, Eliot, Stevie Smith, Liu Yu-hsi, e. e. cummings, and finally some of Joyce's "Finnegans Wake." But it went off well, as did the trip to Dali, as does my life here.

My grad students are back from their research trip which I couldn't go on (and so I was teaching everyone else here), and so now I'll be devoting myself to their questions on all the research material they xeroxed in Beijing and Jinan and Shanghai (I'll have to also read it all), plus teaching the teachers here about modern poetry. Plus anything else they think up for me to do that I'm willing to do. I gave two public lectures on the poetry of war, and will give two more in late May on ten modern British and American poets. Fun. I enjoy giving these public lectures….

Then we (other foreign experts and I) were guests of honor at a banquet. Lots of conviviality and good food and friendliness. I'm getting better and better at making off-the-cuff toasts and speeches. Tomorrow another entertainment for us (and for our Chinese hosts— generosity to us means they also share in the bounteous banquets. Whaddyu expect? Pure altruism?) in honor of May Day. Next day we go on a trip on Dian Lake here in Kunming hosted by (probably) the governor of the province himself. I'm the only furriner to be seated at the V.I.P. table for the banquet following the boat trip. Honors are heaping up on this (once again I have had my head and beard shaved in Lijiang) balding head. Gowing my hair back now and in a few days will stop shaving my grey beard. I look so much younger now. The grey adds aeons."

After my head and beard were shaved in Lijiang, I walked out in that town wearing my usual olive trousers and jacket, and I noticed that people were not staring at me so much, except for an occasional look, as if thinking, "what minority tribe does that guy belong to?" Felt like I belonged, as opposed to feeling like an animal at the zoo, my usual feeling in much of Asia. And as far as my comment above on getting better at making toasts, I said it too soon. At the May Day banquet sponsored by the Central Union of Yunnan Workers at Bayuko near Kunming (I still have my banquet place card), I as the senior foreigner expert (because I'm in charge of graduate students as much as my age and rank) gave the foreigners' toast to our hosts. I had an intricate idea and tried to lay it out clearly, but it drove my head graduate student and translator Jem Li nuts at trying to follow my thoughts, and I realized too late—Keep it simple! I saw all the guests trying to figure out my drift, and finally they just waited till it was over and they could smile and applaud and drink up. It really wasn't that long a toast, but Jem and I laughed about it afterward. Keep it simple!

May 4: "A Chinese professor just came over here while I was writing this letter and played the tape of Pres. Reagan's speech at Fudan University in Shanghai for me so I could help him with some of the words because he has to transcribe them (they transcribe all of Voice of America's broadcasts). Good speech." At the time I thought here I am, a strongly anti-totalitarian type, living in the largest totalitarian country in the world, during the archetypal year 1984, being paid by its government, and helping translate my anti-Communist American president's words when he also was welcomed in China. Performances by several undergraduate classes of plays which were all "directed" by me. "1776" was one of them. Great day for us Yanks!

May 5: Watched China beat Japan in some Davis Cup "doubles" tennis matches. We are getting so international here!

May 15: Celebration of our college being newly named (and raised in status) to Yunnan Teachers University (or as it finally became known—Yunnan Normal University. I argued about this with the college officials. I said "Normal" used to be for training teachers, but this is an old-fashioned use of the word, and many now in the USA don't understand it. The Chinese wanted it to be the same as the famous Beijing Normal University. They won. It's their university after all. Just a problem with translation.) During the speeches, the TV cameras focused on me sitting in the front row, honorable foreign graduate professor. I listened intently as though I understood what I was hearing. I hadn't a clue. Me with my newly shaved head, empty both on the top and inside.

At this celebration, orange soft drinks were handed out to the most important guests, together with a handout explaining that members of our own Chemistry department invented or discovered an extract made from chrysanthemum petals which is 200 times sweeter than sugar. While our president talked, all the speakers and guests on the stage sipped this drink or ignored it. No one finished theirs. The celebratory firecrackers crackled and banged outside the auditorium.

There are booms like a slamming steel door from the artillery practice at the People's Liberation Army (PLA) base nearby in Kunming which at times actually rattle my windows. According to the Voice of America broadcasts which many Chinese listen to, if only in order to practise their English, there are reports of "heavy fighting" on the borders between China and Vietnam. Nothing much though on this in the government sponsored English-language "China Daily" newspaper. In town you see young PLA soldiers on crutches, often with one leg missing. Many soldiers are so young and as they are not carrying guns in the streets, they convey no sense of toughness or aggression. On one street near my apartment, the peasants sell their extra vegetables and food. Here, eels are taken from a bucket filled with water and eels. The live eel purchased is stuck onto a large nail, then sliced down its body all the way, and given to the customer. Eels keep getting stuck on that nail, getting sliced, and their blood, heads, and skin drips down into another bowl. This bowl keeps getting fuller as the day goes on. Animals are just meat, just food.

The comforting buzz of crickets in Green Lake Park, making this exotic Chinese world familiar to me. The amazing show of trees and water is always refreshing. I drink the scenery as the sun sets. On April 8, 1984, I wrote, "Toward sunset: a shift, a pause. In the park the turquoise, yellows, browns, reds of the temples drunkenly shimmys in the water at its base, becomes a wobbly painting, its colors greasing the water. Nearby, an empty ice-cream cup remains more substantial and barely moving, deep and slow next to the painted glaze of the old temple darkening on the pool. Lines of colored electric lights will, after dark, mock the turquoise tiles, the blander blue water." Cut flowers and bonsai trees are on exhibit in the park and at times in front of temples. Sometimes an old woman totters in to pray on tiny, once bound, feet. Beauty relying on the warped and broken. Patriotism too.

At several temples in Kunming, on-lookers, especially the young, often giggle at the few worshippers, who, if they also are young, grin self-consciously. As they bow and perform the rituals, they are obviously embarrassed to be watched. If the worshippers are old, they generally ignore the mockers. In 1984 one could worship the old Chinese gods and use the old rituals more freely than in the past few decades. Temples were even being refurbished, but more for tourists' agendas than for religious ones. I met an old Chinese Catholic priest who, only because of his faith, had been kept in prison for twenty years. He was old and frail and smiling. We all refer to the Communist take-over of 1949 as "Liberation."

I was in China in 1984 for more than one year, 35 years after "Liberation." As a foreign expert (a title, not always an accurate description—like "Liberation") I could say almost anything I wanted, voice many politically incorrect opinions. When I told Dean Yang, before I lectured on the poetry of war, I likely would voice heresy to the Chinese in this public lecture, and how did he feel about that, he told me that anything was O.K. for me to say because I was a foreigner. It seemed to me that my freedom of speech, which Chinese did not have, came a little at the price of being ignored, because I was a "white devil, butter-smelling, round-eyed barbarian." In other words, not Chinese. I tried throughout this year to be polite and diplomatic, which virtues tend to reduce the amount of truth in one's talk. The real sulks and lurks beneath the words.

The vast Kunming bomb shelter is in the hill below Yuentong Zoo, and above the Yuentong Temple. The bomb shelter has stores in it selling plastic flowers and clothing. Long rounded tunnels, painted white. There are photos and drawings of how pleasant life could be down here even in or after a nuclear attack. But also shown are nuclear and chemical and biological warfare and their terrible effects. Photos and drawings show which are the best positions to crouch and to lie to protect yourself. (Think of the word "lie" and two of its meanings.)

Seeing a tiger in the Yuentong Zoo plus my endemic and epidemic sexual and linguistic desires and frustrations pushed me into writing TONGUE:

"It's wonderful, the tongue entering the mouth of a lover, or hers into yours, till none can speak so intertwined the tongues, none knows the end of mine or where yours or you begin, till your senses are stripped of the mind's lingerie, the head flung back, the mind mute.

Like the tiger tonguing meat, no need to chew the tenser flesh, but tonguing can lick all life from the mind, can reduce the mind to flesh and then beneath flesh; to the dark beneath the lights. A sandwich of me and you—meat between meat—between our flesh, our flesh tonguing a telling blow to our slippery separations, between—ah!—between. What of the Christian communion, the true lunch that tongue tastes and twines and twins, and rolls back into the head—like ecstatic eyes, like a bolt into the dark—the flesh.

Bolt: the lightning, the scared leap, the quick gulp—all light this tongue I trip over, unrolled, this red plush carpet leading me deeper into God knows where, this impudent imprudent unrolled tongue, this joining joke, linguistics beyond language, where words gag."

War at a low level was going on between China and Vietnam in 1984, on the borders of my province, Yunnan. During the Cultural Revolution, in which old Chinese culture and new "Western" culture were both brutally crushed out of the people here, from 1966 till 1976, there was a war within China. Not just in ideological terms or chastising individual intellectuals as the world now knows, but so several Chinese told me, also a war between large units of the P.L. Army with one another. It was all over China often a civil war, usually the most uncivil and cruel of conflicts. Here in Kunming you can still see the bullet holes in the walls of the sniping between the Engineering College and ours, the Teachers College. One student had been shot dead by a student sniper of another college while walking down a lane. Even in 1984, so I was told, as the police are not allowed to arrest army people, if someone in the army commits an arrestable offense, the police will arrest that army person's son or other family member who is not in the army. There is a great rivalry between the army and the police. So I was told.

Two public lectures I gave in May and June 1984 were entitled "The Most Important Things: Williams, cummings, Yeats, Stevens" and "Nature in the poems of G.M. Hopkins and D. Thomas." Entertainments during June in Kunming were dances of India, Beijing opera, movies with friends like Richard and Teri, Claire, Ralph, dinners at my Chinese friend Frank He's home, and the evenings having a beer at the Green Lake Hotel or watching the sun set from its 5th-floor open-air balcony with the other foreigners. Rode my bike or hiked to the top, Dragon Gate, of the Western Hills, or out to see the life-size figures of the arhats (disciples) at the Bamboo Temple. Keeping quite busy too with work: "Been reading Eugene O"Neill and E.M. Foster and am now on Henry Fielding's "Amelia" (600 pages of this 18th century novel). Lots of reading on and for my students' researches. They're busy reading the stuff they xeroxed in Beijing, honing their ideas for their theses....keeping on with my class for teachers on poetry. Also, whenever they need someone to take over their classes, the teachers often ask me, and I say "yes." Will help the Juniors to do part of the play "1776" which should be fun."

After late May, the weather changes in Kunming, as then begins the summer rainy season. "As they say here, "when it rains, winter comes to Kunming." Chilly, but not bad, and a contrast to summer heat." Life was sometimes lonely here for me, but easily bearable. The routine is pleasant. "The maid is here now, killing flies, and sweeping under my bare feet, and making my daily three thermoses full of boiled water for drinking." During the summer most foreign teachers left for the academic vacation, but my students asked that I stay around to help them with the work on their theses, and so I did. Butr fewer people to have heart-to-heart talks with, and the grey and rainy weather made my loneliness burgeon some. On July 7, '84 I wrote,"Here I sit watching the rain come down in Kunming, China. (How many poems begin like that?) (Not many because not many poets get to Kunming.) (I'm not talking about Chinese poets.) (But if I knew Chinese poetry....) The rain like tears from the vault of heaven falling.... (The poets' vault door long fallen off its rusty hinges.) (The thieves escaped with all the cardboard prizes long ago.) The rain wears down iron spirits in China as well." Parentheses coop me up here like the rain outside my window. Mildew of the soul? Red rust of the heart? Melodramatic outpourings of me feeling a little lonely during the pouring rains of the summer monsoons.

In July "my Chinese colleagues will be grading 20,000 entrance exams for people trying to get into college. After two weeks of this, they'll be teaching middle school or high school teachers more English. Some vacation!" For me, writing on July 28, "my students are handing in the chapters of their theses....Just got a first chapter of 51 pages from the one student who was slowest deciding on her author, topic, mode of attack. I'll read it tomorrow....Will give a few lectures (question/answer sessions so I don't have to prepare anything) to the 500 middle school teachers (at our high school level) now studying for a month at the college. Also will give a talk for two hours to the heads of the middle schools throughout Yunnan province. Over here, I'm an authority on all sorts of subjects that I'm really a rank amateur on, but the knowledge on various subjects is pretty skimpy here." Many of the questions for me at these sessions are about life in the U.S.A.

Working in a foreign country, especially when I was working being an English and American literature professor, is in many ways not so different from working in the U.S. You read and write and speak a lot. Even my leisure was spent mostly on reading which, while not dull to do, is dull to enumerate. During my seven-week trip in September and October to Tibet and the rest of China (on which more later), I found that none of my graduate students had gone to the two other foreign experts, who were to assist them on their theses while I was gone, nor did the students do much work on their own. So they asked me to postpone their two courses on contemporary American poetry and contemporary American drama. I said "no!" I taught them these two courses for four hours per week on each course, along with pushing them hard toward their theses writing. I also had four hours of "consulting" per week for all other teachers in the foreign language department.

One weekend I went with Dean Guo to Yu Xi, a small town in the south, three hours away by car. For the whole weekend, I was speaking to these teachers till my voice was a charred croak. Exhausting, but very gratifying. After my official lectures were over, they crowded around me, accompanying me everywhere and asking questions. Some had never met a native English speaker, and they had so many questions and so much interest in life in the States, and the English language. Besides this weekend losing my voice, I also lost my money on Sunday July 29. "Talking to two Danish girls, I paid no attention to the small man in blue who pushed me hard while passing down the aisle on the bus in Kunming, and picked my pocket. 42 Yuan gone. What could I do? I had never seen his face, paid no attention, the bus was filled with the same colors—blues and greens—and I didn't speak Chinese. But the loss is small for me, though it's two weeks salary for a worker here." I was told—not that you can always trust what you're told in this country—that

someone in 1984 who stole from a foreigner would get a harsher sentence
than if he had stolen from a native Chinese.

August 8: I gave a lecture to the heads of teacher training institutes and
the administrators of Szetchuan teachers colleges on U.S. high schools—
their different types, their problems and possible solutions, especially
relating to studying languages. As I remember, the theme of mine for
studying foreign languages was "Use it or lose it." (I, however, had given
up studying Mandarin Chinese soon after I arrived in Kunming. Too difficult a tonal language for this boy.)

But now I would need all the Chinese I could muster because I was
soon to be off on vacation traveling around China. My old college friend
Elaine Freeman had come to Kunming for three weeks of travel with me,
and neither of us knew the language. On September 7, 1984, we flew to
Guelin, one of the most beautiful places in the world, with tall limestone
fangs sticking out of the land at the sides of the Li River. I had been there
in frigid January, and now I did the same river boat trip with Elaine in hot
September. Magnificent! Later, in the town of Guelin we climbed a few of
these limestone spires, and on one met an interesting Chinese pharmacist
who specialized in Chinese traditional medicines, but who said if he
wanted to get rid of a medical problem of his own quickly, he used
Western medicine. On the way down one of these spires in a Guelin park,
I almost stepped on a poisonous bamboo viper who was slithering along
slowly on some flagstone steps just in front of me. Elaine and I gave him a
wide berth. He ignored us.

We went to Hangzhou, famous for its West Lake and its vinegar fish,
and islands in the lake, one named "Three pools mirroring the moon."
On this trip I wrote no letters and made no journal entries, and my memory of them is made of water. I remember going out to these islands. I
remember at night it was a full moon at the lake, and we viewed it as
Chinese had done for a couple of thousand years, gaping at and reflecting
on the lunar reflections, symbol of the impermanence and beauty of life.
We ate West Lake fish in a lake-side restaurant, and wandered its shores.

Nearby there are some famous springs, and the most famous is Tiger Running Spring, whose water is so thick with surface tension that I saw coins put on its surface and the coins did not sink. At a small teahouse at the spring, we had an expensive cup of Dragon Well tea made with Tiger Running Spring water. This to elegant Chinese tea connoisseurs is supposed to be the absolutely best cup of tea in the world. We reverently sipped at it. It was good, but my tea-tasting buds must not be so well developed. Just a barbarian, as I suspected

Then on to Suzhou, famous for its gardens and canals. Humble Administrator's Garden and Liu Yuen Garden are lovely, but I was not ravished by most of them. Perhaps too subtle for me to fully appreciate, as were the rock gardens I saw in Japan in 1962. Artfully arranged to make spots for the contemplation of Nature tamed, with pools and rocks and flowering tree branches, all in harmony together—true. Nevertheless, I was hoping for a more powerful revelation than I got, but I more fault me than I do these lovely gardens.

From Suzhou Elaine and I went by overnight boat along the canals into Shanghai. We shared a stateroom with an older Chinese fellow. Fascinating to see all the life that goes on in the waters near Souzhou. The canals in the city are interesting to saunter along, just to watch the goings-on, the ordinary life unconnected to us foreigners or even to anything foreign. Ordinary life in China is interesting to us because it's different. Travel is often most exciting when you are accepted enough to see how people in other cultures live without them paying attention to you. The traveler who can blend in, can be the fly on the wall. But it's rare in China not to be noticed and stared at. Elaine loved just wandering around, and loved it when the people came over to her. I had been broken by so many months of being stared at, I often behaved as would a movie star in the States—just leave me alone. Tried to avoid eye contact. Annoyed at the attention. But Elaine was right. Just smile and stare back at them. Be friendly rather than flee. When I did this, I was happier.

In Shanghai, we tried to get a hotel room at the He Ping Bingwan—the famous Peace Hotel right on the Bund by the river. So unfortunately did everyone else want a hotel room here. Booked solid, the hotel staff assured me. One person manning the lobby desk even said that every hotel in Shanghai was totally booked, so perhaps it would be best that we leave the city. Other tourists told us Shanghai was full! Elaine told them she was just in China for three weeks—we needed a room here. I told them I was the graduate professor—a V.I.P., and with a work card, I was helping their nation, I was…. Nothing seemed to work. Many other Europeans and Americans were wandering the lobby also in despair. Finally after more than an hour of entreaty I told them that "if you did not get us a room, we were prepared to sleep here in the lobby, making it very obnoxious for your other paying guests, and that I knew there were always extra rooms available for your important guests, and damn it, we were they!" Very reluctantly they did "discover" that a room was available for us. Rather than exult publicly I played along that it was just "discovered" and we went up in the elevator with the room key, of course carrying our own packs. In the elevator we danced around in muted and mouth-wide glee. We were in!

In Shanghai we walked along the Bund, a fairly European set of buildings to one side, the river to the other. Folks doing their Tai Chi, airing their singing birds, strolling—the Bund in a good place to hang out on. There's a small section nearby which had old buildings, but Shanghai seemed a city with few real delights to see. The sidewalks and parts of the roads were so crowded with pedestrians and cyclists that walking them felt like being in line, or like rush hour in the subways, but all day long. What if people get rich enough to afford cars? (By the way, during 1984, the first private car was purchased. Before this, all cars were part of work groups. Private cars? There goes the communal Communist revolution. And in crowded Shanghai there goes the neighborhood and all the streets.) Where could they put the new cars or motorcycles? In 1984 the authorities could somewhat keep a lid on population in all of China by controlling everyone's wages. You want to be paid, then your work group rules where you can live. But if you can set up some private business, and you are paid by your customers, not by your work group, then what's to stop you from living anywhere you wish—like in cosmopolitan business-oriented Shanghai. I dreaded the crowds here in the more free future.

From the past in Shanghai came the sounds of 1930s and 1940s jazz, played by the Post Office Band, which we heard perform one evening in some venue by the Bund. Naturally it was packed with foreign tourists, drinking and having one hell of a time. The Post Office Band was frozen in time, older men who had learned jazz before learning anything "Western" and therefore bourgeois and decadent was a crime against the state. It was disjunctive to hear Dixieland tunes played in this Chinese land, although Shanghai was probably mainland China's most European-ized city in 1984.

Then to Beijing, where we toured the Forbidden City, the old Emperor's palace with its many small buildings like the Hall of Supreme Harmony and Palace of Gathering Excellence. Away from it is the Temple of Heaven and the Summer palace with its lake and its marble boat and Jade Belt Bridge. Naturally we ate Beijing duck here. Celebrating Elaine's birthday in the US meant getting together for Beijing duck in New York City's Chinatown. We had not gotten to Beijing by the time her birthday arrived, but we went out looking for Beijing duck and finally came to a place that looked likely. However, no more Beijing duck was available. We pleaded, but to no avail. But we could have duck prepared in the Shandong style—very salty—because they did have one such duck still available. We seized on it. It was delicious. Happy birthday!

Out to the Great Wall of China—there's a restored section open not too far from Beijing that we traipsed along. Seeing the small temples and the old Beijing hutongs—the old-style walled courtyards with the whole extended family living within—quite a wonderful trip for both of us.

Elaine left for the States after her three-week vacation with me, and I continued on traveling.

Datong was next, a several-hour train ride east of Beijing, for its Yungang Grottoes carved out of the soft loess cliffs. In these carved-out caves are huge statues of Buddha and his disciples, the arhats, some of which have their heads smashed off, a result of the religious antipathy Muslims have toward graven images. (Like what the Christians did to the pagan's religious art.)

Hohhot is the capital of Inner Mongolia, and I took a train there, passing grey barren rounded hills, a grey wet day, quite depressing. At the Hohhot train station, the weather and the city seemed so depressing and chilly (it was now October), that I took the next train back into China to Xian. I didn't have warm clothing, and felt—as these past three short paragraphs stylistically may indicate—a desire to get warm and get home, to get my travels through China over with, going through the motions of traveling, with my heart not fully into it.

Xian is great! The most famous sight—and it is stunning—is the terra-cotta warriors of the Emperor Qin Shi Huang Di, still not all the way dug out of the surrounding earth, standing firmly as tomb protectors, now enclosed in a museum which looks like a airplane hangar. There are the carved-stone animals guarding the long path to the Qian Ling tomb, worn down by rain and wind and time, but still somber and elegant and powerful in their persistent presence. In the city, there are the two tall pagodas—the Big and the Small Wild Goose Pagodas, and in the center of the city, there's the big Bell Tower plumb in the middle of the two main streets. Old China still here and vital. I also went out to a romantic pretty spot, about 20 miles outside the city, Huaqing Hot Springs. One feature here is the Imperial Concubine Bath, "said to have been the bath of Yang Yuhuan, the favorite concubine of Emperor Xuan Zong." I got this information from a brochure I kept, but I remember while there trying to conjure up from this chilly pretty place with the hot springs the torrid sexual or romantic atmosphere of Xuan Zong's court, its inevitable "harem" politics, the real life that now is so long gone. Xuan Zong, Yang Yuhuan—just names now, their flesh just dust, their passions cold. (And what then about the rest of us all?)

From Xian I went due east to Luoyang, where I bought a large thick People's Liberation Army coat, wadded with cotton, of a great weight, because by then I had decided to go to Tibet, by middle October, cold at night. Near Luoyang are the Longmen Grottoes, with figures of Buddha and one that looks like Kuan Yin, Chinese goddess of Good Luck, all carved out of a large cliff along a riverbank. I have my notes written on a map of this city: "To White Horse Temple (Bai Ma Si)—bus 8 to Xiguan, then bus 6 to last stop. First to temple, then on way back (bus 8) stop at museum and tombs. Buy sweater at dept. store." How did this museum differ from the other museums I had see on this trip? I don't remember. Since I don't take a camera on my trips anymore, and took few photos even in China, what to hold on to? The postcards I buy? The maps and souvenirs I get? The sights I saw and the intentions I had are worn down in my memory the way the actual places are worn down by time and rain. This whole travel narrative may be a symbol of the way time operates to slowly and softly wipe away all the past.

South then to Yichang on the Chang Jiang, the Yangtze River, where I got a ship upstream to Chongqing, a 2 ½ day voyage. I was the only foreigner in the second-class cabins, which meant I shared a cabin with about six or eight people. Very friendly to me in our packed cabin, double-decker bunks lining the walls. Walking the decks, I struck up a conversation with one of the first-class passengers, a European, and he invited me up to the first-class quarters, where I stayed during the rest of the voyage, except for the nights, when I went below and scrambled into my second-class berth to sleep. We went through the Three Gorges of the Yangtze (Chang Jiang) River, which the current building of the dam will flood. In China and also in the rest of the world, changes are happening so quickly, the old ways and places are being swamped by the new with such speed, anyone wanting to see the world better go very soon! Here these are giant gorges with names like "the Gorge of the Ox's Liver and the Horse's Lung" and "the Shadow Play Gorge." The walls in several places rise steeply up 1500 feet, and even at the very top of some of these precipitous hills you can see rice paddies, made by men's hands over the centuries. In China every bit of arable soil is used and has man's fingerprints on it.

Once the first-class passengers had a banquet which they invited me to, and a dance after with this foreign group who had just been to Bhutan and now were "doing" China in style. The windows to the first-class dining room were filled with the faces of the second-class passengers, all Chinese (except for me), and at one point I noticed a woman who was sleeping in my stateroom who was holding her daughter up to see us all dancing. We previously had exchanged friendly words, though we didn't understand each other's, and I went outside and took her 3-year-old daughter from her arms into mine and took her in and danced with her in my arms. The Chinese outside the windows on the deck were ecstatic—their grins almost ripped their mouths open!— and everyone in the first-class dining room thought it was cute as hell. This woman previously had introduced me to her tiny daughter in our room as "grandfather," a common way to connect each Chinese with every other older Chinese. A young girl I had met in Kunming, asked me if she could call me "old father." I found this connectivity between people charming. So this little girl was easy in my arms, and we danced for a while, all tourists watching, and then I returned her to her mother, all the Chinese around me slapping my back with smiling delight. At times in China, especially in places where they rarely see a white person, some very small children see you, draw themselves up straight with shock, and run screaming and crying to their mothers or older sisters.

Not this 3-year-old charmer.

We docked in Chongqing, a dirty city packed on a bluff above the river. Several Chinese independently approached me and all talked of the terrible Japanese attacks on their city during World War II. History was rarely kind to China. From here I went northeast to Chungdu, where I had one of their culinary specialties, *ma po do fu*, a spicy tofu dish with Szetchuan peppers, which seared my mouth and pruned my taste buds for the rest of the day. In Chengdu there were many houses built as in Tudor England, with timbers in an X-shape through the mortar of the house fronts. I have heard since that these houses are all being demolished to put up apartment buildings which, while they pack in more people in a given amount of land, nevertheless convert a distinctive traditional architectural style into one worthy of Peoria. Same in Kunming. Knock down the old, up with the new. The whole world is changing so quickly nowadays.

From Chengdu I flew to Tibet, on which more later. Back from Tibet, I took the train to Emei Shan, one of China's most sacred mountains. I traveled here with three women, part of a chorus from Switzerland, who now were going around China sight-seeing. On the crowded train (in China they were always very crowded), one of them became sick, and by the time we got a hotel room for us four, she was shitting and had basically collapsed. I remember stroking her head, trying to comfort her, as she, naked and shitting into a small basin on the floor, moaned in agony. The next day she still was pretty sick, but better, and so the other two women and I started to climb Emei Shan, more than 9,000 feet high. They went back to the hotel after a few hours on the slopes, and I continued up alone. I spent two nights on the rainy and chilly mountain wrapped in swirling mists (both me and the mountain).

But it was the sun that was one of the highlights. Hiking to the top by the wide paths in the grey mist made me fear I wouldn't see one of this mountain's magnificent sights—the Buddha light. But looking out from the top over the roiling clouds below the peak, suddenly the sun broke through and sunlight spilled over these clouds. And there it was. The Buddha light. The sun projected my shadow over the clouds below, my shadow which stretched hundreds of yards surrounded by a radiant glow of sunlight. Just to make certain it was really my shadow, I waved my hands over my head. So did my shadow, spikey rays of sunlight glistening around it. Soon a few other Chinese came over and started their wavings and cheerings, and the shadows over the clouds were full of movement. I left the top and headed down.

Trying to get lodging at a hostel below the peak, the manager tried to charge me the foreigner's price. With my work card, I should have gotten the foreign-expert price, somewhat lower. Lower still was the overseas Chinese price, and lowest of all, sensibly enough, was the price for China's Chinese people. The manager insisted, and so did I. The difference in price was small, but we stuck to our principles. Finally I, angry and disgusted with the intransigent Chinese bureaucracy, often even more intransigent than I am, told him I would get lodging lower down, even though it was now very late in the afternoon, and the sun was low. I walked down the misty path at a good pace, and then at an even faster pace. The shadows in the woods were longer, and no one was on the trail now. I had a flashlight, but this would be a bad place to find myself— because I could lose myself—in the dark. I kept quickly striding down, hoping to see the next hut, till at last, as the trail was becoming overwhelmed by the evening darkness, I saw a light ahead of me. It was the hut. I got a cold room (and at the correct price). I was safe.

Next day I first saw the large monkeys I had been warned about. I carried, as did most of the hikers or pilgrims on Emei Shan, a long walking stick which could be used to keep off the monkeys. Walking down to a stream, I saw a pack of monkeys on the other side of it. Now I had heard that they gang up on lone hikers, and that one person had been pushed off a cliff to his death by them. I was nervous, but never good to show fear to an animal, nor is it good to project anger at them. I walked the line between these emotions as I walked across the stream. A couple of monkeys had stayed on the path at its sides, and several were on the six-foot-high raised margin of the path to my right. As I walked past them, projecting more confidence than I felt, one to my left grabbed at my trouser leg. I whirled and raised my stick and waited, staring him down. He looked at me, then sheepishly averted his eyes and turned away. I turned around again and began walking. No problems, mate. But it felt like a close thing.

After a couple of days on Emei Shan, with a cold and a cough brewing, I took the train for Kunming, not far to the south, and that was my seven-week vacation in China.

Busy as soon as I arrived back. My graduate students had done very little on their theses while I was away, so I started pushing them harder and setting tighter deadlines for them. I gave a couple of public lectures that I worked up with another teacher, Diane Gruenberg, on "Literary England"—a series of snippets from novels and poems, to go with Diane's slides, about the English countryside and Oxford. Another public lecture by me also about how to make a phrase or sentence memorable, analyzing various aphorisms and apothegms and proverbs. Got a big raise in salary, because China is having some inflation problems. My salary of 650 yuan per month is about ten times the average teacher's salary here. I feel a bit embarrassed by all these riches (which amounted in total to about $4,000 U.S. per year, so I won't get my Rolls Royce just yet).

A few of us foreign experts were the "talent" for a T.V. commercial for the "Five Spices" factory. For this, I got 20 packages of these spices, plus a couple of banquets, plus a bottle of expensive, powerful, and quite vile Chinese booze. While they filmed us dining in a restaurant on a dish flavored with the famous "five spices," they wanted us naturally to look delighted with the food. Look, even the sophisticated Westerners love these spices! So while I was looking happy and smacking my lips over the chow, I was saying to the other guests, "Hey, man this shit is good! Can't believe these stupid bags of spices can turn this crap into tasty food!" The only sound in this commercial was the announcer talking up the five spices. My words were silent, but I hoped no English-speaking Chinese could read my lips.

Banquets in November, some given by me for my students and the Deans, some given me and the other foreign experts. It honors us, and also gives the Chinese a chance to gorge while getting credit as good hosts.

And they were good hosts to me all through the year. Others had problems with the authorities, but in general I did not. I had a Chinese teacher as helper to naviagate their bureaucracy for me, though once I remember after a particularly frustrating day, my helper told me he felt like taking a machine gun and shooting everyone in the offices he had had to wait in.

We foreign experts had a Thanksgiving Dinner at the Green Lake Hotel, complete with an imported turkey, so we kept the home fires burning.

On Christmas we foreigners had a party in the evening. On Dec. 25, I and my two students, Jem and Jack, and a fellow American teacher Richard, took the poet Allen Ginsberg out to the Western Hills and some temples, showed him around the place. Allen was in town for a couple of days to give a lecture, which I heard. In the afternoon, just Allen and I went to my favorite teahouses in Kunming, walking around in the park, and talked about poetry and life. A lot of fun. That night he came—I invited him—to our Xmas party. When I returned to New York, Allen who had hit it off with my student Jack, helped me get Jack a visa for the States, and Jack ended up living with and cooking and cleaning for Allen for several years, and studying poetry and history.

Of my seven graduate students, five of them are now living in the USA.

December and January I was also busy, but there were moments of calm. On Dec. 22, I wrote to James and Dena, "Just listening to a tape of ancient Chinese music, sitting shirt-less in the sun on my back balcony listening to the cries of the vendors seliing eggs, pickled cabbage, old-newspaper buyers, old-clothes buyers, etc. an irregular cacaphony which mixes as well as it can with the sound of chickens clucking and someone hammering on a new building and (the usual) someone hawking up a lunger. Taking a rest from the thesis-editing I've been busy with these last two weeks. The music on the tape deck and in the street is poignant, reminding me I'll be leaving Kunming soon on Jan. 23 for Beijing, and then on January 30 flying to New York. Longing for the anonymity of Manhattan and a slice of pizza."

Beijing for a week even in the winter was great—and getting back to New York felt very good.

One year and a few days in China was just about the right amount of time.

CHINA4: MIS-SHAPINGS:

An ideogram is defined as a character or graphic symbol representing an idea or thing without expressing a particular word or phrase for it, as the characters in Chinese. Like Chinese characters juxtaposed next to one another making a sentence, some incidents and reflections of mine juxtaposed next to one another also can make meaning. Mis-shapings I'ved noticed can convey through their shapely and significant shape something central to China, itself the Central or Middle Kingdom. The first of two characters that constitute the name of China is a square-ish box with a vertical line slashed through its center. This short section of my memoir can provide one central slice for a biopsy of China in 1984.

YELLOW PERIL: Is it a mirror we throw rocks at, or is the man with bent arm someone else? We think we hear the Chinese down the block singing as he irons worry wrinkles into our foreheads. Yellow stains in our pants betray us....

A road in China winding like someone's character. The road re-shapes the countryside and the fields. It shapes the patterns of life, as the unhusked wheat and rice are deliberately spread out on it so that the trucks and buses that pass can winnow the grain. But peasants still walk across it without looking both ways because they're not used to traffic. They refuse to shape their behavior to cars and bikes, who have to re-shape their movements to avoid these peasants.

On January 17, 1985, I was taken to #2 Provincial Prison in Kunming. Here I learned that with some death penalties, if not carried out for one or two years, and if the prisoner has exhibited good behavior, his sentence can be changed to a life sentence, though later I was told that the maximum term of a sentence was 15 years. Most death penalty sentences are carried out. In this prison there were 2500 prisoners, of whom 10% were women and 10% were reactionaries, or political prisoners. The prisoners produce light-load trucks, red bricks, nails, quilts, furniture, and do printing. The prison factory's name is "The Golden Horse Machinery Factory." No golden horse can you escape on.

Rehabilitation, or re-shaping the person into a proper law-abiding citizen, has four methods, they told me. Punishment, with shortened sentences for doing good work. Punishment, with reform of prisoners' thinking. Punishment and production, with political education and study of technology and skills. And the fourth, tight control and education and persuasion. When I walked around in the prison, no one at that times seemed too tightly controlled, nor did the prisoners seem particularly cowed. I saw the living quarters—rooms with double-decker bunks in them, which were not much different from the bunks and rooms of the Chinese students at my university. I saw the prisoners eating food out in the yards, and the food was the same as I've seen given to our students. Of course, I recognize that if this prison was a nasty one, I would never have been taken around it. I also know that I only got one glimpse of one day of it. But the little I saw did not seem so terrible.

Prisoners here live mixed together, not segregated as to types of crimes. They work six hours a day, and study two hours. The tribal Minority prisoners—those who are not Han Chinese—have their diets and customs respected—Muslims do not get pork, though in China pork is the main meat. In restaurants, if you just ask for "meat" you get pork. Prisoners have group discussions after their political classes. They are asked to write reports on their thinking and their current changes of thinking. Their families come to the prison to try to persuade them to give up their criminal ways. Model workers now who are ex-cons also come to try to persuade them to give up their old criminal ways. Of 150 ex-cons after five years of being released from this prison, only two have commited new crimes. This prison has one of the lowest rates of recidivism in China. All this I was told. When I saw a bunch of old women prisoners, I asked my guides what these inoffensive-looking old ladies were in prison for. They asked them, and was told for opium smuggling. I had been told months earlier that there were problems with opium being smuggled into Yunnan Province from adjacent Burma, and that the Chinese authorities quelled it by executing anyone caught smuggling the stuff. In northern Thailand I smoked opium in the tribal villages, where it is the custom. The old ladies here still lived. One problem for me in China generally is that many different people give you different reasons and stories, and you don't know who to believe. Life in #2 Provincial Prison in Kunming did not seem so terribly different from life in China.

It started when I first arrived. A pat on the bottom of my duffel bag, and I was borne into China at Guangzhou. Monosyllables in nine tones twanged about mine ears. O brave new world! I could understand nothing. So like a baby. Gestures, gestures. My own language; head-shakings. Their language; head-shakings. Classical Chinese, the earlier written characters, are twisted more to mirror the things they name than are modern characters. Many Chinese cannot understand the ancient words, these gestures of lines, the black shadows of things, these lines dangling down the years, past where we can see, just shadows throwing their shadows into the clear light and dark sounds of a new country.

The twig first tied off. The foot first bent down. The line written down, its rhythm twisting about its words. In old China, upper-class girls' toes were bent down and the heel pressed to meet the instep. The bones broken and wrapped tightly, the foot became a bridge, high arching, the toes and heel bent under. This custom was bound up with beauty-as-uselessness, like the long fingernails of the old mandarins, like our Western too-tight trousers, high heels, long nails. In 1984 you still see old women whose shoes—tiny, embroidered—fit their feet. They hobble like amputees, their feet like posts, three inches long, like stilts, like sticks.

The bonsai trees seem more supple. In Kunming's Daguan Park near the water, the twists and reverses, the shapings, the lithe live branches arching out of dead stumps, their directions now man-made. More beautiful, less left to chance or to their own woody promptings. Tiny goldfish will grow into huge carp if they're fed a lot and if the pool they're in be large enough. It rarely is.

For war to change the color on the map is to stain the grass which won't wash out. After the battle, a dead man, who once, craven, flew from his enemy, faced another bright careless foe. A raven beneath the sun changed the shape of his face faster than could any worm, any time. Veterans knew that if you are wounded on a field and might pass out, to turn over and rest your face on the earth, because the ravens first go for the eyes. War is for the birds.

It's shocking what we once did to the Rosenbergs. Their son fears lightning more than he should. The electric cigarette lighter in my car smells of ozone. When I switch on the light, I see what he sees.

In a small alley in Kunming, I see a nose eaten away from inside, a leper's lion-like face, a disease with feet jammed against the door of cure, no way out, changing a profile faster than time can chew on a statue, a little slower than worms.

A Chinese girl says she loves my "smelling." I am confused. Smelling? I use regular Chinese soap. And Old Spice (regular) deodorant. My odor beneath these? The Chinese themselves generally don't smell bad or strong. But liking two-day-old American armpit? "When you smell, I feel happy," she says. Ah ha! Smile, she means. Whew! Almost changed my bathing habits.

Two life choices: change. Or leave it alone. The first requires re-shaping yourself. To leave it alone is to relax, to leave the clay as you find it, to sit at the flower garden, which others have dug and planted, and read a book someone else wrote, and watch the people pass. Let the self be a drain pipe for others' leavings, flowers, sun-struck petals, crisp and ready, all the smelly things we see in this garden, even things passed through the constricted channels of other minds.

But the plumber is your only trade. Sitting out his life, he writes. Sun's scintillations tapped out on yellow foolscap and bleached later by reflection into white bond. After he dies, if he's very good, he becomes immortal for a generation or more, and becomes for the teacher a symbol. Which he deserves. He becomes cold and white as marble, as grey as clouds, green as leaves, as brown as dirt, and as a light, light as fame.

Time gives my face such a squeeze between his hands that the wrinkles stay. They remember the daily caress, that squeeze. Then that blue and red banner wrapping my veins Time gave me too. And that softening flesh. Everything anyone can give me is wrapped in Time's flagging. Look up! It's Time's bright blue vault.

Heel and toes pointed down, feet bound
for beauty, the foot a rainbow of broken bones,
an old woman stilts along a street, feet tiny pegs
to fit in custom's arched holes, thrown up
to us now, still, beauty's rigid misshapen pain.
Striding down the opposite side of the street, bound
for some useful errand, a P.L.A. woman soldier, standing up
with feet squarely on the ground, looks up and down
the street and forges on. Under her leather shoes tiny pegs
of heels. Under her cap, curlers rack her spineless hair.

"He" and "she" are the same, the same sound, same tone—*ta*. Mandarin—the language, not the high court official—blends genders as the falsetto pitch, the sugary roll and sway, the pursing of the face, the eyes, the fruity flutterings of the fan, the role of the woman in the operatic duet in Green Lake Park is taken by a man. *Ta*—the character of man and woman is not the same (the linguistic written character, not the behavioral one—or maybe that too blends). The tone is slightly different in Scotland where "ta" is thanks or good-bye. *Ta*.

The bonsai tree, curved crippled legs, rickets, bowed under the weight of not-so-great grandparents on down, till bearing cannot be bourne, till its bearing thinks straight is curved, thinks twist is tall, up is side, a revolution. And thinks that it's all beautiful, the cripple, the crippling. And it is.

Some smudges on my windows are purely present: dead fly gore smear, yellow dust, a finger's print. My eyes pause not much as they take in, and fly beyond my back door's glass partition to the five-story building across the air. Sunlight points out these smears with mote-filled fingers. The glass comes clean about its past days. But its past, its innate depravity, shows when I cock my head and see a building or a tree branch twist around in a small hole that pulls the light tight around itself, warming itself at memories still molten of inept glass manufacture, now still and still changing the views of things on the other side of air and drifting coal smoke and veils of dust, twisting them around its little pit and pocket.

Mutter. Mutter. To be pronounced very much as a German would, yet this word is Chinese too. But not the word for "mother" here. In Kunming dialect, *mutter* means "not available." Like the Mandarin word *meo.* From some central cavern of language flows this word, slopping over the sides of languages into the tidal pools of dialect, carrying many meanings, a dolphin carrying the god brothers toward Delphi where calm Apollo can be understood by the wild Dionysus, and the mutterings I hear are finally clear.

The shadow of my face changes when I grow a beard or have my hair cut. A friend has a hair transplant; he no longer parts his hair from way down one side. Another friend no longer has her mustache, which was red. Another uses henna to keep her hair red the way perhaps it used to be.

On my passport I still put down that my hair is dark brown although now so much is grey. Dark shadows in my past too.

At the head of Culture Alley in Kunming, near the New Reconstructed Society Cinema, the carmel toffee flows. It flows from a ladle, hot from the smoking wok, it flows with cool calculation from the hand of an old man with shaved head, dressed in faded blue cloth like the peasants standing around him, engrossed in the figures he makes. A greater tilt of his hand and toffee flows off his ladle with no control now but gravity and the tme it takes the molten toffee to cool, harden, and stop, but that gravity and time calculated by his gravity, time and eye. So these swirls, these twists and curls scrawl toffee in their wake till the figure of a bird grows, not flying yet, but with its silence sweet as song.

Ah, China! Words slowly vanish, distilled till drinkable. Ideograms.
Like an old Chinese scroll painting, the smoke
from the Guelin factory mixes with the mist.
Smoke from the cigarette of the old temple attendant
blends with the incense and flaming spirit money.
The temple's turquoise and red tiles shimmer and quiver in the lake
till twilight turns on the colored bulbs circling it.
A night worker blares the night with a acetylene
torch. Near him a wood fire, another light for my illumination.

Ghostly tangles of cigarette smoke and incense,
of factory smoke and mountain mist.
Weathered temple tiles, temple paint,
bleach in glow of colored lights, of acetylene torch
illuminating distinctions.

Man's incense blends with his cigarette smoke.
Turquoise and red paint darken beneath twilight
and bleach by a night worker's acetylene torch.
Wind and wet (and dry) chips paint, dispels mist.

Temple incense. Cigarette smoke.
Mountain mist. Factory smoke.

My 1984 year in China.

TIBET:

The only map I could get in and for Lhasa, the capital of Tibet, was in Chinese. Not in English. And not in Tibetan. The Chinese say that Tibet is a part of China, not a nation of its own, and has been filling Tibet with Han Chinese people who now outnumber the Tibetans there.

In October 1984 Tibet had only been open to independent travelers for about one month when I flew there from Chengdu in China. One week was all I had time for—October 11 till October 18, 1984—and I stayed in Lhasa, sharing a room with two American women, Denise and Randy, who had just graduated from law school at the University of Chicago, and were seeing some of the world before they settled down to work.

The airport for Lhasa is about two hours away from the city by ramshackle road, so pot-holed that we were jounced around, smacking our heads often against the bus's ceiling. The road is being worked on by many Chinese P.L.A. soldiers who double as laborers and soldiers. Lhasa itself is full of Chinese soldiers, and the Tibetan section near the Potala is small compared with the straight streets of the burgeoning Chinese areas.

We were supposed to stay at a Chinese hotel, but the woman behind the desk was so unhelpful and nasty that when a young European traveler told us we could stay in a Tibetan hotel, we made tracks for it. It was the Barnaschou Hotel in the Tibetan area, with big brown window frames, the windows latticed over with strips of red and green and blue wood. We had a room on the upper floor, with the only running water for bathing from the pump outside in the backyard, and the toilet a simple hole, but with a window from which I could see the Potala.

The Potala is the Dalai Lama's Palace, the highlight and huge landmark on a hill in Lhasa. We got into it twice on our own, though there were monks to take us around then, and once got in while a fancy tour of Americans were shown around. These rich people, in this case Americans, could get into Tibet before it really opened up, but they had to pay astronomical prices and had to stay in the one ritzy hotel outside Lhasa, and only could come in rigidly supervised. Denise and Randy and I could stay in Lhasa itself, and wander pretty freely through the town, around the back of the Potala, and into some of the few temples still intact.

From the roof of the Potala you could see the valley of Lhasa, dry and dusty. The floor of the valley is a bit more than 12,000 feet in elevation, so the first day Randy almost fainted in the street from the altitude, and even from just walking up the long stepped ramp to the Potala we were all panting a little. About a week before we arrived here, an older European woman had died from the high altitude. A serious business. The rooms we could see were gorgeously and gaudily arrayed in brass and bright fabrics still glowing in the dim light. More than one monk in the Potala and in the street, after asking me where did I come from, and I answering "American" or in Chinese *mei guo ren,* his creased leather hide of a face lit up more brightly than did the dim bulbs or the yak-butter lamps in the Potala. They would clutch my hand, lean over, and into my ear would whisper, "Dalai Lama." I would grin, squeeze his hand as he squeezed mine, and happy co-conspirators against the heathen Chinee were we.

The only postcards that were sold to foreigners had a few that showed a "Mural painting of the Fifth Dalai making obeisance to the Ching Dynasty emperor Shun Chih" or "Cylindrical clay carving of Princess Wen Cheng" (a Chinese-Tibetan dynastic marriage) or "Portrait and tablet of the Ching Dynasty emperor Chien Lung worshipped by the Dalai." All rather frantically showing that—"see, Tibet was usually part of China, so what's all the fuss about now?" The Chinese in their tourist brochures talk about how the Tibetan serfs were liberated by them, and the Tibetans talk about how their culture and almost all of their monasteries were destroyed and their monks were and are still being tortured.

Many of the Tibetans I saw were religious to an extreme—prostrating themselves on the ground, with knee and elbow patches to protect themselves as they circled the Jokhang Temple, the holiest in all Tibet. Chanting and twirling their prayer wheels, sending prayers aloft to their gods at each turn. Lhasa is full of Tibetans who walk for weeks from their very isolated villages to get here to see their holiest sites, and when they also see us they gape with undisguised amazement as us foreigners, the first they've probably ever seen. We collect very friendly crowds on the streets. One way you know they're friendly is that the women stick out their tongues at you. Several times walking around, women put out their tongues which pointed down their chins, and smiled at me. A sexual come-on? Then I remembered from some anthropology text or other this sign of greeting. I also saw, when I was walking with Denise and Randy, some huge men, young Cham tribesmen wearing red bands around their heads, wiggle their tongues most sexually at my friends. You didn't need to be an anthropologist to get their gist. Mostly people didn't mind if we took their photos, but once a Cham man came over and yelled furiously at Randy after she took his picture, and I had to mollify him by speaking softly to him, neither of us understanding a word of the other's, but our general meanings most clear.

Randy and I went off to see Drepung Monastery near Lhasa, getting a hitch part way from a truck full of armed Chinese soldiers. We climbed into the back of the open truck with these toughened fellows, quite different from the usual P.L.A. soldiers in Kunming who seemed more kids than killers. Drepung was almost deserted, more like a small town than a religious center. A few Tibetans in one family offered us yak butter tea, which tasted of salt and rancid butter. Randy didn't like it, but I told her to keep drinking it all up and smile. She did. Can't say it beats the taste of Earl Grey! We all went out to Sera Monastery another day, which seemed more like a religious center, but also almost no one around. A few monks, that's it.

Our Tibetan hotel was fairly close to the Jokhang (or Jokhand) Temple and we kept trying to get inside, and the authorities stationed in front of it would always tell us to come back tomorrow. So we did. And they told us the same thing each time. However, one day, we were able to enter. The lines were very long of Tibetans, but a monk let us slip past the lines, and the pilgrims were so stunned by seeing foreign white people that they gladly made way for us. The smell of yak butter in the lamps was over-powering. The flickering of the lamps left much of the temple and its tanka hangings and paintings, and the carved and painted altars, still very wavering and shadowy. The people were very nearly all in the most traditional Tibetan clothing, and everyone looked like they hadn't bathed in years. (We three took a hot shower in a Lhasa public bathhouse once. It felt so good to be immersed in hot water, and I wondered if the Tibetans from their small arid villages would ever had had anything like this prodigal outpouring of water.) We three crammed into soffocatingly small rooms, their altar lamps fluttering and sputtering, yak butter continually being added to them by the monks and pilgrims, dim paintings of demons and death on the walls. My friends felt they were going to be sick here, and so we had to leave, much too early for my taste. This scene felt like one from hundreds of years ago, from some medieval place.

That's a tiny chunk of Tibet, being swamped by China and the present.

U.S.A.: HITCHHIKING:

Hitchhiking across the United States during college summers was not my first travel adventure.

For five summers, starting at age eight, I was in Camp Windsor in Belmont, Vermont, on a lake. Travels there were hiking to the top of Mt. Okemo and its firetower, logging in the woods, seeing the marble quarries further north, and the smelly Crowley Cheese Factory nearby. Once on one of our short trips up north several of us kids hiked across a large patch of tumbled grey boulders, hearing them groan and shift under our feet. Scary! So when I entered a contest at age ten or so, having to write on "the greatest adventure I ever had," I thought of crossing this avalanche. The prize was a hand-made "Kon Tiki" raft, named for the Thor Heyerdahl team that sailed on the "Kon Tiki" across the Pacific Ocean, a feat that I had read and dreamed about. But what kind of an adventure could a little middle-class kid from Brooklyn have had by age ten? Walking across these shifting boulders? I won my raft.

At age 13 in 1953 I flew for a summer to Mexico, and in the fall went out for a year at Verde Valley School, several miles outside Sedona,

Arizona. Here I grew to love the desert and its spectacular scenery. We went on trips to the Navajo and Hopi Reservations, among other places, and here I learned to revel in cultures very different from mine. At age 16 my parents and I flew out to the West and saw California and places like Yosemite. We flew down to Florida and Miami. But flying you don't touch the earth. Hitchhiking you do.

After my first summer in college, I planned on getting a job on a Norwegian ship and sailing over to Europe with my friend, Herb Lozoff. The pay was bad, and so were the working conditions, but I heard you could get a job without any experience. Herb at the end of the academic year decided not to do it, and I decided I did not want to do this alone. So I got a job as a camp counselor in upstate New York, not exactly an unexplored region of the world. The next summer I was going to hitchhike across the US with another friend, Frank Tanderjian. He also decided at the last minute not to go. By now, I realized that if I waited for others to accompany me, I may not get anywhere, so I decided to do it myself. I had gotten a job at my old prep school, Verde Valley, at their new summer travel camp, and so, despite my parents' very sensible trepidation about my hitching alone, I packed an old army backpack and was off.

How to shape my writing of this trip? By theme—dangerous or generous characters I met, jails I slept in, scenery gorgeous or desolate (often it was the same scenery)? By my age—earliest trips to later ones? Highlights only? Lowlights or low lifes only? The roads on my maps and my final Arizona destination limited my travel routes somewhat, but I could go the northern way, the southern, by the small roads or by the wide highways. President Eisenhower had not quite gotten us the marvelous intra-continental highway system yet that in the year 2000 we've had for decades, but this was in 1959 when the main Route 66 to California was a two-lane road, and I had to change roads often and get somehow through the towns and cities that clumped along the roads, with few by-passes. Cities often had to be walked through rather than, as now, driven round. The country seemed bigger then, not only because I was smaller with less experience, but because the getting somewhere was literally harder.

So I'll write about it like the trip itself—chronologically, but without the dull bits, avoiding the "imitative fallacy" of my style drooping as I drooped, waiting in the hot sun for hours for a ride, or shivering in staccato choppy chattery phrases to describe standing in the snow in December (or Decembrrr,brrr) watching and hearing the whirr of the Doppler Effect as the cars whizzed by without stopping. Zero to sixty— my life in travel.

It was June 13, 1959 (I have extensive notes on this trip) when I started out from Elizabeth, New Jersey, on Route 1 (my friend Frank drove me to here), and unrolled my lampshade on which I had written, "Arizona or bust, please!" and stuck out my thumb. My first hitch was a Negro in a truck. What did he expect of me as a non-paying rider? Conversation? Offering to share expenses? Agreeing with everything he said? He never had read my lampshade sign. When I told him I was heading to Arizona, I realized how proud and adventurous I felt. But one of the most distressing things about hitching is that everyone looks at you coldly as though you were a bum. I wore my college varsity Track sweatshirt on my trips, which made me out as a college student rather than as a bum, and that did increase my number of rides.

My rides even that first day were with a wide variety of people—a huge and filthy but gentle guy named "Big Bill" whose teeth were either missing or streaked with black oil; an old couple from Michigan; four sailors, two of whom were cooks who told me that cooks had it best in the Navy because of the large amount of time off—then being put off further along than I should have been, and having to back-track in a drizzle. Now where to sleep. Fearing snakes and therefore the woods, I found a large lawn, and tried to fall asleep in a secluded part of it. Crab apples all over it, and therefore some under me. The lawn also sloped at a rackish angle of 30 degrees, and while blowing up my air mattress, I dropped the valve and couldn't find it in the dark, not using my flashlight which light could bring the house's owners and the police down on me. I used my shoes and jacket as a pillow and even the shoe laces seemed sharp. I was glad when dawn came.

Washington, PA was only a short distance away, but distance is deceptive. One hundred miles with a good hitch is shorter than 25 miles with short rides and long waits. Finally I got to Washington and spent 25 cents on bus fare to the other side of town. Before this I spent $2.50 for tolls for Frank to go to and from Elizabeth, N.J. The next 2500 miles to Arizona cost me a total of 40 cents, including this 25 cents bus fare. The full week it took me to get to Arizona—cost me about $19 for everything. Lodging was in my sleeping bag near the road. Food was cherry pie and milk, hamburgers, french fries, the usual road fare. Transportation was free. I was free.

This first trip I wore a brown-and-white-checked shirt, and striped grey-and-black trousers which were pretty good at hiding the dirt. (My second summer hitching around the country I wore blue shorts and a white tee shirt.) After a week on the road—without a shower or a change of clothing—I was quite dirty and smelly. I've little doubt now that several people who picked me up must have wished they never had once they caught a whiff of this stranger from Brooklyn.

Two boys and a girl picked me up, jammed me in the back seat with cartons of new baseballs and away we went in a squeal of rubber. The radio was playing a nasal pop song "Waterloo," which I'll always associate with that wild ride in Ohio.

Got a long ride to Terre Haute, Indiana, with a scientist who very late at night dropped me off on the western side of the city. Outside, I was freezing, so I crossed the bridge to find an all-night cafe. It was a dive, and the food was awful, but the old waitress was friendly and told me of her adventures with hitchhikers. Others came into the cafe, all of whom had stories to tell of the days when they rode the rails, or shot wild Indians. Adventures! Real life! I was thrilled, as well as exhausted, to be meeting the people I'd never meet in Brooklyn in my regular city life.

Rides to Kansas City and then Joplin in Missouri followed. If you get out of one person's car and immediately stick out your thumb, you have a good chance of getting a ride before the first car has pulled away. After all, if you haven't killed the previous driver, you probably won't kill me. Sometimes a short string of rides would happen like this to me.

A really rough looking fellow picked me up and told me of all the trouble with hitchhikers around Missouri. He mentioned Charlie Starkweather and other mass-murder hitchers who I had heard of. If someone pulled a gun on him, he said, he'd speed his car up and tell them he would crash it, if the hitcher did not toss the gun out of the window. He felt if he were going to be killed anyway, he may as well take his killer with him.

A truck let me off at the Big Cabin Exit on the Will Rogers Turnpike in Oklahoma. This was an exit near no town nor farmhouse. Cars roared by me so fast my trousers flapped and snapped in their wind. I stood listening to the snakes rustling and buzzing in the grass on the highway's verge, myself being on the verge of sunstroke, with no breakfast and no water, for more than three hours until a state trooper picked me up. He told me hitching is illegal on this pike, and asked me for my identification. I thought, here goes my first jail record, but he was very nice and wrote me a slip showing I was registered with the Oklahoma police department and was O.K. He took me into Claremore, the home of Will Rogers, where I saw a large gun collection in a hotel.

My scariest time in Oklahoma, and maybe on the whole trip, was getting picked up by a big blond handsome man in Kellyville. He screeched to a stop and told me he'd take me on to the next town, but had to first feed his fighting cocks at his farm. Fine, I'll see his Oklahoma farm and his fighting cocks. We fed them, and sparred a couple of them when a neighbor of his showed up. He let me ride a horse of his bareback around the yard. He invited me to eat an early dinner with him and his old mother who he lived with. Dinner was simple, followed by blueberries and cream. He, H.C. Hopper, known as Hoppy, showed me his newspaper clippings and trophies about when he was one of the best tennis players in the whole country. He was very nice. Then in the barn, after milking the cows, which he let me do, he told me he liked me a lot, and that's when I got this bad feeling. He asked me to give him a hug. Oh, god, one of these, thought I.

Meanwhile, the sun had nearly set, I was in the middle of nowhere, and he was very strong, with a hot temper—one of his roosters pecked him, and he almost wrung its neck. What do I do?

He invited me to stay the night, and offered to share his bed with me. His mom would, he told me, feel this was the hospitable thing to do. I told him I'd stay here for the night, but I had made a vow to myself (I hadn't) that on this hitching trip I would not sleep indoors, and naturally I couldn't break a vow. Finally we compromised, and I slept in the house, but on the floor of the living room.

Before this, but after dinner, he asked me to come out to his car to have a private talk. While sitting in it, he suddenly reached over and tried to kiss me on the mouth. I stopped him by pushing his face away, and told him that if he tried that stuff again I'd break his nose. I think that such a specific and fairly easily accomplished threat, rather than a more generalized "I'll punch you" kept him from trying it again. (This showed me how unpleasant it must be for a woman when a man she doesn't like grabs and tries to kiss her. A little empathy learned.) He was stronger than I was, and I was scared. Beside his neighbor and his mom, who had seen me? Who would know if he killed me and buried my body on his land, and he'd just tell them the hitchhiker continued on his way. Bad situation for me.

In the morning I walked with him as he fed his animals, and finally he said let's go. But his car at first wouldn't start, and I was thinking I'd just walk off to anywhere else just to get away from him. The car eventually did start and he took me to a town right by the road I needed to continue west. That evening, I was picked up by two men outside Oklahoma City, and they asked me if I had gotten any crazy rides. When I named Hoppy, one of the said, "Why, H.C. Hopper, that boy's queer as hell!" This guy was infamous all across the state. I wished I knew that earlier.

Sometimes I had to ask drivers who stopped at gas stations if they'd take me further along Route 66. One fellow was loathe to do it, but after I showed him my college I.D. and my Amateur Athletic Association card (I was on the varsity track and the cross-country teams), he agreed, but asked me to ride up front with him (so I could not choke him from behind, I guess). He told me he didn't pick up hitchers now that a good friend of his had just been killed by a hitchhiker, who had been caught when a policeman who knew this friend's car noticed his friend not driving it, and pulled it over. There are dangers for both hitchers and the drivers who pick them up. But being considered a potential murderer, a bum, an outcast, below the salt, peripheral, is strangely, but not pleasantly, part of the excitement of hitching. Being resolutely middle-class and law-abiding, and then suddenly to be seen as the dregs of society, is a sobering experience. Something like traveling to a different land, one where you don't fit in.

It's being in a society where people who you would never talk to in your regular life will, after they pick you up, tell you secrets they would never tell their wife or their best friend, because they know you'll be long gone and they'll never see you again. It's at times being like a psychiatrist or a priest—confessions pour into your ears. One guy of 35 told me of his six children and of his wife, and said his life is over because he was working seven days a week, every week of the year, just to keep food on the table. He advised me never to get married, to stay free. He felt chained, had not had a vacation in 13 years, and envied me. Another guy, this one quite old, told me of his prowess with a pistol, and said that when he rode the rails in the Depression, guys would kill you for 50 cents. (I talked to a brakeman on the railroad in a small town and he said it wasn't so bad now, but I decided still to stick to cars.) Guys told me of their cheating on their wives, sometimes bragging of it, sometimes ashamed. Lives opened up and I saw down to the bone, to the center. This was better than reading about it in a book! You even got a good sunburn! But it also is a lot more uncomfortable and dangerous.

One long ride I got in New Mexico just at dawn, smelling the desert and facing the rising sun waiting for a ride coming from the east, was from a guy in a ranch bus going all the way to California to bring this bus to his father's ranch. He already had several hitchers aboard, and said he was "picking up anyone except niggers and Indians." Another kind and generous racist. He was of Portuguese descent, very funny and bubbling over with delight at everything we passed. In Albuquerque, we whistled out the windows at all the pretty girls, and once he pulled over to a local city bus stop, flung open the bus's door, and yelled out to the people waiting for the local bus, "California, anyone?" After a shocked second, the waiting people broke into big smiles, and we roared off, pleased with our own sense of humor. Lots of laughs. We stopped and all had a look at Arizona's Meteor Crater, where we thought it would be great to dress up in a space suit and suddenly to emerge from the crater among the tour groups and declare, "At last I am free! Take me to your leader!" Wild guy. Wild ride.

He dropped me off in Flagstaff and I finally got to the camp near Sedona late at night. The first bath I took in a week, left the tub filthy, and so I had to take another bath right after it. The dirt I washed off was from 2600 miles of United States and one week of me. I crossed the country with almost no money spent and with many new experiences and people met. This first trip made me fall in love with hitchhiking and with travel, and for the next couple of years, every vacation I got, I hitched around the country. I couldn't stay still! After this summer, when I first read Jack Kerouac's evocative novel "On the Road," I felt I knew absolutely what he was talking about.

After camp, I hitched out to California and back to Utah, going through Zion and Bryce National Parks. In Ogden, Utah, it was raining hard, and the weather matched my spirits. I was tired and chilled and wet, and I'd just heard about an earthquake in Yellowstone where I was headed, and so I didn't know if the Park was even open. A car stopped and asked me how to get to Route 30 South. I asked them if they'd be passing Yellowstone, but they said they're headed for New York City. I'm from

Brooklyn, I told them, and they offered to take me all the way home. They were a Negro, his white wife with a foreign accent, and their young child. Interesting couple, but I thanked them and said no. Twenty minutes later, wet and cold, I changed my mind, but too late. What an idiot I was! A truck driver stopped and took me to Route 30 South where a one-legged school teacher picked me up. A seat belt kept him from falling out of his seat as he told me of his hiking and camping trips. Taking me a little past Echo, Utah, to a junction, I stood, cursing the rain and the cold and my stupidity in turning down the ride to New York, cursing at the pitted cliffs on the other side of the road. A Studebaker stopped in front of me, and when I asked the driver where he was going, I heard the heavenly words, "Detroit, Michigan." All the way to the east! He was going to study dentistry at the University of Detroit, was also named Chuck, an ex-Army sergeant, about 36 or so, had a pock-marked face and only nine fingers. This great ride lasted 2 ½ days—he slept in the car, and I slept just beside it off the road. Wyoming, Nebraska, Iowa—seeing the corn fields and smelling the alfalfa mills which stunk up the town by burning the alfalfa to make pig food. He put me off at the Ambassador Bridge between Detroit and Canada, and we said our goodbyes. Traveling like this means saying goodbyes very often.

In Canada I teamed up for a while with Derek, a British college student of physics, and we got a few rides together. One old lady picked us both up, and after Derek and I split up, each going to different places, a young pregnant woman took pity on me standing in the rain, and after getting some cigarettes at a store where I was waiting, thumb outstretched, took me to the next town. An old lady and a pregnant woman! Ah, these trusting Canadians (even though both of these women said they don't usually pick up hitchers). But Canada was not all genteel. At Simcoe, a young guy picked me up and wanted to show me how fast his new car could go. Suddenly something flew in the window. He thought it was a bird, I thought it a bat. Unfortunately I was right. It flew around and kept smacking into both of us. Zooming along at 60 miles an hours at night on a winding country road, and having to kill a bat in your car at the same time is no joke. He concentrated on driving, I on the bat. Finally we stopped the car, and pounded the bat into insensibility with my canteen and a map. Later it flew around again, but we beat it up good this time, and put it in the ash-tray so he could show it to his sister. He took me to Welland.

Finally late at night I got to Niagra Falls in Ontario, and wanted to find a jail to sleep in. Asked two women where the jail was, and one of them called them up and made me a "reservation" there. The desk sergeant led me to my cell—a bed and a toilet in it, the bed consisting of interlaced iron strips which served as its springs. After following others' examples by carving my initials in the wall, I went to sleep. The next morning over to the U.S. side and to see the falls. Finally arrived home, tired, smelly, dirty, and utterly exultant!

The jail in Canada was not the only jail I spent nights in. I stayed the night in the jail in St. Augustine, Florida, on Christmas Eve of 1959 on the way hitching to Key West and Cuba for my 10-day Xmas vacation. While there I ate some of the Xmas cookies given me by the guy who gave me my first ride out of Elizabeth, New Jersey. One night in the jail in Panguitch (or Richfield—I'm not sure now which) Utah, where a cop who first thought I was the "wanted" man he was looking for, offered to put me up in the jail if I didn't get a ride out of town.

In Cross City in the Florida panhandle in the Xmas vacation in 1960, heading back from New Orleans after staying in a two-dollar-a-night flop-house on Canal Street there, a deputy sheriff pushed hard to take me to a safe cell for the night because he said "the niggers are acting up tonight," and I needed protection. At his jail crowded with prisoners, I had my own cell which was locked for the night both for my and for the cops' protection. In the morning the warder brought me the first breakfast I ever got in jail: grits with a dollop of melting butter on them, and one small piece of very fatty bacon. Usually in these jails, they'd roust you out of your cell very early so nobody would see you leave. But giving me this breakfast in the Cross City Jail and not kicking me out, made me very nervous. After all, I had to be back for classes in January. I began to think that I was going to be charged for vagrancy—then a crime in the South, and often used to keep someone in jail for 30 days. I saw myself on a chain gang for a month of work and beatings. When I saw one of the warders going around, I asked him when I could leave, half expecting a thick Southern drawl coming back at me: ""When we all is good and ready." However, he told me I could leave any time, and showed me he had unlocked the cell door when he'd brought me the grits. I walked out, got to the end of town, and put out my thumb.

Cycling with my friend Michael Gordon during an Easter Vacation, we ended up in Dingman's Falls in Pennsylvania on a very cold night, and I asked the cops if we could spend the night in their jail. They gave us a cell with a double-decker bunk in it. Beats freezing our asses off sleeping on a golf course, as we had done the night before. And in the summer of 1960, I took a short hitching trip up to Cape Cod, and in Falmouth, Massachusetts, lucked out by getting the "woman's cell" in the jail, the most comfortable of all, because here I could sleep on a sofa instead of the wooden boxes or iron springs of all the other jails. I hadn't bought my sleeping bag on this and other short trips, and so a dry jail cell was better than a baseball field in Newton, the woods, an open-air gazebo in the park where the town held dances, a sofa in someone's house, or a vacant lot, all places on short trips I've spent the night. Spending most of my days, thumb out, hoping for rides, and when getting them, listening to everyone's stories of their lives.

While working in Verde Valley School's summer camp, I traveled too with the campers. A postcard I sent from a trading post in Monument Valley in 1959 on a camp trip noted, like a Walt Whitman catalogue of American Indian names, we've "seen Canyon de Chelley, Spider Rock, a lot of Hopi villages—Schongopovi, Mishongopovi, Hotavilla, Walpi, Oribi—and a lot of the real Hopi kachina dances. Many of these villages look and smell like Mexico. Many Navajos and old Indian ruins—Betatakin, Inscription House, White House, Wupatki. Man, I is seein' da world!" Elsewhere, I wrote that I had found an old Indian ruin that was not on any map, and described it to the ranger, and he didn't know it. I called this discovery "Stickney House," and I still have a photo of it I took.

I noted when I was 19 that the Navajo and Hopi villages smelled like Mexico, and when I was in Tibet at age 44 I noted that the Tibetans smelled and looked like Navajos. The nose provided a probe, a shaft like a geological boring down through my times traveling.

The earthquake in Yellowstone in 1960 that kept me from hitching there then was like the effects of the huge forest fires that were still evident in July 1998 when I spent a couple of days at a campsite in Yellowstone, seeing the river and the bison and the bears, the geysers and the hot springs there. Whole swathes of forest were still blackened and broken, and the roads that had been potholed and melted by the fires of a couple of years ago had not yet been fixed. I had been to Yellowstone hitchhiking also during college at another time, but this trip of 1998 was different. I talked to fewer people, not having to be conversational with the drivers who picked me up during college, because I was the driver. And I did not pick up any hitchhikers myself during this whole six and a half week journey, covering more than 12,000 miles.

On this 1998 drive around the U.S.A. I also stopped at the Grand Canyon, parked in some parking lot during the night and got almost no sleep in the back seat of my Honda Accord because I had no campground reservations, and the Canyon, as always in the summers, was chock full of tourists. Early in the morning I headed down to the Colorado River, made it, doused myself for a short while in the frigid clear rushing water, and headed back up to the rim again. It took me seven hours and forty five minutes, round trip. I took no water, but drank from a spigot in Indian Gardens on the plateau, and once from a spigot on the way up the steeper upper walls. The hike hurt, and at the end I was dragging a bit and resting a lot. I was 58 years old, and remembered the first time I climbed to the bottom of the inner gorge of the Canyon to the river. I was nineteen.

So the Grand Canyon shows not only the geological strata of rocks from ancient times, being laid down over time, but also shows the layering of slices of my own travels, my own life. The first

time I was there was in 1956 with my parents on the South Rim, and went down on a mule to Plateau Point.

In 1959 and 1960 I walked to the bottom of the Canyon, and went on a mule trip for nine miles with some campers of mine down and up from the North Rim, a higher and cooler and less crowded area than the South Rim.

In 1972 my wife Joyce and I walked down from the South Rim on the Kaibab Trail, steeper than the Bright Angel Trail, and met no one on the way. Joyce almost collapsed from the heat and dehydration, and we could find no shade on the trail, and if not for the canteen of water and several salt tablets, she would have been in bad shape. There was no one else around to help us. Once we got lower and the salt had its effect, Joyce was fine and we camped one night at the bottom of the Canyon near Phantom Ranch, the next night part way up at Indian Gardens, and then early in the next morning we walked up to the top.

We also in 1972 took a ten-day raft trip from Lee's Ferry to Lake Meade, running the whole Grand Canyon on the Colorado River. Wonderful rapids, companions, swimming, camping under the moon and stars. Easy and exciting, every bend in the river with grand new views.

And then the hike once again into the Canyon and down to the river and back. Peering down into the Canyon is like looking down into my own past and my travels—hard and rocky in places, hard to make out the details in the distance, changes of color and content in the rock layers as you go deeper, the river fast-moving in places, torpid in others, but always moving.

When I was first at the river in 1959 the Colorado was as reddish as its name, and warm. I drank from it, the suspended sand gritty in my teeth. The last time I drank from it, in June 1998, I drank just a little because it is now supposed to be polluted, but the river was now clear and cold, a legacy from the Glen Canyon Dam way up river. Is that too, like the strata, like my life now?

When you travel you can often go many different routes to get to where you want to, or at any rate where you finally end up.

There's a small town near Mitchell, South Dakota, a town of fewer than 500 residents, a town named Stickney. I have a 1960 photo of me hitchhiking, standing by a signpost pointing to "Stickney—9 miles." I never got there then, but once crossing the country in 1992 with my friend and colleague Sondra Leftoff and her son Avi, in the late afternoon we finally made it to Stickney, and I have a photo of a much older and greyer me standing next to a sign saying "Stickney—pop. 409." Behind me is a small barn-like building which has a sign on it reading "Stickney Body Shop." My face looks like it could use one of those promised tune-ups. In my drive around the nation in 1998 I finally spent some time in Stickney, South Dakota. I bought four tee shirts with "Stickney" printed on them. I got a pair of gloves and some pencils from the man who ran the Feed Store, and he wouldn't accept any payment for them once he heard my name was the same as his town's. I talked with the woman who runs the local newspaper, "The Stickney Argus." I talked with some of the folks in the local ice-cream and sandwich shop. And I spent the night trying to sleep in the water-soaked and mosquito-ridden little park, hot and sweaty from having to keep the windows shut to keep out the bugs. The next morning I walked around the tiny town, and had breakfast in the only place that serves it, the small bowling alley. Then I went off to spend some time in the biggest town around, Mitchell, home of the Corn Palace. Nothing to see of paticular interest in Stickney. It's just my name, just a word.

There's so much left out of any story or any travel narrative, especially one that extends almost half a century. Enough for today.

ZERO TO SIXTY: THE ENDING?

How do you start a chapter called "the ending"? I could have ended these travel memoirs with the last page of the chapter on hitchhiking in the United States, because this country is the return home from my travels around the world, the closing of that great circle route, in my beginning is my end. It is about hitchhiking, which in many ways got me started in adventurous peregrinations.

The word "end" is itself a useful pun. It can mean both the final destination and the purpose of it all, can mean both the where and the why. My final destination has always been home, to be in a place I know and that is truly mine. My purpose? To discover something of the world, its peoples, and myself. Wherever I go, my "I" tags along. TAKE-OFF:
"Taking off from New York, I took off
New York, peeled off its black words,
scrubbed its battling sides, unzipped my
lover, untied my friends, threw off my classes, undid
myself damn near. But caught myself in time."
Travel can change the traveler. But:
"How can you change the shape already fired in a kiln?
I tried travel, hoping change of smells, of air,
of sounds would even re-fuse the shape there
was to new. Sooner change a projector with a new film.
O.K. So say we've now little choice about the shape.
What about the thickness, bumps, depressions?
Can't they change with change of sense impressions
at least like new voices or music change a tape?
Or is each change labeled by our souls a taint,
and as such pushed away until we're dead?
Our past pressing us to its shape is lead,
and change—startling, willful, thin—is paint.
Travel in unaccustomed ways is like a tug
away from the center, a different use for the bowl,
for though the shape stays, what flows through the hole
we can control. We pour water or wine in the jug."
So one reason to travel is to escape from the prison of our ordinary selves or from our ordinary quotidian ruts. Wallace Stevens wrote of "the malady of the quotidian." But the mundane, the ordinary, the quotidian is

also comfortable. We understand it. By seeing and experiencing new things we may perhaps (but only perhaps) become new. But new means unfamiliar, and the unfamiliar can make us anxious. John Cheever in his novel "Falconer" noted, however, that the unfamiliarity of prison—his protagonist is serving time in a literal prison—is similar to the discomfort and unfamiliarity felt by a traveler. "He [Farragut] seemed, in prison, to be a traveler and he had traveled in enough strange countries to recognize this keen alienation. It was the sense that on waking before dawn, everything, beginning with the dream from which he waked, was alien. He had dreamed in another language and felt on waking the texture and smell of strange bedclothes. From the window came the strange smell of strange fuels. He bathed in strange and rusty water, wiped his ass on strange and barbarous toilet paper and climbed down unfamiliar stairs to be served a strange and profoundly offensive breakfast. That was travel. It was the same here. Everything he saw, touched, smelled and dreamed of was cruelly alien...." I remember the distress of Sally when in northern Thailand she didn't get served a "proper English breakfast."

In other countries with other languages, even the familiar can be changed. In Ecuador, for example, a restaurant served steaks such as "Filetminong" and "Chatobrian." "Salad" in Ecuador often meant chopped beets and rice. "Vegetables" were usually both rice and potatoes on the same plate. I noted the spelling in one restaurant in Brasil of "sheesburger." When in Argentina, I ate a long hot dog called "el super-poncho." Lots of English words were spelled correctly on men's tee shirts in Brasil and on truckers' caps in Peru. But even words there in Spanish were sometimes changed in their spellings because Spanish doesn't differentiate well between the letters "b" and "v." The raw fish of "ceviche" became in places "cebiche." "Vende" became "bende" as in "Se bende lotes" ("we sell lots").

Words in other languages may mean something different to us Americans. Traveling around

Europe in 1964-5 I jotted down these amusing names, amusing only to someone speaking English: in Spain, there was "Damn" beer. In France, there was "Pshitt" soda. In Holland, there was "Fochink" vodka. Here's a toast: and the same to you!

There are individual words and then there are the individual arrangements of words, and the possible shapes of a travel memoir. Do I take "traveling" in a wider sense—going off to feelings or situations that are not the usual me? I finally arranged my words in chapters on different countries, but I might have arranged my chapters on different themes—sex; loneliness; time; death. Or arranged it by chronology—each different trip in succeeding years. Or, to play with the pun, succeedings or failings, the good versus the bad on trips. Or slice it into archetypes of travel—the hellos, goodbyes, the strange, the familiar. Or emphasizing the changes in the places—how TV changed things in Banos in Ecuador, or in the tea house in Kunming, China. How Acapulco in Mexico changed from 1953 to 1965 to 1969 to 1986, in biopsies of its now older and more polluted self, or in strata layered like those in the Grand Canyon. Or blend all of the above in places in this book. "Places in this book." Places—another pun. Words again.

Shaving my head is an appropriate motif for much of this book. In Officer Candidate School in the Navy they removed all our hair so we'd all look alike, and we could become one unit of a massive disciplined organization. In Poona, India, at the Raj Neesh Ashram, everyone else was letting their hair grow very long, but I had mine shaved off to clear out all the extraneous stuff in me, to clean me up and out. After my separation from my wife, on Fire Island I wrote of the beach and the sea scouring off my inessentials, making clean and simple my life.

Susan Sontag, in her short story which I just read last week, "Unguided Tour," wrote a dialogue: "I took a trip to see the beautiful things. Change of scenery. Change of heart. And do you know?" "What?" "They're still there." "Ah, but they won't be there for long." "I know. That's why I went. To say goodbye. Whenever I travel, it's to say goodbye." And further on in her story, Sontag continues, "Do you have guidebooks, maps, timetables, stout shoes?" "I read the guidebooks when I got home. I wanted to stay with my—" "Immediate impressions?" "You could call them that." "But you did see the famous places. You didn't perversely neglect them." "I did see them. As conscientiously as I could while protecting my ignorance…." "How did you know where to go?" "By playing my memory like a roulette wheel." "Do you remember what you saw?" "Not much." And, Susan, how little I too remember of all of what happened and of what I saw.

But it is often much more pleasant to think of or talk of your travels after the trip, when you are past the place itself, than it is to deal with the actual **being** in the place. Adventure is often mostly discomfort and danger, but the mind of the adventurer can also see the situation in a romantic glow, can transcend to an extent the leeches nibbling and the mosquitos biting, and think "what a great story!" Once when my parents and I were stuck with our car in a sandy wash in the Valley of Fire near Las Vegas, they were very upset and worried. I, at age 16, told them to relax and enjoy the adventure of it all. We'd get out, we'd live, so relax. And you know—I was right! Adventure is danger and discomfort filtered through a sensibly romantic sensibility. It's certainly not all, but it is partially, all in our head.

But what about the natural world? Does it care about what shape or meanings we give it? Hell, no! And VIVE LE INDIFFERENCE!

"When I woke up from napping on the beach, the sea didn't even notice. No one was collecting tickets for its show, and the hermit crab was just interested in enough sand to scoot across.

The party went on, and when the astronomers and poets pleaded previous engagements, or got drunk and incoherent and had to leave, the stars stayed and talked intensely way past sunrise to each other."

The world and time proceed at their own paces, and our minds trying to follow them may make us mis-step. The world and time are indifferent to us, pay little attention to us, and sometimes we, doused in our own minds' internal wanderings, lost in our preoccupied and convoluted paths, pay little attention to them. So I wrote of these two characters, TIME AND MIND:

"Mind stands, restless, bored, at a party, idly sweeping with eyes the room for someone else, never catching your eyes, muttering.

Time strolls at his habitual pace around the 18th century square in his usual dusk-blue pin-striped suit tapping methodically his cane each time his right foot steps. He seems very pleased with himself.

Mind sits down to Chicken Marengo with raspberries and cream washed down with dry champagne. Mind reads the papers throughout the meal, abstracted, as he toys with his food.

Time walks to the refrigerator to get the beer he was thinking about for the past hour, stands

with his hand on its door, unopened, while he dreams of talking to Doris on the phone tomorrow.

Mind goes to the movies with his pal, Time. Time thinks of his work tomorrow. Of his vacation, thinks Mind. Afterwards they walk and discuss the movie as though they had been there."

I have been in many exotic places where I might be thinking or writing mostly about something relating to my life in New York. I am often not fully in wherever it is I actually literally am.

We take from our traveling whatever experiences or poetic symbols we need at that particular time. We cluster our souvenirs and memories in meaningful patterns, the way I'm doing now with these poems and quotations and memories. And with these, my poem

THREE MEDITATIONS: NATURE IDEAS:
"I take from the sea what I need.
Ideas are washed clean up on the beach.
New trails the waves lick are followed.
Convoluted shells decorate my mantle.
I wear the seaweed like sages' hair.
Plane lines in the sky cable me meanings
I myself devise. Just by looking I
take from everywhere all. Yet I do need
mirrors and also dust with no glisten, glimmer.

I am a landowner of all that animates me.
Titles, even great deeds of land, are just dirt.
I use whatever comes to hand: an arm, a palm
tree, a temple, light. All ideas we ever get—
love, death, the ways we resemble things—wrapped up
with different colors, coded to where they come from.
Granite headlands or policeman's paunch flash power.
Rain pours life on the dry, death on those who've slogged
through mud. What startles or pains you into poetry
depends on what you stumble on, on what hits your eye.
Death sees itself mirrored in a lake or in the road's dust.
I've seen it in both. I've traveled.
Swift found the spider ugly, spinning out
of itself only, venom and dirt. Whitman called
the soul a spider launching forth filaments out
of itself. Alone, I spin out of control
webs. Control this asymmetry by light filaments
of sticky stuff from corners of the eyes,
by wet from fingers turning telegram pages,
by white fleck foam from edge of lips.
Whatever sticks to world, I'll stick to it.
From webs of self to catch someone who flies."

Like Whitman's child who, whatever he saw, he became, we too are
changed and shaped by what we see, and we hope, as we grow, to fully
understand these sights and sites. Words are what we use as tools for grasp-
ing, but the world does not always open to the blunted screwdriver of our
language. The world speaks in its own way. It's often our hearing that is
feeble. I wrote,

"Before Adam, before words, all things signed their names,
some rigid, the cuneiform of coral, some sloppy
like whitecapped wave speech. We listen and try
to learn their names. We eavesdrop when wind shouts

to trees in autumn, and hear the leaves of words the trees fling back.
Ocean clears its throat and jellyfish wash up. It shushes for silence,
and we wait by the shore for oracular boomings. Our ships
scrawl the water, but their engines stutter.
While ocean, tree and wind persist in wet, wooden, or windy,
small shells wander in casual crabbed doodles on the sand.
Let us also footprint her shore as the sea's tide tongue
forces us to speak louder, longer, deeper, and again."

We must speak, and some poor bastards have also to write. But the
word "grass" is blue ink. The word "sea" is always and only ink blue. The
word "red" is not, but blue. The word "wind" never cools, never blows,
never blew.

Susan Sontag ends her story "Unguided Tour" with:

"**Advice.** Move along, let's get cracking, don't hold me down, he travels fastest who travels alone. Let's get the show on the road. Get up, slu-
gabed. I'm clearing out of here. Get your ass in gear. Sleep faster, we
need the pillow....

If I go this fast, I won't see anything. If I slow down—

Everything. —then I won't have seen everything before it disappears.

Everywhere. I've been everywhere. I haven't been everywhere, but it's
on my list.

Land's End. But there's water, O my heart. And salt on my tongue.

The end of the world. This in not the end of the world."

Zero to 60—my age now and my speeding through the world—
although I have gone at all speeds and by many conveyances from camel
to car, from bus to water buffalo. My speed despite the title is now decel-
erating due not merely to age but to having done it and been there. My
profession as a professor has given me the time and enough money to
travel the world, and how can you end a book on travel round the world,
when there's always more world, and world enough?

Robert Graves wrote one of his poems about how things continue on even after the poem about them ends. I'll have to paraphrase it here because I can't find this poem, and my memory can't re-capture it all— such as I've been saying this whole book long about any full travel experience. Graves wrote that this poem itself should end "like a gander on the wing, at a careless comma,"

A comma implies it is to be continued somewhere. Age 60 has no period.